State Organized Terror

SERIES ON
STATE VIOLENCE, STATE TERRORISM,
AND HUMAN RIGHTS

Series Editors
George A. Lopez, University of Notre Dame
Michael Stohl, Purdue University

State Organized Terror:
The Case of Violent Internal Repression,
edited by P. Timothy Bushnell, Vladimir Shlapentokh,
Christopher K. Vanderpool, and Jeyaratnam Sundram

International Armed Conflict Since 1945:
A Bibliographic Handbook of Wars and Military Interventions,
Herbert K. Tillema

World Justice? U.S. Courts and International
Human Rights, edited by Mark Gibney

State Organized Terror

The Case of Violent Internal Repression

EDITED BY

P. Timothy Bushnell,
Vladimir Shlapentokh,
Christopher K. Vanderpool,
and Jeyaratnam Sundram

Westview Press

BOULDER • SAN FRANCISCO • OXFORD

Series on State Violence, State Terrorism, and Human Rights

This Westview softcover edition is printed on acid-free paper and bound in library-quality, coated covers that carry the highest rating of the National Association of State Textbook Administrators, in consultation with the Association of American Publishers and the Book Manufacturers' Institute.

Copyright © 1991 by Westview Press, Inc.

Published in 1991 in the United States of America by Westview Press, Inc., 5500 Central Avenue, Boulder, Colorado 80301, and in the United Kingdom by Westview Press, 36 Lonsdale Road, Summertown, Oxford OX2 7EW

Library of Congress Cataloging-in-Publication Data
State organized terror : the case of violent internal repression /
   edited by P. Timothy Bushnell ... [et al.].
      p.   cm. — (Series on state violence, state terrorism, and
   human rights)
   Includes bibliographical references.
   ISBN 0-8133-8307-2
   1. Political persecution.   2. Terrorism.   I. Bushnell, P.
Timothy.   II. Series.
JC571.S786   1991
323.4′9—dc20   91-20259
                                                                           CIP

Printed and bound in the United States of America

The paper used in this publication meets the requirements
of the American National Standard for Permanence of Paper
for Printed Library Materials Z39.48-1984.

10   9   8   7   6   5   4   3   2   1

Contents

PART THREE
Terror as an Instrument
of State Policy

PART FOUR
The Social and Political
Psychology of State Terror

Acknowledgments

This book grew out of an international conference entitled State Organized Terror: The Case of Violent Internal Repression, which was conceived and directed by Vladimir Shlapentokh and Christopher K. Vanderpool. Neither the conference nor the book would have been possible without the financial and moral support and encouragement of several foundations and organizations, various offices and departments within Michigan State University, and numerous individuals and outstanding scholars in the field who gave freely of their time and expertise. We would like to thank each and every one of them for their support and for increasing our understanding of state organized terror and repression.

Among the foundations and organizations who supported us are The Earhart Foundation, The National Council for Soviet and East European Research, and The Michigan State University Foundation. We would like to thank the following individuals within Michigan State University: David Scott and the Office of the Provost; John Cantlon, the former vice president for research and development; Ralph Smuckler, the former dean of International Studies and Programs; Gwen Andrews, the former dean of the College of Social Science; John K. Hudzik, associate dean of the College of Social Science; Myron S. Magen, dean of the College of Osteopathic Medicine; Donald Weston, former dean of the College of Human Medicine; John W. Eadie, dean of the College of Arts and Letters; Barbara Steidle, dean of James Madison College; Marvin Olsen, former chair of the Department of Sociology; Joseph Papsidero, chair of the Department of Community Health Science; Brian Silver, chair of the Department of Political Science; Tom Carroll, director of the Center for the Advanced Study of International Development; Munir Sendich, director of the Russian and East European Studies Center; David Wiley, director of the African Studies Center; Marc Van Wormer, former conference consultant with University Conferences and Institutes; and David E. Wright, professor and former assistant to the vice president for research.

We would also like to thank members of our staff, including Tammy Dennany, Jane Noice, Cindy Struthers, and Wes Pitts, who gave unstintingly of their time and whose efforts contributed much to the success of the conference, and also Debi Hogle, Irene Unkefer, and Melissa Hefty for helping us to complete the preparation of this book. Thanks go as well to Richard Yuille for his talented editorial assistance in the last stage of the project.

Last but not least, we would like to thank our conference advisory panel: Jonathan Adelman of the Graduate School of International Studies at the University of Denver; George Lopez, fellow of the Institute for International Peace Studies at the University of Notre Dame; Alfred Meyer, professor of political science at the University of Michigan; and Richard Hellie, professor of history at the University of Chicago.

P. Timothy Bushnell
Vladimir Shlapentokh
Christopher K. Vanderpool
Jeyaratnam Sundram

PART ONE

Introduction

1

State Organized Terror: Tragedy of the Modern State

P. Timothy Bushnell, Vladimir Shlapentokh, Christopher K. Vanderpool, and Jeyaratnam Sundram

The use of terroristic violence and repression by states against their own citizens is a common phenomenon. In this century alone, tens of millions of people, living in most regions of the world, under communist, democratic, military, and theocratic governments have been and continue to be victims of state organized repression and violence. The prototypical episodes of state violence against its own citizens were those perpetrated by the Nazi and Stalinist regimes in the 1930s and 1940s. The unprecedented evils of the Nazi Holocaust and the Great Soviet Purges have often been viewed as the special consequences of Nazism and Soviet communism. Yet, with the frequent recurrence of massive and violent state repression in other parts of the world since the 1940s, there has been greater awareness that these horrors are not restricted to a narrow range of cultures or types of regime. It has become evident that the phenomenon has deeper, more global roots and is tied to the increasingly sophisticated and continuously expanding bureaucratic and technical capabilities of states everywhere for violence and repression.

In spite of this increased awareness, there is little theoretical knowledge available about the nature and sources of state organized terror. Unfortunately, the severe scholarly neglect of the subject of violence and terror is just a part of the neglect of the more general subject of repression. Even when histories and political accounts of extremely repressive regimes have been written, they usually have not analyzed the origins, the instruments, the politics, and the effects of terror itself. At least three fundamental factors are responsible for this lack of attention. First, information on violent internal repression is extremely scarce since most of the relevant documents have been intentionally destroyed or kept secret, while journalistic investigation is severely restricted. To compound the problem, victims of violent terror often disappear or fear bearing witness to events.[1] Second, outside investigation of the state's terroristic exercise of power over its own population has been viewed as interference with state sovereignty. Only recently has the protection of human and civil rights become a legitimate issue of international concern. Third, predominant theoretical frameworks have failed to identify repressive state violence and terror as phenomena that are central to the modern state and which therefore require explanation. The principal varieties of theory concerning the state have either been analyses of the ideological and economic underpinnings of the state or have focused on the play of politics within the context of a legally sanctioned political consensus that limits the way state violence is deployed.

The development of the comparative perspective has been frustrated by scholarly specialization in different regions of the world and by differences in orientation associated with the variety of social scientific and humanistic disciplines.[2] Divergent sets of policy problems posed by various regions of the world have contributed to differences in research emphasis that discourage the integration of knowledge. Much of the literature on state terror has also been politically polarized by the tendency of authors to choose nations for discussion on the basis of their political views.[3]

The neglect of the subject of internally directed state terror has been compounded by the fact that although many theoretical insights on state terror have been gained through descriptive studies of individual cases, there have been very few efforts to link these insights together. In the field of political theory, only theories of totalitarianism, which have been used to understand the Nazi and Stalinist regimes, have explicitly attempted to explain the state's political use of violence against its own citizens.[4] Since the 1960s, however, as the division of labor between those studying fascism and those studying Stalinist Russia has deepened, totalitarianism, as a theory, has ceased to guide scholarship.[5]

Two serious attempts were made at the end of the 1960s toward extending the theoretical understanding of state organized terror by broadening the comparative framework. Alexander Dallin and George Breslauer,[6] in their book *Political Terror in Communist Systems*, took the logical step of searching for parallels between China and the Soviet Bloc countries by looking at the relationship of terror to political and economic development. E.V. Walter,[7] in his book *Terror and Resistance*, attempted to provide a new perspective on totalitarian terror by examining terror in the Zulu empire of the nineteenth century. Surprisingly, virtually no one built on either of these works until the 1980s.[8] The most notable works are a volume on secret police in communist states by Jonathan

Adelman,[9] and three volumes on state violence and repression edited by Michael Stohl and George Lopez,[10] which aim to provide a framework for a broader comparative analysis and to define the relevant body of literature. The present volume is meant to complement their efforts, though casting the comparative net somewhat differently.

Recent developments in Eastern Europe and the Soviet Union seem to indicate a global trend toward the liberalization of society and the diminution of state organized terror. Politicians, journalists, and scholars, around the world, are already trumpeting the coming of a better and more humane world. A closer look at the nations of the world, however, shows that the phenomenon of state organized terror is far from vanquished. Even as Eastern Europe and Soviet Russia liberalize, other states continue unabated in the repression of their own citizens. The salient case is China and that new symbol of state terror, Tiananmen Square. Others that come to mind easily are the cases of South Africa, Iran, El Salvador, Burma, and Sri Lanka. These are but the most obvious cases that have been subject to the glare of media attention. There are numerous others that are little known because of state control and secrecy or because the violence has not been dramatic enough to draw media attention. North Korea, Guatemala, and Burundi are but a few of the examples that would fit into this category.

Even in the case of Eastern Europe and the Soviet Union, we cannot be certain that state organized terror is a thing of the past. There is no certainty that the struggle to develop socially and economically and to rationalize the new social order will be successful. What will happen if some of the problems are not politically resolved? Take the cases of the Baltic states, Armenia, Azerbaijan, Moldavia, and other parts of the Soviet Union, their desire to leave the Soviet federation, and the Soviet resolve not to let them go. Would the Soviet Union, under pressure, resort to repression? The same can be asked of Romania in regard to its ethnic problems. What will happen if the newly free Eastern European states and Soviet Russia itself cannot deliver on their economic promises and the people become disaffected and restless? Could they resolve the problem without resorting to repression? Hence, even as we hope for and anticipate the dawning of a more humane world, we need to recognize that state organized terror will be a continuing problem. It needs to become a stronger focus of political attention and inquiry if we are ever to work effectively to reduce its occurrence.

The State: Its Glory and Tragedy

State organized terror during the middle and late twentieth century has revealed and discredited the dark side of the modern state. If we follow Max Weber,[11] the essential distinguishing feature of all states, as sets of institutions, is their monopoly or pretense of monopoly over legitimate acts of violence. It is then logical to suppose that the scale and illegitimacy of violence in episodes of state organized terror develops as a frequent, if not necessary, consequence of the symbolic, organizational, and physical resources intrinsic to the modern state. But state organized terror cannot be considered simply a manifestation of the state's essential nature. It is also a pathology and a perversion of the state. By extension, it is a pathology of civil society as well, for state and society are in symbiotic relationship, each with its own dimensions of autonomy, while each conditions and shapes the other.

The ideal relationship of state to society was articulated by such thinkers as Hobbes, Hegel, and Rousseau[12] prior to the disasters of the twentieth century. It may be said that most of them saw the state as an institution which, like a gift from the heavens, could bring peace to humankind, prevent people from mutual destruction, and introduce some measure of order into their lives. It was unthinkable to them that the state could, like a maniacal beast, assail its own citizens. Glorifying the state as the embodiment of a social contract, Rousseau contended that "the subjects do not need guarantees against sovereign power because it is impossible to assume that the organism will want to damage its members."

Much of this respect and admiration for the state was based on its performance of three essential functions: (1) the maintenance of internal peace and order, (2) the organization and protection of economic activity, and (3) the defense of national independence and national interests. The origins of our respect for the state's function of maintaining internal peace and security for its citizens lie in the Middle Ages, when internal wars frequently made life unbearable. Other wars as well, such as the one between the Gibbelines and Gwelfs in thirteenth century Italy, the "War of the Roses" between Lancaster and York in fifteenth century England, and the so-called "Thirty Years War" which reduced the population of Germany by one-third in the seventeenth century, formed the backdrop for the writings of Hobbes, Rousseau, and finally Hegel, who saw in the state "the implementation of the moral and divine idea."

The notion of the state as organizer of social and economic life was introduced by such utopians as Campanella[13] and Thomas More, who were both inspired by Plato.[14] They each envisioned a powerful state organization that would be able to bring equality and fairness to human life. Marx,[15] and especially Lenin,[16] developed the idea of the state as an organ which could carry out the radical transformation of society into a planned collectivist paradise. In the Great Depression of the 1930s and during the American New Deal, growing responsibility for economic management and social welfare was popularly thrust upon the state. This, in a country which is known for its antipathy toward "big government," further contributed to the prevailing esteem for the state. Furthermore, socialist states, as well as states in the West, can be credited with having made many positive strides in the realms of education, health services, and assistance to the elderly and poor.

In recent years, the state has also gained legitimacy as a vehicle of nationalism. National liberation movements have always had as their primary goal the creation of their own state. This has greatly enhanced the prestige of the state in the minds of the hundreds of millions of people across the world who, in recent times, have emerged from colonialism in Asia, Africa, and Latin America. Nationalists of all kinds have emphasized the defense of national independence and an ideology of patriotism that demands the subordination of all values to one, namely, service to the motherland, thus justifying any action performed by the state and its rulers.

Today, the state has lost some of its authority as the guardian of order and as the protector of its own citizens. This book is about many of the most important events that have brought this about. In the twentieth century, the state, like an unchained beast, has ferociously attacked those who claim to be its master, its own citizens. In most cases, people could not understand the cause of this rage or the desire to destroy those who seemingly were an important means of support for the state, and ultimately its very reason for existence. The fruit of these perversions of the state has been the human rights movement whose theme has been liberation from the iron grip of the state and whose greatest fulfillment and validation has been the processes set in motion by Gorbachev's *glasnost*.

While there were isolated instances of state intervention for humanitarian reasons in the internal affairs of other nations before World War II, the Universal Declaration of Human Rights of 1948, inspired by reaction to the Holocaust, marked the beginning of a period of a rising hope and a determination to establish the legitimacy, and means for international protection, of human rights. In the wake of the Helsinki Accords of 1975 and President Carter's human rights initiatives, a dynamic has now been created at the grassroots level which cannot be entirely controlled and predicted by the states that have taken advantage of it or encouraged it at various points. In fact, we seem to have witnessed an increasing ascendancy of the sovereignty of the individual relative to the sovereignty of the state. Even in the face of sharp increases in chauvinistic nationalism, the recognition that people have a right to basic human needs and dignity has made remarkable headway. Human rights now seem firmly established as an important subject of international diplomacy and bargaining in a way unimaginable only fifteen or twenty years ago.

The state, having failed to protect its individual citizens, has been increasingly exposed as a deeply flawed and destructive vehicle for nationalism and the promotion of economic and social welfare. The last decades have witnessed widespread disillusionment with the state in the economic sphere. Gone are the times when the state was assumed capable of stimulating economic growth through careful planning and other regulatory activities. The newly free Eastern European countries and Gorbachev's Russia lead in a frontal attack against the state as manager. Meanwhile, Reaganomics and Thatcherism reflect pessimism in the West about the state and a validation of the rush to free enterprise in the East.

The image of the state as the defender of national integrity and independence has also been seen as misleading in its neglect of the state's behavior in multi-ethnic and multi-national dominions. The state tends to be chauvinistic and jingoistic, often seeing in the persecution of minorities in its territory the best way to gain the support of the majority and secure itself against potential opposition. We find that the state in the twentieth century has acted aggressively against the members of minority ethnic groups much more often than it has come to their defense. The states of Hitler and Stalin are just the most terrible examples of this general tendency.

State Organized Terror:
A Pathology of State and Society

What has given the state the capacity and impetus for terroristic violence in our age? Part of the answer may be found in the violent nature of the modern state's origins.[17] With every stage in its development, it overwhelmed local sources of power and undermined communal and particularistic forms of authority. At the same time, its own power was built on its capacities for organization and communication, which were used effectively to deploy resources over an extensive territory. In particular, the state's power was manifested in development of mandatory public education, regulation of health and sanitation practices, collection of taxes, the courts and systems of conscription, as well as the police and the military. The experience of the population under these broader structures of power gave them a common orientation and identity as citizens of the state thus making them a "mass" in the political sense.

As the state grew in power, its institutions expanded to meet the social needs of its citizens. At the same time, the rights of citizens were increasingly protected and expressed in more universal terms. The state, in its attempt to control, mobilize and exploit society, relied on society to sustain its own matrix of social and economic structures that produce the human material and physical wealth necessary for the exercise of state power. Requiring regularity and legitimacy in its activities, the state had to shape itself to respond in some measure to society's resistance to its power and to society's claims upon its capacities. Thus, the concept. and defense of citizens' rights developed as a part of the process of formation of the apparatus of the state. State organized terror becomes, in this perspective, a phenomenon in which the relationship between the apparatus and power of the state and the rights of citizens has become severely distorted and one-sided.

The spread of terroristic violence to society at large involves a two-fold transformation of the state and its relationship to society. On the one hand, citizens' rights and the boundaries of legitimate violence are redefined, while on the other the state's agencies of violence undergo an extensive, malignant development.

In the political life of most modern states, individuals and the groups they form are recognized, to a substantial extent, as having "rights" that are inherent in human nature and the nature of social life. The best-known classical statement of this view is Locke's theory of government,[18] in which the individual is considered as having a natural right to "life, liberty, and the pursuit of happiness." Such rights are based on a conception of individuals as decision-makers who govern their own thoughts and actions and a conception of society as self-determining in its evolution.

In highly repressive states, on the other hand, there is a lack of acceptance by the state of the role individuals and groups play as initiators of social, political, and economic change. Change is only believed to be appropriate and good when it is initiated at the top of the power structure and pushed down through the masses. The state takes upon itself the right to impose, through violence, its definitions of reality and correct behavior throughout the whole field of human action. As terror penetrates the sinews of every organization and association in social life, people are numbed into subservience and repress any independent thought or impulse to action. Life becomes pervaded by the symbols of the all powerful state and its agents and tools of repression—the political police, their weapons and prisons, and their wider cultural manifestations, all conveying the ever-present threat of violent reprisal for transgressions of all types. A culture of terror develops in which no one is to be trusted. Only the state is good and only the leader has the vision and rationality to carry the state and people to their destiny. As these norms become "accepted," a darkness descends on society and repression becomes part of the taken-for-granted reality of everyday life.

In its most advanced forms, the state can become so effective and efficient in the use of terror that it can decrease its reliance on overt and direct use of violence. As repression becomes increasingly subtle, selective, and restricted from public view, violence is more easily defined as a legitimate exercise of power by the state and its agents.

This suggests the other side of transformation in state terror. Not only behavior changes, that is, state policies and culture, but the instruments of violence do so as well. These tend to achieve a heightened status, autonomy, and dynamism. The various agents and administrative apparatuses of the state begin increasingly to substitute normal due process and the routinized practices of government with "extraordinary" measures. Acting with a sense of urgency and mission, they may even act beyond the control of the regime itself, accelerating the spread of violent repression through the population. Often, personnel more closely identify with the state and its leadership than before. The state is felt to be a living organism whose life must be protected and enhanced. In return, a means for transcending the normality, morality, and banality of everyday life is provided through attachment to the higher good of the state. Potential is created for the emergence of a demonic cult of violence with disastrous consequences for the citizenry.

What causes such terrible and destructive invasion of society by the state? Elite structure theory provides part of a general framework within which to construct an answer. When the state views its monopolization of power and authority as absolute, society's institutions loom larger as potentially competing centers of power. The state then operates to preclude that competition. The focal point for the jealousy of the state and its agents may be a political party, educational or religious institutions, an ethnic group, business interests, an economic class or even a cultural trend. Beyond these foci is the vast, ill-defined group termed the "masses" or the "people." This mass is generally unorganized, mostly apathetic, and in general it is a quiet audience or witness to the power struggle between the regime and its supposed opponents.

This division of society between the state, threatening sectors or institutions of society, and the general citizenry recalls the elite structure described by Mosca and Pareto.[19] At the center of the regime is the governing elite controlling the ongoing processes and structures of power and authority in the state. Surrounding the center are a series of peripheral power centers parallel to what Pareto called the non-governing elite. Below these two groups are the masses.

These divisions may or may not be empirically evident. What is important, though, is that the state views political reality in such terms.

The more threatened the state and its leaders feel from the existence, real or not, of a competing elite stratum, the more likely is terror and repression. The peripheral power groups of the non-governing elite are generally the direct targets of repression.

The masses or general citizenry are not usually, then, the major victims or real targets of terror. They are, however, affected by the repression of elite groups. When such groups as the intelligentsia, the military, business leaders, and religious figures are terrorized and their "crimes" and punishments publicized, the masses wonder whether they too can fall victim to the power of the state. As anxiety spreads through the populace, the more "silent" the citizenry become. They withdraw even further from the public arena of politics and isolate themselves in the private routines of everyday life.

If, however, the regime begins to think that the masses may become a pivotal factor in the competition with the peripheral elites for power, they too will suffer the violence of the state. The routines of everyday life will no longer provide them with shelter from the shifting political winds of the state. Such was the case during the generalized mass terror of the Soviet Union during the thirties, the radicalization of Chinese society in the Cultural Revolution, and the massacre of millions in Kampuchea.

Conditions Associated with
the Emergence of State Organized Terror

What follows is proposed as a theoretical template for the phenomenon of state organized terror. It has been constructed out of an analysis of all the papers presented at the conference that was the basis for this volume.[20] The reader should test it against the papers that appear here as well as against others. This portrait of conditions conducive to state terror is meant to encompass the prototypical episodes in Nazi Germany and Stalinist Russia as well as more recent episodes in a wide variety of political systems throughout the world.

Four general conditions seem to be associated with the emergence of state organized terror. They are: (1) distorted conceptions of the state and society and their inter-relationship, (2) the disarray of state institutions, (3) the presence of deep economic and/or ethnic conflicts in society or between the society and the state, and (4) state dependence on a foreign power. Terroristic regimes are typically animated by ideologies sharply at odds with reality and by unrealistic ambitions for social and economic control. Communist regimes, such as those in the Soviet Union, China, Afghanistan, and Kampuchea, see society in terms of class struggle and attempt to radically transform feudal and capitalist structures of land tenure and enterprise. One-party, military-dominated regimes, on the other hand, tend to see the nation as an organism that must be dedicated to survival in the face of external aggressors whose agents are seen behind all independent political movements within the country. The "National Security Doctrine" of the Argentine military in the 1970s and the concept of "total onslaught" guiding the South African government until very recently are examples of this world-view.

The imperative for state action supplied by distorted ideology is typically and tragically linked to an assumption that the agencies of the state possess nearly unlimited power to command social change (or maintain stability) and that the state's leader possesses the power to comprehensively control the agencies of the state. Progress is conceived as depending upon the strength of the leader's power to command and the destruction of anyone who would threaten to disrupt the implementation of command. The image of a strictly top-down, pyramidal exercise of power is often legitimized and reinforced by a personality cult or a belief in the religious authority of the head of state. Thus, most cases of state terror are closely associated with the concentration of power in a single leader such as Stalin, Hitler, Pol Pot, Jim Jones, Khomeini, Pinochet, etc.

The frequent presence of personality cults suggests that the exaggerated estimation and rigidly hierarchical view of state power is reflected also in the attitudes of the general population. Although terror is often a response to social unrest and popular resistance to state actions, the state's use of terror for political control tends to occur where the citizenry has traditionally been politically passive. While popular resistance is aimed at reversing the violence and injustice of state actions, it does not necessarily aim at democratic participation in state affairs and it may not be coupled with a capacity to see and understand the political instabilities and rivalries in ruling circles. Such was the case in Iran, where people rebelling against the repression of the Shah were willing to submit to Khomeini's authority. Terror can even be justified to a naive population, as it was by Stalin, as a method of purging those elements in the leadership and bureaucracy that supposedly are at fault for the violence of the terror itself, as well as for the economic and military failures of the state. The general population remains unable to distinguish the war against society from the war against society's enemies and is ready to accede to violent political upheavals and terror as legitimate attempts by the leaders of the state to return state and society to "the right path."

The second fundamental condition associated with state organized terror is great institutional chaos and disorganization, which breeds particularly intense political rivalries within the state apparatus. Terror has grown out of such a context even in cases, such as Nazi Germany and Stalinist Russia, where the state has seemed monolithic and all-powerful to its victims and external enemies. The chaos of the state may exist because its various agencies have no clearly defined missions or means of carrying out their duties, or have overlapping responsibilities. Chaos is often great in states in early stages of formation, when concepts of public service to the nation and bureaucratic order have a weak hold on ill-trained personnel. The danger in such political chaos, particularly where the state is facing obvious and severe economic problems or a military threat, is the emergence of political rhetoric emphasizing boundless will and energy and simplistic absolutes. Such rhetoric can take root and thrive because there are no established bureaucratic structures of decision making or political norms to support measured evaluation of policies.

A regime of terror, once in place, has a tendency to further increase the disarray of state institutions. A regime such as Stalin's in the 1930s, for example, requires the use of vast numbers of informants to identify the ubiquitous enemy; these informants are largely motivated to accuse others by a need to demonstrate their own loyalty and escape blame for malperformance of duties. In addition, the criteria for targeting victims are arbitrary and the standards of evidence low or nonexistent. Self-protective falsification of reports and clandestine personal alliances throughout the bureaucracy for the purposes of mutual protection and promotion make matters worse. In such a context, the quality of information received by the agencies and leaders of the state is likely to be very poor and its quantity likely overwhelming. There is a corresponding decline in the ability to monitor events and impose detailed accountability.

Loss of control of state institutions is furthered by terror in another way as well. Radical social change and political domination through terror require a vast number of agents to which a great deal of power must be delegated, despite the ideology of total command by the state's leader. Such extensive delegation of power to lower levels of the state apparatus or to people outside the government can lead to a loss of control and unwanted social unrest, as it did in the Soviet and Chinese cases. Terror also sometimes threatens to seriously disrupt private sector organizations in industry and commerce, as it did in Nazi Germany. This can motivate a return to less arbitrary and massive use of violence which is likely to take the form of a restriction of powers of violence to the official police and military. However, terroristic regimes also give secret police and military units much authority to act on their own; the result can be operations that political leaders know little about, as was recently discovered in South Africa.

Economic and ethnic divisions are the third general condition associated with state organized terror. Economic growth has often created a large group of landless peasants and a new industrial working class that have lost their economic security while commercial and political elites have grown wealthy. The resulting political volatility and mobilization of large sectors of the population has motivated severe repression in response or has caused revolutions that have installed repressive regimes. Economic factors in state terror have been most salient in Latin America and are becoming more important in Africa with increased industrialization. The volatility of the economically suffering Soviet peasants and workers amidst the visible wealth of ruling elites played an important role in bringing about Stalin's Great Terror as well.

The violence of a state against its own citizens is also often built upon or reinforces preexisting racial and ethnic conflicts. Ethnic conflicts, however, rarely lead to massive violence unless cultural and religious differences correspond to some degree with differences in economic or political status. Often, ethnic differences will be exaggerated by a regime such as Hitler's as a way of crystallizing a definition of the enemy which will add the force of ethnic antagonisms to their own political support.

Where subjugated ethnic groups are culturally cohesive and engage in subversion or violence against the dominant group, as Indians have in Guatemala, the way is clear for legitimation of mass political murder by the dominant group. This is the case in many Third World states which were set up by colonial powers to rule over different ethnic groups which had not previously developed a common political culture or ways of balancing interests.

The fourth condition associated with state organized terror involves its international context. Repressive and terroristic regimes have often been regimes that have gained power with the military, financial, and political support of another, more powerful state. The clearest examples are the Eastern European nations and Afghanistan, but several severely repressive regimes in Latin America and elsewhere have come to power as a result of U.S. support. Such externally installed regimes tend to lack legitimacy and an orientation and ability to be responsive to citizens' needs, and so are more likely to resort to violent repression for control.

Many violent regimes in Africa, Asia, the Middle East, and Latin America, though not installed by external powers, have built up their security and police forces with heavy foreign assistance, leaving other state institutions relatively underdeveloped. Such foreign aid has been aimed largely at maintaining secure conditions for production and trade by keeping volatile opposition political activity in check, and at increasing influence to achieve geopolitical goals. However, the relative overdevelopment of the state's means of coercion has meant that leaders are heavily influenced by military doctrine and are more likely to deal with internal political problems by force and, by extension, terror.

Organization of the Book

This introduction is extended by Alfred Schmid's paper which elucidates some imprecisions and suggests some refinements in the way we use the terms repression, terror, and genocide and distinguish them from each other. The second section of the book is comprised of five papers that address themselves primarily to the antecedent structural factors conducive to state organized terror. The first, by John McCamant, proposes a way of situating state organized terror within the context of a multifaceted analytical scheme for conceptualizing the relationship between different forms of power on the local, national and international levels. McCamant describes the erosion in the twentieth century of traditional structures of authority and economic domination on the local level as markets become national and international in scope and modern media penetrate the culture. In his view, the economic and political dislocation this causes tends to be dealt with through repressive violence because the power of the state has developed much more rapidly in the military domain than in the institutions needed for stable democracy and effective action for public welfare.

Charles Brockett attempts to isolate the roots of repressive violence through a comparative study of the Central American countries, most of which experienced roughly equal levels of popular political mobilization in opposition to the state but differing amounts of repression. He finds that lack of peasant access to land or the unavailability of underused land to the state for redistribution correlates with the use of repressive violence. Another important correlate of repression is the degree to which police and military forces are developed and are geared to defending the interests of large landowners involved in export agriculture. Finally, he notes, violent repression has been deeply embedded in the political culture of some nations, especially where Native Americans have traditionally been viewed as subhuman and permissible targets of violence.

Rhoda Howard examines the rise in government-perpetrated political violence in Kenya since 1982 with a view to determining whether the factors that explain it are similar to those that have been linked to violent repression in Latin America. She argues that the extent of economic inequality and displacement of peasants from the land, the development of ideological opposition among the political elite, and geopolitically motivated, foreign (U.S.) build-up of the military all have contributed to the conditions for Kenyan violence.

The papers by Jonathan Adelman on the role of the secret police in the communist states and by William Maley on terror in Afghanistan concentrate less on economic factors, but join McCamant, Brockett, and Howard in identifying foreign support for the security apparatus as a source of violent repression. Adelman maintains that a regime that comes to power through protracted and popular struggle develops governmental and military institutions that are effective enough to reduce the need for a secret police to keep itself in power. Where no such broad-based struggle takes place and power is attained quickly with the help of foreign military aid, the secret police becomes much more critical for control. Finally, the wider the scope of regime ambition for military or economic mobilization, the more use is made of secret police.

It is primarily the unrealistic ambition for rapid socioeconomic transformation that Maley places at the root of Afghan terror, along with the enormous military intervention of the Soviet Union. State institutions were vastly underequipped to carry out a naively conceived plan of land reform or to break down extremely stable traditional modes of local self-governance. Escalation of violence was a tragic and futile response to the peasant resistance generated by land reform.

The third section of the book focuses on terror as government policy. The papers by David Pion-Berlin, Bernd Wegner, and Stanley Shernock all address the question of how far terror can be viewed as a rationally employed instrument of power. Pion-Berlin shows how state terror rose in Argentina in the 1970s while political opposition was actually declining. This, he argues, is because of the influence upon the military of the "National Security Doctrine" and associated counterinsurgency techniques learned from the French. This doctrine facilitated the linkage of the most minor sorts of opposition, both real and imagined, to a larger geopolitical battle requiring "total war" by the nation state to maintain itself and survive. So distorted were the perceptions of the military that there was little apparent political or ethnic pattern in their targeting of victims.

Wegner's paper on Nazi Germany, the original source of much of the thinking behind the National Security Doctrine, also makes the point that terror was largely dysfunctional as an instrument of power. It was extended to the point where it undermined the authority of the regime by violating moral and legal norms of the German population and brought Germany to defeat when unleashed outside its borders under cover of war. Wegner places the responsibility for terror, as well as genocide, upon an ideology of politics as a competitive, Darwinian fight for survival that was able to erupt in an extreme, racially based form in the context of tremendous chaotic rivalries in a disorganized state.

The verdict on terror as a functionally rational instrument of power is more complex in Shernock's paper. In his comparative study of Nazi Germany, Stalinist Russia in the 1930s, and the early Cultural Revolution in China, he claims that very little of the terror can be seen as unintended or out of control. At the same time, terror did reduce regime legitimacy, threaten the integrity of state and private economic institutions, and strike many victims who were no part of any genuine opposition. The leaders of these states appeared to have used terror rationally from the point of view of their personal power but not from the point of view of regime stability and effectiveness of state institutions.

The papers by Ben Kiernan and Chanthou Boua give stark documentation of the techniques used in the destruction of three clearly defined target groups in Pol Pot's Cambodia, namely, peasants of the Eastern Zone, the Muslim minority, and Buddhist monks. Kiernan explains that the first group was targeted because of its social and political ties with the neighboring Vietnamese enemy and shows how the manner in which they were rounded up and marked for execution, based on an ideology of national purification, was reminiscent of the Nazi treatment of Jews. While the Muslims (discussed by Kiernan) were a minority community, and the Buddhist monks (discussed by Boua) were at the center of Khmer social life, both were victimized because they represented potentially competing sources of social authority rather than because of their political opposition.

The papers in the fourth section of the book, while relevant to the structural sources of terror and terror as a strategic instrument of state power, also provide deeper insights into the political and social psychology of state terror. The show trial is a key political device of some terrorist regimes which is particularly useful in revealing the psychology of both perpetrators and target populations. William McCagg's paper analyzes the Rajk trial and the turn toward terror in Hungary at the end of the 1940s. The Hungarian leaders who designed the trial were themselves terrorized into mimicing Stalin and forcing a violent, contradictory shift in direction upon the Hungarian Communist Party. The trial was, in turn, a vehicle for the crystallization of the Hungarian population's "captive mind"—dependent, fearful, and credulous of the Party's rationalizations of its actions.

Dmitry Shlapentokh's study of Soviet show trials early in the Stalinist period reveal how they were designed to play to the deep political resentments of workers who wanted to see the accused severely punished. The victims of these trials were high-level managers and bureaucrats who were popularly perceived as corrupt, debauched, and economically over-privileged. The trial aided Stalin in painting a contrasting portrait of himself and "loyal" party officials as puritanical and egalitarian.

Helen Fein's paper examines the relationship between leader and led in a very different cultural context. She examines the Jonestown, Guyana, People's Temple community of the 1970s as a microcosm of the politics and psychology of totalitarianism. Just as Stalin did, the leader, Jim Jones, was able to portray himself as a savior from the enemies of society. Though the threat was depicted as coming mainly from outside the community's borders, the leader employed violence and public humiliation against his followers to break down normal interpersonal relationships that could serve as a frame of emotional and cognitive reference to deny Jim Jones the total allegiance he sought.

The last paper in this section is one that takes us away from the focus upon leaders and provides a personal account of the experience of state organized terror as it moves downward and outward through society. Jane Wu tells of the suicide of her brother and identifies several of those groups in Chinese society who were most vulnerable to committing suicide during the Cultural Revolution despite their lack of any connection to genuine political opposition. Utterly alone in taking their lives, they left behind them loved ones who, out of fear or opportunism, denounced them as anti-revolutionaries. Wu contends that the social and political progress of China requires the Chinese and especially China's current leaders to speak not only of their experience as victims of terror but as victimizers who isolated and condemned those who took their own lives.

The book concludes with an evocative essay by Robert Solo who finds the concept and phenomenon of the demon to be at the center of the great twentieth century slaughters of the innocent. In Solo's scenario, once a society is captured by the belief that demons lurk everywhere behind the facade of normalcy, the demons themselves multiply. For those who participate in stalking and unmasking the demon or who are merely afraid of being identified as the demon, do everything they can to conceal their thoughts and suspicions and in this way become like demons themselves. Universal distrust of one's neighbors leaves only the leader as a guide to the demon's true identity.

Notes

1. In a survey of fifty prominent scholars of terrorism, twenty nine of the respondents said the data on state or regime terrorism was the type "required the most urgently in order to advance our knowledge on the subject of terrorism." Alex P. Schmid, *Political Terrorism: A Research Guide to Concepts, Theories, Data Bases, and Literature* (Amsterdam: North-Holland Publishing Company, 1984),

274. For more information on the paucity of data and research on terroristic repression, see the more recent edition of this guide: Alex P. Schmid and A. J. Jongman et al., *Political Terrorism: A New Guide to Actors, Authors, Concepts, Data Bases, Theories and Literature* (Amsterdam: North-Holland, 1988).

2. Schmid (1984, p. 418), states, in reference to literature on terrorism of all types, that "Scholars from different fields such as psychology, criminology, law, political science, sociology, history and the military sciences have contributed to it. But these writers have often not taken cognizance of each others work when it is from another discipline, which might go some way to explain the lack of cumulativeness in the literature of terrorism."

3. Schmid, 174.

4. Schmid, 171.

5. See the "Introduction," in Ernest A. Menze, ed., *Totalitarianism Reconsidered* (Port Washington, New York: Kennikat Press, 1981).

6. Alexander Dallin and George Breslauer, *Political Terror in Communist Systems* (Stanford: Stanford University Press, 1970).

7. E.V. Walter, *Terror and Resistance* (New York: Oxford University Press, 1969).

8. Schmid (1984, p. 174) points out: "Given the ubiquity of rule by terror, the uneven attention given to regime terrorism in contrast to insurgent terrorism by social scientists is depressing." According to Jonathan R. Adelman, ed., *Terror and Communist Politics: The Role of the Secret Police in Communist States* (Boulder: Westview Press, 1984), p. 2, "What Dallin and Breslauer found in 1971 is still valid in 1984, 'We soon discovered to our surprise, that the theoretical literature on political terror was not nearly so well developed as we had expected, and that in particular, there are almost no systematic efforts in this field to compare and to explain differences among various Communist (and non-Communist) systems.' (Dallin and Breslauer, vii)."

9. See Adelman.

10. See Michael Stohl and George Lopez, eds., *The State as Terrorist: The Dynamics of Governmental Violence and Repression* (Westport, Conn.: Greenwood Press, 1984); Michael Stohl and George Lopez, eds., *Government Violence and Repression: An Agenda for Research* (Westport, Conn.: Greenwood Press, 1986); George Lopez and Michael Stohl, eds., *Dependence, Development, and State Repression* (Westport, Conn.: Greenwood Press, 1989).

11. See H.H. Gerth and C. Wright Mills, *From Max Weber: Essays in Sociology* (New York: Oxford University Press, 1958).

12. See Thomas Hobbes, *The Leviathan* (Buffalo, New York: Prometheus Books, 1988). See also, G.W.F. Hegel, *Hegel's Political Writings*, trans. T.M. Knox (Oxford: Clarendon Press, 1964). Also see Jean Jacques Rousseau, *The Social Contract* (Harmondsworth: Penguin, 1968).

13. See T. Campanella, *The City of the Sun: A Poetical Dialogue*, trans. D.J. Donno (Berkeley: University of California Press, 1981).

14. See Thomas More, *Utopia*, ed. G.M. Logan and R.M. Adams, (New York: Cambridge University Press, 1989). See also, Plato, *The Republic*, trans. R.W. Sterling and W.C. Scott (New York: Norton, 1985).

15. See John Maguire, *Marx's Theory of Politics* (Cambridge: Cambridge University Press, 1978).

16. See V.I.Lenin, *State and Revolution* (New York: International Publications, 1971).

17. This paper draws heavily from Anthony Giddens, *The Nation State and Violence* (Berkeley and Los Angeles: University of California Press, 1987).

18. John Locke, *Two Treaties of Government* (Cambridge: Cambridge University Press, 1963).

19. Gaetano Mosca, *The Ruling Class* (New York: McGraw-Hill, 1939); Vilfredo Pareto, *The Rise and Fall of the Elites* (Totowa, New Jersey: Bedminster Press, 1968).

20. A list of conference papers appears at the end of this chapter.

Papers Presented at the International Conference Entitled State Organized Terror: The Case of Violent Internal Repression Michigan State University, November 2–5, 1988.

Adams, Richard C. *The Reproduction of State Terrorism in Central America.* Adelman, Jonathan R. *The Development of the Secret Police in Communist States.*

Bacon, Walter. *Cult and Terror in Communist Systems.*

Boua, Chanthou. *Genocide of a Religious Group: Pol Pot and Cambodia's Buddhist Monks.*

Bowen, Gordon. *Legacies of Latin American State Terrorism: Barrier to Democratization?*

Brockett, Charles D. *Sources of State Terrorism in Rural Central America.*

Coser, Lewis. *The Power and Limits of Terror.*

Doan, Van Toai. *Terror and Ideology in Rightist and Leftist Regimes.*

Eley, Geoff. *Racism, Genocide, Holocaust: Putting Nazi Anti-Semitism in Context.*

Fein, Helen. *The Politics of Paranoia: Jonestown and Twentieth Century Totalitarianism.*

Friedman, Edward. *The Origins of Mao's Mass Terror in Pre-1949 Leninist Institutions and Robespierrian Legitimations.*

Harff, Barbara. *State Perpetrators of Mass Political Murder Since 1945.*

Howard, Rhoda. *Repression and State Terror in Kenya: 1982–1988.*

Kiernan, Ben. *Genocidal Targeting: Two Groups of Victims in Pol Pot's Cambodia.*

Lewellen, Ted. *State Terror and the Disruption of Internal Adaptations by the CIA.*

Lopez, George. *Humanitarian Intervention and International Law: The Search for New Insights.*

Maley, William. *Social Dynamics and the Disutility of Terror: Afghanistan 1978–1989.*

Mahdi, Akbar. *Islam, Human Rights, and Violence.*

McCagg, William O. *The Experience of Terror: The Rajk Trial and the Captive Mind in 1949.*

McCamant, John F. *Domination, State Power, and Political Repression.*

McKay, John. *Internal Order and Ecology of Repression in Northern Ireland: Public Policy and Sociospatial Organization in Belfast and Derry.*

Meyer, Alfred. *A Mismanaged Political Purge: The U.S. Army Denazification Program.*
Montville, Joseph. *The Psychology of the Khmer Rouge Terror.*
Ndibongo, Manelisi. *Policing in South Africa: Apartheid's Black Police.*
Perlmutter, Amos. *The Role of the Political Police, Vanguard of the Modern Authoritarian System: A Comparative Institutional Analysis of Nazi Germany and the USSR.*
Pion-Berlin, David. *The Ideological and Perceptual Causes of Terror.*
Richter, Helena. *In the Shadow of Stalin's Terror: The Course of the Development of the Opposition During the Post-Stalinist Era in the USSR.*
Riordon, Rory. *Murder by Proxy: The Modernization of South Africa's Security Juggernaut.*
Rittersporn, Gabor T. *State Organized Terror and the Disorganization of the Soviet State.*
Salehi, Mohammad. *Visibility of Repression.*
Schmid, Alex P. *Repression, State Terrorism, and Genocide: A Conceptual Framework.*
Shernock, Stanley. *The Refractory Aspect of Terror in Movement-Regimes.*
Shlapentokh, Dmitry. *Bureaucracy and the Public Response to the Political Trials of the Late 1920s.*
Sloan, Stephen. *State Organized Terrorism: New Trends, Capabilities, and Tactics: The Privatization of Terror.*
Solo, Robert. *Enter the Demon.*
Suny, Ronald G. *Ideology or Social Ecology: Rethinking the Armenian Genocide.*
Thaxton, Ralph. *State Repression and the Origins of Popular Protest in Modern China, 1915-1949.*
Wegner, Bernd. *Violent Repression in The Third Reich—Did it Stabilize Hitler's Rule?*
Weissman, Susan. *The Role of the Purges in the Formation of the USSR.*
Wheatcroft, Stephen G. *The Scale and Significance of the Terror in the USSR in the 1930s.*
Wu, Jane Jiajing. *Suicides and Suicide Survivors of the Cultural Revolution.*

2

Repression, State Terrorism, and Genocide: Conceptual Clarifications

Alex P. Schmid

All I ask is that, in the midst of a murderous world, we agree to reflect on murder and to make a choice.

—Albert Camus

I take it that the intent of science is to ease human existence.

—Bertold Brecht

Von Clausewitz held that "War is . . . a continuation of political commerce, a carrying out of the same by other means."[1] By implication, normal politics is apparently conducted without the use of (warlike) violence. That is, by and large, our experience in the postwar Western world. However, this is an experience of the happy few. In the majority of nations, politics is not like that. Charles Humana noted in the mid-1980s that four out of five persons on earth live in states where human rights are violated.[2]

Why has so little attention been given in social science research to such massive violations? It seems, as John F. McCamant has suggested, that "the models of politics lacked the conceptual tools to make repression visible."[3] Extreme but not unusual political behavior by states, such as the unilateral use of instruments of war against unarmed civilians for the enforcement of allegiance or compliance, has only in the last decade

I wish to thank A.V.D. Wateren, a student at Leiden University, who not only assisted in screening the literature, but also made useful suggestions.

begun to emerge as a topic in its own right. The sole, important exception to this "rule" was the study of "totalitarian" communist and fascist regimes and the Jewish Holocaust.

The recent rediscovery of the dark side of politics by political scientists has not yet produced consensus with regard to terminology and conceptualization. Yet this is necessary in order to make the ongoing research cumulative and to advance the field. The purpose of this chapter is simply to present and review three concepts currently available. Each of these will be discussed in domestic contexts, although it is recognized that there are important links between international conflict and internal repression.

Repression

Repression, like oppression and suppression, involves pressure, which can be exerted either physically against the members of a class of subjects, or in a psychological form, affecting the emotional, mental or spiritual well-being of target groups.

Tilly has characterized repression as one of three reactions a regime may opt for when challenged by groups attempting to improve their own (power) position, the other two types of responses being "toleration" and "facilitation." The choice of reaction depends, according to Tilly, on the character of the regimes: facilitation is somewhat greater in democracies than in other regimes; toleration is much greater in weak regimes than in totalitarian states. Also important are the characteristics of the groups striving for greater influence. Tilly held that "the weaker or less acceptable the challengers and the larger their scale of action, the more likely they are to be repressed."[4]

Most authors use the concept of repression only in connection with political control measures taken by governments against opponents or potential opponents. While this is understandable since incumbent regimes are the main utilizers of this mode of influencing target populations, it is not wise to confine the term in such a way to official establishment violence. Hosmer has analyzed the activities of a national liberation movement with the help of this term. He used it to refer to a broad range of measures by which the Vietcong sought to eliminate, neutralize, punish, and reform their known enemies. The spectrum ranged from execution to such relatively mild disciplinary actions as compulsory indoctrination.[5]

It makes sense to consider in the same category both official repression and private repression by non-state actors. To use privileged terminology for the actions of a certain actor considered either more or less legitimate than other actors engaged in the same actions is a sin against the universality principle of science. T.R. Gurr has, in our view, correctly emphasized that such coercive tactics are available to all participants in the political process.[6]

Another issue is whether repression always involves physical violence or whether what Hosmer terms "relatively mild disciplinary actions" also fall under it. A sliding scale of the severity of means of coercion utilized might be helpful. Thus, Stohl and Lopez[7] and Sederberg[8] have linked the concepts of oppression, repression and terrorism by placing these in three concentric circles, starting with oppression at the outer edge and ending with terrorism in the center. As one moves toward the center, denial of social and economic privileges (oppression) gives way to threat or use of coercion (repression) which in turn gives way to threat or use of violence (terrorism).

In sum, it would appear useful to use "oppression" for referring to a continuing situation of involuntary subordination with an emphasis on acts of omission by the government against its citizens, while reserving "repression" for a more active process of social control by neutralization or elimination of actual and potential opponents by a variety of coercive sanctions, such as those specified in Table 2.1.

This table contains categories which, on the one hand, border on oppression, and, on the other hand, border on state terrorism and genocide. Thus, the problem of overlap exists between repression and each of these concepts.

Hannah Arendt, who distinguished four forms of "political oppression," (totalitarianism, despotism, tyranny, and dictatorship) utilized the term "repression" in contrast to "authority," stating that "where authority fails, repression begins."[9] Building on this distinction, Marjo Hoefnagels created a diagram which illustrates a correspondence between the degrees of authority and the degree and form of government violence. Thus, she constructs an increasing scale of violence starting with influence, then manipulation, followed by coercion and finally repression. In this scheme, a decrease in authority of a regime is likely to be accompanied by the use of more violent forms of governmental force, and ultimately, repression.[10]

An alternative framework for situating the concept of repression is offered by McCamant. He identifies "coercion" as one of three means of domination, the other two being "purchase" and "persuasion." He sees repression as an illegitimate extension of state domination, especially of a coercive form. Finally, according to Wilkinson, repression can be distinguished from terrorism because it is a form of coercion affecting only actual dissenters. Terrorism, since it is meant to deter potential dissenters, is more arbitrary, unpredictable and indiscriminate in its effects.[11]

Table 2.1: A Sample from the Repertoire of Repressive Tactics

---

1. Entry and search of homes without warrant,
2. Destruction of private property, including arson,
3. Suppression of newspapers and other media,
4. Prohibition of the use of a native language,
5. Suppression of political parties,
6. Prohibition of religious services,
7. Physical attacks on trade union meetings,
8. Physical attacks on political meetings,
9. Eviction from office,
10. Use of "agents provocateurs" to create violent incidents, justifying repressions,
11. Beatings and physical assaults on individual opponents,
12. Excessive police brutality during arrest,
13. Security force baton assaults against unarmed and peaceful demonstrators,
14. Forced exile or prevention of departure,
15. Arbitrary arrests and incarceration,
16. Threats and reprisals against the families of opponents,
17. Torture and mutilation,
18. Political assassination,
19. Execution of prisoners without trial or after show trial,
20. Secret individual abductions followed by torture and murder (disappearances),
21. Pogroms,
22. Deliberate massacres,
23. Extermination in slave labor camps by means of inadequate rations and sleep control, and long hours of hard work,
24. Death marches under the pretext of deportation.

Source: Partly based on Major Henry J. Chisholm, "The Function of Terror and Violence in Revolution," (M.A. Thesis: Georgetown University, 1948), 29.

A crucial question is raised by this analysis: Is repression illegitimate by definition? If a state has a monopoly over violence, this violence can be used against external opponents or internal opponents. Few would doubt the legitimacy of the first option, at least when this is a defensive operation aimed at maintaining rather than expanding state power. The legitimacy of the second option depends upon whether those who control the state can be persuaded to relinquish this control on the request of a majority. If those who control state power trample on the rights of the majority of citizens and refuse to allow nonviolent change by rule-based mechanisms such as elections, popular resistance is legitimate and repression consequently illegitimate.[12] On the other hand, if a legal regime is attacked by an armed section of the population, selective repression based on the principle of proportionality would seem legitimate. It seems useful to make a distinction between legitimate acts of repression—comparable to legitimate acts of war—and illegal "crimes of repression."[13]

Henner Hess defines repressive crime as illegal acts "committed to maintain, strengthen—or above all—defend privileged positions, in particular those of power and property."[14] Two problems with this definition are that repressive crimes are implicitly limited to "crimes of government," and that all repression is considered illegal. If a majority-based government is attacked by a non-democratic minority, repression can, in our view, be legal if certain conditions are met. According to Kirchheimer, these conditions are (1) the existence of a framework of substantive and procedural norms binding both the government and the governed as well as public prosecutors, and (2) that sanctions against opponents be subject to public criticism.[15]

The line between legal, reactive, proportionate repression against lawless "enemies of society" and illegitimate repression against political "enemies of the government" is not always a clear one. An occasional overstepping of this line by organs of the state (if punished by the authorities) does not make a state an *état criminel*, a criminal state. Yet when repression is directed preventively against the whole society, a majority of society, or an oppressed minority, this line is clearly overstepped.

State Terrorism

The sovereign state is often considered as an impartial arbiter between the groups and classes in society, wielding the legitimate monopoly of violence to maintain public order. How can such a state be "terrorist"? Part of the answer lies in the elusive concept of the "state." There are many definitions. A recent one by James N. Rosenau defines the core phenomena of states—those authority structures that are as easily torn down as built up—as consisting of the norms governing relationships, the habits of voluntary and coerced compliance, and the practices of cooperation through which large numbers of people form and sustain a collectivity that possesses sovereign authority with respect to them. It is these patterns of compliance and cooperation, as they unfold in response to the application of law and the exercise of force, that fluctuate under changing circumstances.[16]

In such a definition there is no room for a recognizable state terrorist actor. A more legal definition, like the one of the 1933 Montevideo Convention, on the other hand, defines a state as a political unit with four characteristics: (1) a permanent population, (2) a defined territory, (3) a government, and (4) a capacity to enter into relations with other states.[17]

It might be more useful to speak of government terrorism or, even better, regime terrorism. The latter term would then include sectors of the government and sectors of the population wielding power together[18] through certain types of violent acts. However, the term state terrorism is currently used more widely for patterned and persistent atrocities by state or state-sponsored actors than the preferable term "regime terrorism."[19]

Neither non-state nor state terrorists usually take pride in being labelled terrorist. They shift responsibility and use the cover of "plausible denial" as a standard device. State terrorists can, through censorship, obtain "partial anonymity" to hide atrocities, while the non-state terrorist cannot and usually does not want to hide them.[20] The state controls various agents of surveillance and physical coercion—the army, the police, the secret police and various para-military units—which can move freely on the state's territory. Non-state terrorist actors have to hide; usually they control no territory (except when guerrillas have "liberated" part of the territory and use tactics of terrorism in combination with more rule-based tactics of protracted guerrilla warfare). The incumbent state terrorist can mobilize (or demobilize) great numbers of people while the non-state terrorist usually has no large following, at least at the beginning of an insurgency. (As a terrorist group gains a following, it sometimes dispenses with the tactics of terrorism.)

One reason for using the term terrorism for the actions of both state and non-state actors, is that it would make no sense to stop labelling a non-state actor a terrorist when that actor manages to conquer state power by means of terrorism and subsequently continues to rule by his proven instrument. The National Socialist movement in Germany did not cease to be terrorist after taking state power in 1933.

What does change when a terrorist actor manages to take state power is that his repertoire broadens enormously. While a numerically small terrorist group often uses acts of terrorism as its sole tactic, a state actor can usually, certainly after the consolidation of power, draw from any of the three sanction systems identified by Dallin and Breslauer:

1. "normative power" (e.g. socialization, education, the offer of prestige, recognition, or love),
2. "material power" (e.g. wages, rewards, bonuses, bribes, and promotions), and
3. "coercive power" (e.g. penalties, regulatory and police power, and terror).[21]

Besides a wide range of policy options, as compared to non-state actors, a state actor also has the means to formally legalize his terror. The legislative body is under the political control of the ruler and passes laws that fit the requirements of the executive, while the judiciary is either a bypassed actor or an auxiliary instrument of state terror and repression. If we look, for instance, at Nazi Germany in the 1930s, we notice that more than 250 laws and decrees were issued against the Jews, long before genocide started. While many of these authorized tactics of harassment fell short of terrorism, the legal system itself became, in part, an instrument of terror. An example was the People's Courts which were set up in 1934 and which were instructed by Hitler to "pass sentences which were mercilessly hard and brutal."[22]

The concentration camps set up by the National Socialists were probably legal in a formal sense, but they were pure instruments of terror, as were the Stalinist show trials. When the state does not only punish those who violate laws, but also punishes some people who are not guilty so that others are deterred from violating them, we have moved beyond the rule of law. Where the law has become unpredictable in its application because individual guilt is less important to the regime than collective obedience, we are clearly no longer dealing with a legitimate monopoly of violence, but with state terrorism.

State terrorism goes beyond the legitimate use of violence by those holding the reins of power, just as war crimes go beyond what is considered permissible in warfare. Many acts of terrorism such as hostage taking, killing of prisoners, and deliberate attacks on civilians are prohibited by the rules of war.[23] If a state deals with political opponents by tactics which include selective and random murder, abduction and secret torture, massacres, and the use of concentration camps, it engages in methods which might be legalized by the state's own lawmaking machinery, but which are widely considered as contrary to humane and civilized behavior. These violent methods of control are also contrary to covenants of international law that most states have signed.

While a narrow legal definition of terrorism or state terrorism is desirable, such a definition might not be helpful in understanding terrorism in social scientific terms. The attempt to find a "scientific" definition of terrorism has led to a large number of proposals. I myself have tried to construct an academic consensus definition by means of polling scholars and analyzing existing definitions in the literature. A first attempt to arrive at a consensus definition in 1984 received a high degree of support (81 percent of the respondents could agree or partially agree to it). However, there was also criticism. On the basis of both agreements and disagreements, I have constructed a second definition:

> Terrorism is an anxiety-inspiring method of repeated violent action, employed by (semi-) clandestine individual, group, or state actors, for idiosyncratic, criminal, or political reasons, whereby—in contrast to assassination—the direct targets of violence are not the main targets. The immediate human victims of violence are generally chosen randomly (targets of opportunity) or selectively (representative or symbolic targets) from a target population, and serve as message generators. Threat—violence—based communication processes between terrorist (organization), (imperiled) victims, and main targets are used to manipulate the main target audience(s), turning it into a target of terror, a target of demands, or a target of attention, depending on whether intimidation, coercion, or propaganda is primarily sought.[24]

One of the aims of this definition is to cover both state and nonstate terrorism. Since we are concerned here with state terrorism, I will contrast this conceptualization with two quotes attributed to practitioners of state terrorism. The first quote is allegedly from a Stalinist source; the second is attributed to Adolf Hitler himself. A Soviet NKVD "Document of Terror" which surfaced in the early 1950s from behind the Iron Curtain refers to "enlightened terror." It states:

> The only tool which general terror knows and uses is force . . . [The] tool used by enlightened terror is any means which is able to produce the planned psychological effect . . . As has already been frequently emphasized, the aim of any action in the system of enlightened terror is to evoke a psychological process and implant and amplify its effects in the consciousness of the resonant mass. This goal can be attained if one repeats the same action constantly and systematically. But naturally such a method—the repetition of action—is uneconomical . . . The same goal can be attained if one is able to cause the resonant mass to experience the same action repeatedly through clever propaganda. It consists of

executing a typical, planned action in classic form. Subsequently this action is brought home to the resonant mass through printed statements, the radio, the motion picture, the press—in short, through all the means of propaganda available. Naturally such propaganda cannot be dry and factual reports . . . Its propaganda must be lively, colorful, dramatic—that is, dynamic. But it is not important that it follows the truth in details.[25]

Adolf Hitler was quoted as saying:

> I shall spread terror through the surprising application of all means. The sudden shock of a terrible fear of death is what matters. Why should I deal otherwise with all my political opponents? These so-called atrocities save me hundreds of thousands of individual actions against the protestors and discontents. Each one of them will think twice to oppose us when he hears what is [awaiting] him in the [concentration] camp.[26]

Such premeditated, state organized terror which transgresses the boundaries of conventional law and public order enforcement, can deter the formation of opposition. Once the overwhelming fear has entered the hearts and minds of the target population, it will linger on for some time before it has to be reinforced by a new collective shock treatment. In this special sense, there can apparently even be terror without violence.[27]

In sum, state terrorism can be seen as a method of rule whereby some groups of people are victimized with great brutality, and more or less arbitrarily by the state or state supported actors, so that others who have reason to identify with those murdered, will despair, obey or comply. Its main instruments are summary arrests and incarceration without trial, torture, political murder, disappearances, and concentration camps.

Genocide

Genocide can be viewed as either the highest stage of repression or as something "sui generis." The first view is expressed by George A. Lopez and Michael Stohl, who place genocide at the end of a continuum that stretches from bad to worst. They consider

> state terror [to be] a very particular form of violence which unfolds as a subcategory of oppression and repression. . . . When this type of violence increases to the point where the aim no longer appears to be coercion and intimidation, but elimination of the minority population, the policy moves from one of state terror to genocide. For state terrorism . . . does

leave many of its victims and targets still living; genocide clearly does not.[28]

This is a logical but formal approach. In reality, the charge of genocide is often raised to describe a situation where far from all people of a race or ethnic group are eliminated. Raphael Lemkin who created the term "genocide" in his book on *Axis Rule in Occupied Europe* (1944), describes "genocide" as the annihilation of the "essential foundations of life of national groups" which leads to the disintegration of "the political and social institutions of culture, language, national feelings, religion, and the destruction of the personal security, liberty, health, dignity, and even lives of the individuals belonging to such groups."[29] One of the prerequisites for "genocide" is, in Lemkin's conceptualization, the existence of a coordinated plan, consisting of different actions aiming at annihilation of a group by destroying its essential foundations. Lemkin was one of those who took the initiative for the United Nations Convention on the Punishment and Prevention of Genocide (1948), according to which:

> genocide means any of the following acts committed with intent to destroy, in whole or in part, a national, ethnic, racial or religious group, such as: (1) killing members of the group, (2) causing serious bodily or mental harm to members of the group, (3) deliberately inflicting on the group conditions of life calculated to bring about its physical destruction in whole or in part, (4) imposing measures intended to prevent birth within the group, and (5) forcibly transferring children of the group to another group.[30]

The weaknesses of this definition have been pointed out by several authors, including Leo Kuper. He focused in particular on the problem of demonstrating "intent," the problem of how many lives have to be taken to justify the label "genocide" (stemming from the formulation "in whole or in part"), and the problem created by the words "such as," which expands the initial qualification even further.[31] Kuper noted as a major omission "the exclusion of political groups from the list of groups protected."[32]

This omission prompted Barbara Harff and Ted R. Gurr to coin the term "politicide." For them:

> in genocides the victimized groups are defined primarily in terms of their communal characteristics; i.e., ethnicity or religion or nationality. In politicides the victim groups are defined primarily in terms of their hierarchical position or political opposition to the regime or dominant groups.[30] . . . whether an episode of mass killing is a genocide or a politicide depends

on the combination of a state's objectives, the motives of its ruling elite, the prevailing ideology, and the power relations within its authority structure.[33]

Though others have disagreed, I think that it is possible to regard genocide as "sui generis" and still place it within the repression-state terrorism-genocide continuum. The most concise definition of genocide is the one offered by Michael Freeman who conceptualizes it, in the tradition of Lemkin, as "the destruction of a nation by the state." Yet this definition, which begs the question, "what is a nation?" is not yet widely shared. Freeman himself has identified, in a list that is not complete, six different current uses of the term "genocide." They are:

1. the murderous attack by a state on a distinct ethnic, national or religious group, the Holocaust being the extreme example,
2. the attack by a state on the continued existence of an ethnic, national or religious group by attacking the foundations of its way of life (e.g. banning its language or religion, murdering its cultural leaders), so-called "cultural genocide,"
3. same acts as (1), but carried out by non-state groups,
4. same acts as (2), but carried out by non-state groups,
5. the murderous attack by a state on what it perceives, rightly or wrongly, to be its political opponents (this would include Stalin's attack on the kulaks as well as Ceausescu's order to shoot to kill the Timisoara demonstrators),
6. same act as (5) carried out by non-state actors (massacres in Lebanon might fall into this category).[34]

These are meanings of genocide in political and political science discourse. In legal terms, genocide is a crime under international law (Geneva Convention, 9 December 1948).

Conclusion

The discussion above, sketchy as it is, makes clear that repression, state terrorism and genocide are more than slogans in the political arena. These concepts cover important and still largely unexplored areas of state behavior. While there is no consensus about the meaning of these terms, there is enough common ground to engage in fruitful and cumulative research. Let me summarize some crucial elements of these concepts:

Repression denies individuals or groups the ability to develop their capacities freely. It is not necessarily illegitimate (let alone illegal), if the principles of proportionality and distinction are observed. The principle of proportionality is that the degree of repression should not be greater than necessary to re-establish control over the public order. The principle of distinction is that immunity must be granted to those who choose not to take part in the conflict.

Terrorism creates chronic fear for one's individual existence as a member of a targeted group through the random use of unprovoked acts of extreme violence which occur intermittently and without warning. The physical survival of the group as a whole is, however, not in doubt. Acts of terrorism are peacetime equivalents of war crimes. When they are committed by non-state actors, they are usually treated as criminal despite the underlying political intent. The prohibition from using criminal acts for political purposes should be extended to state and state-sponsored actors as well.

Genocide denies a national or other group the right to exist. This makes genocide different. It is a policy sometimes applied in the process of (attempted) state formation where a population (usually a minority, sometimes a majority in a minority position) is categorized as expendable by the powerholders and consequently not just repressed and denied its identity, but exterminated. Genocide can be viewed as a kind of war fought by a regime against a largely unarmed section of the population. It differs from war in that it is waged unilaterally, with complete disregard for rules of war which demand the protection of the civilian population. While war can be seen as a series of battles, genocide can be viewed as a series of massacres for which the perpetrators are usually not brought to justice due to the sovereignty of the state defined as "independence from any outside power and final authority over men who live within certain boundaries."[35]

At the beginning of this chapter, I quoted Clausewitz's statement that war is the continuation of politics by other means. A contemporary writer, the Chilean sociologist Jorge A. Tapia-Valdes, has observed the rise of national security states with a new "neo-Clausewitzian" ideology according to which "politics is the continuation of war by other means."[36]

International law has established some ground rules about what is licit and illicit in inter-state war. There are also some rules emerging about internal warfare between security forces of the state and guerrilla fighters. What is lacking are international laws and concomitant international sanctions for conflict situations when regimes wage war against unarmed citizens. International law should, in such situations, be able to withdraw sovereignty from a criminal killer state. International respect for a nation state's sovereignty should be made conditional by the international community. To confront situations of illegitimate repression, state terror, and genocide, an array of sanction mechanisms should be devised, representing varying levels of coercion. The basis for action should be a scientific, global monitoring system, acting like a meteorological monitoring system, to issue warnings and calls for protective action when the foul weather of repression, the storms of state terrorism and the hurricane of genocide are approaching.

Notes

1. See K.M. Von Clausewitz *On War* (London: Keagan Paul, (1908), vol. 1, book 1, 85.

2. "Only about one person in five, in total fewer than 1 billion out of a world population approaching 5 billion, enjoys the security of knowing that he or she is protected by laws and constitutions that are respected by his government." See Charles Humana, comp., *World Human Rights Guide* (London: Pan Books, 1987), 1.

3. John F. McCamant, "Domination and Political Repression" project description, manuscript, (1989), 1.

4. See Charles Tilly, *From Mobilization to Revolution* (Reading, Mass.: Addison-Wesley, 1978).

5. Stephen T. Hosmer, *Vietcong Repression and Its Implications for the Future* (Heath, Mass.: Lexington Books, 1970), 1.

6. See T.R. Gurr, "Persisting Patterns of Repression and Rebellion: Foundations for a General Theory of Political Coercion," in M.P. Karns, ed., *Persisting Patterns and Emergent Structures in a Waning Century* (New York: Praeger, 1986), chap. 6.

7. See Michael Stohl and George A. Lopez, eds., *The State as Terrorist. The Dynamics of Governmental Violence and Repression* (Westport, Conn.: Greenwood Press, 1984).

8. Peter C. Sederberg, *Terrorist Myth: Illusion, Rhetoric, and Reality* (Englewood Cliffs, N.J.: Prentice Hall, 1989).

9. Hannah Arendt, *The Origins of Totalitarianism* (New York: Harcourt, Brace, and World, 1966), 460.

10. Marjo Hoefnagels, ed., *Repression and Repressive Violence* (Amsterdam: Swets and Zeitlinger, 1977), 32–36.

11. Paul Wilkinson, *Political Terrorism* (London: The Macmillan Press, 1976), 40.

12. Karl Popper wrote, "In fact, there are only two types of states: those, in which it is possible to get rid of a state without the spilling of blood in an election, and those, where this is not possible." "Zur Theorie der Demokratie," *Der Spiegel* 41, no. 32, (August 1987): 54.

13. The term "repressive crime" has been proposed by Henner Hess. See Henner Hess, "Repressives Verbrechen," *Kriminologisches Journal* 8, no. 1, (1976): 1–22.

14. Ibid.

15. Otto Kirchheimer, *Political Justice: the Use of Legal Procedures for Political Ends* (Princeton, N.J.: Princeton University Press, 1961), 120–121.

16. James N. Rosenau, "The State in an Era of Cascading Politics: Wavering Concept, Widening Competence, Withering Colossus, or Weathering Change?" in James A. Caporaso, ed., *The Elusive State: International and Comparative Perspectives* (Beverly Hills: Sage, 1989), 18.

17. Ibid., 1.

18. See, for example, Stohl and Lopez, *The State as Terrorist*.

19. See Gurr, *Persisting Patterns*.

20. Eugen Kogon, *De SS-Staat: Het systeem der Duitse Concentratiekamp* (Amsterdam: Amsterdam boek, 1974), 35.

21. Alexander Dallin and George Breslauer, *Political Terror in Communist Systems* (Stanford, Calif.: Stanford University Press, 1970), 2.

22. J. Klaassen, "Historici Moeten Oordeel Vellen Over Nazi-rechters," *Volkskrant*, October 1986, 5.

23. Elsewhere, I have pleaded for a legal definition of terrorist acts as "peacetime equivalents of war crimes," following a suggestion first made by A. P. Rubin.

24. See A.P. Schmid and A.J. Jongman et al., *Political Terrorism. A New Guide to Actors, Authors, Concepts, Data Bases, Theories and Literature* (Amsterdam, North Holland Publications, 1988), 28.

25. David C. Rapaport and Yonah Alexander, eds., *The Morality of Terrorism: Religious and Secular Justifications* (New York, Pergamon Press, 1983), 189.

26. These "Conversations with Hitler" were a forgery by a gifted journalist in need of money. However, his perception of how Hitler's mind worked was remarkably accurate. See Herman Rauschning, *Gesprche mit Hitler* (Wien, 1940), 82.

27. Dallin and Breslauer adhere to this view when they write: "whereas he [E.V. Walter] considers all terror to be violence designed to control (p.14), and Alfred Meyer speaks of terror as 'violence, applied or threatened' (The Soviet Political System, p.318), terror in our usage does not necessarily include violence; just as some violence involves no terror, some terror (e.g. intimidation) requires no violence." (Dallin and Breslauer, 1n–2n).

28. Stohl and Lopez, *The State as Terrorist*, 2,9.

29. Raphael Lemkin, *Axis Rule in Occupied Europe* (Washington, D.C.: Carnegie Endowment of International Peace, 1944), 79.

30. Leo Kuper, *Genocide* (Harmondsworth: Pelican Books, 1981), 210–214.

31. Ibid., 33–38.

32. Ibid., 39.

33. Barbara Harff and Ted Gurr, "Toward Empirical Theory of Genocides and Politicides: Identification and Measurement of Cases since 1945" *International Studies Quarterly* 32 (1988): 360.

34. Michael Freeman, "Speaking About the Unspeakable: The 'Genocide' Problematic: Reality, Ethics, Discourse," paper presented at the Workshop on Theories of Political Violence at the ECPR Joint Sessions, Bochum, 2–7 April 1990, 20.

35. Joseph Strayer, *On the Medieval Origins of the Modern State*, as cited by Stephen D. Krasner, "Sovereignty: An Institutional Perspective" in James A. Caporaso, ed., *The Elusive State: International and Comparative Perspectives* (Beverly Hills, Sage, 1989), 58.

36. See Jorge A. Tapia-Valdes, *National Security, The Dual State and The Rule of the Exception: A Study on the Strategocratic Political System* (Rotterdam: Erasmus Universiteitsdrukerij, 1989), 567.

PART TWO

The Structural Sources of State Organized Terror

3

Domination, State Power, and Political Repression

John F. McCamant

The twentieth century has brought political freedom to many people, but to others it has brought imprisonment and death for their political views. In fact, we in the twentieth century have experienced the worst cases of political repression in history, and together these have been responsible for as many deaths as international and civil wars.[1] South America experienced its most repressive decade by far during the 1970s, and Central America did so in the 1980s. Iran, Kampuchea, and Uganda remind us that unprecedented bloody repressions have occurred in every part of the Third World. Germany and the Soviet Union experienced extraordinary repression in the 1930s.

Political repression is significant not only in its human toll but also in its political consequences. It has strongly conditioned the patterns of communications media, interest groups, and political parties in all parts of the world, and it is a necessary accompaniment to many cultural and economic policies. The importance of political repression stands in sharp contrast to the comparatively little attention it has received in either popular or scholarly writing.

Political repression would be almost invisible if it were not for human rights activists, who have documented abuses—often at considerable risk to their own lives and freedom. National and international organizations investigate and record cases of violations, and the established press sometimes relays this information to the general public. Political repression basically covers the same phenomena as violation of civil and political liberties, but seen in terms of their connections to political actions and struggles rather than as separate legal rights and duties. Thinking of these phenomena as "political repression" rather than "human rights violations" better leads to considering explanations and suggesting nonlegal policy remedies or structural reform.[2]

Political scientists have failed to explain or predict the repression of this century and only in the 1980s have they begun to work on the question. Harry Eckstein[3] suggested one reason for the failure in pointing out that political scientists of the first part of this century emphasized democracy because of "an almost universal belief in the inevitability of representative democracy in the development of nations . . . it seemed pointless and superfluous to write about contemporary predemocratic, obviously transitional, systems." The Nazi record should have awakened social scientists to another possibility, but instead they deflected the problem into the concept of totalitarianism, which after the 1940s was given only communist expression. Political development writing after 1950 returned to the easy optimism of the first part of the century. The assumption that the development of democracy was automatic and inevitable not only prevented scholars from examining authoritarianism and political repression, but also had the insidious side effect of depreciating the struggles of those who committed themselves to bringing about or defending freedom.

The naive assumption of progress is not the only reason that social scientists have failed to see and appreciate the significance of political repression. None of the principal models of the social sciences provide a place for the use of coercive action against dissidents or others who stand in the way of the powerful.[4] Thus, in order to understand state terror and political repression, we must create a model that allows us to envision and interpret the way rulers use force against opposition and potential opposition. That is the intention of the model of domination presented here.

Political repression is one technique of domination. Wherever one finds repression, one finds struggles of domination. Nevertheless, most attempts to dominate involve noncoercive means, and only by seeing repression in this larger context can we begin to analyze how and why rulers attack domestic "enemies." After discussing the general concept of domination and the various means and modes of domination, we will point out how the development of the state has radically changed the ways in which domination takes place. As more traditional patterns of domination break down, rulers at certain places and times may have the will and the capability to use massive amounts of repressive force. These conditions are new to the twentieth century, making the current epoch the century of repression as well as of freedom. In conclusion, we will outline the conditions that could move the world toward freedom rather than repression, for the model should also serve as a guide to action.

Domination

One sees the term "domination" increasingly in the social science literature, but there is still missing a systematic treatment of the concept that would give it theoretical meaning. The two realms of discourse where the concept is clearest are those concerned with human/nature and man/woman relationships.

The development of environmental concerns and ecological models has provided a perspective from which humans' (usually men's) domination of nature becomes clear. What seemed the normal relationship for several hundred years is now seen as only one type of relationship, and not necessarily a sustainable one. Human domination of nature implies that nature is exploited and used solely for human benefit, without consideration of any independent concerns of nature. The earth is penetrated and reshaped, forests are cut down, rivers are dammed and diverted, and deadly chemicals are poured on the soil, all motivated by exclusive consideration for human material welfare. Preservation of endangered species and protection of animal rights do not fit easily into this logic and require considering nature as something more than a resource for humans. Such an alternative view, the ecological, would see humans as only a part of a larger system, which may be modified but not controlled by humans.

The exploration of the meaning of domination has perhaps gone furthest in feminist writings on gender relations. Remarkably, men's domination of women was invisible in the social science literature as long as men ruled the social sciences.[5] In a comparison of 139 societies, Sanday[6] operationalized male dominance as the exclusion of women from political and economic decision-making and male aggression against women, the latter "measured by the following five traits: the expectation that males should be tough, brave, and aggressive; the presence of men's houses or specific places where only men may congregate; frequent quarreling, fighting, or wife beating; the institutionalization or regular occurrence of rape; and raiding other groups for wives." Thirty-two percent of pre-westernized societies sampled were free of such indicators of domination.

Domination, as an aspect of social relationship, refers to both the use of power by some to control others and also the structure of control that persists over a period of time. It appears in fleeting relationships between two persons, and it is also crystallized into social and political structures in a more permanent way. It is a vertical relationship between persons of unequal power. It is the relationship of two or more persons or groups where choices are interdependent and one party's choices carry greater weight than the others. Domination occurs at many levels—personal, household, local, national, international—and also between these levels.

Domination varies greatly in degree. At one extreme is near total domination, as seen in a master/slave relationship. The other extreme of little or no domination is characterized by two different situations: autonomy, where no relationship exists, and free and equal association, where relationships may be close but no one party prevails over the others. Autonomy can exist in pure form only when people are not dependent upon one another. If societies are integrated and interdependent but still ruled by a few, a totalitarian society exists. It is ameliorated insofar as association becomes free and equal with wide participation in collective decision making. As will be shown, the historical development of modern Europe, too, moved from high domination with considerable autonomy toward freer association with less autonomy. A strong state does not necessarily imply strong domination even though the state has become the most powerful instrument of domination ever developed.

Domination does not just appear; it results from the struggle between individuals and groups in which the outcome depends in large part on the distribution of the *means of domination*. Very broadly, the means of domination can be divided into three general types: persuasion, purchase, and coercion. One type of means can be used to acquire other types. Priests can motivate generals through persuasion; landowners can purchase priests; generals can conquer land and the ability to purchase that comes with the land. The three types of means are seldom used separately; rather, they are used in combination by both those seeking to dominate and those resisting domination. The combination of the gun and the bible—overwhelming force and arrogant self-righteous arguments—brought about the domination by Europeans of most of the rest of the world.

The degree of actual domination is not simply a reflection of the distribution of the means of domination. There must be relations among the parties before there is a struggle of domination. Both the will of the parties and the intelligence of their use of means of domination will affect the outcome. The use of means is complicated by the difficulty of determining the relative values of the three types of means in any given situation. A common error has been for a party to use strong-arm tactics when gentler means would have been more effective. Once a pattern of domination is set, it may last for a considerable time without being challenged, even though the distribution of the means of domination changes.

In any particular instance, *relations of domination* can be described. Consensus, exchange, or command will prevail in the formation of the overall structures of society and can be considered the *mode of domination*. When a *command* relationship, which relies primarily on coercion, exists, one can order another without the other having any choice. Industrialization of agriculture transformed traditional person/nature relations of exchange or consensus into command relationships. Patriarchy instituted the command authority of the father in the household. Slavery, the military, and some business organizations rely on command relations, but communities cannot exist on such a basis. Command relations characterize dictatorships at the national level, and empires rely, at least formally, on command.

When rulers provide a reward for acceptance of the relationship, through their means of purchase an *exchange* relationship exists. Unequal exchange implies domination. In economic theory, market exchange is an independent act of short duration, but in broader social relations exchanges are interdependent, may be prolonged over an extended period, and are almost always unequal. Peasants thought of their relationship with nature as one of exchange. The breakdown of patriarchy led to the prevalence of exchange relationships in the household. Anthropologists have documented prevalence of exchange in patron-client relationships in traditional communities around the world. Exchange forms the basis of most local government relations. When exchange becomes the basis for a larger system and is organized around a political party, it may be called a "machine." If it is organized around an upper class, it is an oligarchy or plutocracy. Spheres of influence of the great powers rely primarily on exchange for control.

A *consensus* relationship exists where issues are discussed and agreed upon by all involved. Consensus may mean an agreement to disagree and respect for each other's autonomy, and it is more important for decision-making procedures than for substantive questions. Inequalities in the means of persuasion create domination even with consensus. Where persons treat natural objects as spiritual, as have such Native American cultures as the Hopi, the relationship is based on consensus. Consensus is common in contemporary marriages, but we do not seem to have a name for such families. In interpersonal relations, consensus requires dialogue; in larger organizations, it requires participation. Consensus lies behind the acceptance of democratic decision-making rules that allow for popular participation, but it may also undergird stable monarchical rule. Consensus can provide the basis for international relations where equality of states and noninterventionist policies exist, so that treaties and decisions of international organizations are freely arrived at.

More or less autonomy may exist at each level. Where parts of nature are kept apart from human activity in a state of wilderness, there is autonomy rather than a relationship between persons and nature. Likewise within a family—husband and wife may have most of their activities in separate domains, providing each with relative autonomy. Communities may be no more than isolated subsistence settlements; ethnic groups may live as separate segments with little interaction between them. Nations can be formed from a loose confederation of local communities, and nations can live in isolation from one another.

The historical trend has been toward increasing inequality of the means of domination in the world, both as a whole and in its parts. However, the concentration of the means of domination in the institutions of the state complicates the outcome of this trend and makes the social control of domination possible.

State Power

When the state came to monopolize coercion, tax and regulate the economy, and collect and disseminate information, any person or group who sought to dominate others had to take state power into account— either to neutralize it or to seize it and use it. Struggles of domination became political struggles.

Growing state power means more and more concentration of control over coercion by the central government, until the state has a near monopoly. The means of coercion, as Giddens[7] has noted, becomes separated from the means of production. If non-state institutions use commands, they can no longer enforce them by coercion except through the state.

Orwell and Giddens[8] emphasized the growth of surveillance as a necessary complement to coercive means of domination. The huge bureaucracies of modern government have the capability to monitor nearly every action of everyday life. The revenue-collecting agency extracts a large proportion of society's production and, in doing so, keeps track of most economic transactions. Big Brother is always watching. The threat of being removed from society and lodged in prison is ever-present in the world and lies heavily in the subconscious of every member of society.

It is harder to trace the state's increasing control of the means of persuasion. Control of information more or less coincided with the growth of surveillance power. The fully developed state, whether democratic or authoritarian, has become the source of nearly all news; it licenses or owns the electronic media, provides resources for the majority of research, controls most education, and the president or prime minister is guaranteed prime time exposure whenever he or she asks. If we could quantify control of the means of persuasion in the same way that expenditures can be quantified, we would certainly find that the modern state controls more than fifty percent of the means of persuasion.

In Europe and the European offshoots, state growth resulted from a dialectic of internal and external forces, between responses to nationally-developing commercial and production needs and to threats from foreign states. Business required a strong state to enforce property rights, regulate trade, and provide an economic infrastructure. People and businesses needed to have a state to represent them in dealings with other states, and international conflict required the strengthening of coercive forces and resource capacity. At the same time, the commodification of life and growing exchange of goods and services provided an opportunity for the state to extract greater revenue. Foreign conflict provided incentive to expand citizenship and increase revenues.

The opposite dialectic operated in the Third World. External commercial and production pressures demanded expansion of regulation and public services while most of the conflict was internal. When European people wished to do business with the rest of the world in the 16th through the 19th centuries, they turned them into colonies in order to have the state services and regulation necessary for doing business. After independence, foreign aid encouraged the continual expansion of services and infrastructure. As powers of the state grew, internal conflicts were exacerbated, and state coercive powers tended to be directed more toward internal "enemies" than external ones.

The growth of state institutions and the expansion and integration of the economy provide instruments for domination at a distance—for dominating others impersonally in ways that can be disguised. In earlier stages, the means of domination were applied personally by rulers or close agents of the rulers. Now the state serves as an intermediary between those who dominate and those who are dominated, and laws and governmental policies establish who will be on top and who will be on the bottom. Even the conflict of workers and management is mediated by the state, though more in some polities than in others. The landed and landless find their positions conditioned by impersonal but not impartial laws. The lending of money was once a personal exchange between money lenders and debtors, and the exchange rate was determined through unequal bargaining between them. Now, world interest rates are primarily the result of Federal Reserve Board actions in the United States, and debtors in the Third World have no contact with the bond holders and bankers for whose benefit the interest rates are regulated.

The growth of state institutions also provided a powerful independent base for domination. Those holding state positions could use them to dominate for their own self-interest as well as to protect the interests of established social classes. Anastasio Somoza of Nicaragua provided a classic example in the early 1930s of how a person with no social base could use the military of a fractured society to make the country his private "hacienda." A few decades later, bureaucratic and military classes would follow his example in Africa.

Changing Patterns of Domination

Despite the considerable differences between societies, they all have to face similar changes: in the economy, from the processes of the commodification of life and integration into the world economy; and in the polity, from the process of increasing state power. These changes have profound effects on the modes of domination as the principal locus of domination changes from the local to the national, which in turn is increasingly affected by the international. The changing locus generates instability at local levels and creates possibilities for shifting modes of domination at all levels. The countries that went through these economic and political changes in earlier centuries experienced them at a slower pace and had more time to respond—to reestablish equilibrium (if such a thing exists in societies). The countries that have gone through these changes more recently experienced them at a far more rapid pace.

The same loss of isolation that brings instability to local patterns of domination also brings a loss of autonomy. The struggle for domination is enlarged, now involving conflict or competition with other regional rulers, with national groups, and with international power holders. Both the scope and the intensity of struggles of domination increase. Autonomy is no longer possible.

Local patterns of domination are undermined from every direction. As the local economy becomes integrated into the world economy, goods that were once personally exchanged and used to cement community relations become commodified in the impersonal market, and community relations are weakened. Those who have control of the key resources and skills needed to produce for the larger economy enrich themselves and gain power at the expense of those with more outdated resources. Control of both the economy and coercion shift away from the hands of those living in the locality. Both public and private investment decisions come to be made elsewhere. The central government replaces local institutions in the provision of welfare. The state often imposes officials on the local community.

As traditional means of domination are eroded, local rulers can maintain their dominant status only by gaining access to resources and power at a higher level. A common pattern has been for those who dominate locally through exchange relations to use that power in order to gain access to national institutions, and then to use the resources of the national institutions in order to maintain their local domination. At the same time, middle classes, and then lower classes, come to understand that they can weaken the domination of established rulers and perhaps change the mode of domination through the use of state power.

National rulers are in turn strengthened by the innumerable advantages bestowed by international forces upon those who occupy positions of state power. Foreign trade and investment provide easy sources of bribes and tax revenue. By virtue of forming a government they can print money and channel it into circulation through themselves. They can receive international technical assistance, grants, and loans. They can receive military aid and form alliances. They can enhance their status by representing the state at international forums. Of course, foreign powers bestow these privileges much more readily on persons who cooperate. Those who occupy state positions exchange with foreign powers, which in turn enhances their ability to exchange with lower levels of their own societies.

For the most part, the internationalizing of power works to the advantage of established classes. They are in a position to benefit from international connections and so are not likely to oppose them. They have had the benefit of better education, often in the country of the dominant international power, and can speak the language of the foreigners. If there had been a colonial occupation or foreign intervention, those who cooperated with colonists or interveners would have the advantage, and these opportunists sometimes replace traditional elites.

Working classes have much more difficulty in taking advantage of the resource of the growing power of the state. Smaller proportions, both in First and Third World countries, work in factories, where labor organization is easier than in services and construction. High levels of unemployment and underemployment further weaken their bargaining position. Workers cannot forge autonomous unions and political parties as they did in Europe because the state and the established classes contain their efforts through corporatist methods. In their weak position, workers are easily co-opted by international institutions controlled by the rich and powerful states working with national elites.

Ethnically divided societies suffer from an additional difficulty, and the expansion of the state system through colonialism created a great number of ethnically divided states. Integration of the economy and growth of state power increase the interactions among cultural groups and raise the question of whose culture will dominate in these emergent relationships. Questions of official language, officially sanctioned religious and ethnic symbolism, interpretation of historical events, and receipt of economic benefits from growing corporate and state power intensify the struggle of domination among ethnic groups. If one group can take control of the instruments of the state, it can enforce its own cultural view.

Twentieth Century Repression

Why, then, has the twentieth century been the century of repression? Any answer must allow that the twentieth century has also been the century of freedom. Why does freedom come about in some places and times and repression in other places and times? Eckstein suggests, "Thus, the modern counterpart of coping with conspiracy in order to retain control over the princely domain is either mass suppression or the search for mass support."[9] With the politicization of nearly all aspects of everyday life, twentieth century rulers have had to deal with citizens in a way not found before.

The development of the coercive and surveillance power of the state makes gross repression possible for the first time. In earlier centuries, rulers could commit massacres but they lacked the capabilities to know what most people were doing and to constrain them. Giddens[10] has made this point forcefully: "But we also conclude that aspects of totalitarian rule are a threat in all modern states, even if not all are threatened equally or in exactly the same ways. Whether we like it or not, tendencies toward totalitarian power are as distinctive a feature of our epoch as is industrialized war." Modern bureaucracies, police, and armies provide the capability for large-scale repression. Whether and how this coercive power will be used against political opposition depends upon the configuration of struggles of domination.

Rulers in France, the Netherlands, Scandinavia, Great Britain, and its offshoots, the United States, Canada, Australia, and New Zealand, never did choose to use the coercive power of the state in order to establish a command mode of domination over large numbers of their populations. Coercive power was used on occasion (in the United States against workers until 1932; against Black, Hispanic, German, and Japanese minorities at various times and places; and against left-leaning political leaders and intellectuals and foreign policy dissidents during wars), but rulers did not attempt mass suppression. In Scandinavia and the British offshoots, no landed aristocracy dominated local populations (except in the South of the United States); small landholders developed a relatively equalitarian consensus mode of domination at the local level and carried this same mode into national politics. In Britain and France, the landed aristocracy failed to increase its power through commercial agriculture and was defeated by revolutionary wars. Barrington Moore's[11] thesis seems even more persuasive when reconsidered in terms of patterns of domination. He suggested that the democratic route to modern society required that two conditions be met: (1) the weakening of the landed aristocracy and (2) the prevention of an aristocratic-bourgeois coalition against the peasants and workers. The mode of domination used in highly inequalitarian land tenure systems had to be broken before the growth of the state allowed local rulers to call upon state coercive means to maintain local domination.

In the rest of the world, intense domination struggles and the growth of the state tended to coincide in the twentieth century, while problems developed more rapidly and intensely. In the Third World, these developments occurred mostly after 1950. The period has been full of crosscurrents in which any mode of domination at the national level seemed possible. Local patterns of domination were disrupted by economic changes. Both established rulers and the ruled saw the opportunities for change that the growth of the state offered. Urbanization and the expansion of education created some of the preconditions for democracy. Economic surpluses generated by foreign investment and trade and international loans provided possibilities for machine politics. At the same time, however, national police, militaries, and intelligence apparatuses established the bases for military dictatorships. With these contradictions, the only determined outcome was instability. With national conditions making any mode of domination possible, the primary factors for pushing rule in one or another direction came from local and international levels of domination.

The struggles in the international world were of a different sort than the local struggles but, with the general loss of autonomy, all levels became connected. What was available for national rulers to use in support of local elites depended upon alignments at the international level.

After World War II, the Cold War preoccupied the foreign policies of the two superpowers and conditioned the ways in which they related to their client states. Eastern Europe and Latin America, although as different as conceivable at the local and national levels, had nevertheless a great deal in common because of their client status with the superpowers. The international relationship bordered on command or imperialism, and both superpowers resorted to coercion if the overall relationship was threatened. The client military was strengthened through aid and training and, in fact, became something of a subsidiary force of the patron. If the national coercive power should prove to be insufficient, the patron's military force stood ready to intervene. Nevertheless, day-to-day relationships were based on exchange, as rulers of the client states exchanged loyalty for economic and military aid and other forms of open and covert support. The rhetoric was framed in terms of security, but elites of the client and patron states were also busy enriching each other.

In the U.S. sphere of influence, the patron and clients developed the national security doctrine to justify the use of military force to preserve the domination of the ruling classes. The doctrine claimed, roughly, that since the Soviet Union was contained through Western military might, it would seek to expand through subversion in the weaker countries allied to the United States. Anyone who sought to subvert ties with the United States was a communist and should be eliminated. In the Soviet sphere of influence, a mirror image doctrine made similar claims against opponents.

During crises, the primary concern was security: the preservation of the pattern of domination. However, economic issues were intertwined with security matters. Obviously, those who advocated anything but the closest of economic relationships between client and patron were subversive. In 1948, for instance, the Rio de Janeiro meeting of the Organization of American States declared that communists were attempting to sabotage "defense industries," and most of the Latin American governments went home and outlawed Communist parties. In the Third World, maintaining an open door to U.S. investment and trade was a sign of loyalty to the U.S. In Eastern Europe, maintaining a centrally planned system and trade with the Soviet bloc was a sign of loyalty to the Soviet Union.

While the superpowers were extremely touchy about deviations in loyalty to international relationships, they were much less concerned with how client rulers treated their subjects—as long as order was maintained. Corruption and violations of human rights received little attention.

Thus, the superpowers furnished their clients with more than enough coercive power to institute highly repressive regimes, and they also provided a rationale for applying repression. Nevertheless, the amount and use of political repression depended on local struggles. There were three types of local struggles that brought on political repression: (1) the attempt of landholding/business elites to maintain established patterns of extreme domination; (2) the use of state power by a dominant ethnic group to impose its cultural mores on other ethnic groups; and (3) the use of state power by an ideological true-believing party to impose its vision on the rest of society. While the motives were quite different in each of these routes to repression, the outcomes were rather similar.

In 1950, most Third World countries were still primarily rural. The mode of domination depended primarily on land tenure patterns, and rural areas still enjoyed a good deal of autonomy from the rest of society. Despite the common tendency to lump the characteristics of the many societies in the Third World together under the label "traditional," there was a great deal of difference among them, and the changes they experienced also varied.

Unequal land tenure systems operated in most of the Third World, which meant that a few families ruled through exchange modes of domination, but the degree of inequality differed among countries and regions. The most unequal systems prevailed where ethnic differences reinforced land holding differences and led to dehumanization of the labor force.

Many of these rural areas were suitable for export agriculture as the world economy became more integrated. In these places, local landlords moved into export crops, introduced machines and chemicals, dispossessed tenant farmers or small landholders, and in general increased their income and wealth while the newly landless rural workers became worse off. The economic changes also disrupted the established exchange mode of domination as changing technologies of production broke down interpersonal relations. Commercial exporting landlords sought to bring in the coercive weapons of the state to maintain and increase their domination, now through a command mode. Working class leaders were branded as terrorists and were "disappeared."

The second route came when one ethnic group was able to take over the new state power put in place by the expanding state system and use it for its own purposes. Unlike the cases of the first route, ethnic communities in these countries maintained separate cultures and enjoyed sufficient autonomy to enable them to keep their own institutions. Usually they resided in separate regions. What brought them together and created conflict were the changing economy and the accident of sharing state boundaries. At times, the dominant ethnic group simply wished to see its own cultural values expressed in the state. At other times, it felt intense antipathy toward other ethnic groups. In both cases it was necessary to use repression to impose the particular cultural values of the ethnic group, but repression was more viciously applied in the second case. Where the dominant ethnic group composed only a minority of the population, it felt more threatened and put down opposition more ruthlessly. Where regional separation of ethnic groups allowed both to build armies, civil war resulted, with high levels of repression in regions of mixed population. Within conditions of an integrated economy and a strong state, an ethnic minority can rule only through a command system based on coercion. It is not surprising that many, perhaps the majority, of cases of large-scale political repression in the twentieth century have occurred in ethnically divided states: Guatemala, South Africa, Uganda, Central Africa Republic, Sri Lanka, Israel, Pakistan, Soviet Union, etc.

The third route to political repression occurred when an ideological minority seized state power, often with the aid of a foreign power, and, in much the same manner as an ethnic minority, imposed its views on the rest of the population. It is important that the minority be true believers—that is, that they feel that their ideology represents the only correct view and provides answers to society's major problems. Whether a party vanguard or University of Chicago trained economists, they feel that they have scientific answers that the majority of the population are too ignorant to understand. In the first half of the twentieth century, racist and communist ideologies were thought to represent true science. In the second half of the twentieth century, neoliberal economic doctrine and a few resurgent religious faiths are the ideologies that grip the faithful.

The worst cases of political repression have occurred where there is an overlap between these three paths. Nazi Germany incorporated some aspects of all three. Eastern Germany had highly unequal land tenure systems with a threatened landholding class wishing to use state power to maintain its domination. An ethnic majority wished to impose its cultural values on the few minorities. And ideological true believers were able, through intimidation and manipulation, to take over the full power of the state. The Soviet Union combined true belief with ethnic domination. Guatemala combined highly unequal landholding and ethnic domination.

Eliminating Political Repression:
Building Free and Equal Association

The world has often suffered high degrees of domination without political repression, but wherever a high degree of domination exists, political repression is a possibility. Systems of unequal exchange have been stable in both premodern and modern times. The British at the end of the nineteenth century and the North Americans at the end of the twentieth demonstrate the possibilities of maintaining a consensual exchange system with great economic inequalities. Nevertheless, a ruling group that finds itself losing its grip, or feels it needs additional power to carry out some policy objectives, and which has the coercive forces of the state at its disposal, is likely to use them. Only as the art of free and equal association is developed will the threat of political repression be eliminated.

Since World War II there have been strong parallels between the international structures of domination in the Third World and in Eastern Europe, which have both provided coercive backup to challenged national leaders and encouraged them to turn to political repression to secure their rule. In 1989, Eastern Europe's structure suddenly dissolved, and with it political repression. Removing the international structure was sufficient to bring about political freedom. Would removing the international structure in the U.S.-dominated part of the world lead to a similar burst of freedom there?

The cases of Chile and El Salvador would suggest yes. The U.S. furnished coercive resources to both countries for dominant classes to maintain rule when their own local and national power resources had declined. The landed/business class of Chile had already lost its power when it solicited the support of the U.S. government to overthrow the representatives of a more equalitarian system. The land-owning oligarchy of El Salvador had not yet been replaced, but was severely threatened, when the United States stepped in to guarantee its survival. In both cases, it was the ability to draw on outside resources that made the difference and allowed large-scale repression.

Yet, the parallel between East and West may not be as good as it appears at first glance. The situation in Eastern Europe may be far more propitious for democracy than in most of the Third World. Even though the Russian Revolution kept the mode of domination of the Czars, the new rulers adopted policies that radically changed the distribution of the means of domination. In particular, they eliminated the huge disparities in the means of purchase and through an equalitarian education program provided potential for equality in the means of persuasion. Women achieved a great deal of progress toward equality in the household, in the workplace, and in politics. The conquest of Eastern Europe after World War II transposed the same mode of domination and policies from the Soviet Union to these states. Thus, by 1989, it was primarily the command mode of domination of the state, rather than the structures of society, that stood in the way of a more equalitarian system of rule. Furthermore, the Marxist ideology of Eastern Europe was at odds with the corrupt and selfish societies that had been created, and always foresaw the implementation of democracy.

The most encouraging aspect of changes in Eastern Europe is that, except in the case of Romania, they have occurred without violence. The peaceful changes establish a precedent for relying on persuasion and entering into dialogue to achieve a consensus.

The societies of the Third World are more contradictory. Education has expanded but remains very uneven. Women are breaking out of some of their bonds but have not come close to their position in Eastern Europe. The Catholic Church, so important in Latin America and the Philippines, is riddled with contradictions; formally, it maintains as hierarchical a system as the Pentagon, but it contains at its roots the most democratic institutions in the Third World. Sadly, in this contradictory tangle of authority patterns, the hierarchy is using its power to weaken the democratic elements. As the world capitalist system extends its reach, more and more Third World people become part of the hierarchical business structures of the transnational corporations. And, what is most problematic, the distribution of the means of purchase is as unequal as has ever existed anywhere.

It is customary to measure income inequality only within the boundaries of single states, but the poor of the Third World are part of the same economy and system of domination as are the rich of the First World. The difference in the means of purchase between the rich of the First World and the poor of the Third World has never been greater and continues to grow. Probably the worst deterioration has occurred in the Western Hemisphere.

The aggressive marketing of "free enterprise" economics by right-wing organizations, the U.S. government, banks and transnational industries, and the International Monetary Fund and World Bank seeks to persuade the world that the rich deserve to rule. There is a strongly anti-democratic aspect to this set of ideas as it blames organized popular groups for presumed distortions in the economy.[12] This ideology and the huge exchange power of the same organizations have been remarkably successful in extending the power of this narrow group with only limited use of coercion. What will happen after their economic project fails to provide welfare for much of the world? Will they back off like the Communist leaders of Eastern Europe have?

Fortunately, there are countercurrents in the West. Probably the most promising is the fostering of the growth of solidarity between First and Third Worlds by nongovernmental not-for-profit organizations. Nonprofit development organizations work in most communities of the Third World. One count a couple of years ago found 16,000 NGO development agencies in the Philippines. This type of foreign assistance works to favor freedom, as it empowers local groups and communities and encourages consensus rule. It is always on a smaller scale than official assistance, but it has become quite significant in its overall reach.

In the troubled times of recent decades, nongovernmental human rights organizations have provided the greatest force for freedom in the world. A dense network of small and medium-size groups has come into existence in the last twenty years, which support national and local groups struggling for human rights, bring violations to the attention of international organizations and foreign governments, and generally cause discomfort to repressive states. It is possible to build far stronger international structures to support human rights.

In the long run, civil society must regain some of its autonomy vis-a-vis the state and transnational corporations in all parts of the world. Occupants of state offices will not, and perhaps cannot, do anything to foster a more autonomous civil society. Managers of transnational corporations, likewise, have no interest in autonomous communities that might resist their demands. People, then, must work outside of governments to increase their capability for collective and consensual action, and to be truly independent they will also have to become more economically self-sufficient. Autonomy may require partial withdrawal of individuals and communities from the state and world economy—creating local solidarity groups similar to what previously existed in small agricultural family farm communities. People in these communities would have the independence to influence national policies without being manipulated or coerced.

Notes

1. See Barbara Harff and Ted R. Gurr, "Towards Empirical Theory of Genocides and Politicides: Identification of Cases Since 1945." Paper delivered at the International Studies Association meeting, (1987).

2. See John McCamant, "Critique of Current Measures of 'Human Rights Development' and an Alternative" in V. Nanda, J. Scarritt, and G. Shepherd, eds., *Global Human Rights: Public Policies, Comparative Measures, and NGO Strategies* (Boulder, Colo.: Westview Press, 1981).

3. Harry Eckstein, "A Perspective on Comparative Politics, Past and Present," in Harry Eckstein and David E. Apter, eds., *Comparative Politics: A Reader* (New York: Free Press, 1963), 24.

4. See John McCamant, "Governance without Blood: Social Science's Antiseptic View of Rule, or the Neglect of Political Repression," in Michael Stohl and George Lopez, eds., *The State as Terrorist: the Dynamics of Governmental Violence and Repression* (Westport, Conn.: Greenwood Press, 1984).

5. See Sandra Harding, *The Science Question in Feminism* (Ithaca: Cornell University Press, 1986).

6. Peggy Reeves Sanday, *Female Power and Male Dominance* (Cambridge: Cambridge University Press, 1981), 164.

7. See Anthony Giddens, *The Nation-State and Violence* (Berkeley: University of California Press, 1985).

8. See George Orwell, *Nineteen Eighty Four* (New York: Harcourt Brace Jovanovich, 1949); and Giddens, *The Nation-State and Violence*.

9. Harry Eckstein, "The Idea of Political Development: From Dignity to Efficiency," in Harry Ekstein, *World Politics*, 483.

10. See Giddens, 310.

11. See Barrington Moore Jr., *Social Origins of Dictatorship and Democracy* (Boston: Beacon, 1966).

12. See David Pion-Berlin, *The Ideology of State Terror, Economic Doctrine and Political Repression in Argentina and Peru* (Boulder, Colo.: Lynne Rienner Publishers, 1989).

4

Sources of State Terrorism in Rural Central America

Charles D. Brockett

A number of studies have contributed valuable knowledge about the tragic phenomenon of state terrorism in Latin America. These include both cross-national aggregate data analyses[1] and case studies of individual countries.[2] Major deficiencies persist in our understanding, however, because of a dearth of systematic, comparative case studies. Thus, while many hypotheses have been advanced to explain both the causes of state terrorism and its spread in recent decades,[3] there is little comparative analysis to substantiate the purported relationships between state terrorism and hypothesized causal variables.

This study undertakes such a comparative analysis for the countries of Central America. Some of the most terrible examples of state terrorism during the past decade have been located in this region, posing serious problems for U.S. foreign policy and for concerned U.S. citizens. At the same time, the region provides especially appropriate conditions for comparative analysis; although the five Central American countries included in this study share many characteristics, there have been major variations among them in the recourse to repression.[4]

Regimes ruling El Salvador and Guatemala in recent years have been notorious for their reliance on widespread and systematic terrorism to repress the considerable popular mobilization confronting them; equally notorious was the Somoza regime in Nicaragua. More than forty thousand civilian noncombatants were murdered in El Salvador during 1980–1984 by government forces and allied death squads.[5] Estimates for Guatemala vary widely; the most careful of them place the number of victims between fifty thousand and seventy-five thousand from 1978 to 1985.[6] Most of the state violence in Nicaragua occurred in the context of the Somoza regime's failed effort to stay in power in the face of a popular revolution. Some fifty thousand people were killed, largely as the result of the regime's indiscriminate killing.[7] This extraordinary violence is often simply explained as an elite response to mass political mobilization. When Honduras is included in the analysis, however, it becomes clear that other factors were at work as well. Honduras also has experienced substantial popular mobilization in recent decades, but it has largely escaped the state terrorism plaguing its neighbors. The last of the five cases, serving to expand the variation among them, is Costa Rica, which has neither suffered from state terrorism nor experienced levels of popular mobilization similar to those of the other four.

Through the comparison of these cases this study will evaluate the following two hypotheses. One, the incidence and severity of a repressive response by the state to popular mobilization is determined by the level of perceived threat, the capacity for repression, and the propensity for repression. Capacity refers to quantitative and qualitative characteristics of the repressive apparatus; propensity refers to individual dispositions as they are collectively expressed. The second hypothesis is this: the level of threat perceived by ruling groups when confronted by popular mobilization is not directly a function of the level of mobilization itself but is also the result of at least three other factors. The first is the larger political context. The second factor is the supply of resources available with which popular demands can be met. The third factor is the inequality and rigidity of the class structure and its relationship to the state (especially the relationship between the agrarian bourgeoisie and the state).[8]

In order to keep this study manageable, attention will be concentrated on repression in rural areas, which have been the most important sites of state terrorism in the region. Accordingly, the discussion of popular mobilization will be restricted to the peasantry.[9]

The Perception of Threat and the Political Context

The comparative levels of peasant mobilization in the Central American countries cannot be accurately gauged, and even less so can the perception of degrees of threat by economic and political elites. However, rough inferences that are sufficient for the purposes of this study can be made on the basis of the available evidence. When the countries are examined at the point just prior to the onset of widespread state violence (i.e., Guatemala before 1978, Nicaragua before late 1978, El Salvador before late 1979), there do not seem to be substantial differences in the level of peasant mobilization or its threat, although it might be said to be somewhat less in Nicaragua. What is most important is that the levels reached in Honduras during the mobilization peaks of the 1968–1975 period were easily equal to those of the other three countries during comparable periods. Accordingly, the recourse to state terrorism cannot be explained as a consequence solely of the level of rural mass mobilization itself.

Two political factors, though, do distinguish Honduras from the other three countries, although a third political factor weakens the political context as an explanation for state terrorism. First, popular mobilization in urban areas was far less in Honduras than in the others, especially El Salvador. Second, and particularly important, radical organizations and demands were more prominent in the other countries than in Honduras, creating a greater overall atmosphere of danger to elite interests. In Nicaragua by late 1978, the Sandinistas were a serious threat to the regime; furthermore, much of the population agreed with demands for an end to the regime and for major socio-economic reforms. In El Salvador by late 1979, radical mass organizations were the most dynamic political force in urban areas, gathering some 200,000 demonstrators in the capital, for example, on January 22, 1980. Behind these non-violent groups were five revolutionary organizations, although of much less importance at this point than they would soon become. That El Salvador was on the brink of civil war was clear to all sides. Yet too much should not be made of this factor as an explanation for state terrorism. Radical and violent organizations in Guatemala were substantially less significant prior to the onset of widespread state violence than in Nicaragua and El Salvador, though certainly more prominent than in Honduras.

The analysis of the role of political factors becomes even more confused when the external context of these situations is included. The acceleration of state terrorism in Nicaragua and El Salvador did roughly correspond to a deteriorating international situation, from the regimes' perspective. U.S pressure on Somoza intensified from late 1978 on, while Cuban (and other) assistance to the Sandinistas increased. The fall of Somoza heightened the perception of threat in close-by El Salvador, as did the evidence of some assistance to the Salvadoran revolutionaries from Nicaragua during late 1980 and early 1981. However, the external context should be regarded as more threatening to Honduras than to Guatemala. Honduras shares substantial borders with both Nicaragua and El Salvador but the areas of greatest turmoil in Guatemala were isolated from the region's centers of conflict. Nor is there evidence of important contributions of outside support to the Guatemalan revolutionaries. Human rights abuses did increase in Honduras in the early 1980s as the international context became more dangerous; yet, they greatly improved during 1984, unlike the geopolitical situation.

As repression increased throughout the region, so did popular resistance. This mass mobilization developed into the greatest threat to the established powers in Nicaragua, where the regime was overthrown and replaced by a revolutionary government, and then El Salvador, where the same goal was almost achieved. Although the threat was substantial in Guatemala, it did not approach the same level as in the other two. The major point, then, is this: the level of mobilization, the prominence of radical organizations and demands, and the international environment do not explain the two central questions with which this study is concerned. They are, first: Why was state terrorism the most widespread in El Salvador and Guatemala (especially compared to Nicaragua)? and second: Why has state terrorism been at far lower levels in Honduras?

Constraints on Resources

Guatemala and El Salvador entered the twentieth century with the most exploitive and coercive rural class structures in Central America. Because of variations in the availability of land, labor, and capital,[10] the ability to expand the production of export crops, such as indigo and coffee, had been the greatest in these two countries. Elites in El Salvador and Guatemala had often relied on coercion to obtain the land and labor they required, especially if the peasants were Indians (more likely in these two countries). Similar developments did occur in Nicaragua, but less extensively because of less propitious conditions. Coffee agriculture was as important to Costa Rica as to the first two countries, but it spread in Costa Rica with little coercion and under more egalitarian circumstances, for reasons following from its divergent colonization pattern. In contrast, Honduras had little export agriculture until recent decades because of the lack of the necessary capital and infrastructure and because of its difficult terrain (with the exception of its important but isolated banana enclaves).

The consequences of these historical patterns for the region's contemporary agrarian structures can be seen in Table 4.1. The first column shows that Guatemala and El Salvador confront the most severe land scarcity, while Honduras and Nicaragua are less constrained, as measured by cropped land per economically active person employed in agriculture. Costa Rica also falls into the first group but it has far less of its population employed in agriculture. Furthermore, rural poverty is much less pervasive in Costa Rica than in the other four countries, which group closely together in their rates of total rural poverty, but with Honduras significantly the worst in "extreme" rural poverty.

The final column in Table 4.1 reports a rural inequality score for the early 1970s. This measure gives equal weight to three dimensions of

TABLE 4.1 Indicators of Rural Economic Security in Central America

Country	Land Availability[a] (1978/1979)	Population in Agriculture[b] (1979)	Percent Population in Rural Poverty[c] (1980)		Rural Inequality Score[d]
			Extreme	Total	
Costa Rica	1.7	36	18.7	34.2	99
El Salvador	1.3	51	55.4	76.4	162
Guatemala	1.8	56	51.5	83.7	149
Nicaragua	4.5	44	50.0	80.0	101

(a) Hectares of cropped land (arable land plus land in permanent crops) in 1978 per economically active person employed in agriculture in 1979. Calculated from International Agricultural Development Service, *Agricultural Development Indicators* (New York: IADS, 1978), pp.16, 17.

(b) Percentage of economically active population employed in agriculture. (IADS, 16)

(c) Aria Eugenia Gallardo and José Roberto López, *Centroamérica: La Crisis en Cifras* (San José, Costa Rica: Instituto Interamericano de Ciencias Sociales, 1986), 158.

(d) Gives equal weight to three dimensions of rural inequality in the early to mid-1970s: (1) "minifundización" (smallholders as percentage of all farm operators divided by the average size of smallholder farms); (2) landlessness; (3) percentage of all land held by large estates. For sources and further explanation, see Charles Brockett, "Cycles of Protest and the Impact of Repression in Central America," paper presented athe the Fifteenth International Congress of the Latin American Studies Association, Miami, December 4–6, 1989, table 2.

the land issue: the concentration of most of the land in large estates owned by a few, the concentration of most peasants on the smallest plots of land, and landlessness. For each of the three dimensions (this data is not included in the table), El Salvador and Guatemala feature the worst rural inequality, followed by Honduras. As a result, that is the ranking on the overall score given in the table, followed by Nicaragua and Costa Rica, which are virtually tied.

These empirical indicators demonstrate that El Salvador and Guatemala clearly have the most unequal agrarian structures in the region. They combine sizable populations employed in agriculture with the worst land scarcity and concentration of land ownership. The agrarian problem has not been as extreme in Honduras nor especially Nicaragua (although it is certainly serious in both). Costa Rica is in a separate category. It is apparent why peasant mobilization and agrarian conflict in Costa Rica have been at significantly lower levels than in the rest of the region since it has the lowest rates of rural poverty, the smallest agriculture-based population, and the lowest rural inequality score. In addition, the Costa Rican peasantry has not experienced the same degree of land expulsion as elsewhere.

As peasants mobilized and asserted their interests, especially the primary demand for land, the region's governments varied in the availability of resources with which they could meet peasant demands. Land distribution was facilitated in Honduras and Costa Rica up to the mid-1970s by the availability of public lands; this was especially true in Honduras where up to one-third of the land was still public as late as 1974. Large tracts of unused or under-used lands owned by foreign multinational fruit companies also were most plentiful in Honduras and Costa Rica. Although underutilized, domestically owned lands are plentiful throughout the region and therefore potential targets of agrarian reform programs, in reality they are extraordinarily difficult to expropriate since they are the economic base of the landed elite. Consequently, they are available for redistribution only under the most exceptional of circumstances—namely those of revolutionary Nicaragua and El Salvador in 1980.

In summary, the existence of public lands and underutilized foreign fruit company holdings facilitated meeting peasant demands for land by governments in Honduras especially, but also in Costa Rica (and Guatemala in the reform period of the early 1950s). Although Honduras has had a relatively large and assertive peasant movement, its demands were less radical than elsewhere since Honduran peasants and their supporters were more likely to believe that solutions could be found short of attacking the holdings of large domestic land owners. Similarly, land owners and public officials were less likely to perceive peasant demands as fundamental attacks on the existing agrarian system. Of course, as some peasant demands were met through land distribution, fewer resources were "available" to meet demands in following years; that is, constraints have seriously tightened in recent years. (Similar dynamics have occurred in Costa Rica.)

Land pressures worsened during the 1970s throughout the region due to the further expansion of commercial agriculture and population growth.[11] These land pressures were the worst in El Salvador and Guatemala, intensifying elite opposition to any serious consideration of land reform or other needs of the peasantry. As popular pressures accelerated, this elite opposition degenerated into institutionalized state terrorism on a massive scale. Nicaragua falls between the two groups of countries. In the 1970s, its land pressures were not as acute as in El Salvador and Guatemala, but its ruling elites were just as intransigent.

The Agrarian Bourgeoisie and the State

Country differences in resource constraints have been reinforced by differing patterns in the relationship of the agrarian bourgeoisie to the state. Given both the extreme rural inequality and the scarcity of land, elites in El Salvador and Guatemala have perceived the land issue as zero-sum in nature. Consequently, government inflexibility on the issue has been expected and was ensured by the militarized state's willingness to serve the agrarian bourgeoisie's fundamental interests in both countries. Indeed, both military regimes originated at times of social crises engendered by the land question (i.e., El Salvador in 1932 and Guatemala in 1954).

The notable contrast with Nicaragua in this respect has been usefully analyzed by Midlarsky and Roberts.[12] They identify the military regime of El Salvador (and Guatemala in passing) as an "instrumentalist state"— that is, one where "the state is essentially . . . [though] never entirely an instrument of class domination."[13] Somoza's Nicaragua, though, was an "autonomous personalist state"—a clear example of an instance in which the "interests served by the state are those of the personal ruler and his cohorts, rather than those of a unified dominant class, [or] that state as an institution."[14]

The agrarian bourgeoisie of Nicaragua had never been able to develop the coherence or the political power of its counterparts in El Salvador and Guatemala, because it was pre-empted by the Somoza dynasty and, in an earlier period, because it suffered interventions by Great Britain and the United States.[15] Even though the policies of the Somoza governments often did benefit the landowning class, Somoza interests and those of landowners could also diverge, as they did increasingly during the 1970s. Accordingly, an anti-dictator coalition including both peasants and landlords could, and did, form. Society polarized in Nicaragua, not along class lines, but instead as a broad multiclass coalition against the dictatorship.

Somoza employed indiscriminate violence against the peasantry with impunity earlier in the decade, but in later years he confronted greater constraints on his ability to achieve his objectives through state terrorism. As an "autonomous personalistic state," two constraints were particularly relevant. First, the Somoza regime was the most dependent on the United States in the region. Although the dynasty was relatively autonomous from and superior to economic elites domestically, internationally it was a client of the regional hegemonic power (and clearly the two facts are related). The rural repression of 1974–1976 was relatively unnoticed in the United States but Somoza faced (and responded to) a more concerned U.S. public, Congress, and administration in 1977–1979.[16] This U.S. concern helps to explain why oppositional leaders did not disappear with as great a frequency as in the neighboring terrorist states (which is not to deny that his "mop-up" operations after insurrections were horrendous). Furthermore, as an "autonomous personalistic state," its capacity for systematic state terrorism was inadequately developed, as will be explained in the following section.

Different patterns of elite-state relations are provided by Costa Rica and Honduras. From the first years of the coffee boom, the coffee bourgeoisie of Costa Rica was larger, less wealthy, and less parasitic. It was, therefore, less of an obstacle to the development of a more pluralistic political system, especially as society became more urban and less agriculturally based.[17] Finally, both the agrarian bourgeoisie and state in Honduras were quite weak in comparison to their neighbors as late as 1960, largely because of the lack of a significant domestically-controlled exportable crop to provide the capital necessary for either to expand. Although that expansion followed rapidly in the subsequent decades, Honduras, through the mid-1970s, still presented the best possibility for the redirection of government policy toward the peasantry's interests without prior changes in fundamental class-state relations.[18] As a consequence of these factors, then, the state was far less likely to be used as an instrument of violence against the peasantry in Costa Rica and Honduras than in the other three countries.

Capacity of the State Security Apparatus

Central American countries also differ in their coercive capacities, as measured both quantitatively and qualitatively. Given their histories and more rigid agrarian structures, one would expect El Salvador and

Guatemala to have larger and more competent security forces than the other countries. The data, as presented in Table 4.2, indicate that this is true. The first column gives the number of the principal security force personnel in each country during the late 1970s. For Guatemala, Honduras, and Nicaragua, the figure given is for armed forces personnel only. Costa Rica disbanded its military after its 1948 "revolution;" the figure in the table is for the Civil Guard. The figure for El Salvador includes its large and important National Guard which has responsibilities for rural order. The five countries vary widely in area and this must be taken into account in determining their relative coercive capability, especially since the subject of this study is repression in rural areas— often remote areas difficult to reach.[19] A rough measure of coercive capacity—the number of security force personnel per square mile— indicates a much stronger coercive capacity in Guatemala and especially in El Salvador. This more highly developed capacity facilitated the implementation of systematic state terrorism in these two countries, while the lesser capacity acted as a constraint in the others. The contrast with Nicaragua is especially notable.

When other security forces are taken into consideration, the magnitude of the difference becomes even greater. In addition to the personnel already listed, El Salvador, at the end of the 1970s, also had a National Police notable for its size (two thousand), as well as the over one thousand members of the Treasury Police, notorious for their brutality.[20] Finally, there was the Democratic Nationalist Organization (ORDEN, i.e., "order") a 100,000 member rural paramilitary organization linked to the National Guard.[21] Similarly, well-organized paramilitary death squads tied to the military have been operating in Guatemala since the mid-1960s.[22]

The greater coercive capacity of El Salvador and Guatemala is also clear when the competence of the security forces is examined. The Salvadoran National Guard, for example, was described in 1960 by a U.S. security specialist as providing "the most complete and beneficial [!] civil police services ever observed by us in Latin America."[23] Similarly, the professional competence of its National Police has been praised in comparison to the rest of the region, including Guatemala.[24] The development of a modern army in Guatemala began in 1871 at the time of the coffee revolution. By 1922 the military had garrisons in the smallest towns throughout the country, and during the following decade they penetrated into remote rural areas.[25] The military continued to modernize in the following years, and by the mid-1960s, it had become "a coherent political institution capable of dominating the country's political life" like its counterpart in El Salvador had for decades.[26]

In contrast, it was not until the early 1950s that the military of Honduras "began to achieve a certain primitive level of institutionali-

TABLE 4.2 Security Forces of Central America

Country	Security Force Personnel[a]	Area (Square Miles)	Security Force Personnel Per Square Mile
Costa Rica	3,000	20,000	.15
El Salvador	8,930	8,200	1.09
Guatemala	17,960	42,000	.43
Honduras	11,300	43,000	.27
Nicaragua	7,500	57,000	.13

(a) Total number in armed forces in late 1970s, except the following: Costa Rica, number in Civil Guard; El Salvador, includes the 2,000 man National Guard.

Sources: Armed forces (except Nicaragua): George T. Kurian, *Encyclopedia of the Third World*, 3 vols. (New York: Facts on File, 1982), 451, 572, 693, 770. Nicaragua: George Black, *Triumph of the People: The Sandinista Revolution in Nicaragua*, (London: Zed Press, 1981), 52. El Salvador National Guard: Michael McClintock, *The American Connection: Volume I: State Terror and Popular Resistance in El Salvador*, (London: Zed Press, 1985), 215.

zation."[27] Further development was promoted by the country's humiliating loss in the "Soccer War" of 1969 with El Salvador. By the mid-1970s, the military had consolidated a central position within the national political system,[28] but still did not penetrate rural society as it did in the other two countries, although substantial efforts have been made in this regard since 1963.[29]

The National Guard of Nicaragua was small by comparison with its neighbors. Furthermore, it was a personal instrument of Somoza family rule, undermining its effectiveness as a military force. Continual intervention by the Somozas into Guard personnel and policy decisions secured for the family a compliant force that did not threaten its power. But, this interference corroded the Guard's effectiveness as a coercive institution capable of maintaining the status quo.[30]

Propensity for Repression

As peasants mobilized throughout Central America in response to their growing economic crisis of the 1960s and 1970s, they also encountered different government responses because of differences in political cultures and elite subcultures. As Ted Gurr has pointed out, "historical traditions of state terror . . . probably encourage elites to use terror irrespective of . . . structural factors."[31] Indeed, there are important differences among Central American countries in the extent of historical reliance on repression.

The elites of Guatemala and El Salvador had been more likely to utilize violence in the past to obtain the land and labor they required for their economic enterprises and to rely on repression to keep those economic structures in place. The point here is two-fold. First, the agrarian class structures of these two countries were more exploitive than in the other countries and were protected, therefore, by more elaborate and extensive repressive institutions. Consequently, mass mobilization in these two countries would be perceived by elites (correctly) as more of a fundamental threat than would similar levels of mobilization elsewhere. Second, given the scope of the violence that had been used in the past, elites, reinforced by their subculture, would be more likely to believe violence an acceptable and effective response to any perceived threats in the present. Elites in El Salvador could and did look back to the massacre of 1932 as "a model response to the threat of rebellion" and to the four decades of "peace" that it brought.[32] Guatemalans contemplating violence needed to refer back only to 1966–1976 and 1954, or they could go back to the twenty-two year "reign of terror"[33] of Manuel Estrada Cabrera early in the century. Going progressively further back in time, the patterns of violence employed in the conversion of food land to coffee cultivation, in maintaining colonial society, and in the Conquest, distinguished Guatemala and El Salvador from the other three countries. In overly reductionistic terms, the essential reason for the greater propensity for repression in these two countries was this: opportunities for the creation of an export economy based on forced labor (Indian and mestizo) were greater in Guatemala and El Salvador than in the other three countries.[34]

If we assume, however, that the "massive slaughter of members of one's own species is repugnant" to humans,[35] then the existence of such "incentives" as those discussed above is an incomplete explanation for state terrorism; attention must also be given to factors that facilitate the dehumanization of potential victims.[36] The two most important such factors are probably political ideologies and social cleavages.

Ideologies can portray "foreign" ideas as threats to society, thereby turning (suspected) advocates of these ideas into mortal enemies, regardless of whether these advocates intend to employ force. Most salient in contemporary Latin America, of course, has been a national security ideology imbued in the militaries and among economic elites, that identifies radicalism with Communism and Communism with the Soviet threat to the hemisphere.[37] This national security ideology is important to explaining the prevalence of state terrorism in the region, but it is difficult to distinguish any meaningful differences in this variable among the four countries under study here. More significant to the explanation of country differences in the propensity for repression are social cleavages.

Gurr[38] claims that "the greater the heterogeneity and stratification in a society, the greater the likelihood that a regime will use violence as a principal means of social control." Similarly, both Kuper[39] and Duvall and Stohl emphasize the importance to dehumanization of "the perceptual social distance between the government and the victim population."[40]

In terms of class, this social distance has been the greatest in El Salvador and Guatemala with their more polarized rural structures. As Table 4.1 demonstrated, in these two countries there has been a much smaller intermediate category of farms separating the small landed elite from the large and impoverished majority. A social cleavage of perhaps even greater importance has been ethnicity. The Indian population of Guatemala in the 1970s is estimated at around 44 percent with the comparable figure for the other three countries ranging between 5 percent and 7 percent.[41] Among these three there are important differences. The Indian populations of Honduras and Nicaragua are largely isolated in the remote and underpopulated Caribbean lowlands, but such physical segregation is not present in El Salvador. Furthermore, the 1932 massacre in El Salvador was particularly aimed at Indians, causing many of the survivors to relinquish their cultural identity. Although they and their descendants may not be culturally distinct from the European and mestizo elites and security forces, they are nevertheless distinctive in physical appearance.

The noncombatant group most likely to supply the innocent victims of state terrorism in Central America in recent decades has been the Indians of Guatemala's western highlands. This is the contemporary manifestation of the racism that stretches back to the Liberal reforms of the nineteenth century, which expropriated land and labor from the Indians, and back further to the Conquest. The reinforcing effect of this racism and of the national security ideology in promoting the dehumanization necessary for this brutality is clearly shown in Michael Richards's[42] interviews with military personnel involved in the subjugation of the remote Ixil region of northeastern Guatemala in the early 1980s. Both officers and soldiers perceived the Ixil "as backward and culturally, and even mentally, less developed."[43] As a consequence of such attitudes, "the Ixiles are not afforded real human status."[44] When combined with the national security doctrine, this racism produced the following closed-hearted attitude: "the death, destruction, and displacement of the human population were simply unfortunate consequences of a strategy couched in the clinical design of counterinsurgency."[45]

Conclusion

The application of systematic state terrorism in El Salvador from 1980 to 1983 and in Guatemala up to 1984 accomplished, for the time, its purpose. Although revolutionary forces continue their struggles in both countries, the tens of thousands of murders in each country were sufficient to destroy popular organizations and restore fear and passivity to the countryside. In Nicaragua, by contrast, Somoza's willingness even to destroy the nation's cities with his air force was not sufficient to save his regime. During the final battles of the civil war, his forces killed on levels approaching those of the other two countries but, unlike in the other two, his personalistic dictatorship had alienated all sectors of society and did not possess the institutional capacity to implement state terrorism on the same widespread level.

Land pressures in El Salvador and Guatemala, due to both the further expansion of commercial agriculture and to population growth, intensified elite opposition in the 1970s to any serious consideration of land reform or other needs of the peasantry. Given that both systems were based on highly exploitive labor systems, intensifying land pressures heightened the probability that peasant mobilization would be experienced as an intolerable threat to the existing system. The pattern of state-class relations, the well developed security apparatus, and the history of repression ensured that the necessary coercive measures would be taken to eliminate that threat. In Nicaragua, however, land pressures were not as acute, nor was the labor system as coercive (speaking only relatively). Furthermore, the landowning class had been pre-empted from exercising state power by the Somoza dynasty. These are the reasons why the agrarian bourgeoisie in Nicaragua did not at first experience the popular mobilization there as posing the same degree of threat as that perceived by their counterparts in Guatemala and El Salvador.

In contrast, Costa Rica and Honduras entered the contemporary period with less repressive structures, as well as fewer constraints on the ability of their governments to meet peasant demands for land. Although serious agrarian problems remain in both, relative to the other three countries, regime responsiveness (and "mild" repression in Honduras) has been sufficient to hold rural discontent below the level where it would represent a serious threat to the maintenance of the system. Furthermore, neither has a tradition of rural repression similar to El Salvador and Guatemala; nor have their security forces as thoroughly penetrated rural society.

What about the future? The cyclical nature of repression in El Salvador and Guatemala suggests, tragically, that another reign of terror is probable in their futures unless the fundamental conflict between economic elites and a desperate majority is ameliorated. The fate of Nicaragua is as imponderable as the future of United States policy toward the Nicaraguan Revolution. In terms of the variables analyzed in this study, the most interesting country is Honduras.

Along certain dimensions, Honduras is becoming more like the other countries, increasing the possibility of a state terrorist response to future mass mobilization. Although much delayed compared to its neighbors, the spread of important domestically controlled export crops has created a modern agrarian bourgeoisie and the financial resources for the expansion of the state. This development has given both a motive and the resources for the growth of the security forces and their further penetration of rural areas. This growth was accelerated in the 1980s with the generous backing of the United States government because of concerns about the geopolitical situation shared by Honduran and U.S. elites. Finally, constraints on resources are much tighter now than they were in the past and they will be even tighter in the future. The easiest land to distribute is now gone, but the number of landless and land-poor peasants will continue to grow.

Yet, there are still differences in the Honduran situation that might sufficiently inhibit any future recourse to widespread repression. Honduran political culture still has lower propensity for repression compared to El Salvador and Guatemala, as clearly demonstrated in the 1980s. There are other notable differences in their political systems as well.

Honduras is described as having "a plethora of relatively independent groups, structures, and organizations . . . at both the state and societal level."[46] Although these actors emerged only after 1945, their development was concurrent with that of a modern agrarian bourgeoisie and centralized state. In El Salvador and Guatemala, on the other hand, the coffee-based elite, the military, and the state were well established and inter-connected prior to the organization of most non-elite groups. These differing relationships between classes and between the state and classes have important implications for expectations concerning social control by both elites and popular forces and for the ability of elites to implement control.

When a significant level of popular mobilization challenges elite interests in Honduras in the future, two additional factors will probably determine the balance between the influences of the two sets of factors already discussed. The first is whether a revolutionary movement emerges with sufficient strength to justify, for the relevant actors, a resort to draconian measures. The second factor is the international situation which comprises two elements, one regional and the other concerning the probably crucial role of the United States. The peak of peasant mobilization in Honduras in 1975 occurred in a relatively non-threatening regional context, but in the 1980s, peasant organizations were constrained by the regional crisis in which the United States was heavily involved.

This study has demonstrated that human rights abuses in Central America are largely a function of domestic forces. However, the impact of the hegemonic power can also be important. The state terrorism of 1980–1984 coincided with the electoral campaign and first term of a U.S. president whose administration refused to apply any serious coun-tervailing pressures on the guilty regimes until the end of 1983. Such pressures, under certain circumstances, can have an effect, as demon-strated by the case of the Carter administration and the Somoza regime.

Notes

1. See, for example, Ernest A. Duff and John F. McCamant, *Violence and Repression in Latin America: A Quantitative and Historical Analysis* (New York: Free Press, 1976).

2. See, for example, for Guatemala, Gordon Bowen, "The Political Economy of State Terrorism: Barrier to Human Rights in Guatemala," in *Human Rights and Third World Development*, ed. George W. Shepherd, Jr., and Ved P. Nanda (Westport, Conn.: Greenwood Press, 1985), 83–124; and Bowen, "Prospects for Liberalization by Way of Democratization in Guatemala," in *Liberalization and Redemocratization in Latin America*, ed. George A. Lopez and Michael Stohl (Westport, Conn.: Greenwood Press, 1987).

3. See, for example, George A. Lopez, "Terrorism in Latin America," in *The Politics of Terrorism*, 3d ed., ed. Michael Stohl (New York: Marcel Dekker, 1988); and John W. Sloan, "State Repression and Enforcement Terrorism in Latin America," in *The State as Terrorist*, ed. Michael Stohl and George A. Lopez (Westport, Conn.: Greenwood Press, 1984).

4. Rather than define repression and state terrorism as distinct (e.g., Lopez, "Terrorism in Latin America," 512; Stohl and Lopez, *State as Terrorist*, 7), it seems more appropriate to conceive of state terrorism as "the most extreme form of governmental repression"(Sloan, 83). Repression is the use of coercion to gain compliance; state terrorism is "life threatening," (Ted R. Gurr, "The Political Origins of State Violence and Terror: A Theoretical Analysis," *Government Violence and Repression: An Agenda for Research*, ed. Michael Stohl and George A. Lopez [Westport, Conn.: Greenwood Press, 1986], 46) that is, not aimed only at the direct victims but at "some target observers who identify with that victim in such a way that they perceive themselves as potential future victims" (Christopher Mitchell et al., "State Terrorism: Issues of Concept and Measurement," in *Agenda*, ed. Stohl and Lopez, p. 5). The objective of state terrorism, then, is not only to eliminate its direct victims, but also to terrorize others into acceptable behavior.

5. Cynthia Brown, *With Friends Like These: The Americas Watch Report on Human Rights & U.S. Policy in Latin America* (New York: Pantheon, 1985), 115.

6. Bowen, "Prospects," 42; Chris Krueger and Kjell Enge, *Security and Development Conditions in the Guatemalan Highlands* (Washington, D.C.: Washington Office on Latin America, 1985), p. 2. Altogether, over the past three decades, the death toll climbed to over 100,000 killed and 38,000 disappeared, according to the British Parliamentary Group on Human Rights (Congress, House, Committee on Foreign Affairs, *Developments in Guatemala and U.S. Options: Hearings before the Subcommittee on Western Hemisphere Affairs*, 99th Cong., 1st Sess., 20 February 1985, 63); another one million were internal refugees (Bowen, "Barrier," 106). This was in a country whose population during these three decades grew from 3.5 million to 7.5 million people.

7. Thomas W. Walker, *Nicaragua: The Land of Sandino* (Boulder: Westview Press, 1981), 41.

8. Secondary hypotheses could be generated, of course, specifying interactions between these three variables.

9. The terms "peasant" and "peasantry" will be employed loosely in this study, conforming to the definition of the peasant as "any rural cultivator who is low in economic and political status" (Henry A. Landsberger and Cynthia N. Hewitt, "Ten Sources of Weakness and Cleavage in Latin American Peasant Movements," in *Agrarian Problems & Peasant Movements in Latin America*, ed. Rodolfo Stavenhagen [New York: Doubleday Anchor Books, 1970], 560). This usage does not assume any particular set of values or agricultural practices.

10. Charles D. Brockett, *Land, Power, and Poverty: Agrarian Transformation and Political Conflict in Central America*, (Winchester, Mass.: Allen & Unwin, 1988), 13–39.

11. As one important manifestation, per capita domestically produced food supply declined by 17 percent for the region as a whole from 1948/1952 to

1976/1978, while the amount of land devoted to export crops relative to that in food crops increased 53 percent (Brockett, *Land, Power, and Poverty*, 56; Robert G. Williams, *Export Agriculture and the Crisis in Central America* (Chapel Hill: University of North Carolina Press, 1986).

12. Manus I. Midlarsky and Kenneth Roberts, "Class, State, and Revolution in Central America: Nicaragua and El Salvador Compared," *Journal of Conflict Resolution* 29, no. 2 (June 1985): 163–193.

13. Ibid., 181. It can be argued, though they do not, that this characterization no longer applied to El Salvador after the 1979 coup, nor to Guatemala by the 1970s. The Guatemalan military's control of the state was more secure and total during the 1970s than in El Salvador and more autonomous from economic elites.

14. Ibid., 183. For a similar characterization of the Marcos regime in the Philippines, see Gary Hawes and Gretchen Casper, "President Marcos, Multinationals, the World Bank, and the U.S. Government," in *Agrarian Reform in Reverse*, ed. Birol Yeshilada, Charles Brockett, and Bruce Drury (Boulder: Westview Press, 1987).

15. Jeffrey M. Paige, *Agrarian Revolution: Social Movements and Export Agriculture in the Underdeveloped World* (New York: Free Press, 1985), 94.

16. William M. LeoGrande, "The United States and the Nicaraguan Revolution," in *Nicaragua in Revolution*, ed. Thomas W. Walker (Boulder: Westview Press, 1982).

17. See Mitchell Seligson, *Peasants of Costa Rica and the Development of Agrarian Capitalism* (Madison: University of Wisconsin Press, 1980).

18. See Charles D. Brockett, "Public Policy, Peasants, and Rural Development in Honduras," *Journal of Latin American Studies* 19, no. 1 (May 1987): 69–86.

19. A more complete analysis might also consider differences in terrain and transportation infrastructure. The rankings shift if other, less salient indicators are used, such as military expenditure as a percentage of gross national product and military manpower per thousand working age persons. See Charles L. Taylor and David A. Jodice, eds., *World Handbook of Political and Social Indicators*, 3d ed. (New Haven: Yale University Press, 1983).

20. Michael McClintock, *The American Connection: Volume I: State Terror and Popular Resistance in El Salvador* (London: Zed Books, 1985), 215–216.

21. Brockett, *Land, Power, and Poverty*, 145–147.

22. Michael McClintock, *The American Connection: Volume II: State Terror and Popular Resistance in Guatemala* (London: Zed Books, 1985), 85–90.

23. Quoted in McClintock, *Volume I: El Salvador*, 197.

24. Ibid., 198.

25. McClintock, *Volume II: Guatemala*, 8–18.

26. Ibid., 69. This source and McClintock, *Volume I: El Salvador*, provide thorough and well documented discussions of the role of the United States in the development of the security forces of these two countries.

27. James A. Morris and Steve C. Ropp, in *Latin American Research Review* 12, no. 2 (1977): 27–68.

28. Ibid., 44–45.

76	Charles D. Brockett

29. Steve C. Ropp, "The Honduran Army in the Sociopolitical Evolution of the Honduran State," *The Americas* 30, no. 4 (1974): 521.

30. George Black, *Triumph of the People: The Sandinista Revolution in Nicaragua* (London: Zed Press, 1981), 70–72.

31. Gurr, 66.

32. McClintock, *Volume I: El Salvador*, 99–100.

33. Dana G. Munro, *The Five Republics of Central America* (New York: Oxford University Press, 1918), 53–54.

34. Brockett, *Land, Power, and Poverty*, 15–28. Both countries elaborated and enforced legal codes that coerced labor, such as laws making "vagrancy" a crime and requiring "vagrants" to work on private farms (Mcclintock, *Volume I: El Salvador*, 125; Brockett, *Land, Power, and Poverty*, 24).

35. Leo Kuper, *Genocide: Its Political Use in the Twentieth Century* (New Haven: Yale University Press, 1981), 84.

36. Raymond D. Duvall and Michael Stohl, "Governance by Terror," in *The Politics of Terrorism*, 2d ed., ed. Michael Stohl (New York: Marcel Dekker, 1983), 209–210; Kuper, 84–100.

37. See, for example, George A. Lopez, "National Security Ideology as an Impetus to State Violence and State Terror," in Stohl and Lopez, *Agenda*.

38. Gurr, 58.

39. Kuper, 84–85.

40. Duvall and Stohl, 209.

41. George T. Kurian, *Encyclopedia of the Third World*, 3 vols. (New York: Facts on File, 1982).

42. Michael Richards, "Cosmopolitan World View and Counterinsurgency in Guatemala," *Anthropological Quarterly* 58, no. 3 (1985): 90–107.

43. Ibid., 101.

44. Ibid., 102.

45. Ibid., 99.

46. Morris and Ropp, 51.

5

Repression and State Terror in Kenya: 1982–1988

Rhoda E. Howard

Repression and Terror

In Kenya in the 1980s repressive tactics were used by the state against some of its real and perceived opponents. Under certain circumstances such tactics could become terrorist. Both repression and terror are deliberate and preventative rather than merely punitive in nature, and both affect the audience as well as the object of the act. My decision to label the coercive activities of the Kenyan state in the 1980s repressive rather than terrorist rests on the following criteria. First, with regard to degree, Kenya's repressive activities hardly resembled those of countries such as Chile. The number of victims of political murder was very low, and even those imprisoned numbered in the hundreds rather than in the tens of thousands. Second, with regard to the kind of coercive activity, Kenya, unlike state terrorist countries, did not arrest, torture, or murder "innocents" who merely happened to be connected with the targets of state violence. While real or perceived opponents of the regime were arrested, their wives, children, friends and fellow villagers were (with a few significant exceptions) left alone.

Repression can become terrorism when violence is used by the state as a first, not a last, resort against its real or perceived opponents and against the audience that might be affected by its coercive activities. Stohl and Lopez[1] distinguish among oppression, repression, and terrorism. Oppression is a situation in which "social and economic privileges

For their comments on earlier drafts of this paper, I am most grateful to Bruce Berman, Jack Donnelly, Barbara Harff, John Lonsdale, Richard Stren, Gavin Williams, and the editors of this volume. I am also very grateful to Susan Dicklich and Lisa Kowalchuk for their research assistance.

are denied to whole classes of people regardless of whether they oppose the authorities." Repression is "the use of coercion or the threat of coercion against opponents or potential opponents in order to prevent or weaken their capability to oppose the authorities and their policies." Finally, terrorism is "the purposeful act or threat of violence to create fear and/or compliant behavior in a victim and/or audience of the act or threat." Hence, when political imprisonment, torture, and murder are used *in preference* to co-optive activities, such as bribes or the offer of a position in government, or milder punishments, such as involuntary exile, then terror is a better description. In Kenya, repressive activity became widespread after an attempted coup in 1982. By the end of 1988, severe curtailment of civil liberties and threats against almost all opposition figures suggested that the state was moving toward a policy of using violence as a first resort.

In what follows, four factors influencing the rise of terror in Kenya are posited. The first factor is a regime change[2] that resulted in a weakening of the Kenyan state. The "weak" state is more characteristic of sub-Saharan Africa than of Latin America. The other three factors, however, resemble the Latin American model of terrorism. They are the increasing salience of class politics; the injection of ideologies into political discourse; and the effects of external influence on internal politics (in Kenya's case, influence from the United States).

I do not propose that these four factors are sufficient to result in state terrorism. Certain variables such as the idiosyncratic natures of individual political leaders are not easily, if at all, susceptible to prediction. Further, it may be the case that some or all of the four factors are unnecessary to state terrorism. These conditions are derived from literature on the emergence of state terrorism in South and Central America, especially in Chile, El Salvador, and Guatemala.[3] Thus one purpose of this chapter is to consider whether the "Latin American model" of state terrorism is likely to arise in Africa. Kenya is chosen as an example of an African country that is developing social and political conditions that may, in the future, resemble those of state terrorist countries in Latin America.

Background

Kenya achieved independence in 1963 under the leadership of Jomo Kenyatta, an ethnic Kikuyu who remained President until his death in 1978, when he was succeeded by Daniel Arap Moi, a member of the minority Kalenjin nationality, who was still the President in 1991. The country became a *de facto* one-party state in 1969; this was changed to *de jure* status in 1982. In both cases, the changes were in reaction to political challenges by Oginga Odinga, an ethnic Luo whose public utterances frequently had a populist bent and who was particularly critical of the acquisition of large, private, landed estates by (often Kikuyu) capitalists. Kenya has regular competitive intra-party elections, with many ministers and members of Parliament defeated at each one. Electoral participation rates are low, however, as it is not possible to change the government, merely to change one's own representative in the Parliament. In 1988 public "queue-voting" (in which voters lined up behind a picture of the candidate of their choice) replaced the secret ballot in the intra-party primaries. There were also serious allegations of vote-rigging, fraud, and violence during the general election.[4]

There was a dramatic increase in political repression (arbitrary arrest, detention without trial, and torture) in Kenya from 1982 to 1988. These activities were precipitated by an unsuccessful attempted coup on August 2, 1982, by members of Kenya's Air Force, supported by many students at the University of Nairobi. The popularity of the coup was evidenced by celebratory looting both in Nairobi and in the rural areas.[5] The actual suppression of the attempted coup was very violent; for example, it appears that one to three busloads of students were machine-gunned.[6] The entire Air Force was disbanded and hundreds of officers and men were arrested and court-martialed. Several hundred were shot.[7]

From 1982 to early 1988, while some people were released, at least 600 others were imprisoned or taken into preventive detention. Most of them were professionals, academics, and businessmen, although a few were from the popular classes. A few of the detainees were lawyers whose only "crime" was attempting to defend already-detained clients.[8] Repression of students also characterized the ensuing six years; for example, in April 1985 one student was reported shot and fifteen arrested on the University of Nairobi campus.[9] There were several new arrests and re-arrests of prominent opposition politicians in late 1988.

Most of the prisoners whose cases were documented (there may very well have been many more whose arrests were not documented) were convicted of publishing, reading, or being aware of the existence of written material connected to the allegedly clandestine Mwakenya movement (of which more below), although, in one case those arrested were accused of railway sabotage.[10] In 1988 the government began accusing some of its perceived opponents of belonging to two new, hitherto unheard-of, underground groups, which it named as the Kenya Patriotic Front and the Kenya Revolutionary Movement.[11] The prisoners underwent trials without counsel at which presumably false confessions extracted by torture were used as evidence against them, although a few who refused to confess were detained instead under indefinite preventive detention legislation. The most notable torture was water-logging, in which prisoners were kept naked in water-filled cells for days or weeks at a time. Other tortures, such as electrical shocks, were also used. Up to early 1988, only three deaths of political prisoners were documented, and one, the death of a Ugandan refugee illegally in Kenya but not presumably involved in Kenyan politics, was immediately investigated. However, several more deaths occurred in 1988.[12] In early 1988, some of the prisoners detained under the Preservation of Public Security Act, who had never actually confessed to anything, were released; this was interpreted as a move to put a good face on Moi's regime prior to the March 1988 one-party elections.[13] Despite the releases of these prisoners, many others were still in jail.

In all fairness, it should be noted that the increase in repression after 1982 occurred after a real incident of political insurgence. It did not occur "out of the blue," or in anticipation of an event that might happen; the event, namely, the attempted coup, did happen. Moreover, the Kenyan regime did not resort to the very brutal tactics of state terror used in many other countries, such as murder of political opponents' wives, children, or fellow villagers. Nevertheless, the post-coup detentions followed a pattern that suggested the government was strongly worried by the emergence of an articulate, professional elite that had not been and could not be co-opted by the spoils of office. Although some observers noted the prevalence of Luo in the Air Force,[14] it appears that the opposition to the regime was not entirely ethnically based, and therefore not completely manageable by the regional/ethnic redistribution of resources.

Nevertheless, by the end of 1988, when the Air Force, which had been reconstituted and put under Army control,[15] was no longer a threat, the general state of civil liberties in Kenya was very poor. Options for dissent were almost completely closed off. All meetings of more than three people—even for social events such as weddings—required a police permit.[16] Student organizations were closely monitored, and student leaders were frequently arrested or expelled from the university; spies were placed in classrooms.[17] The independence of the judiciary was severely eroded on August 2, 1988 (perhaps not coincidentally the sixth anniversary of the failed coup), when the President was given the power to dismiss judges of the Appeal Court (the highest court in Kenya) and the High Court. At the same time, the police were given the power to detain people suspected of capital crimes, including treason, for 14 days without charge, up from the previous legal limit of 24 hours.[18] Religious leaders who objected to the imprisonments and tortures and who criticized the new queue-voting system were harassed and warned to stop meddling in politics. In October 1988, a member of Cabinet warned that the Government might "abolish the constitutional guarantee of freedom of religion."[19] A New Ministry of National Guidance and Political Affairs was established in 1987, with the explicit objective of controlling political debate and the explicit responsibility of censorship.[20] Three prominent journalists were jailed or harassed in 1988 for criticizing the government.[21] Families of dissidents also began to suffer harassment: the uncle of a prominent exile was arrested and the wife of Raila Odinga, the imprisoned son of Oginga Odinga, was fired from her job (although she was subsequently reinstated).[22]

Parliamentary debate, which until the late 1970s had been quite free and lively, was severely restricted. All discussion of Mwakenya was cut off by Moi in 1987, at which time he also ordered a stop to all public discussion of the topic.[23] In 1987 Moi explicitly announced that the sole legal political party, KANU (Kenya African National Union), was now supreme over the Parliament.[24] A KANU membership campaign was undertaken in 1986 and people who did not wish to join were frequently intimidated.[25] There were indications that the government intended to abrogate Kenya's 1982 Constitution;[26] suggestions were made that it was a colonial legacy, presumably because it contained clauses guaranteeing human rights and fundamental freedoms.

As freedom of speech, the right to association, and the rule of law are more tightly controlled in a country, actual physical coercion frequently becomes the weapon of first, rather than last, resort against the opposition. The erosion of civil liberties in Kenya in the late 1980s was unprecedented in that country's history, and suggested a trend toward a terroristic state in the 1990s.

Regime Change and the Weakened State

In the academic literature on sub-Saharan Africa, scholars now question whether the state as such actually exists. For example, Naomi Chazan attributes the decline of the Ghanian state to the non-institutionalization of state power, legitimacy and authority. Ghana, she argues, has merely the "shell" of a state.[27] And Goran Hyden maintains that, in general, in sub-Saharan Africa, the state is "soft," and "suspended in mid-air" over a society that could easily escape its attempts at organizational control.[28]

At minimum, a state consists of a set of institutions including the government, judiciary, and bureaucracy, whose orderly functioning can continue even when the politicians in charge of the government change. According to Alfred Stepan, "The state must be considered as more than the 'government'. It is the continuous administrative, legal, bureaucratic and coercive systems that . . . structure relationships between civil society and public authority."[29] In part, an effective state apparatus is considered legitimate by the citizenry, and its authority generally acknowledged, because it controls—through the mass media, the educational system, and other such institutions—the boundaries and content of ideological discourse. In the modern world, an orderly and effective state adheres to rational-legal norms of bureaucratic efficiency, so that even when policies or personnel change, there is no interruption in functioning.[30] The relations between government and society are strongly affected by the degree and methods of institutionalization and legitimacy of a state. The higher the degree of institutionalization and legitimacy, the lesser the amount of physical coercion that one ought to expect. Physical violence will be used only as a supplement to efficiently coercive rational-bureaucratic rule, and only in cases in which the ruler or government has not been able to co-opt or incorporate its opposition through other means.

A major characteristic of sub-Saharan African "states" is their weak institutionalization and the low degree of legitimacy accorded to actions taken by bureaucracies formally possessed of authority. In many cases the government is simply the personal preserve of one strongman and his clique of followers. Personal rule is arbitrary, non-institutionalized, and based on the individual decisions of the ruler.[31] Violence is endemic under personal rule and tends to be characterized as much by inter-citizen conflicts such as private vendettas, ethnic hostilities, and factional infighting, as by coercive activities undertaken by the state against its citizens. The "type" of personalist ruler and of the degree of coercion on which he must ultimately rely does, however, vary by the degree and kind of institutionalization and legitimacy of the state. Jackson and Rosberg divide personalist rule in sub-Saharan Africa into four types: "prince, autocrat, prophet and tyrant."[32] In Uganda, Idi Amin was a tyrant who, after a very brief "honeymoon" period of charismatic popularity, was left with very little claim to legitimacy other than his ethnic ties to tribes in the northwest of the country. In consequence, he relied on genocidal massacres perpetrated against sectors of the Langi and Acholi (real or perceived ethnic clients and supporters of his predecessor Milton Obote) and random terror against ordinary citizens by his personal henchmen.[33] Amin's rule was so terroristic that the state effectively disintegrated.

In Kenya, the opposite occurred. The Kenyan state exhibited a relatively high degree of legitimacy and authority, especially under the princely rule of Jomo Kenyatta.[34] Kenyatta's charismatic-revolutionary legitimacy was substantial, rooted in his nationalist activities and a perceived connection to the revolutionary Land and Freedom Army ("Mau Mau") of the 1950s. Moreover, he successfully cloaked himself with traditional authority through use of an African language (KiSwahili), adoption of chiefly symbols such as the ceremonial flywhisk, and encouragement of African culture—for example, on ritual occasions he would join in public dancing. Kenyatta set up a relatively successful constitutional system in which an indigenized bureaucracy operated relatively efficiently, albeit largely in the interests of the ruling family and elite. He also manipulated both class and ethnically-based clients through a reward system of power and wealth, so as to forestall any organized opposition.

Nevertheless, Kenyatta also resorted to violence on occasion. Although there was very little preventive detention during his rule, there were at least three political murders. There were 26 political prisoners in Kenya when Kenyatta died, all of whom were released by Moi.[35]

The interesting theoretical question in Africa is not why non-institutionalized states such as Uganda turn to violence, but why efficiently institutionalized states turn to it as a major method of control. What conditions, that is, facilitate the emergence of state terrorism where previously it did not exist? The Kenyan state has a relatively high degree of institutionalization and legitimacy in the context of sub-Saharan Africa. Yet the amount of political violence in Kenya increased significantly from 1982 to 1988. A major reason for this change was that Kenyatta's successor, Daniel Arap Moi, did not possess the same degree of legitimacy as Kenyatta himself. It is generally acknowledged that from 1978 to at least 1983, Moi had less control over the Kenyan political scene than his predecessor. He was not a member of the Kikuyu elite that had dominated politics in the 1960s and 1970s. There was no assurance that he would be able to ease this elite out of its dominant political position. However, by 1984, two years after the attempted coup, Moi's control over both the personnel and the bureaucratic apparatus of power seemed to be much surer. He had subtly managed to ease out of office his chief political rival, Charles Njonjo, who had been Kenyatta's most powerful advisor.[36] Further, he began to gradually replace senior Kikuyu bureaucrats or subject them to the informal scrutiny of non-Kikuyu, often Kalenjin, "subordinates."

Nevertheless, even in the late 1980s, Moi's control of Kenya was still insecure. Kenyatta had been able to control the country through his Kikuyu power-base and through distribution of wealth—especially of formerly white-owned land—to both Kikuyu and non-Kikuyu clients. After the economic recession of the late 1970s, there were fewer spoils of office for the new President to distribute. His reaction was to accuse all potential opponents of disloyalty. Instead of co-optation, Moi turned to repression in order to manage the political system, accusing almost all known or potential opponents of being a member of Mwakenya. (Mwakenya stands for Muungano wa Wazalendo KuKomboa Kenya, or Union of Nationalists to Liberate Kenya).[37] Moi was particularly fearful of the professionals and intellectuals known to be critical of his regime, whom he decried as "unpatriotic, educated elites serving foreign masters" and "intellectuals with passports."[38]

Thus, one reason for the repression of the 1980s was a regime change in a situation in which leadership was incompletely institutionalized and still heavily dependent on personalist skills. Long-term changes in Kenyan social and political conditions suggest, however, that there could be reoccurrences of the extreme state violence of the 1982–88 period, even if the state were more completely institutionalized. Class formation along capitalist lines, peasant landlessness in particular, is already quite severe in Kenya. Politics is increasingly being interpreted from below, and reacted to from above, in an ideological manner. And the United States' interest in Kenyan affairs is growing.

The Development of Class Politics

In much of Africa, politics is still an intra-elite game. The "masses" are incorporated into politics through patron-client relations, often based on ethnic or regional ties, or through an elite-controlled one-party state in which there is limited opportunity for political expression and participation. A ruling class, based particularly on access to and control of the state is emerging and consolidating in its own interests. It is comprised of a combination of the state elite, the bureaucratic elite, budding local capitalists, and traditional chiefs/rich farmers. However, there is very little coherent class formation from below. Peasants are notoriously difficult to organize on a political basis owing to their physical isolation, ethnic and linguistic fragmentation, and relatively high rates of illiteracy. Although they will sometimes take political actions in their own interests, peasants can be expected to be relatively quiescent recipients of national economic and political policies as long as they have access to some land. In Commonwealth Africa, rates of peasant landlessness do not yet approach those of Central American countries given over to extensive foreign agribusiness investment. But, one of the distinguishing characteristics of Kenya is its relatively high rates of peasant landlessness.

Of those Africans who are neither part of the ruling class nor peasants, very few can yet be considered to be members of a permanent, wage-earning proletariat. Large percentages of urban dwellers are non-wage earners subsisting in the "informal" (uncontrolled services and petty manufacturing) sector of the economy. Many people in both the wage-earning and the informal sectors still maintain close ties to their rural villages, and many still have use rights to land should they wish to return. Thus, proletarian political consciousness is not yet highly developed; the society is not as clearly bifurcated into rich property-owners and the poor propertyless as it is in Latin America. In most of sub-Saharan Africa the elite is not yet frightened by the possibility of peasant and proletarian political action. One does not encounter peasant-based guerilla movements against independent, black African governments.

In Africa, the intelligentsia tends to be politically influential. In the past it was incorporated into the elite; higher education was a scarce good that obtained privileged employment for its owners. This situation is changing, however, as new generations of university-educated young men (and a few women) find that they cannot obtain employment as privileged as that which was available to their post-independence predecessors. Unemployed, educated young men tend to become disaffected; this was one of the reasons for the student support of the August 2, 1982 attempted coup in Kenya. In any case, thought can have its own influence, even when the intelligentsia is fairly well-paid and highly privileged in material terms in comparison to the population at large, as in Africa. Much political action is undertaken by university professors, lawyers, writers, and students in Africa, and they are frequently the objects of repressive activities. Embryonic links are being made, especially in Kenya, between intellectuals and the rural and urban poor.[39]

Thus, one can expect that as independent Africa becomes more divided in class terms, and as rates of landlessness increase, class consciousness from below will result in political repression and possibly state terrorism from above. Kenya is a country that is relatively advanced in this process. By 1982, 22 percent of Kenyans were estimated to be landless.[40] Among those who did have land, distribution was highly uneven. In 1984–85, 2.5 percent of Kenyan land holdings accounted for 46 percent of arable land, while 97 percent of the holdings accounted for only 40 percent.[41] 3,433 large farmers occupied half the arable land.[42] Although the very high population growth rate was one reason for landlessness, an important political reason was that Kenya had been a settler colony and many Kikuyu had been forced off the land during the colonial period to make way for Europeans. After independence, land was "redistributed," primarily to wealthier Africans who could buy it. Landlessness in the 1980s was exacerbated by an increasing shortage of urban jobs. Only about 20,000 new jobs were created every year for about 300,000 school leavers.[43] Thus poverty is endemic and severe in Kenya. In the 1977–1986 period, 10 percent of the urban and 55 percent of the rural population were considered to be living below the absolute poverty level.[44]

By the 1980s, Kenya's ruling class was much more consolidated than that of many other African countries, and much more closely identified with Marx's early stage of "primitive accumulation" of capital. The elite, especially Kenyatta's own family, used access to the state to line its own pockets. Moi himself was extremely wealthy and owned, among other properties, the most prestigious skyscraper in Nairobi.[45] Civil servants were encouraged to become businessmen. There was no routine distinction made between the state's wealth and one's own, either by politicians and civil servants, or by private individuals who could gain privileged access to the state's resources through bribery. Income distribution was highly skewed. In 1976, it was estimated that the top 10 percent of the Kenyan population received 45.8 percent of the income, and the top 20 percent received 60.4 percent, while the bottom 20 percent of the population received only 2.6 percent of the income. The ratio of the top to the bottom quintiles of income earners, that is, was 23:1. Of 26 low-income and middle-income countries for which the World Bank had income distribution figures in 1989, only four (Brazil, Panama, Peru, and Ivory Coast) had more inequitable distributions than Kenya.[46]

Such ruling class consolidation suggests the increased possibility of large-scale popular unrest in both urban and rural areas in the 1990s.[47] Despite the persistence of ethnic ties that cut across class cleavages, in the desperate economic situation that characterized the 1980s and which continues in the 1990s, urban unrest, riots, and revolutionary tendencies may become unrestrainable except through institutionalized state terror.

The Introduction of Ideologies into Political Discourse

Terror is more likely to appear when politics become ideologized, either from above or from below. In Kenya, there is no official state ideology other than the so-called "African Socialism" (actually capitalism)[48] introduced in 1965, and the slogan of "nyayo" (following in Kenyatta's footsteps) invoked continuously by Moi to induce political loyalty. But the Kenyan elite has adopted a form of ideological minimalism typical of non-welfarist capitalist societies. In this perspective, the claim of non-ideological rationality is frequently used to cover a preoccupation with private property and profit, while articulation of political grievances in class terms from below is denigrated as unwarranted ideological interference. Those aspects of liberalism that protect civil and political liberties are discarded.[49] Frequently, as was the case in Kenya by the late 1980s, this minimalism is accompanied by an ideology of national security, such as is described by David Pion-Berlin in his chapter on Argentina in this volume. Internal opponents of the regime are identified with external threats, and all dissent is quashed on the pretext that it weakens the state.

In Kenya, the formally non-ideological but pro-capitalist stance of the elite is opposed by an embryonic liberal/socialist-oriented movement. Most of the people imprisoned after 1982 were accused of belonging to the elusive, and possibly non-existent, organization known as Mwakenya. Mwakenya appeared to be an embryonic political movement that interpreted politics in specifically ideological terms. It fit well within the national security ideology exploited by Moi to claim that Mwakenya had a communist ideology, thus, like South Africa, identifying an internal threat with an external threat. In fact, publications associated with Mwakenya articulated a populist critique of Kenyan politics and class rule incorporating strong liberal elements.

Part of the "evidence" used in the accusations of membership in Mwakenya was alleged possession of a journal called *Pambana*, published by a group called the December 12 Movement (after Kenya's date of independence). Even to have known of the existence of *Pambana* and not to have reported it was considered a crime. One *Pambana* pamphlet is readily available to researchers. In this pamphlet, the viewpoint is populist. *Pambana* claims to represent the "majority poor, dispossessed Kenyans" and calls for "revolutionary change," threatening to reclaim Kenyans' rights "forcibly if necessary." Moreover, it explicitly condemns the ruling class.

> The broad masses of Kenya are materially and politically worse off than ever before. The criminally corrupt ruling clique . . . has isolated itself from the concerns of our daily life. . . . They have silenced all opposition and deprived us, forcibly and otherwise, of the very right to participate in Kenya's national affairs. The sacred rights of expression and association have been cast aside.[50]

This issue of *Pambana* is dated May 1982, three months before the attempted coup. It is not surprising, then, that it should have been perceived to be connected with the attempted coup, or with students and academics. It is probable that a later-formed London exile group, Ukenya, had a similar social composition. Ukenya, like *Pambana*, interpreted Kenyan politics in populist terms, although many of its specific demands were liberal. Its political objectives, published in September 1987, included "democracy and freedom"; equality of all Kenyan nationalities and of Kenyan men and women; the rights to freedom of expression and association; abolition of laws facilitating the arbitrary arrests and imprisonments described above; and abolition of state-of-emergency regulations in the northern provinces of Kenya, where Somali pastoralists have sometimes been massacred as a result of the state's fear of ethnic irredentism.[51]

Thus, if the elusive political group Mwakenya existed at all, it was probably small and representative of a variety of political tendencies, including liberalism, populism, and perhaps Marxism. It was also probably dominated by members of the professions and the intelligentsia. The capacity of such individuals, themselves members of the educated elite, to seriously organize the dispossessed peasantry or urban masses for political action is questionable. Presumably, President Moi could have chosen to ignore Mwakenya or to control it by means other than repression, perhaps by some concessions in the direction of greater freedom of speech or merely by ceasing the violence which apparently was one of the major impetuses of Mwakenya's formation in the first place. But informed observers suggest that Moi was obsessed by Marxism to the point of paranoia.[52] Thus, apparently the notion of making concessions to his opponents or co-opting them—perhaps by appointing them to senior academic positions—was anathema to him.

In the 1980s, many observers assumed that Mwakenya was politically irrelevant.[53] Throup,[54] for example, stated that "this group is a powerless clique of discontented intellectuals and former student leaders," and he assumed that their activities "provide[d] the government with an excuse to clamp down and to demonstrate the power of the state" against Moi's real challengers, namely, "discontented factions in the army and among Kikuyu businessmen." But Moi's judgement of Mwakenya's potential may have been more astute than that of such academic observers. While it could not, in all likelihood, organize a mass political revolution, Mwakenya could influence future coup attempts by educated young military officers, along the lines of the successful coups d'etat in Ghana in 1979 and 1981. Evidence from confessions (highly suspect since most were extracted by torture) suggested that Mwakenya included in its ranks "farmers and the country's influential middle class—clerks, bankers and the like."[55]

It is quite possible that by the very act of accusing its opponents of belonging to a new, cross-ethnic and national underground opposition, the Kenyan government helped to create it. Although the organizers of the 1982 coup attempt were primarily Luo,[56] many of the alleged members of Mwakenya are Kikuyu,[57] among them many prominent intellectuals and professionals. The common prison experience of dissidents from various ethnic sectors of the Kenyan elite may well have brought them together in a manner otherwise impossible.

External Influence on Domestic Kenyan Politics

Increased external interest in a country by a major power (or, in the case of the United States, its private citizens) increases the chances that state terrorism will be used by the government. The greater the interest that an external power has in a country, either ideological, geopolitical, or economic, the greater its costs should the internal regime change.

The interests of privately-owned American multinational corporations are also relevant. A multinational corporation that aspires to long-term profits is likely to desire government stability and control over any possible trade union or general political unrest. It can be hypothesized that increased transnational investment in Kenya, especially in the agribusiness sector, could increase external interest in Kenya's having a "stable" government.

In the mid 1980s, however, many American corporations left Kenya. The stated reason was, essentially, that corruption has been unpredictable.[58] Whereas under Kenyatta foreigners had been guaranteed relative stability as long as they paid an agreed-upon bribe to bureaucrats or politicians, under Moi the elite was rapacious and unpredictable. American firms such as Firestone found that they could not do business unless they sold majority shares (under new legislation providing for Kenyan ownership in joint ventures)[59] directly to companies controlled by President Moi or by members of his family. It was easier to leave Kenya than to continue doing business under such conditions, since, presumably, Kenya is not important enough to American business interests for them to become involved in fomenting a coup d'etat. The American interest in Kenya is more geopolitical and ideological than economic.

During the Reagan administration, the U.S. defined more and more African countries as strategic to its interests. In the 1980s, the United States had two treaties with Kenya which, as far as is known, allowed it to use the port of Mombasa and the airfields at Embakasi and Nanyuki, and which may have given it other rights.[60] (The treaties, known as the Mutual Defense Assistance Agreement [1980] and the Agreement for Consultation and Expanded Relations Concerning Security Assistance [1980],[61] are not available for perusal by researchers.)

Under both the Carter and the Reagan administrations, U.S. interests in Kenya were clearly articulated. Kenya is a strategically important country in the Horn of Africa. The immediate motivation for the U.S. to become involved in the Horn was to assist it in establishing a permanent presence in the Indian Ocean, as a reaction to the Afghanistan and Iranian crises of 1979.[62] The port of Mombasa was large and modern enough to accommodate ships engaged in transporting oil in the event of a crisis in the Gulf or Middle East area;[63] it was in fact "the only modern working port between Durban [South Africa] and Port Said."[64] An additional motive of the Carter administration was to seek Kenyan support of the U.S.-sponsored peace process between Israel and Egypt. Carter also sought to limit Soviet influence in the Horn, especially in

Ethiopia.[65] Thus U.S. interest in Kenya was quite clearly motivated by geopolitical concerns, although this interest was masked by frequent reference to such "common goals" of Americans and Kenyans as the values of human rights, democracy, and the free market.[66]

In return for allowing the U.S. to use its port and airports and for supporting overall American geopolitical interests, Kenya received various benefits. U.S. aid in the 1980s included helicopters, aviation equipment, and engineering and construction assistance,[67] presumably to make Mombasa more usable by large American navy ships and more accessible by land. The United States also provided Kenya with logistic and communications programs.[68] The U.S. trained Kenyan military officers through its International Military Education and Training Program, which it considered a very worthwhile investment, as it resulted in long-term close ties between the U.S. and foreign military personnel.[69] In the American view, this program promoted "respect for human rights . . . [and] respect for the United States and democratic institutions among individuals who play a key role in determining the level of freedom and stability in African countries."[70] However, in 1986 Moi announced that Kenyans would no longer receive military training abroad.[71] Perhaps the formal commitments of the U.S. military establishment to human rights and democracy were considered by Moi to be too inflammatory for the Kenyan army.

The military and strategic interests of the United States had an impact on internal Kenyan politics. Opposition figures viewed the U.S. presence in Kenya as more evidence of the arbitrary and pro-capitalist nature of the Kenyan government, especially as neither the Kenyan people nor even the Kenyan Parliament had been consulted about the U.S.-Kenya agreements. As the exiled Kenyan writer Ngugi wa Thiong'o noted, the treaties could be debated by the American people but not by the Kenyans, who were much more immediately affected.[72] The exile movement Ukenya explicitly demanded "the immediate removal of all USA military facilities and all other foreign military presence from our soil."[73] U.S. interest in Kenya contributed to both the tendency of the opposition to interpret Kenyan politics in ideological terms and the tendency of the state to repress that opposition.

Conclusion: The Likelihood of State Terror in the 1990s

This chapter used the case study of Kenya to investigate the possibility that an African state might become terrorist in the future. It is hypothesized that the increase in repressive tactics in Kenya from 1982 to 1988 was not merely a response to the attempted coup in the former year. Class formation and peasant landlessness were relatively advanced in Kenya; some ideological dimensions were being introduced into political debate; and the United States did have an increased interest there. Kenya appeared to be developing characteristics that resemble the "Latin American model" of social structure and politics.

The tactics used by the government of Kenya in the 1980s against various real or perceived members of the opposition are best considered, following the definitions of Lopez and Stohl, as repression rather than state terrorism. In the case of Kenya, the targets appeared to be only the actual people suspected of subversion, not their families and villages. The repression was deliberate and probably intended to be in part preventative, a warning to others considering opposition. But the numbers affected were relatively small.

In the future, Kenya could resort to state terrorism because of its accelerating class formation, the introduction of ideology into its politics, and increased external (U.S.) interest in it. There is no reason to assume that the high degree of social inequality in Kenya will be ameliorated in the near or middle future; nor that the trend toward peasant landlessness will lessen; nor that employment opportunities will appreciably improve, although it is possible that the population growth rate will decrease. The state has fewer goods to deliver in the 1990s than earlier in Kenya's history. These factors could result in heightened class consciousness and political organization.

The strongest barrier to such class consciousness and organization will be the continued ethnic basis of Kenyan politics. The use of clientilist politics (by which ethnic patrons distribute resources to co-ethnic clients) in Kenya still seems relatively effective. As long as ethnic ties between rich and poor crosscut class ties, the psychological impact of impoverishment will be ameliorated by pride in and ties to one's more successful ethnic kin, who in their turn will dispense part of their gains from corruption (access to the state and its resources) as jobs, donations to village self-help projects, and privileged places in the lineup for state and foreign development projects.

The continuation of ethnically-based clientilist politics will make the interpretation of politics in strictly ideological terms difficult to generalize to large sectors of the population. Nevertheless, the educated community, especially professionals, students and academics, and university-trained military officers, will still be attracted to interpretations of social injustice that are populist in tone. A major difficulty will be the state's reactions to such interpretations.

Many of the criticisms that *Pambana* and Ukenya have made of the government are essentially liberal and reformist. A liberal reformist option in Kenya, coupled with African populist concerns for equitable distribution of wealth, could well be one that promotes genuine social justice. But, if the state's reaction to such liberal and populist concern is to reinforce its own minimalist preoccupation with private property by resorting to a strengthened national security ideology, then the potential for political polarization and a resort to state terror is increased.

Continued U.S. interest in Kenya will increase the tendency to resort to state terror in the defence of so-called national security. It is quite possible that the United States has already trained the Kenyan military and police in counter-insurgency techniques. It is also reasonable to assume that its program of training Kenyan military officers was meant, in part, to counter the left-populist tendencies in the military that seemed to be part of the reason for the 1982 attempted coup. The U.S. clearly wishes to see Kenya remain a pro-Western, capitalist state, with respect for "human rights" as the U.S. interprets them (i.e., with very little concern for economic security or equitable distribution of wealth). The official U.S. view of human rights is clearly indicated by then President Reagan's welcoming address to President Moi in June 1987. According to President Reagan, "Under President Moi's leadership, Kenya has enjoyed economic development and political stability . . . Our peoples share a commitment to the principles of representative government, private ownership and individual freedom."[74]

Outside Kenya's borders, the United States' interest will be most clearly influenced by events in the surrounding region. In 1989, the end of the Iran-Iraq war and Soviet withdrawal from Afghanistan temporarily lessened United States military concern in Southwest Asia. As political repression in Kenya intensified during the first half of 1990, the United states ambassador in Nairobi openly pressured Moi to change his one-party state to a multi-party system.[75] But the frequency of reports of such open pressure declined markedly as soon as Iraq invaded Kuwait. Moi's authority over the port of Mombasa may well have outweighed concern for internal human rights in Kenya as the United States and its allies faced warfare in the Middle East. The political stability of the Kenyan government was more important, even if Moi resorted to more terroristic tactics to maintain it.

It cannot be assumed that all class-divided capitalist countries in which the United States has an interest will resort to state terrorism, even when there is an increasingly ideological content to politics. These conditions are not necessarily sufficient to cause state terrorism. State terrorism is not merely a matter of kind (severe abuse of civil rights) but also of degree. To be terroristic, a state would have to systematically use coercion in the absence of any more effective control mechanisms, such as rational-bureaucratic "order" or ideological legitimation of the ruling class's control. There are also incidental historical variables, such as the character of the ruler, that will affect the likelihood of a regime becoming terrorist. Unfortunately, by the early 1990s it appeared that Daniel Arap Moi had chosen violence over other means of controlling the Kenyan political system.

Perhaps counteracting this development was mounting international concern regarding human rights in Kenya. From 1986 to 1988, President Moi and other members of the Kenyan elite were reported to be extremely annoyed by international criticisms of repression in Kenya. Moi cancelled a state visit to Norway and Sweden and threatened to reject their development aid because of their criticism and because two former M.P.'s, considered to be Mwakenya members, had been granted political asylum in Norway.[76] The KANU party chairman accused Amnesty International of being a foreign agency with no business interfering in Kenyan affairs, going so far as to claim that it was in collusion with Mwakenya and with those who had been behind the 1982 coup.[77] Amnesty International's report on Kenya was rejected as "not only unfounded but also malicious, fueled mainly by dissident Kenyans abroad."[78] Two U.S. human rights observers were also expelled from Kenya in early 1988 for allegedly subversive activities, after taking notes in a courtroom without permission.[79]

Angered as he was, Moi was nevertheless obliged to respond to such criticisms of his human rights violations, as indeed was the U.S. government itself. In January 1987, Howard Wolpe, a U.S. Congressman and Chairman of the Sub-Committee on Africa of the U.S. House of Representatives, visited Kenya and criticized its treatment of dissidents.[80] Shortly after that visit, the U.S. Department of State Bulletin printed a speech by the Deputy Assistant Secretary for African Affairs acknowledging concerns with Kenya's human rights practices. "As a close friend, we are concerned about the human rights situation in Kenya, particularly the Kenyan government's recent actions against political dissidents."[81] A factor counteracting increased repression, then, is the existence of freedom of speech outside Kenya's borders, particularly in the United States. It is thought that one reason for the release of those in preventive detention in 1988 was U.S. and international criticism.[82]

Taking all of these variables into consideration, it would be unwise to conclude that Kenya's repressive tactics in the 1980s implied an inevitable drift toward state terrorism. Nevertheless, the possibility was there. Although it might be argued that the degree of coercion lessened in the later 1980s, the range of targets—including students, clerics, lawyers and newspapermen—widened. In a few cases, family members of dissidents were arrested or harassed. Coercion became a more frequent first resort, rather than a tactic resorted to when all else failed. Most of the formerly legal avenues of dissent were effectively closed off by the end of 1988. As more and more people came under government suspicion, so more and more had cause to resent the government. Tragically, a country formerly viewed as an exemplar of democracy in Africa seemed to be turning to terror as a means of controlling an increasingly restive, class-divided and class-conscious population. While the extent of terror was minuscule compared to most Latin American examples, the causes and trends were similar.

Notes

1. Michael Stohl and George A. Lopez, "Introduction," in Stohl and Lopez, eds., *The State as Terrorist: The Dynamics of Governmental Repression and Violence* (Westport, Conn.: Greenwood Press, 1984), 7–8.

2. George A. Lopez, "A Scheme for the Analysis of Government as Terrorist," in Stohl and Lopez, eds., *The State as Terrorist*, 69.

3. Jinny Arancibia, Marcelo Charlin, and Peter Landstreet, "Chile," and Liisa Lukhari North, "El Salvador," in Jack Donnelly and Rhoda E. Howard, eds., *International Handbook of Human Rights* (New York: Greenwood Press, 1987), 49–73 and 117–134; Gordon L. Bowen, "The Politics of State Terrorism: Barrier to Human Rights in Guatemala," in George W. Shepherd and Ved P. Nanda, eds., *Human Rights and Third World Development* (Westport, Conn.: Greenwood Press, 1985), 83–124.

4. On this and other events in 1988, see U.S. Department of State, "Kenya," *Country Reports on Human Rights Practices for 1988,* (Washington: U.S. Government Printing Office, 1989), 155–168; and Manfred Nowak and Theresa Swinehart, eds., *Human Rights in Developing Countries: 1989 Yearbook* (Arlington: N.P. Engel, 1989), "Kenya," 182–209.

5. *Weekly Review* (Nairobi), 6 August 1982, 10–17.

6. The Committee for the Release of Political Prisoners [*University Destroyed: Moi Crowns Ten Years of Government Repression in Kenya,* (London: May 1983), 14] states that "two, possibly three buses crowded with students and other youths were machine-gunned." A Canadian observer saw one bus being machine-gunned. James Reid "Kenyan Academics, Students Victims of Government Purge," *CAUT (Canadian Association of University Teachers) Bulletin,* (May 1983), 11, 13.

7. "Kenya: Post Mortem," in *Africa Confidential* 23, No. 17 (25 August 1982), 2. See also *Defense and Foreign Affairs Handbook* (Washington D.C.: The Perth Corporation, 1986), 521.

8. Amnesty International, *Kenya: Torture, Political Detention and Unfair Trials* (London: Amnesty International, July 1987).

9. Colim Legum, ed., *Africa Contemporary Record* 17 (1984–85), B269.

10. "Now It's Sabotage—Mwakenya members jailed for damage to railway line," *Weekly Review,* 11 July 1986, 5.

11. Human Rights Watch, letter to President Daniel Arap Moi, (7 December 1988), 2. See also "Kenya," in Nowak and Swinehart, *Human Rights,* 193.

12. Amnesty International, *Kenya.*

13. *Christian Science Monitor,* 15–21 February 1988, 10.

14. David W. Throup, "The Construction and Deconstruction of the Kenyatta State," in Michael G. Schatzberg, ed., *The Political Economy of Kenya* (New York: Praeger, 1987), 64.

15. *Africa Contemporary Record* 19 (1986–87), B331.

16. U.S. Department of State, "Kenya," *Country Reports*, 162.

17. Personal communication.

18. "Kenya Restricts Independence of Judges," *New York Times*, 4 August 1988, 3.

19. *New York Times* (International Edition) 5 October 1988, Y7.

20. U.S. Department of State, "Kenya," *Country Reports*, 161.

21. Human Rights Watch, letter to President Daniel Arap Moi (7 December 1988), 3.

22. Ibid., 10; "Raila Inside, His Wife Out," *Weekly Review*, 16 September 1988, 24; "Continuing 'get tough' Measures," *Weekly Review*, 7 October 1988, 6.

23. "Kisuya Accuses Central Province of Oathings," *Weekly Review*, 13 March 1987, 5.

24. *Africa Contemporary Record*, 19 (1986–87): B321. See also "Kenya," in Nowak and Swinehart, 189.

25. *Africa Contemporary Record* 19 (1986–87), B324–25.

26. Article 19 [*Information, Freedom and Censorship: World Report 1988* (London: Article 19, 1989), 31] states "It is believed that . . . publication and circulation [of the Constitution] are now prohibited." Nowak and Swinehart ("Kenya," in *Human Rights*, 199) report that a prisoner who asked for a copy of the Constitution to prepare his defense was denied it.

27. Naomi Chazan, *An Anatomy of Ghanaian Politics: Managing Political Recession, 1969–82* (Boulder: Westview Press, 1983), 353.

28. Goran Hyden, *No Shortcuts to Progress: African Development Management in Perspective* (Berkeley: University of California Press, 1983), 60–63.

29. Alfred Stepan, *The State and Society: Peru in Comparative Perspective* (Princeton: Princeton University Press, 1978), xii, as cited in Theda Skocpol, "Bringing the State Back In: Strategies of Analysis in Current Research," in Peter B. Evans, Dietrich Rueschemeyer, and Theda Skocpol, eds., *Bringing the State Back In* (New York: Cambridge University Press, 1985), 7.

30. On the state in general, see Max Weber, *The Theory of Social and Economic Organization* (New York: Oxford University Press, 1947), 324–41.

31. Robert H. Jackson and Carl G. Rosberg, *Personal Rule in Black Africa: Prince, Autocrat, Prophet, Tyrant* (Berkeley: University of California Press, 1982).

32. Ibid.

33. Rhoda E. Howard, *Human Rights in Commonwealth Africa* (Totowa, N.J.: Rowman and Littlefield, 1986), 159–160.

34. Jackson and Rosberg, 98–112.

35. Rakiya Omaar, "Moi's Growing Power Is the Real Threat to Kenyan Stability," *Christian Science Monitor*, 24–30 October 1988, 30.

36. *Africa Contemporary Record* 17 (1984–85), B260–62. *Africa Confidential* 26, No. 1 (January 1985), 5.

37. *Africa Contemporary Record* 18 (1985–86), B331.

38. "One Chorus—Leaders All Over Kenya Condemn Secret Society," *Weekly Review*, 18 April 1986, 10.

39. Kate Currie and Larry Ray, "State and Class in Kenya—Notes on the Cohesion of the Ruling Class," *Journal of Modern African Studies* 22, No. 4 (1984), 581.

40. Anonymous, *In/Dependent Kenya* (London: Zed Press, 1982), 55.

41. *Africa Contemporary Record* 17 (1984–85), B257.

42. Kate Currie and Larry Ray, "The Kenya State, Agribusiness and the Peasantry," *Review of African Political Economy* 38 (April 1987): 94.

43. Throup, "Construction and Deconstruction of the Kenyatta State," 71.

44. UNICEF, *The State of the World's Children 1989*, (New York: Oxford University Press, 1989) table 6, 104.

45. *Africa Contemporary Record* 18 (1985–86), B327.

46. World Bank, *World Development Report 1989*, (New York: Oxford University Press, 1989), table 30, 222.

47. Throup, "Construction and Deconstruction of the Kenyatta State," 72; and Kate Currie and Larry Ray, "The Pambana of August 1—Kenya's Abortive Coup," *Political Quarterly* 57, No. 1 (January-March 1986), 49.

48. Republic of Kenya, *African Socialism and Its Application to Planning in Kenya* (Government of Kenya, 1965).

49. Rhoda E. Howard and Jack Donnelly, "Human Dignity, Human Rights and Political Regimes," *American Political Science Review* 80, No. 3 (September 1986), 806–807.

50. "*Pambana:* Organ of the December 12 Movement," printed in Committee for the Release of Political Prisoners in Kenya, *Law as a Tool of Political Repression in Kenya*, pamphlet (London: August 1982), 5, 6 and the back cover.

51. "Manifesto of the Ukenya Movement for Unity and Democratic Democracy in Kenya" *Review of African Political Economy* 39 (September 1987), 60. On the Somali problem see Howard, *Human Rights in Commonwealth Africa*, 95–96.

52. *Africa Contemporary Record* 17 (1984–85), B261, and 18 (1985–86), B327.

53. Ibid., 13, B327; Michael G. Schatzberg, "Two Faces of Kenya: The Researcher and the State," *African Studies Review* 29, No. 4 (December 1986), 11.

54. Throup, "Construction and Deconstruction of the Kenyatta State," 71–72.

55. Michael Paul Maren, "Kenya: The Dissolution of Democracy," *Current History* 86 (May 1987), 211.

56. Currie and Ray, "The Pambana of August 1," 54.

57. *Africa Contemporary Record* 19, (1986–87) B317.

58. Michael A. Hiltzik, "Kenya Corruption Overwhelms Investors," *Los Angeles Times*, 25 June 1989, part 1, p. 4.

59. *Africa Contemporary Record* 19 (1986–87), B316.

60. U.S. Department of State, *American Foreign Policy: Current Documents 1982*, Document 546, "Changes in Africa and Challenges for U.S. Policy in Africa," 1147. See also *Keesing's Contemporary Archives*, 25 July 1980, 30379.

61. *Lambert's Worldwide Dictionary of Defense Authorities 1984* (Washington, D.C.: Lambert Publications, 1984), 698.

62. *Keesing's Contemporary Archives*, 9 May 1980, 30235.

63. Chester A. Crocker, "FY 1987 Assistance Requests for Sub-Saharan Africa," *U.S. Department of State Bulletin* 86, No. 2112 (July 1986), 30.

64. Frank Wisner, "FY 1986 Assistance Requests for Sub-Saharan Africa," *U.S. Department of State Bulletin* 85, No. 2098 (May 1985), 53.

65. U.S. Department of State, *American Foreign Policy: Basic Documents 1977–80*, Document 666, "United States Objectives in the Horn of Africa," 1236. A similar statement is in *Current Documents 1982*, Document 541, "U.S. Goals in Africa," 1127.

66. U.S. Department of State, *American Foreign Policy: Current Documents 1982*, Document 551, "A New partnership with Africa," 1162, and Document 613, "Bush Voices U.S. Support for Kenya," 1264.

67. U.S. Department of State, *American Foreign Policy: Current Documents 1983*, Document 528, "Security and Development Assistance Proposals for Africa," 1112.

68. U.S. Department of State, *American Foreign Policy: Current Documents 1982*, Document 543, "Proposed Foreign Assistance Budget for Africa," 1135.

69. U.S. Department of State, *American Foreign Policy: Current Documents 1981*, Document 583, "The Administration's Request for Assistance to Africa for Fiscal year 1982," 1069; and *Current Documents 1982*, Document 543, "Proposed Foreign Assistance Budget for Africa," 1135.

70. "Feature: National Strategy," *U.S. Department of State Bulletin* 88, No. 2133 (April 1988): 26.

71. *Africa Contemporary Record* 19 (1986–87): B330.

72. Ngugi wa Thiong'o, "The Commitment of the Intellectual," *Review of African Political Economy* 32 (April 1985): 24.

73. "Manifesto of the Ukenya Movement for Unity and Democratic Democracy in Kenya," 80.

74. "Visit of Kenyan President" (remarks by President Reagan and President Moi after their meeting on March 12) *U.S. Department of State Bulletin* 87, No. 2123 (June 1987): 28.

75. *The New York Times* (International Edition), 9 July 1990, A3; 26 July 1990, A4; and 29 July 1990, 6.

76. "Straightening up the Record—Foreign Affairs," *Weekly Review*, 11 September 1988, 14–15.

77. Ibid., 15.

78. "The Realities of Kenyan Society," *Weekly Review*, 18 December 1987, 21.

79. "Another Diplomatic Flap," *Weekly Review*, 15 January 1988, 6.

80. "Sour Diplomacy—U.S. Congressman Riles Kenyan Authorities By His Human Rights Violation Claims," *Weekly Review*, 23 January 1987, 11–12.

81. Roy A. Stacy, "FY 1988 Assistance Request for Sub-Saharan Africa," *U.S. Department of State Bulletin* 87, No. 2122 (May 1987), 16.

82. "Detainees: Harsh Rejoinder," *Weekly Review*, 19 February 1988, 20.

6

The Development of the
Secret Police in Communist States

Jonathan R. Adelman

There is little doubt of the importance of secret police forces for the development of Communist political systems. On the topic of the secret police in the Soviet Union, theorists of totalitarianism have often echoed the statement by John Dziak that, "in the Soviet Union the intelligence and security services have enjoyed a pervasive and powerful position since 1917 . . . the position of the Soviet security organizations . . . is a special one unmatched by any other Soviet institution, including the military."[1]

Indeed, a historical account of Soviet politics would be very limited without reference to the role of the Cheka and its successors during the times of the civil war period, the Great Purges, the Gulag, the Doctor's Plot, and Khrushchev's "secret speech" denouncing the secret police. Barrington Moore even titled his classic work on Stalinism, *Terror and Soviet Progress*, epitomizing the central role of the secret police in Soviet politics.[2] As Seweryn Bialer points out, this role was by no means clandestine:

> Far from acting as an anonymous, discreet and secret force, the "secret" police was an open and recognized political force, glorified and praised in the media, highly visible at all official ceremonies and political assemblies, and extolled by Soviet propaganda as a prime example for emulation. Its high officials were "elected" to the Soviet parliament and constituted, in fact, from 1936 until Stalin's death, the second largest homogeneous group of deputies.[3]

Similar words could be penned about the secret police in many other Communist states. If anything, the role of the secret police was even more pervasive in Eastern Europe, where a lack of any national/

indigenous revolution deprived the Communist regimes of the kind of popular support enjoyed by the Bolsheviks. For the alienated masses of Hungary, Romania and Czechoslovakia, the bloody show trials of the late Stalinist era epitomized the essence of Communist rule. The depth of popular animosity towards the secret police was demonstrated during the Hungarian Revolution; in the early stages of the revolution, crowds stormed the headquarters of the AVH (secret police) in Budapest and killed many of the agents on duty. Similarly, Czech reformers, casting about for a symbol for the Prague Spring of 1968, decided on the abolition of censorship and removal of KGB control over the Czech secret police; moves which were immediately reversed when Soviet troops invaded in August 1968, toppling the reformist regime led by Alexander Dubcek. Again, in the case of Poland, local secret police forces (ZOMOs) predictably took the lead in bloodily imposing martial law in December 1981, in their attempt to crush the solidarity movement.

The centrality of the secret police in perpetuating Communist rule is also evident in the Third World. In Asian Communist regimes, the role of the secret police forces was nowhere more noticeable and evident than in Cambodia, where the Khmer Rouge committed genocide on an unprecedented scale between their seizure of power in April 1975, and their demise at the hands of the Vietnamese invaders in December 1978.

The Paucity of Literature
on the Secret Police

Despite enduring popular fascination with the general topic, the secret police of Communist countries have been almost totally neglected by Western scholars. Academics have either largely ignored the role of the secret police in Communist systems or have given it inappropriately brief coverage. Most of the writings that have appeared on the subject have been produced either by Soviet defectors and emigres, such as Deriabin and Solzhenitsyn, or by Western non-academic analysts writing for popular consumption, such as Barron. Wolin and Slusser, in their seminal work on the Soviet secret police published in 1957, expressed the hope that the "bleak picture of general paucity of recent scholarship of studies of the secret police" would change.[4] Their hopes went largely unfulfilled. In the subsequent 15 years, there was but one doctoral dissertation (unpublished) on the topic.

As recently as 1973, after a review of the extant literature, Slusser would again lament the "confusion and uncertainty which characterize this field of study." He concludes that:

despite its fundamental and recognized importance, the secret police continues to be the neglected stepchild of Soviet studies. . . . As far as the scholarly community in this country is concerned, the study of the secret police still seems to be regarded as somehow discreditable, marginal or unfeasible. To judge by the titles of doctoral dissertations being completed in this area, strikingly few scholars are turning their attention to this subject.[5]

To date, the literature on the secret police remains remarkably weak. Although scholars have repeatedly acknowledged the powerful role played by these forces in Communist regimes, there is virtually no literature, in the last two decades, on the secret police forces of any Communist states, except for China and the Soviet Union.[6]

Only two comparative works on Communist secret police forces or terror have ever been assayed—by Dallin and Breslauer (1970) and Adelman (1984). The Dallin work does not deal primarily with the secret police *per se* but with the role played by terror in Communist regimes and with the functionality of terror in various stages of political development.

The writers of these general works substantiate this critical evaluation of the literature. In 1970, Dallin and Breslauer began their work in the field by observing:

We soon discovered, to our surprise, that the theoretical literature on political terror was not nearly so well developed as we had expected and that, in particular, there are almost no systematic efforts in this field to compare and to explain the differences among various Communist (and non-Communist) systems.[7]

In my 1984 work I asserted that these comments by "Dallin and Breslauer in 1971 are still valid in 1984" with no new works having been completed in the field.[8] In addition, no further works have appeared on the subject since my 1984 volume, leaving the field very sparsely populated indeed. As John Dziak observed in a study of the KGB, "the serious study of foreign, and specifically, Soviet intelligence and security systems is a recent development in nongovernmental circles in the West and as such still has a limited literature, whether theoretical or operational."[9]

There are a number of reasons which help to account for this sad state of affairs in an area of undoubted importance. First, there has been, until the move to "bring the state back in" to political science in the mid-1980s, a distinct lack of interest in any kind of institutional study, whether focused on the state bureaucracy, on the armed forces, or on the secret police. For several decades the study of institutions was seen as an atavistic and potentially ill-fated return to the pre-war days of fruitless study of legal formalism, a long-dominant analytical trend in Western political science.[10]

Second, the weakness of studies on the secret police in Communist states reflects broader shortcomings in the study of Communist systems as a field of academic inquiry. Among the approximately 5,200 political scientists active in American graduate departments, only 150 list any specialization in Soviet politics, and only another 100–150 specialize to any extent in the politics of other Communist systems. Of these approximately 300 scholars, perhaps 200 actually concentrate primarily on Communist politics. These two hundred scholars constitute less than 4 per cent of political scientists working in the foremost American graduate departments where most research is done.[11]

The serious decline in the number of new doctorates granted in political science in the last 15 years has further exacerbated the problem. This has caused Marshall Shulman at Columbia to speak of the "loss of a generation of scholars in Soviet studies."[12] And the problem is even more acute in less favored areas of inquiry, such as Eastern European studies and studies in Communist systems in Asia, excluding China. The magnitude of this problem is also manifest in the ranks of the American Political Science Association; about five years ago the association's Section on Communist Studies was simply eliminated. The weakness of the field is even reflected in the state of such journals as *Studies in Comparative Communism*. Contrary to expectations aroused by the journal's title, most of the articles are case studies with no comparative focus. Overall, then, there is a great shortage of area specialists in Communist studies in general, let alone scholars focusing on a specific area of notoriety.

Third, the study of secret police forces has been seen as ideologically distasteful by most scholars, imbued with mainstream liberal or radical Marxist views. A similar problem affects the comparative study of armed forces which has become an orphan of the social scientific profession, nurtured only by military historians and a few other political scientists. The armed forces, however, can at least be considered legitimate bodies for the defense of a nation. The secret police forces, on the other hand, are seen as illegitimate repressors of the natural will of the people. Ideological opposition to studying them is thus all the stronger among Western (especially American) scholars, with their deep desires for the universalization of democratic and humanitarian values. The fact that the only academic journal to systematically run articles on secret police forces in the Communist bloc is *Orbis*, a conservative journal run by the Foreign Enterprise Research Institute in Philadelphia, illustrates this point well.

Fourth, the historical legacy of the past century has served to dampen enthusiasm for the study of secret police forces, both in and out of the Communist World. Given the totalitarian equation of Nazi Germany and the Soviet Union, the study of Communist secret police forces is still shadowed by the reign of terror of the German SS, preceding and including the period of World War II. All the horrors committed by the German secret police forces—summarized in the one apocalyptic phrase "Holocaust"—have given the entire subject a revolting flavor, one which scholars of nearly all persuasions wish to avoid.

Fifth, there is the historical legacy of the 1950s, 1960s, and early 1970s with which to contend. The role of the American FBI in harassing the civil rights movement in the 1950s and 1960s as well as the Vietnam War movement in the 1960s, further aided in depressing any innate American interest in the study of such subjects. Abroad, the palpable role of the CIA in overthrowing populist regimes in Guatemala and Iran in the early 1950s, in attempts to overthrow the Cuban regime in 1962 and in instigating the collapse of the Allende government in Chile in 1973 further deepened the revulsion of most American intellectuals to the study of any kind of secret police forces, who came to epitomize "the enemy" to all forms of intellectual freedom and progress in the world.

Sixth, there is a substantial informational problem. The problems of evidence and documentation are well nigh overwhelming. Communist studies in general are data poor, given the inaccessibility of most archives and leaders and the general secrecy of Communist politics. This secrecy is nowhere more closely guarded then in the area of secret police activity. Given the resulting paucity of information, there always seem to be much better topics whose study more closely approximate academic norms of intellectual rigor than the Communist secret police forces. And the very lack of prior analysis further inhibits scholarly interest in this field.

Determinants of Secret Police Development

1. The Threatening Foreign Environment

Given the paucity of literature on the subject, explaining the nearly universal emergence of secret police forces in Communist systems becomes an urgent task indeed. What factors helped the secret police to acquire a central role in the world's Communist systems? Part of the answer can be derived from the international environment of revolutionary Communist regimes. For Communist regimes that came to power by revolutionary means, such as the Soviet Union, China, Vietnam, Cambodia, Yugoslavia, Albania and Cuba, there was the strong counterrevolutionary pressure from abroad common to all revolutionary regimes. The strong foreign opposition to Communist revolutionary regimes came from forces similar to those that have threatened revolutionary regimes throughout history, from France in 1789 to Iran in 1980. Foreign countries traditionally have been deeply dismayed by and hostile to revolutionary regimes. Revolutionary regimes threaten to upset the international political order and the rule of the dominant powers. In response, the dominant powers, or their allies, often intervene to try to crush the revolutionary regimes.

Foreign intervention was significant in the early years of these Communist revolutions. The Bolsheviks faced the intervention of 26 countries, including Japan, the United States, Germany, France and England; countries which sought, in Winston Churchill's picturesque phrase, "to strangle Bolshevism in its infancy." Only the end of World War I, the defeat of Germany, and the limited size of the intervention forces and of foreign aid to the White Russians, saved the Bolsheviks.[13]

Until the latter half of 1948, The Chinese Communists also struggled against foreign intervention by the United States. The United States provided several billion dollars worth of military aid to Chiang Kai Shek, transported his troops back to major population centers after the end of World War II, and trained many of his elite divisions for combat. With no offsetting Soviet help, except for some limited assistance in Manchuria, the Chinese Communists stood alone in their civil war with the Nationalists.[14]

The situation was little different with Vietnam and Cuba. The Vietnamese Communists endured a thirty year struggle, first with France and then with the United States before the final triumph of their cause in 1975. Both Western powers spent tens of billions of dollars (the United States alone spent 120 billion dollars), deployed hundreds of thousands of troops and utilized massive amounts of modern weaponry to aid in the struggle against the Viet Minh and the Viet Cong. Similarly, the American incursion into Cambodia created a direct and dire threat to the Khmer Rouge, as did massive American bombing.

In the cases of Yugoslavia and Albania, due to the special circumstances of World War II, the Communists did not face Western democratic opposition to their rise to power. But, here there were the massive depredations of Nazi Germany in Yugoslavia that killed 1.7 million Yugoslavs. This was a higher civilian death toll than that of any country other than Poland and the Soviet Union or of any people other than the Jews of Europe. Only in Cuba, due to the rapid rise of Castro to power in January 1959 was there no significant anti-Communist foreign intervention; and this was at least in part because Castro was not a proclaimed Communist at that time.

Furthermore, high levels of foreign hostility to these Communist movements persisted well after the regimes were in power. The Soviet Union endured a very hostile international environment in the interwar period. This was highlighted by the lack of American recognition until 1933, exclusion from the crucial Munich conference until 1938, border clashes with the Imperial Japanese Army in 1938 and 1939, and the German invasion in June 1941. The German invasion would leave in its trail the horrid specter of 20 million Russians dead, 1,700 cities and towns destroyed and 25 percent of the Soviet production capacity destroyed. Even after the war, the brief allied interlude would come to an abrupt end with the rapid onset of the Cold War, which would last, with an intermission in the 1970s era of detente, well into the 1980s.

For the People's Republic of China too, final victory would bring no respite from international pressures. The proclamation of the People's Republic of China in October 1949 was rapidly followed by General Douglas MacArthur's swift march to the Yalu in November 1950 and the ensuing Korean War, the Taiwan Straits crisis of 1958, and the border conflicts with India in 1959 and 1962. Throughout the Cold War era, the United States was strongly anti-Chinese, keeping China out of the United Nations and enforcing a costly economic blockade. The U.S. sought to isolate China for almost a quarter of a century, reversing these attempts only in 1972 with the sending of the Shanghai Communique and with President Nixon's subsequent visit to China.

U.S. intimidation of China found its parallels in measures taken by the Soviet Union, which, for the last 30 years, has been strongly anti-Chinese. The Soviet Union has aggressively sought to oust China from the international Communist movement, cripple it by trade and economic sanctions, and intimidate it by placing 46 heavily armed divisions on its border. The Vietnamese invasion of Cambodia in 1978, the Soviet invasion of Afghanistan in 1979, and the continued strengthening of Soviet-Indian ties were all, in part, motivated by Soviet desires to isolate China. Only with the rise of Gorbachev to power in 1985 has this pressure eased, although the troops have remained menacingly in place.

The same was true for Vietnam and Cuba. In the thirteen years following the Communist victory in Vietnam, the United States has worked assiduously to keep Vietnam isolated, both politically and economically. The United States has refused to recognize Vietnam and has encouraged other Vietnamese enemies, such as China and Thailand, in their hostility towards Vietnam. This has helped deepen Vietnamese dependency on the Soviet Union, especially given deep Chinese hostility to Vietnam and its invasion of February 1979. In the Cuban case, the

United States has maintained a strict and very costly economic embargo on the island nation throughout the three decades of Castro's rule, thereby pushing it towards the Soviet Union. The U.S. has also consistently worked to isolate Cuba internationally by refusing to recognize it. In 1961 the United States actively backed the anti-Castroite invasion attempt at the Bay of Pigs, and in 1962 it again menaced Cuba over the missile crisis.

As for Yugoslavia and Albania, they have also not escaped extensive international hostility. For Yugoslavia the threat came not from the West but from the East. In 1948 the Soviet Union expelled Yugoslavia from the Cominform. Subsequently, it tried hard to overthrow the Tito regime, using political, economic and psychological pressure, even threatening military invasion. As for Albania, it has become progressively more isolated by successive splits with Yugoslavia in 1948, the Soviet Union in 1960, and China in 1970.

Finally, of course, Cambodia did not survive a hostile international environment. In 1978 Vietnam invaded Cambodia and ousted the genocidal Pol Pot regime. Only recently have the Vietnamese begun a withdrawal from Cambodia, with unknown consequences for the future.

The foreign environment for those Communist regimes that came to power in the wake of a soviet Red Army invasion (Eastern Europe, Mongolia, North Korea) naturally differed significantly from those that came to power by indigenous force. Seen as Soviet (or occasionally Chinese) dependencies, they generally received far less international attention. At the same time, lacking an indigenous revolutionary movement or distinctive ideology, they were seen as, sui generis, less threatening than the other revolutionary regimes. Their obvious internal weakness and external dependency, in contrast to the much stronger capabilities of the revolutionary regimes, reinforced this image. When they did take important international action, as in the North Korean invasion of South Korea in June 1950, they were usually seen as pawns of other greater powers, regardless of the truth of the matter.

2. The Threatening Domestic Environment

The greatest threat to the new Communist regimes in the first several decades of their rule inevitably came from domestic opposition. Historically, of course, this too has been true of all revolutionary movements. The French Revolution faced the Vendee Uprising, while the English Revolutionaries of the 1640s fought three civil wars before finally attaining success. The Spanish Revolution of the 1930s did not survive the Spanish Civil War, won by General Francisco Franco's fascist forces in 1939.

In general, Communist regimes have also been internally driven to adopt radical programs for the transformation of their societies. These programs, such as collectivization, nationalization, industrialization and modernization, inevitably entail great hardships that will arouse strong opposition from significant elements of the population. Were Communist regimes content to become status quo authoritarian regimes and adopt policies on the lines of the Soviet NEP in the 1920s, this would hardly be the case. But the civil peace espoused by Nikolai Bukharin has generally been rejected in favor of radical social measures that have often entailed a virtual declaration of civil war with large and influential segments of the population.

Here we will differentiate three paths to power taken by Communist parties. The situation was worst of all in non-revolutionary regimes. There the lack of a civil war or national liberation struggle ensured that elements hostile to Communism usually formed the great majority of the population. Indeed, apart from Bulgaria and Czechoslovakia, where the Communists were generally popular at first, all of the other countries had a tradition of deep hostility to Communists and their Soviet patrons. Sometimes there were special circumstances that exacerbated the problem. In Poland a store of passionate anti-Russian sentiment had been built up by 140 years of Tsarist Russian suppression of Polish independence. In East Germany, 13 years of Nazi propaganda and resentment over the Third Reich's defeat at Soviet hands ensured a particularly deep East German enmity towards the Soviet Union. In general, then, a very weak Communist party needed extensive Soviet support to maintain itself in the face of serious and widespread domestic opposition. The non-Soviet revolutionary regimes naturally face the least opposition after their rise to power. They have mobilized far more active political support on their behalf through the use of nationalist and reformist discourse. Their defeat of the counterrevolutionary enemies on the field of battle, and the terror which ensued, generally intimidated the natural foes of the regime. At the same time, large scale emigration from countries such as China, Vietnam, and Cuba helped weaken the opposition.

At the same time, even in these countries, there remained strong elements, especially in the cities, hostile to the revolution. Rural based revolutions, such as those in China, Vietnam, Cambodia, Cuba, and Yugoslavia, were often weak in the cities. The cities were often strongholds of the counterrevolutionaries who were generally of a relatively cosmopolitan, Westernized capitalist spirit which placed them in unalterable opposition to the usually puritanical revolutionaries. Despite substantial emigration, the former urban ruling classes remained largely intact in the cities after liberation, thereby posing a major threat to the regime's radical programs.

The final case is that of the Soviet Union. Any reading of Merle Fainsod's 1957 work based on the Smolensk archives, or of Teodor

Shanin's work on the Russian peasantry in the 1920s, will vividly highlight the broad range of opposition to the regime.[15] The bulk of the Russian peasantry were either noncommittal or hostile in their view of the regime and maintained largely traditional forms of social organization in this period. Members of the bourgeoisie and aristocratic remnants were generally hostile, as were the emerging NEP men. Religious believers of all denominations resented deeply the government's active promotion of atheism. Clearly, the narrow base of the October Revolution was reflected in the enmity of the majority of the rural population, and of much of the urban population, to the Bolsheviks.

3. Institutions and Revolutionary Paths

The Communists, as Samuel Huntington has maintained, may be very good at institution building, but they face serious problems in this area nonetheless.[16] In this realm, the influence of the path taken to power is critical. For those non-revolutionary regimes that came to power with the help of the Red Army, the problem is extremely acute. The lack of an indigenous revolutionary struggle, comparable to the anti-colonial wars fought by many Third World countries for their independence, prevented the creation and legitimation of strong institutions. The result was that, at birth, these Communist regimes were very fragile; they were dominated by a weak and divided party commanding an insignificant army and secret police force and with only the remnants of the pre-revolutionary government bureaucracy at its disposal. It is therefore no accident that many of these non-revolutionary Communist regimes witnessed popular revolts—East Germany (1953), Hungary (1956), Czechoslovakia (1968) and Poland (1956, 1970, 1980s). Yet, given the assured level of support from a Communist superpower, these regimes never had to worry about being overthrown.

For the second class of Communist states, the situation was quite different. Although they had fewer allies in general, they could also count on far greater institutional capabilities and popular support. In over two decades of struggle up to 1949, the Chinese Communists created three very capable institutions, (army, party, and government) whose capability was demonstrated in their impressive performance in the Korean War. Yugoslav institutions under Tito were sufficiently strong to resist all Soviet attempts to overthrow the regime in the late 1940s. The Vietnamese too, after their victories in 1954 and 1975, were sufficiently capable to oust the Pol Pot regime from Cambodia in 1978 and resist Chinese incursions in 1979. The Bolsheviks, although significantly weaker than the other revolutionary regimes, were still able to survive the interwar era and go on to defeat Nazi Germany in World War II.[17]

There was a marked disparity in institutional capabilities between the three kinds of regimes. Yet, it is important to note that even victorious revolutionary regimes face serious institution-building problems. The kinds of governmental institutions built up in rural base areas by the Chinese, Vietnamese, Cambodian, and Yugoslav Communists were of limited relevance to governing major urban centers or to transforming a backward national economy. Similarly, the relatively primitive, yet effective, mass guerrilla armies of these four movements also would have to be massively modernized in order to be competitive against modern, high technology, enemy forces. And the parties, so painstakingly built up in rural areas and oriented to peasant problems, would now need a whole new set of ideas, cadres, and orientations to deal with the potential hostility of the urban population to the Communists.

Thirdly, the Communists were far from unified. Bourgeois nationalists and fanatical Communist ideologues, intellectuals and laborers, ethnic majorities and minorities, atheists and believers, all vied for control of the Communist parties. Cleavages appeared along other lines: pro-Soviet versus pro-Chinese, underground revolutionaries versus revolutionary exiles, gradualists versus proponents of immediate change, careerists versus Communist believers, army and secret police versus government and party cadres. Under these circumstances, creating a relatively unified and capable party organization was a difficult task.

Three patterns of party structure development can be discerned. In the case of nonrevolutionary regimes, the problem was extremely acute. The Rumanian Communist Party, for example, had less than one thousand members before liberation and several hundred thousand members a few years later. The party was filled with careerists, monarchists, Iron Cross members and numerous others unfit for such a party. The North Korean party faced an even worse problem with members returning from Yenan, Manchuria and Moscow vying for control with those from Korea itself. In all such cases the lack of authenticity of the party and its servile dependence on the Soviet Union severely retarded its effective development. A similar situation developed with regard to the military which generally had to be massively purged and reconstructed almost from the bottom up, given the almost total lack of reliable Communist officers or even soldiers. The party organizations in these revolutionary regimes were by far the best unified. This reflected the lengthy gestation period before the seizure of power (often 10–20 years) and the intensity of the life and death struggle that welded the party together. The Yugoslav party resisted Stalin's attempts to overthrow Tito as the Chinese party withstood all Soviet efforts to undermine Mao's leadership. The Cuban party rallied around Castro to defeat American attempts to overthrow him. In short, the revolutionary regimes generally started with a far more advanced institutional capability than the other regimes.

The second pattern was characteristic of revolutionary regimes outside of the Soviet Union. Here there was a strong development of Communist parties in countries such as China, Vietnam, Cambodia and Yugoslavia before the takeover. Only in Cuba did the brief insurrectionary phase preclude this development. In the wake of revolution, however, all of the parties now needed to find cadres with much higher levels of education and technical knowledge to face the new tasks of governing large cities and managing the national economy.

Finally, there was the Soviet example. Although the Bolsheviks did seize power in an insurrection in October 1917, they lacked a well developed party. As late as February 1917, the party numbered but 23,500 members compared to 400,000 members in October. Furthermore, there were serious differences in the party between exiled intellectuals such as Trotsky, Zinoviev, and Radek, and undergrounders such as Stalin and Dzerzhinsky. Other cleavages emerged along lines specified by ethnicity (Russians/Jews), class (middle/upper) and educational attainment (university/technical school/primary school). After Lenin's death in 1924, these differences helped fuel a fierce intraparty struggle that was resolved only in 1929 with Stalin's final victory over the Right Opposition.

The Political Context

A constellation of internal and external threats, combined with political institutions of varying strengths and origins, provided different conditions for the development of Communist secret police forces. In the first set of cases, that of non-revolutionary regimes, the regimes' high expectations for radical change were weakened by weak regime capabilities and institutionalization as well as strong popular resistance. Mitigated only in part by powerful dependence on the Soviet Union (which, of course, further weakened the domestic bases of support for the regimes), these nonrevolutionary regimes required powerful roles for the secret police from the very beginning. In the early days, the very weak base even for secret police development further promoted a powerful role for the Soviet secret police in domestic secret police development.

In the second set of cases, that of revolutionary regimes formed on the rural insurrectionary model, the need for either heavy foreign dependence or for a prematurely powerful secret police role in smashing especially powerful internal enemies was avoided. In the course of a lengthy rural gestation period of 10–25 years, these regimes created strong and capable institutions. At the same time, the protracted military campaigns against internal and external enemies promoted a very popular and capable party, army, and government, capable of demoralizing the enemy in the wake of the Communist takeover. In this context, the secret police role was, at least in the early stages, noticeably less significant than in other Communist regimes.

The last set of cases was that of revolutionary regime development in the Soviet Union. Given its unusual pattern of development (urban, rather than rural), the narrow base of the October Revolution and minimal pre-takeover gestation pattern (eight months rather than 10–25 years as in other cases), the need for secret police development was strong from the start. Here too, there was no friendly Communist regime to take part of the load in repelling foreign threats or developing the secret police. This, too, generated a strong secret police role but without the context of foreign dependency and with the strong urban support, both missing in the prior case.

Stages in Development of Secret Police Systems

Here we elaborate a basic scheme to account for the development of the secret police in Communist states. We see that the role of the secret police depends most heavily on the nature of the takeover in that particular Communist state. In addition, it reflects the degree of popular support enjoyed by the regime (the higher the support, the lesser the need for coercion), the scope of ambition of the regime, the capabilities of other institutions, and the degree of international legitimacy of the regime. Thus, in the urban insurrectionary mode, exemplified by the Soviet case, the degree of popular support is moderate and concentrated in the cities, the level of capabilities of other political institutions is moderate to low, and the degree of legitimacy of the regime is moderate to low. This creates a strong need for the secret police. In rural insurrections, as in China and Vietnam, the degree of popular support and capabilities of other political institutions, developed in a lengthy gestation period, is high, as is the legitimacy of the regime. This dictates a relatively low demand for using the secret police forces. And, finally, in cases of external takeover, as in Eastern Europe and North Korea, the degree of popular support for and capability of the other political institutions is very low, and the degree of legitimacy of the regime both internally and internationally is similarly low. This dictates a strong need for developing domestic secret police forces in coordination with the invading external power, usually the Soviet Union.

The role of the secret police in Communist states remains a relatively unexplored topic. There has been very little systematic work, except on the Soviet Union, and even in this case, much remains to be done.

Without a strong case study base on which to build, it is hardly surprising that little theoretical literature exists on the topic. Yet, the very importance of the topic mandates greater attention. In this work, we have reviewed the state of the field and advanced a neo-structural functionalist perspective to encapsulate some of the material that is available.

Notes

1. See John Dziak, "The Action Arm of the CPSU," in *Problems of Communism* 30, no. 4 (July/August 1981): 53–54.
2. Barrington Moore, *Terror and Soviet Progress* (New York: Harper and Row, 1954).
3. Seweryn Bialer, *Stalin's Successors* (Cambridge: Cambridge University Press, 1980), 14.
4. Robert Slusser, "Review," *Slavic Review* 32, no. 4 (December 1973): 828.
5. Ibid.
6. See Alexander Dallin and George Breslauer, *Political Terror in Communist Systems* (Stanford: Stanford University Press, 1970), and Jonathan Adelman, ed., *Political Terror and Communist Politics* (Boulder, Colorado: Westview Press, 1984). The literature on China, it should be added, is very scanty and impressionistic.
7. Dallin and Breslauer, ix.
8. Jonathan Adelman, *Terror and Communist Politics* (Boulder, Colorado: Westview Press, 1984).
9. John Dziak, *Chekistry—A History of the KGB* (Lexington, Mass.: Lexington Books, 1988), 1.
10. See Peter Evans, Dietrich Rueschemeyer and Theda Skocpol, eds., *Bringing the State Back In* (Cambridge: Cambridge University Press, 1985).
11. See Jonathan Adelman, "A Profile of the Soviet Field: Or Who Will Study Stalin's Successors?" *PS* (Winter, 1983), for a detailed study of the Soviet field.
12. See *Columbia* (1983).
13. Lenin himself acknowledged that only the small size of the foreign intervention forces saved the Bolsheviks. For further details see Jonathan Adelman, *The Revolutionary Armies* (Westport, Conn: Greenwood Press, 1980).
14. Indeed Moscow continued to recognize the Chiang Kai Shek regime until the end and signed a Sino-Soviet Treaty with it in 1945.
15. See Merle Fainsod, *Smolensk Under Soviet Rule* (Cambridge: Harvard University Press, 1957).
16. Samuel Huntington, *Political Order in Changing Societies* (New Haven: Yale University Press, 1968), chap. 1.
17. For the great improvements in Russian capabilities manifested in World War II over World War I, see Jonathan Adelman, *Prelude to the Cold War: Tsarist, Soviet and American Armies in Two World Wars* (Boulder, Colorado: Lynne Rienner Publishers, 1988). For the differences in the impact of the paths to power on the development of the role of the armed forces in politics see Jonathan Adelman, *The Revolutionary Armies* and Jonathan Adelman, *Superpowers and Revolution* (New York: Praeger, 1985).

7

Social Dynamics and the Disutility of Terror: Afghanistan, 1978–1989

William Maley

Afghanistan provides one of the saddest recent examples of a country in which state organized terror has been deployed by a regime against substantial elements of its own population. It is also an example that illustrates the circumstances propitious for the deployment of terror to aid the controlled transformation of society and the consolidation of Marxist-Leninist regimes. For that reason it merits close attention. This paper identifies a number of factors that may help explain the blatant failure of terror to serve those ends in Afghanistan. Principal among these are the strength of Afghan *society* and the weakness of the Afghan *state*.

Terror and violence have much in common, but not all violence qualifies as terror. According to Aron,[1] one labels terrorist an "action of violence of which the psychological effects are out of proportion to the purely physical results." This stipulation has five aspects that are important and worth noting. First, it limits the violence under discussion to physical violence. Second, it does not exclude the state as a potential actor. Third, it does not confine state terror to actions carried out through agents or proxies. Fourth, it does not set up an artificial distinction between actions carried out in peacetime and those carried out in war. Fifth, its content depends on the prevailing norms within a society, as it is these norms that determine the character of the general psychological reaction prompted by a particular action.[2]

Yet, by virtue of the fact that the stipulation emphasizes effects rather than motivations, it fails to capture fully the flavor of a terrorist action. Thus, it seems useful to add one additional element: that the action be carried out to produce certain *political consequences*. This limitation (which would in any case apply almost by definition to *state* organized terror) excludes such phenomena as conflict between anomic interest groups whose activities challenge each other but not the political order of the society in which the conflict occurs. It also provides a criterion for distinguishing epiphenomenal violence, which frequently accompanies war and revolution, from purposeful, systematic practices carried out by servants of the state as part of a conscious plan to bolster a new regime.[3] Of course, this distinction between epiphenomenal and systematic violence is, in practice, difficult to draw: even if an act of terror has not been specifically sanctioned by a regime, it may be that the regime should nevertheless be held responsible, by virtue of having fostered an environment in which acts of terror are deemed right and appropriate.

When a regime is brought to office by a coup, its most pressing need is usually to establish a basis for its continuing exercise of power. This has been the case in a range of European Leninist regimes, which in Jowitt's[4] terminology have faced successively the core tasks of transformation of the old society, consolidation of the revolutionary regime, and, finally, inclusion. These different stages tend to draw on different strategies for bolstering the regime's position. In the transformation stage, *coercion* may assume a dominant role, as traditional institutions come under attack. In the consolidation and especially the inclusion stages, however, the use of coercion becomes increasingly costly. Although institutions may be established to deter the voicing of unorthodox opinions, thereby reducing the need for overt coercion, it is much easier for a regime to survive if it can achieve generalized normative support, or *legitimacy*. This entails most importantly the control of "the personal executive staff and the material implements of administration" identified as essential for organized domination,[5] but it also requires, at the very least, compliance from the politically significant powerholding sectors within society. Having become legitimate, a regime's coercive practices are thereby less likely to generate the psychological disproportion that characterizes terror.[6] For this reason, state organized terror is most often found in regimes going through transformative or consolidative stages.

Afghanistan, on the eve of the Communist coup of April 27, 1978, was structured on distinctive lines not readily captured by models designed to describe and explain social and political developments in other societies. It most closely resembled what Migdal[7] has called a "web-like" society, in which "social control is spread through various fairly autonomous social organizations." It emerged as a territorial unit, from a tribal confederation, during the reign of Ahmad Shah Durrani (1747-1772); many remnants of its tribal origins were carried into the twentieth century. It would be inaccurate, however, to depict Afghanistan simply as "a tribal society." The reality is far more complex. One can argue that Afghanistan as a territorial unit initially consisted of not one but *many* "societies." Furthermore, the very notion of "tribe" proves, upon closer inspection, to be elusive and variously conceptualized by scholars.[8] It is only by going *beyond* the tribal label to investigate specific behavioral patterns of particular segments of a patrilineal structure that one can hope to shed light on a historical case such as the Afghan.

The Afghan territorial unit in 1978 encompassed a range of groups with diverse internal structures and functioning norms. The numerically predominant Pushtuns were divided among different tribes, as were the Qizilbash and the Hazaras, whereas other significant groups, such as the Tajiks, were organized on non-tribal lines. Furthermore, although the population was overwhelmingly Muslim, it was divided between Sunni and Shiite elements. The bulk of the Shia were Qizilbashis or Hazaras; the latter occupy the lowest stratum of the Afghan social structure.

Two points are particularly worth nothing vis-a-vis the politically important groupings within Afghanistan. On one hand, it has historically been only under certain circumstances that *deep-rooted* culturally determined sources of identity, such as ethnicity and tribe, have formed the bases for distinctive patterns of political action.[9] On the other hand, *ephemeral* political groupings, what one might loosely call coalitions, can emerge in response to particular political circumstances.[10] The superficial pluralism within the Afghan population has thus tended to mask an underlying propensity to act concertedly in the face of generalized threat, and it is in part this capacity for concerted action that allows us now to speak of the strength of a single Afghan society. Ethnicity has provided one basis for such action: in Dupree's words, feuds before 1880 "occurred between neighboring vertical-structured, segmentary groups, but when an *external horizontal* force intruded and threatened indigenous *vertical* structures, regional traditional enemies often united and attempted to throw out the invader."[11] Islam, which has been called "the central nerve of Afghan culture,"[12] has supplied an even broader foundation for collective action, and has proved a source of cohesion at a number of different levels. During the "Hazara War," mounted in 1891-1893 by Amir 'Abd al-Rahman Khan, different Shiite Hazara tribes united to defend their *heterodox* Islamic perspectives in the face of Sunni persecution.[13] Yet, following the Communist coup in April 1978, both Sunni *and* Shia rose spontaneously against the new rulers, who were perceived to pose a fundamental threat to the religion, and through it the culture of the Afghan population.

The state, according to Poggi,[14] is "a complex set of institutional arrangements for rule" which "reserves to itself the business of rule over a territorially bounded society." Yet the Afghan state, while territorially bounded from the 18th century, was in institutional terms hardly a state at all until the reign of 'Abd al-Rahman Khan (1880-1901).[15] The institutions which arose from the rule of Ahmad Shah Durrani proved fragile, reminiscent of what John Kautsky[16] has called "conquest empires." Ahmad Shah's son had no standing army to defend his position, and the dynasty's authority disintegrated, leading to over a century of instability complicated by the manipulation of Afghan domestic politics by Russia and Great Britain. It was only with the accession of 'Abd al-Rahman Khan that the key instrumentalities of the state were consolidated. Most notable among these were the standing army and a system of tax gathering which increased the emphasis on taxes in cash rather than in kind.[17] However, the "Iron Amir" was well aware of the limits of his authority, in particular with respect to the tribal aristocracy and the religious establishment, for it was these forces rather than the feeble central state that had proven vital in the struggle against invaders during the First and Second Anglo-Afghan wars. During his reign, he managed to use coercive means to alter the character of these forces, but not altogether to subordinate them.[18] This was to prove crucial to popular resistance to the state following the April 1978 coup.

Although the upper echelons of the state structure were largely dominated from 1826 to 1978 by the Mohammadzai family from the Barakzai clan of Durrani Pushtuns, this did not provide a secure basis for the exercise of state power. During the reign of 'Abd al-Rahman Khan's son Amir Habibullah (1901-1919), there emerged in Afghanistan the first major intellectual push for social modernization, promoted by the journalist Mahmoud Tarzi through the pages of his newspaper *Seraj al-Akhbar*. Amir Amanullah, who took the throne following his father's assassination, made a serious attempt to further the subordination of rival social forces commenced by his grandfather.[19] In this he proved unsuccessful; in 1929, after nearly a decade in office, he was overthrown in a popular uprising in which ethnic, regional, and religious forces were activated, and coalesced, in the ephemeral fashion that has characterized Afghan political opposition. Although the rebellion was short-lived—Amanullah's successor ruled for less than a year before being overthrown by Durrani forces led by General Mohammad Nadir—it confirmed the structural weakness of the state. At the moment of crisis, loyalties to non-state institutions and values had proven more compelling than loyalties to the central authorities. Neither Amanullah *nor* his successor had been able to derive from the state the necessary resources or the mobilizational capacity to secure their rule.

The Musahiban dynasty, which ruled from 1929 to 1978, in general took great care not to antagonize social groupings with the capacity to mobilize opposition to its rule. One of the reasons that this dynasty survived so long was its paternalism, and the years of Musahiban rule were notable for relative political stability. Mohammad Nadir moved rapidly to secure legitimacy for his rule by acquiring the sanction of a Pushtun Great Assembly (*Loya Jirgah*), which promulgated a constitution patently intended to satisfy the demands of the Islamic establishment.[20] Following Nadir's assassination in November 1933, his son Zahir Shah was content for almost two decades to preside over a tacit compromise between the state and society, under which modest economic development and financial reform were conducted at a pace acceptable to all parties.[21] Although military forces were increasingly used to assert the authority of the state within the countryside, notably in suppressing the Safi Pushtun revolt in 1947-1949,[22] *terror* was not used in any serious fashion.

The appointment of the King's cousin, Mohammad Daoud, as Prime Minister in 1953 brought important changes in public policy. The education system was expanded in rural areas, electrification in towns was increased, and steps were taken to improve transport and communications networks.[23] Daoud, however, was inspired by Pushtun chauvinism to a much greater extent than his predecessor. This led to a ferocious border dispute with Pakistan, which claimed as its citizens many Pushtuns separated from the Afghan Pushtun population by the frontier between Afghanistan and British India demarcated in 1893. Daoud's feuding with Pakistan led him to turn to the Soviet Union for development assistance, rather than to Pakistan's ally, the United States.[24] Unfortunately, this set the scene for increased Soviet penetration of Afghanistan, which took three forms.

First, the Soviet Union attempted to make the Afghan economy more dependent on the Soviet economy by providing low interest loans for the purchase of (frequently overpriced) Soviet capital equipment and by diverting Afghan trade from free world markets.[25] Second, the USSR provided significant military aid, so that by the time of the 1978 coup the Afghan armed forces were substantially Soviet-trained and equipped.[26] Third, the Soviet Union encouraged the emergence of pro-Soviet political groups within the minute Kabul-based intelligentsia. This process was muted while Daoud remained Prime Minister, but in 1963 Zahir Shah obtained Daoud's resignation and inaugurated the so-called "constitutional period," which lasted until his own overthrow in July 1973. The constitutional period brought a new climate of pluralism, which allowed the pro-Soviet groups to come together in 1965 to form the People's Democratic Party of Afghanistan.[27]

The People's Democratic Party posed no obvious political threat to the regime. One reason was that, after a brief period of unity, the party split into its constituent factions, which then engaged in internecine sniping. Babrak Karmal headed the *Parcham* or "Banner" faction, while the *Khalq* or "Masses" faction was led by Nur Mohammad Taraki and Hafizullah Amin. Another reason was that neither faction could claim significant support from the elements of rural society upon which the survival of Afghan governments significantly rested. These factors long hid the fact that while pro-Soviet forces indeed had no foundations upon which to base a revolution, they increasingly had at their disposal the forces necessary to mount a coup in Kabul.

The first such coup was mounted in July 1973, when Zahir Shah was vacationing in Europe. Its leader was Daoud, but his closest collaborators were members of the *Parcham* faction, many of them middle-ranking officers of the Afghan Air Force and Tank Brigade. Daoud's ambitions had for years been frustrated by a term of the 1964 constitution excluding members of the Royal Family from political activity, and he was eager to return to office. The *Parchamis* were also keen to make a bid for power, as they had felt particularly threatened by the appointment of Mohammad Musa Shafiq as Prime Minister in 1972. For a number of reasons, the coup met with little resistance. Daoud was, after all, a member of the Mohammadzai family and a former Prime Minister: this supplied him with a degree of traditional legitimacy, and the transition to a republic under his presidency therefore did not strike either the public or the Kabul bureaucracy as particularly dramatic. More importantly, the constitutional experiment prior to Shafiq's appointment had not delivered a strong and decisive government, and its inadequacies were readily apparent during the 1971 famine emergency.[28] This left the pre-coup government extremely vulnerable to the armed forces, which, as a result of Soviet penetration and the frustrations of non-elite Pushtuns and members of other ethnic groups denied promotion, were far from firmly committed to protecting the monarchy.[29]

Daoud at first had some success in consolidating his position, but as part of this process he took the perilous step of purging those *Parchamis* who had held office in the Cabinet formed in the wake of the coup. The purge met with strenuous Soviet objections. In April 1977, during an official visit to the Soviet Union, Daoud took the even more imprudent step of clashing openly with Soviet Party Leader L. I. Brezhnev.[30] The reuniting of the *Khalq* and *Parcham* factions under Soviet pressure in July 1977 was therefore an ominous portent.[31] It set the scene for a second coup, staged nine months later by supporters of the People's Democratic party in the armed forces, most prominently the *Parchami* Colonel Abdul Qader.[32] The new regime, established with Taraki as President and Prime Minister and Amin and Karmal as Deputy Prime Ministers, was at once accorded diplomatic recognition by the Soviet Union.

This coup, which cost the lives of Daoud, many members of his family, and hundreds of other Afghans, led to terror of two different kinds. Immediately after the coup, there were major purges of the urban elite. These purges had definite political purposes and their psychological effects were certainly out of proportion to their physical results, but they had only a marginal impact on rural society. Within a short space of time, however, the regime extended its purges to embrace *rural* elites, and as it encountered opposition in the countryside to its radical social and economic policies, it increasingly responded with massacres and other atrocities which constituted *widespread* terror.

The regime made no secret of its willingness to resort to terror. "Those who plot against us in the dark will vanish in the dark," threatened Taraki.[33] In Kabul, the use of terror began well before the regime had any chance to offend important social elites through the implementation of policies. Numerous prominent figures were arrested, including former Prime Ministers Nur Ahmad Etemadi and Mohammad Musa Shafiq,[34] neither of whom survived incarceration. On occasion, whole families disappeared; on January 18, 1979, Mohammad Ibrahim Mojadiddi, a prominent sufi known by the title *Hazrat-i Shor Bazaar* and leader of one of the most important religious families in Afghanistan, was arrested with 29 male relatives ranging in age from 19 to 65. Only one was ever seen again. Intellectuals, supporters of previous regimes, and other individuals identified as enemies of the "revolution" were particular targets. Arrests were carried out by a political police called the Afghan Interests Protection Service or AGSA (*Da Afghanistan da Gato da Satalo Adara*) and headed by the sadistic *Khalqi* Asadullah Sarwari.[35] Thousands were arrested and held without trial in the Puli-Charkhi prison near Kabul, in conditions of the utmost squalor. A number of eyewitness accounts are available of mass executions, torture of prisoners, and random brutalities. According to one witness, during one month 250-300 people were executed every night.[36] On occasion victims were buried alive; one witness, a professor at Kabul University, concluded that the purpose was "to terrorize the prisoners."[37] Dr. Abdullah Osman, formerly Professor of Psychiatry at Kabul University, overheard the Commandant of Puli-Charkhi, Sayid Abdullah, make the following statement: "A million Afghans only must remain alive; we only need a million *Khalqis*; the others, we don't need; we will eliminate them."[38]

The reference to *Khalqis* was no slip of the tongue; within months after the coup, the long-standing hostility between the two factions of the People's Democratic Party had resurfaced. Karmal and his principal associates had been shunted into diplomatic appointments, from which they decamped when subsequently expelled from the party. However, a very large number of middle-ranking *Parchamis*, including such prominent figures as Abdul Qader, Sultan Ali Keshtmand, and Sulaiman Layeq were arrested in Kabul and survived only because of Soviet protection,[39] which Soviet advisors were in a position to provide.[40]

In rural areas, there were also purges of prominent figures. They amounted to what Lemercier-Quelquejay and Bennigsen have called "the slaughter of the tribal aristocracy."[41] At first the purges were selective, amounting to the elimination of social elements such as the clergy and other notables.[42] Nonetheless, they provoked considerable antagonism towards the regime and, as I shall argue shortly, advanced none of the regime's political objectives, as the groups under attack were not structurally vulnerable to decapitation.

The hostility produced in rural areas by the spread of the purge was fueled by the specific character of the party's policies. The regime rapidly promulgated a number of ambitious measures which unfortunately paid no attention to the values embodied in the religious and tribal codes that gave meaning and shape to the lives of a large number of rural Afghans, and which frequently had unforeseen consequences that negated their purpose. The most ill-considered initiative was undoubtedly the regime's "land reform," which imposed an ownership ceiling of 30 *jerib* (6 hectares) of fertile land per family.[43] This rested on the crudest of ideological premises.[44] In the view of the *Khalq*, most rural dwellers were exploited peasants whose craving for liberation from feudal bonds was hidden from them by false consciousness. The reality was quite different. In Afghanistan in 1978, rural society was *not* in crisis. First, while commercialization was beginning to threaten traditional patterns of power and exchange in rural areas,[45] the process had not led to widespread social dislocation. Second, the empirical evidence of inequalities in land distribution was defective. As Roy points out, "under the royalist regime, local communities, confronted by a government functionary who demanded that lands be attributed to a single proprietor and who did not recognize the notion of communal property, registered communal lands in the name of the chief of the clan or tribe, which resulted in the creation on paper of false *latifunda*".[46] Third, the impact of inequalities in land distribution was frequently ameliorated by social obligations upon nominal landowners to use the fruits of the land for the benefit of others. The beneficiaries of these obligations were often as offended by the land reform as those whose holdings were legally affected.[47] Furthermore, the reform was demonstrably unworkable, neglecting reforms of water and seed supply to such an extent that Roy has suggested that it was intended not to achieve its stated goals, but rather to break down traditional social structures.[48]

The People's Democratic Party was in no position to attempt such reforms. First, there was no popular demand for such radical policies.

Second, the party was organizationally unequal to the task of implementing its policies, for it had only a small and factionalized membership amounting to little more than a party of "teahouse political talk."[49] The state bureaucracy, particularly frail in rural areas, was equally inadequate for the task.[50] Third, the Party had no particular basis upon which to secure legitimacy.[51] As a result, there was a major discrepancy between the Party's objectives and the instruments at its disposal to further those objectives without coercion. The regime, its options crucially narrowed by the weakness of the ruling party and of state instrumentalities, then made the fatal mistake of adopting an obvious but flawed strategy: it resorted to *widespread* terror as a transformative and consolidative device, rather than the painful but more promising strategy of modifying its grandiose ideology and policies. The regime's resort to *widespread* terror in response to the emergence of opposition to its policies set it on a collision course with the *mass* of Afghan society and prompted the activation of popular opposition from both established segments of society and local coalitions.

The eruption of mass opposition even *after* the purge of rural elites was possible because, in a number of respects, the main elements of Afghan rural society were far less hierarchically structured than the regime had believed. Political mobilization therefore did not crucially depend upon direction from above. It is dangerous to generalize on this matter,[52] but a number of points stand out. First, the *Khans*, who to the outside observer appeared the most salient figures in Pushtun society, performed roles that were much more complex than their mere salience would suggest. Given the nature of these roles, the elimination of individual *Khans* did not constitute a lethal blow to the lineage structure within which they operated. Others could emerge to fill their shoes. Second, major decisions among the Pushtuns often fell to a pluralistic assembly (*jirgah*), the existence of which reproduced a distinct diffusion of power.[53] Third, the behavior of individuals within Pushtun society was influenced more by custom than command. When Pushtun *Khans* came under attack from the *Khalqis*, the customary law of the Pushtuns, known as *Pushtunwali*, created an obligation to exact revenge (*badal*). All these factors meant that Pushtun society proved quite robust in the face of the tribal purge.

The policies of the regime, and the attack on rural notables, prompted mass opposition, which first broke out in the region of Nuristan during the summer of 1978. As it spread, the regime made increasing use of *widespread* terror. This took the form of indiscriminate bombing and atrocities carried out by ground forces. The town of Kamdesh in Nuristan was attacked with incendiary bombs in September 1978,[54] and, in March 1979, following a bloody uprising against the regime in the city of Herat,

Soviet pilots from Dushanbe carried out a bombing raid that, by conservative estimates, cost 5000 lives.[55] Of the attacks by ground forces, the most widely publicized was undoubtedly the massacre of the male residents of the Kunar village of Kerala. The unfortunate victims were summoned by soldiers and Soviet advisers to a field outside the village, denounced by officers as supporters of the resistance, and machine-gunned. The dead and wounded were then buried with a bulldozer.[56] Yet this was by no means the only atrocity of its kind. At the end of April 1979, over a thousand young Hazaras were bound, blindfolded, and thrown into the Oxus river, where they drowned; and in the same region, between two and three hundred elders were trucked into the desert and flung from a cliff into a ravine. Witnesses attested to the involvement of Soviet advisers on each of these occasions. Soviet advisers were also present when, on August 8, 1979, 650 residents of the village of Qal'a-e Najil were buried alive in sixteen trenches.[57] Similar atrocities occurred in the cities. On June 23, 1979, there were serious disturbances in the Hazara quarter of Kabul. Troops fired on the demonstrators, and a grim reprisal followed: three hundred Hazaras were trucked to a field outside Kabul, where half were buried alive with a bulldozer, and the other half drenched with gasoline and set on fire.[58]

The circumstances that led up to the Soviet invasion are by now reasonably well-documented, and need not be restated at any length.[59] In March 1979, Amin became Prime Minister, and the use of widespread terror escalated. The USSR became increasingly perturbed by the obvious disorder growing within the country, and officials of the Soviet Embassy attempted to pressure Amin to modify his policies. When this failed, they plotted with Taraki to secure Amin's removal. However, their attempt to eliminate him in mid-September 1979 miscarried disastrously: Amin survived an attempt on his life and removed Taraki, whose death was reported by the Kabul Times in a terse backpage report in early October. Secret police chief Sarwari sought refuge in the Soviet Embassy, and the political police was retitled the Workers' Intelligence Institute, or KAM (Kargari Astekhbarati Muassessa), and headed first by Aziz Ahmad Akbari and then by Hafizullah Amin's nephew, Asadullah Amin.[60] The atrocities that followed Amin's seizure of the presidency were especially brutal, but the regime was living on borrowed time. Apparently ignoring specialist assessments of the situation in Afghanistan,[61] the USSR dispatched its intervention force in December 1979, killing Amin and replacing him with Babrak Karmal.

The introduction of Soviet forces greatly increased the intensity of the opposition facing the regime, and contributed nothing to the unity of the People's Democratic Party. By late 1988, the Soviet television journalist Mikhail Leshchinskii could still complain that "the party, as before, is being torn by contradictions between factions and wings," and that it had no support from the people.[62] Although resistance to the regime had spread rapidly before the invasion, it was still confined to specific localities. After the invasion, the conflict became a full-scale war.

The war brought immense suffering for the Afghan population. First, Afghanistan in places was so physically devastated that a British journalist, visiting the once-fertile countryside, remarked that it was as though someone had dropped a bomb in the Garden of Eden.[63] Second, the war produced massive population shifts, creating large external and internal refugee populations. In September 1988, the United Nations estimated that approximately 5.6 million Afghans had sought refuge in Pakistan and Iran.[64] Third, a staggering number of Afghans were killed. Academician Andrei Sakharov, in a speech to the Congress of People's Deputies in Moscow on 2 June 1989, estimated the death toll at one million.[65] According to a study by Marek Sliwinski of the University of Geneva, aerial bombing raids, shootings, artillery attacks, anti-personnel mines, and exhaustion and other traumas between 1979 and 1987 cost the lives of roughly 1.24 million Afghans, or 9 percent of the Afghan population.[66] It would be incorrect, however, to suggest that the violence the Afghans encountered was simply an epiphenomenal aspect of military conflict. On the contrary, there is abundant evidence that civilian non-combatants were deliberately exposed to violence by the regime and its backers in order to bolster their position. Nonetheless, the terror practiced between the Soviet invasion, and the signing in Geneva on April 14, 1988 of accords providing for the withdrawal of all Soviet forces by February 1989, proved no more successful in securing the position of the regime than the terror carried out by the *Khalq*.

It is again necessary to distinguish between events in the cities and developments in rural areas. In early 1980, a new secret police was established, known as the State Information Agency, or KHAD (*Khedamati Atela' at-i Dawlati*). Until November 1985, it was headed by a dedicated *Parchami*, Dr. Najibullah; he was succeeded by his deputy, General Ghulam Farouq Yaqubi, and in January 1986 the organization was renamed the Ministry of State Security, or WAD (*Wazirat-i Amaniat-i Dawlati*). This organization, with substantial Soviet assistance, masterminded significant coercion of the urban population. It was responsible for the forcible silencing of protest against regime measures and for the administration of the system of arrest, interrogation, and imprisonment.

The mistreatment of Afghan political prisoners after 1979 has been documented in detail in a series of reports prepared by the United Nations Special Rapporteur on Human Rights in Afghanistan (Professor Felix Ermacora).[67] The most famous of KHAD's targets was the distinguished historian Professor Hasan Kakar, arrested in March 1982 for attempting to establish an independent association of teachers at Kabul University,[68] and imprisoned until 1987, when he was released for publicity purposes. At a press conference in Peshawar on January 12, 1988, Kakar reported that political prisoners were "subjected to inhuman and untold physical tortures in jails in Afghanistan," and referred to a prisoner whose body was injected with a solution of salt.[69] Abundant eyewitness testimony pointed to the use of torture to intimidate political detainees.[70] Some of the worst abuses involved women prisoners. Mrs. Fahima Nasery, a mathematics teacher at a Kabul high school, was arrested in May 1981. She subsequently described the following grim experience: "I was taken to a room where I witnessed the most horrible sight of my detention. Cut fingers, noses, ears, legs, hands, breasts and hair of women were piled there. In one corner, a decayed corpse was lying. The smell of blood and the decayed corpse were intolerable. I remained in that chamber of horrors until the following morning."[71] In rural areas there developed a sustained pattern of atrocities by ground forces, comparable to those that occurred between April 1978 and December 1979—atrocities for which, according to a Soviet journalist, there are now "mountains of evidence."[72] These atrocities took many forms, of which the following are merely examples. In the village of Mata lived two blind brothers, aged 90 and 95. According to a native of the village, "they stayed behind when the rest of the villagers fled during the spring offensive. 'The Russians came, tied dynamite to their backs, and blew them up'."[73] Explosives were also used to blow up bound captives inside the mosque in the village of Kolalgu near Ghazni on January 16, 1988.[74] On October 20, 1984, in a village near the Kabul-Gardez road, twelve men and four women were driven from their houses, doused with kerosene, and set on fire. "We aren't going to squander our ammunition for the Afghans," remarked one of the Soviet soldiers responsible.[75] A Turkmen woman from the region near Mazar-i Sharif reported harassment by a Soviet search party in August 1985: "They asked me if I knew where the *mojahedin* were hiding. I had my little boy in my arms. I said I didn't know. So they took a *kalashnikov* and just shot my little boy in front of me."[76]

The failure of this terror to improve the position of the regime is again something that should be understood in terms of the relations between state and society. On one hand, the arrival *en masse* of Soviet forces did nothing to strengthen the indigenous instrumentalities of the Afghan state, let alone provide them with legitimacy. In fact, it had the very opposite effect: the Kabul regime, headed first by Karmal, and from May 1986 by Najibullah, was ineradicably associated in the eyes of the population with the repulsive Soviets, whose virtues as neighbors the regime was obliged ceaselessly to extol. On the other hand, the arrival of Soviet soldiers galvanized disparate elements of Afghan society to mount further attacks on the state and its plenipotentiaries. There were several reasons for this.

First, the notorious atheism of the Soviets provided a basis for cooperation between different social units in common defence of the Islamic faith. Canfield has noted among Afghans "a special repugnance for the Soviets because of their avowed atheism, which to the Afghan moral consciousness implies filthiness, gluttony, drunkenness and sexual promiscuity."[77] At a higher level, Islam fortified the resistance in several ways. It provided an ideological basis for the act of resistance and a positive set of values to be defended. Furthermore, the eschatological notion of salvation through martyrdom gave rise to an indomitability among believers that terror could not easily displace.

Second, the bombing of the Afghan countryside had mixed effects. While it drove thousands of Afghans from their wrecked villages (as was intended), it also left many of these refugees with little to do *but* fight the regime and its backers, and thus the Afghan resistance groups found a ready source of volunteers. This tended to reinforce the determination which the notion of martyrdom produces, as is illustrated by the following remark made by a member of the resistance to a Western journalist: "I died five years ago when I left Kabul. My soul has gone to heaven; this is just my body. If I die, it is finished. People will say, 'he was a brave freedom fighter; we can be proud of him.' It is an honor to be martyred."[78]

Third, the leadership roles in the resistance were increasingly filled by younger, better educated figures, who took the places vacated by those tribal and religious leaders eliminated during the periods of rule by Taraki and Amin. This by no means occurred uniformly throughout the countryside, but, where it happened, it increased markedly the professionalism of the resistance. The clearest example was in the Panjsher Valley, where Tajik Ahmad Shah Massoud fashioned an extremely efficient *Mujahideen* force and parallel civilian administration.[79]

At the heart of the dilemma that the Soviet Union came to face in Afghanistan lay the failure of the state to penetrate and dominate society. This failure was affirmed in an interview by the Soviet Major-General Kim Tsagolov, in which he remarked that "a significant part of the population abandoned the PDPA, ceased to believe in it as a vanguard force, capable of implementing its policies."[80] The reconciliation of Afghan state and Afghan society was inherently a task which the Soviet forces could not perform directly, yet one which their Afghan associates were in no better position to accomplish. By the time Karmal was depicting his policies as moderate and Najibullah was calling for "national reconciliation," the regime was so discredited that there no longer existed a basis from which to build normative bonds with the Afghan population. Coercion was therefore needed simply to prevent the regime's collapse. At the same time, however, coercion held out no particular hope of permitting transition to the inclusive stage of regime development: all it could do, in fact, was fan the fires of resistance. This, together with the increased military costs imposed by the U.S. supplying to the resistance Stinger and Blowpipe anti-aircraft missiles from late 1986 onwards, was almost certainly a major consideration behind the Soviet commitment to withdraw its troops from Afghanistan by February 1989.[81]

The Afghan case highlights a point of considerable importance. State organized terror is employed, quintessentially, for political purpose. Terror directed by a state against its subjects is designed to give rise to a situation in which the subjects' normative commitments to non-state political actors are subordinated to the *prudential* concern to avoid becoming victims of the terror, thereby fracturing the bonds of social solidarity upon which the functioning of organized resistance depends. However, where strong bonds of social solidarity are liable to intensify in the face of a threat from outside the social unit, terror is highly likely to prove counterproductive. This is exactly what happened in Afghanistan.

Notes

1. Raymond Aron, *Paix et Guerre Entre les Nations* (Paris: Calmann-Levy, 1984), 176.

2. On the importance of such norms, see David Rapoport "Messianic Sanctions for Terror," *Comparative Politics*, 20, no. 2 (January 1988): 196.

3. Paul Wilkinson, *Terrorism and the Liberal State* (London: Macmillan, 1977), 48.

4. Kenneth Jowitt, "Inclusion and Mobilization in European Leninist Regimes," *World Politics*, 28, no. 1 (October 1975): 69–96.

5. Max Weber, "Politics as a Vocation," in *From Max Weber: Essays in Sociology* (London: Routledge & Kegan Paul, 1948), 80.

6. Grant Wardlaw, *Political Terrorism: Theory, Tactics, and Counter-measures* (Cambridge: Cambridge University Press, 1982), 7–8.

7. Joel S. Migdal, *Strong Societies and Weak States: State-Society Relations and State Capabilities in the Third World* (Princeton: Princeton University Press, 1988), 34–35.

8. Olivier Roy, *L'Agfhanistan: Islam et Modernité Politique* (Paris: Editions du Seuil, 1985), 23; Richard Tapper, ed., *The Conflict of Tribe and State in Iran and Afghanistan* (London: Croom Helm, 1983), 9.

9. M. Nazif Shahrani, "State Building and Social Fragmentation in Afghanistan: A Historical Perspective," in *The State, Religion, and Ethnic Politics: Afghanistan,*

Iran, and Pakistan, ed. Ali Banuazizi and Myron Weiner (Syracuse: Syracuse University Press, 1986), 24.

10. Robert L. Canfield, "Islamic Coalitions in Bamyan: A Problem in Translating Afghan Political Culture," in *Revolutions & Rebellions in Afghanistan: Anthropological Perspectives,* ed. M. Nazif Shahrani and Robert L. Canfield (Berkeley: Institute of International Studies, University of California, 1984), 211–229. 11. Louis Dupree, "Cultural Changes Among the Mujahidin and Muhajerin," in *The Tragedy of Afghanistan: The Social, Cultural and Political Impact of the Soviet Invasion,* ed. Bo Huldt and Erland Jansson (London: Croom Helm, 1988), 28.

12. Michael Barry, *Le Royaume de L'Insolence: La Resis Afghane du Grand Moghol l'Invasion Sovietique* (Paris: Flammarion, 1984), 57.

13. David Busby Edwards, "The Evolution of Shi'i Political Dissent in Afghanistan," in *Shi'ism and Social Protest,* ed. Juan R.I. Cole and Nikki R. Keddie (New Haven: Yale University Press, 1986), 205–206.

14. Gianfranco Poggi, *The Development of the Modern State: A Sociological Introduction* (London: Hutchinson, 1978), 1.

15. Barnett R. Rubin, "Lineages of the State in Afghanistan," *Asian Survey* 28, no. 11 (November 1988): 1188–1209.

16. John Kautsky, *The Politics of Aristocratic Empires* (Chapel Hill: The University of North Carolina Press, 1982), 62–72.

17. Vartan Gregorian, *The Emergence of Modern Afghanistan: Politics of Reform and Modernization 1880-1946* (Stanford: Stanford University Press, 1969), 129–192; Hasan Kakar, *Government and Society in Afghanistan: The Reign of 'Abd al-Rahman Khan* (Austin: University of Texas Press, 1979), 73–114.

18. Ashraf Ghani, "Islam and State-Building in a Tribal Society: Afghanistan 1880-1901," *Modern Asian Studies* 12, no. 2, (1978): 271.

19. Leon B. Poullada, *Reform and Rebellion in Afghanistan, 1919-1929: King Amanullah's Failure to Modernize a Tribal Society* (Ithaca: Cornell University Press, 1973).

20. Mohammad Kamali, *Law in Afghanistan: A Study of the Constitutions, Matrimonial Law and the Judiciary* (Leiden: E. J. Brill, 1985), 20.

21. Maxwell J. Fry, *The Afghan Economy: Money, Finance and the Critical Constraints to Economic Development* (Leiden: E. J. Brill, 1974), 82–88.

22. Louis Dupree, *Afghanistan* (Princeton: Princeton University Press, 1980), 537.

23. Gilbert Etienne, *Rural Development in Asia: Meetings with Peasants* (New Delhi: Sage Publications, 1985), 32–33.

24. Leon B. Poullada, "Afghanistan and the United States: The Crucial Years," *The Middle East Journal* 35, no. 2, (Spring 1981): 187.

25. M. S. Noorzoy, "Soviet Economic Interests in Afghanistan," *Problems of Communism* 36, no. 3, (May-June 1987): 43–54.

26. Henry S. Bradsher, *Afghanistan and the Soviet Union* (Durham: Duke University Press, 1985), 27–28; Muhammad R. Azmi, "Soviet Politico-Military Penetration in Afghanistan, 1955 to 1979," *Armed Forces & Society* 12, no. 3, (Spring 1986): 334–335.

27. For detailed discussion see Anthony Arnold, *Afghanistan's Two-Party Communism: Parcham and Khalq* (Stanford: Hoover Institution Press, 1983).

28. Michael Barry, *Afghanistan* (Paris: Editions du Seuil, 1974), 175–183.

29. Ralph H. Magnus, "The Military and Politics in Afghanistan: Before and After the Revolution," in *The Armed Forces in Contemporary Asian Societies*, ed. Edward A. Olsen and Stephen Jurika, Jr. (Boulder: Westview Press, 1986), 335.

30. Abdul Samad Ghaus, *The Fall of Afghanistan: An Insider's Account* (McLean: Pergamon-Brassey's, 1988), 178–179.

31. Anthony Arnold, *Afghanistan: The Soviet Invasion in Perspective* (Stanford: Hoover Institution Press, 1983), 52–56; Bradsher, *Afghanistan and the Soviet Union*, 261.

32. For a detailed account of the coup see Louis Dupree, *Red Flag Over the Hindu Kush Part II: The Accidental Coup, or Taraki in Blunderland*, American Universities Field Staff Reports, no. 45 (Asia).

33. This remark was attributed to Taraki by Hafizullah Amin. See "Our Revolution Is Secure," *Asiaweek* 4, no. 45, (17 November 1978): 40.

34. Dupree, *Afghanistan*; Amnesty International, *Violations of Human Rights and Fundamental Freedoms in the Democratic Republic of Afghanistan*, ASA/11/04/79, London, September 1979.

35. Bruce J. Amstutz, *Afghanistan: The First Five Years of Soviet Occupation* (Washington: National Defense University, 1986), 264.

36. See Michael Barry, "Répressions et Guerre Soviétiques," *Les Temps Modernes* July-August 1980, p. 177. This article, which contains transcripts of interviews recorded in early 1980 with prison survivors, is an indispensable source of information on atrocities in Afghanistan following the April 1978 coup.

37. Ibid., 194.

38. Ibid., 183.

39. Anthony Hyman, "Afghan Intelligentsia 1978–81," *Index on Censorship*, no. 2, (1982): 9.

40. Barry, "Répressions," 189–190.

41. Chantal Lemercier-Quelquejay and Alexandre Bennigsen, "Soviet Experience of Muslim Guerilla Warfare and the War in Afghanistan," in *The USSR and the Muslim World*, ed. Yaacov Ro'i (London: George Allen & Unwin, 1984), 209.

42. Roy, *L'Afghanistan*, 127.

43. Latif Tabibi, "Die Afghanische Landreform von 1979: Ihre Vorgeschichte und Konsequenzen," (Ph.D. Diss.: Freie Universität Berlin, 1981).

44. Olivier Roy, "Le Double Code Afghan: Marxisme et Tribalisme," *Revue Francaise de Science Politique* 36, no. 6 (December 1986): 853–856.

45. Jon W. Anderson, "There Are No *Khans* Anymore: Economic Development and Social Change in Tribal Afghanistan," *The Middle East Journal* 32, no. 2, (Spring 1978): 167–183.

46. Roy, *L'Afghanistan*, 117.

47. David Busby Edwards, "Origins of the Anti-Soviet Jihad," in *Afghan Resistance: The Politics of Survival* ed. Grant M. Farr and John G. Merriam (Boulder: Westview Press, 1987), 40.

48. Roy, *L'Afghanistan*, 120.

49. Henry S. Bradsher, "Communism in Afghanistan," in *Soviet-American Relations with Pakistan, Iran and Afghanistan* ed. Hafeez Malik (London: Macmillan, 1987), 339.

50. Richard S. Newell, *The Politics of Afghanistan* (Ithaca: Cornell University Press, 1972), 88–95; Hasan Kakar, "The Fall of the Afghan Monarchy in 1973," *International Journal of Middle East Studies* 9 (1978): 200–201; Thomas J. Barfield, "Weak Links on a Rusty Chain: Structural Weaknesses in Afghanistan's Provincial Government Administration," in Shahrani and Canfield, *Revolutions and Rebellions*, 170–183.

51. William Maley, "Political Legitimation in Contemporary Afghanistan," *Asian Survey* 27, no. 6, (June 1987): 705–725.

52. For a more detailed discussion on this subject see Pierre Centlivres and Micheline Centlivres-Demont, *Et Si On Parlait de l'Afghanistan?* (Paris: Editions de la Maison des Sciences de L'Homme, 1988).

53. Bernt Glatzer, "Political Organisation of Pashtun Nomads and the State," in Tapper, *Conflict of Tribe and State*, 222.

54. Edward R. Girardet, *Afghanistan: The Soviet War* (London: Croom Helm, 1985), 114.

55. Jonathan C. Randal, " 'Grim' Nickname Fits Afghan Tales of Torture, Murder," *The Washington Post*, 11 May 1979, p. A23.

56. For accounts of this massacre, see "Massacre Described by Afghan Refugees," *The New York Times*, 17 February 1980, p. 10; Girardet, pp. 107–110; Barry, *Le Royaume de L'Insolence*, p. 270; and Mohammad Wasim Lodin, "A Pilot Survey of the Displacement, Loss of Life and Disablement of the Population in Three Afghan Villages," *WUFA: Journal of the Writers' Union of Free Afghanistan* 3, no. 3, (July-September 1988): 45-71.

57. Barry, "Répressions," 211–214.

58. Ibid., 204.

59. See Bradsher, *Afghanistan and the Soviet Union*; Thomas T. Hammond, *Red Flag Over Afghanistan: The Communist Coup, the Soviet Invasion, and the Consequences* (Boulder: Westview Press, 1984); Arnold, *Soviet Invasion*; Raymond L. Garthoff, *Détente and Confrontation: American Soviet Relations from Nixon to Reagan* (Washington: The Brookings Institution, 1985); and Joseph L. Collins, *The Soviet Invasion of Afghanistan: A Study in the Use of Force in Soviet Foreign Policy* (Lexington: Lexington Books, 1986).

60. Amstutz, 265.

61. On the military advice available to the Soviet leadership, see Sergei Belitsky, "Authors of the USSR's Afghan War Policy," *Report on the USSR* 1, no. 17 (April 1989): 11–12; and Cynthia Roberts, "Glasnost in Soviet Foreign Policy: Setting the Record Straight?," *Report on the USSR* 1, no. 50 (December 1989): 4–8. Louis Dupree ("Afghanistan 1984: Crisis After Crisis, Internal and External," in *Escalation and Intervention: Multilateral Security and Its Alternatives*, ed. Arthur R. Day and Michael W. Doyle [Boulder: Westview Press, 1986], p. 112) states that before the invasion the Soviet leadership received advice from scholars that, "given known Afghan historical and cultural patterns, the Afghans would resist." Oleg Bogomolov, ("Kto zhe oshibalsia?," *Literaturnaia Gazeta*, 16

March 1988, p. 10) specifically points to the lack of attention paid by the leadership to specialist advice.

62. See BBC, *Summary of World Broadcasts*, SU 0309/A3/1, 15 November 1988.

63. Gavin Bell, "Paradise Lost in Afghan Valley of Death," *The Times*, 21 July 1987, p. 7.

64. See the Office of the United Nations Co-ordinator for Humanitarian and Economic Assistance Programmes Relating to Afghanistan, *First Consolidated Report*, UNOCA/1988/1, Geneva, September 1988, p. xxi. For a more detailed discussion of the refugee problem, see William Maley, "Afghan Refugees: From Diaspora to Repatriation," in *Refugees in the Modern World*, Canberra Studies in World Affairs, no. 25, ed. Amin Saikal (Canberra: Department of International Relations, Research School of Pacific Studies, The Australian National University, 1989), 17–44.

65. See BBC, *Summary of World Broadcasts*, SU/0480/C/10, 12 June 1989.

66. Marek Sliwinski, *Evaluation des Consequences Humaines, Sociales et Ecologiques de la Guerre en Afghanistan* (Paris: Bureau International Afghanistan and Médecins Sans Frontières, 1988), 5.

67. United Nations, Human Rights Commission, Economic and Social Council, *Rapport Sur la Situation des Droits de L'Homme en Afghanistan*, 19 February 1985, E/CN.4/1985/21; *Situation of Human Rights in Afghanistan*, 17 February 1986, E/CN.4/1986/24; 26 February 1988, E/CN.4/1988/25; 16 February 1989, E/CN.4/1989/24; 9 January 1987, A/41/778; 23 October 1987, A/42/667; 24 October 1988, A/43/742; 30 October 1989, A/44/669.

68. Amnesty International, *Democratic Republic of Afghanistan: Background Briefing on Amnesty International's Concerns*, ASA/11/13/83, London, October 1983, p. 6.

69. BBC, *Summary of World Broadcasts*, FE/0050/C/4, 16 January 1988.

70. For detailed discussion of torture, see Amnesty International, *Afghanistan: Torture of Political Prisoners*, ASA/11/04/86, London, November 1986; and *Afghanistan-Unlawful Killings and Torture*, ASA/11/002/88, London, May 1988.

71. Fahima Rahimi, *Women in Afghanistan* (Liestal: Stiftung Bibliotheca Afghanica, 1986), 108.

72. See Leonid Batkin, "Two Worlds Meet at the Congress of Deputies," *Moscow News*, 11 June 1989, p. 9. Specific atrocities had earlier been mentioned in Vladimir Snegirev, "Pro Voinu," *Komsomol' Skaia Pravada*, 9 February 1989, p. 4; and Gennadii Bocharov, "Afghan," *Literaturnaia Gazeta*, 15 February 1989, pp. 13–14. It is notable that Batkin's demand that the Soviet authorities "punish the guilty to clear ourselves of the filth" was not taken up. Instead, the Supreme Soviet in November 1989 issued a general amnesty for crimes committed in Afghanistan: see "Postanovlenie Verkhovnogo Soveta SSSR Ob Amnistii Sovershivshikh Prestupleniia Byvshikh Voennosluzhashchikh Kontingenta Sovetskikh Soisk v Afganistane," *Pravda*, 30 November 1989, p. 1.

73. Jeri Laber and Barnett R. Rubin, *A Nation is Dying: Afghanistan under the Soviets 1979–87* (Evanston: Northwestern University Press, 1988), xi.

74. See Arthur Kent, "Massacre," *The Observer*, 3 April 1988. I wish to thank Bernard Levin for sending me a copy of this report.

75. Bernard Dupaigne, ed., *Les Droits de L'Homme en Afghanistan* (Paris: AFRANE, 1985), 20.

76. Michael Barry, Johan Lagerfelt, and Marie-Odile Terrenoire, "International Humanitarian Enquiry Commission on Displaced Persons in Afghanistan," *Central Asian Survey* 5, no. 1, (1986): 95.

77. Robert L. Canfield, "Western Stakes in the Afghanistan War," *Central Asian Survey* 4, no. 1 (1985): 128.

78. Jan Goodwin, *Caught in the Crossfire* (London: Macdonald, 1987), 175.

79. Roy, *L'Afghanistan*, 244–245.

80. "Afganistan-predvaritel'nye Itogi," *Ogonek*, no. 32 (July 1988): 26.

81. William Maley, "The Geneva Accords of April 1988," in *The Soviet Withdrawal from Afghanistan*, ed. Amin Saikal and William Maley (Cambridge: Cambridge University Press, 1989), 12–28.

PART THREE

Terror as an Instrument
of State Policy

8

The Ideological Governance of Perception in the Use of State Terror in Latin America: The Case of Argentina

David Pion-Berlin

Considerable attention has been paid to the rise and fall of authoritarian regimes in South America. However, the nature and causes of state terror which sustained those regimes have still not been adequately explained. Nowhere has state terror assumed such regularity and taken on such proportions in recent decades as it has in Latin America. For years, human rights offices have been flooded with reports of the abduction and murder of members of the clergy, the mysterious disappearances of trade unionists or the mass detention of students. The abuses have been widespread and the governments seem to strike arbitrarily, unpredictably, and nearly everywhere against alleged enemies of the state.

Acts of political repression are not always unprovoked. During the 1960s and the early 1970s, some governments were faced with formidable rural and urban guerrilla movements. Sparked by the victory of Castro's forces in Cuba and the daring exploits of men such as Che Guevara and Camilo Torres, these rebels were determined to redress social inequities by overturning the political and economic order. Acts of armed aggression and unarmed violence (riots, mass demonstrations, politically motivated strikes) increased 30 percent from the 1950s to the 1960s.[1] This was a turbulent period, one which gave meaning to the phrase "violence begets violence." But the political repression that emerged by the mid 1970s in South America was less reactive in nature, undertaken, in fact, without regard to levels of dissent.

This paper will explore some underlying motives for this peculiar brand of state terror. After the defeat of rebel forces, governmental coercion persisted with increased frequency and intensity. The worst forms of human rights abuses were not committed by the authorities against violent organizations, but against civilians who had already acquiesced to the power of the authorities. These were individuals who, for the most part, had neither violated any laws, nor participated in any clandestine activities, nor shown any interest in radical causes. Defendants were genuinely surprised by their detentions, having had no reason to suspect they would be placed under surveillance and treated as enemies of the state. Specific charges were rarely brought against them. Instead, the authorities accused them of subversive or terrorist activities. These terms were broadly and arbitrarily defined, making a legal defense against such charges virtually impossible. In Brazil, those who allegedly committed subversive acts were seeking the "transformation of the existing order." Argentina employed even less precision: Military President General Jorge Videla labelled a subversive as "anyone who opposes the Argentine way of life."[2]

Policies of overkill resulted in the detention and trial by military tribunal of over 7,400 Brazilians between 1964 and 1979. In Argentina, it took the form of a "dirty war" which claimed the lives of as many as fifteen thousand individuals.[3] Some ten thousand Chilean citizens were thought to be murdered shortly after the 1973 coup.

Several features of this brand of state terror should be noted. First, these assaults on human freedom were neither unintentional nor were they miscalculations. Elaborate state security apparatuses were purposefully devised to repeatedly and systematically brutalize political opponents. Second, there were no clear racial, ethnic or religious lines drawn, though other characteristics (as opposed to the activities) of those victimized were probably significant. Third, terror was rarely selective: there were few clear demonstration effects, meaning there was no separation of victimized populations either spatially or temporally so as to send a warning to relevant target populations. Instead, repression was more scattered and pervasive, though inevitably it induced tremendous fear in the population nonetheless. The form of state terror, in other words, resisted any easy classification. So did its causes.

A motive for terror can be traced to the perceptual and ideological biases of the regimes. Despite the near absence of effective and violent oppositions, the military regimes of the region, to one degree or another, sensed a clear and present danger. Some regimes were simply obsessed with the security dilemma: how best could they defend the regime, state and nation against an elusive and ubiquitous foe? All other policy considerations were quickly made subordinate to the issue of security.

Threats were everywhere, or so they perceived them to be. The perception
of threat was grounded not in a careful appraisal of "enemy" resources
and intentions, but in a set of ideas about the political order. With the
adoption of French and American security doctrines, beginning in the
1950s, the armed forces discovered ideas which, to them, were persuasive,
seductively simple, and self-serving. For those reasons, the ideas were
accepted and ultimately regarded as cardinal truths, despite the fact that
they were neither contemporary nor congruent with Latin American
realities. With doctrines in hand, the military launched a crusade against
"revolutionary and terrorist subversion" which they believed threatened
the social and political fabric of their nations.

Threat Perception: The Objective Dimension

Theorists acknowledge the importance of threat perception to the
study of coercion, but little has been written on it, outside of psychology
and, more recently, in international relations literature. Threat perception
can best be understood as "an anticipation on the part of an observer,
the decision maker, of impending harm—usually of a military, strategic
or economic kind—to the state."[4] States assess the relative capabilities
and intentions of their alleged adversaries and then formulate perceptions
based on the combined impact of those capabilities and intentions.[5]

The use or intended use of coercion indicates that a government
already anticipates danger, and the higher the levels of force employed,
the greater the government's sense of threat.[6] If threat perception were
grounded squarely in the assessment of evidence, then what would be
the relevant facts for governments to consider were they to resort to
terror against their adversaries?

First, they must be able to identify alleged "agents of destruction."
States do not lash out indiscriminately. As unpredictable and as widespread as the terror may be, it is always directed toward some target
population or populations. Second, governments will make some estimate
about capacity. If adversaries are to inflict harm, they must have some
ability to do so. The presumption is that opponents can mobilize at
least enough resources to undermine the regime's authority and, at most,
to place in jeopardy the social and political order. Resources may be
broadly defined to include masses of people, economic resources, coercive
capacities, and organizational assets.

Third, some consideration will be given to motives and intentions.
Projections of potential for rebellion are complicated by the uncertainty
of the future, the absence of reliable information about opponents, or
the vested interests of certain state actors in distorting the evidence. As
in international relations, the authorities may rely on historical precedent.

If hostile actions occured in the past, and relations have not improved, such actions are predicted to occur in the future. Often, governments are faced with new situations in which historical precedent does not help. They must sort through a maze of data and options and select the facts which may reveal hostile and aggressive intent. Failure to gauge intent accurately is evident in the case of Argentina. The government of General Juan Carlos Onganía failed to anticipate the groundswell of opposition among workers and students that was building against his regime in the city of Córdoba. The "Cordobazo" riots of May 1969 precipitated the demise of the unprepared Onganía dictatorship.

Fourth, the nature of the act must be considered. Governments which perceive threats assume the worst, that opponents will choose aggression and generally destructive forms of behavior, or that even where peaceful and non-violent forms of dissent are manifested, that these will have as their ultimate purpose the subversion of the current order. Fifth, timing is important. Governments must have some sense that danger is impending. Threats which are far in the future are less worrisome. Finally, there is direction. Authorities normally assume that hostile and aggressive acts are aimed directly at them, or at least at some definable symbols of national economic, political or military security which they are called upon to defend.

These considerations enter into the government's overall assessment of its opposition. Once that evaluation is made, the authorities must next decide what course of action to take. To employ force, the authorities must believe that they have a reasonable chance of overcoming their opponents. That probability estimate would be based on the assessment that (1) the state has ample resources with which to assault the opposition; (2) those resources can be marshalled effectively and efficiently; (3) the opposition is vulnerable, meaning that it lacks resources, is organizationally fragmented, and/or is marginalized from the rest of society; (4) the absolute costs of employing terror can be minimized, and (5) the opportunity costs are low, meaning that alternative strategies foregone would be much less desirable.[7] In short, from this perspective, military regimes would be conceived of as utility maximizers who minimize costs, weigh the benefits and risks associated with terror, and base their judgment about the degree of impending danger on a rational appraisal of the evidence.

These theories seem particularly appropriate where governments encounter formidable and armed domestic opponents. Even the strongest military government would be unwise to engage in wreckless (uncalculated) counterinsurgent activities in the face of skilled guerrilla or terrorist insurgents. However, the approach seems less appropriate to the study of unprovoked terror against compliant populations. The authoritarian regimes which ruled South America during the 1970s and early 1980s enjoyed unrivalled power. For instance, the share of defense in the Argentine central government budget increased 50 percent between 1975 (prior to the coup) and 1977 (a year after the coup). By 1982, military expenditures as a proportion of gross domestic product reached 8 percent, the highest in Latin America and in Argentine history.[8] A good portion of these sums went to internal security operations. Similar increases occured in Chile after the September 11 coup there. The armed forces were resource-rich while most of their opponents were not.

In a pure calculation of relative capabilities, the probability of success for the authorities should have been extremely high, and the degree of uncertainty surrounding both the capabilities of the opposition and the decisions to use terror should have been extremely low. The financial, moral and/or political costs of armed confrontation should also have been low. Political costs should have been especially low since, comparatively speaking, military regimes are much less preoccupied with public image and quick to confer upon themselves legitimacy with the assumption of state power and historic responsibilities. They are less likely to sense an erosion of support or morale as a result of repressive action. The sense of impending harm should subside as the risks and uncertainties are reduced, and even more so once terrorist practices commence. Yet scholarship indicates that the military's sense of insecurity seems to grow over time in proportion to its preoccupation with threat.[9]

This returns us to the question of threat perception. Why should the strong military regimes such as those found in Brazil and the Southern Cone of South America have perceived any threat at all? And why would they need to rely so much on terror to overcome those perceived threats?

Threat Perception: The Subjective Dimension

It is tempting to pass the military's fears off as a mere rationalization: the armed forces have simply created a pretext to justify the political murder of particular groups whom they wish eliminated. They devised an image of a nation besieged from without and from within by hostile revolutionary forces bent on the total destruction of the political and social order. This clever ruse disguises the regime's more focused political objectives.

Such an argument will not wash for two reasons. First, the ideas which sustained the image of a regime and nation at peril were not conveniently invented and espoused just prior to the onslaught of terror. They had permeated the ranks of the military years before, and were elaborated upon in military journals, speeches, and hemispheric security conferences. Secondly, despite the defeat of guerrilla forces in Argentina and Uruguay, and the defeat of the organized left in Chile, the armed forces did not abandon their views when no longer needed. Even during current episodes of relative calm under democratic rule, members of the armed forces in Argentina and Brazil have continued to repeat the same security themes. Perception in this instance appears to be conditioned by an image of reality formed independently of the objective environment or prior to the assimilation of information.[10]

Such perceptions, of course, do not emerge in a vacuum; they must be anchored in a belief system or ideology. Ideologies provide authoritative world views, with a general set of principles and arguments from which more specific policy positions can be deduced. The process of deduction is seductive to those who are wed to an ideology. Ideologies act as "maps" or "blueprints" of reality[11] for policymakers who would rather fall back on a few guiding principles than be forced to make numerous new judgments in an uncertain environment. Those "maps" sharpen some images of the political landscape while blurring others, facilitating the selection of information and the making of decisions by greatly simplifying a rather complex and problematic political situation.

Ideologies which are conceptually flawed, anachronistic, or simply incompatible with contemporary realities are sure to incorrectly "map" the political terrain and thus generate serious misperceptions. The more firmly perceptions have become embedded in doctrine, the more glaringly discordant they become with the observable world. Exaggerated or implausible accounts of national conditions are then fully internalized, and make the mistaken options (such as the excessive use of violence against complacent populations) seem imperative.[12]

The problem with ideological predispositions themselves is that, once formulated, they tend to persist unchanged. Growing disparities between old doctrines and modern realities makes it more likely that misperception will occur. "The easy thing is to predict today what you predicted yesterday," according to Knorr,[13] but it is also likely to cause serious errors in judgment. Unless policymakers are prepared to render new interpretations of old ideologies that are more relevant, or abandon them entirely, they are bound to become trapped within a cognitive and attitudinal shell from which they will not easily escape.

Conceivably, the ideologically driven regime could be acting rationally. Regimes with a missionary approach to politics and sufficient resource strength are more likely to discount current difficulties. Even where some uncertainty still surrounds the decision to resort to terror, that uncertainty will be counterbalanced by the vision of achieving the ultimate objectives associated with the ideological framework.[14] Thus, the missionary state will prefer state terror over other policy options since it perceives the costs of terrorist action to be minimal and the benefits of goal-oriented behavior to be extensive.[15]

Scholars have noted that mass murder is a calculated choice of policymakers[16] predicated upon the pursuit of specific objectives. As Fein argues,[17] (concerning genocidal acts, though her point bears relevance for state terror as well) such calculations are rational not insofar as they are reasonable, but to the extent that they are "goal oriented acts *from the point of view of their perpetrators*" (emphasis mine). Policymakers with strong ideological predispositions may logically take terror to be the most sensible instrument of policy for the achievement of desired ends.

To an ideologically minded military regime concerned about the security of the state, there is nothing necessarily inconsistent about obsessing over an opposition and pursuing state violence at any cost. The regime is so convinced of the enormity of the potential dangers facing the nation and of the overriding importance of achieving security, that it unleashes a wreckless and uncontrollable fury of political violence. The mission becomes so central a task that the uncertainties of action (where they exist) are displaced by the overriding, imperative achievement of final objectives.[18]

These arguments provide a means for conceptualizing the specific problem of ideology and terror in Latin America. The task is to demonstrate how the prevailing ideologies of Latin American authoritarian regimes helped to misguide policymakers towards the excessive and unnecessary use of force. Using Argentina as a test case, we will explore how the military's ideologically grounded and misinformed perceptions about national security risks and political oppositions were causal agents in the resort to state terror.

The Latin American National Security Ideology

Scholars concur that most Latin American armed forces of the 1960s and 1970s were under the strong influence of the National Security Doctrine (hereafter, NSD).[19] Though interpretations of the doctrine have differed, and though the doctrine is more variegated than convention would have it,[20] there are a set of core features of the doctrine which repeatedly emerge within the writings and pronouncements of Latin American officers.

In Argentina, for example, politicians, scholars and human rights advocates alike take it as an article of faith that the "Proceso" Government was principally inspired by this doctrine to launch a campaign of state terror against its rivals.[21] The prestigious Argentine National Commission on the Disappeared called the NSD "the doctrine behind the repression" in that country.[22] It is alleged that the armed forces' misplaced and exaggerated fears of opposition were driven by a doctrine that focused on the identification of conspiratorial threats to national security and which urged state leaders to engage in a form of permanent warfare against those security threats.

With roots planted in German, French, North American and Latin American military literature, the NSD is a set of ideas and principles about achieving national security. All states are security conscious. But within the NSD, national security assumes overwhelming proportions; it is the yardstick by which policy success is measured, and the beginning and the end of political life itself.[23] The state, as the central institution of society, is charged with guaranteeing that security, and state managers are therefore granted special prerogatives. States are thought of as brain centers of an organism and the public as cells who must cooperate if the "body politic" is to survive. Rudolf Kjellen (1864–1922) took the organic metaphor furthest, claiming that states were conscious, rational entities with interests, prejudices and an instinct for self preservation.[24] As political life-forms situated in a hostile environment, they must prevail over rivals in order to survive and do so by acquiring territory.

Though largely anachronistic in most parts of the world, a number of Latin American military officers, including General Augosto Pinochet of Chile, still take Kjellen's ideas seriously. Many observers have been surprised at the resurrection and retention of geopolitical themes in Latin American military literature after World War II. Largely discredited as a result of the defeat of Nazi Germany (whose leaders took geopolitical themes seriously), geopolitics seems to have found a receptive audience in South American military and non-military circles. However, owing to the difficulties of territorial acquisition, other Latin American strategists have transformed geopolitical thinking, shifting the focus from the conquest of physical space to the conquest of political space, while preserving the organic concept of the state.[25] To achieve security, states must organize and marshall their own natural and human resources. Geopolitical theorists are consequently preoccupied first with the integration of underdeveloped and ignored regions with centers of power, and secondly with the establishment of tight political control over all subjects within the territorial confines of the state.[26]

Perhaps the most pertinent borrowed doctrine is that of counterinsurgency. Counterinsurgency (CI) doctrine developed in the late 1950s in France and in the early 1960s in the U.S. in response to revolutionary warfare in Vietnam, Algeria and Cuba.[27] Having established rules for combatting rural guerrillas, it is often thought of as the operative arm of the NSD. Actually it is more than that. It is a conceptual framework that has extended and modified the rules of conventional war between states in order to combat an elusive and unconventional enemy that struggles from within. In war between states, regular forces would engage in direct combat in a clearly defined terrain for purposes of grasping and holding physical space. In guerrilla war, the enemy, using a mixture of regular, paramilitary and irregular forces, would attack and disperse, thereby avoiding direct engagements with the opposition, and remain well-intermingled with the population.[28]

Favorite targets of CI were "insurgents" or "subversives." These were clandestine operators who used their tactical expertise to undermine constitutional regimes. Since they were presumed to be highly skilled, dangerous, and unorthodox in their approach, counterinsurgency manuals provided detailed instructions to Latin American officers on how to combat these forces.[29] This was the operational arm of the doctrine. Though these internal "enemies of the state" fought differently than conventional forces, their battles were not waged in isolation. They were participants in an international revolutionary conspiracy against "Western civilization and ideals." Third World states were simply theaters of operations in a global confrontation.[30] Consequently, according to CI, internal wars would persist along with and in coordination with wars between states, and domestic subversion and international communism were two sides of the same coin.

CI was developed by the French and Americans in reaction to revolutionary struggles waged far from their shores. These were doctrines not intended for use against their own political subjects. Certainly, the possible success of revolutionary nationalist movements in Algeria and in Southeast Asia jeopardized French colonial holdings. But these movements posed no threat to the French Republic itself; nor did a potential Vietcong victory pose any direct threat to the U.S. Because CI was intended for use elsewhere, its proponents could afford to be somewhat callous in their conceptualization and application of the doctrine. The political fallout resulting from an unpopular anti-nationalist or anti-revolutionary campaign in Algeria was less likely to reach back to the homeland (or so they thought) and could therefore be more easily disregarded. The same could be said of the Americans who, blessed by distance, were able to treat Vietnam as a testing ground for new CI concepts like strategic hamlets which would never be tolerated at home.

The doctrine of counterinsurgency was purposefully universalistic in quality. It did not take into consideration the peculiarities of Third World countries. Dan Shafer points out that CI proponents operated according to the politics of principle: the correct application of sound ideas in any context would produce the desired effects.[31] The reality and constraints of local politics seemed to be a distant blur for CI experts, who were confident that CI held out the promise of development and stability for troubled societies if it were only faithfully administered.

Given such blindness to actual conditions, importation of CI by Latin American regimes was destined to produce problems. Spatially, the ideology of counterrevolution was twice-removed from Latin American reality. Not only were the fundamental principles devised by First World states, but they were intended for use in other parts of the Third World. Secondly, the ideas were temporally discordant. Created in the 1950s during the Cold War, by powers desparately trying to hold on to colonies and spheres of influence, they were now to be resurrected for application in the much changed world of the 1970s. Detente had replaced the Cold War and colonies were a thing of the past. How could regimes, whether authoritarian or democratic, adhere to antiquated, colonial-minded doctrines in the treatment of their own citizens? Of course, one solution would have been to amend CI in substantial ways so that it would conform to country-specific conditions. A "homegrown" version of CI would be equally distasteful to those desiring fundamental and radical change, but its chance of success would certainly be greater. Unfortunately, most Latin American regimes swallowed CI whole and unrevised.

Specifically, what was it about CI doctrine and its depiction of national security threats which was incongruent with the Latin American reality? Let us examine the Argentine case which, because it was somewhat typical of the region, will throw light on situations elsewhere.

The Argentine military government of the "Proceso de Reorganización Nacional" (PRN) ruled from 1976 to 1983. During this period, the authorities conducted a "dirty war" against alleged political opponents which left an estimated fifteen thousand citizens dead and unaccounted for, and which was marked by numerous acts of state terror, the most frequent of which was disappearance. Many of the Argentine generals were enamored with a doctrine which they had first been exposed to some twenty years before. The CI views made their way to Argentina during the late 1950s with the visit of French military missions to that country. Those officers who would later rule during the *Proceso* had their formative training and indoctrination into military life at about this time. The French were already entrenched in counterinsurgency operations in Algeria and Vietnam, could speak from experience, and thus were taken very seriously by these future heads of state. A flurry of articles (many authored by French officers) soon appeared in Argentine military journals such as the *Revista de la Escuela Superior de Guerra* warning of the country's vulnerability to international communism and preparing the country for countersubversive struggle. Writing in 1964, an Argentine colonel stated categorically that the hardline French views had thoroughly penetrated the Argentine armed forces at every rank.[32] Even then, the ideas seemed out of place. Immediately after the Cuban revolution, when Castro's victory sent shock waves through the Western

Hemisphere, Argentina had less to worry about than most countries. Castroite and Maoist-styled revolutionary movements which began to flourish in Peru, Colombia and Central America, did not appear in Argentina. Few Argentines at the time had any sympathies with communist parties or movements. The most progressive party with any clout was, of course, the labor-based Peronist Party. But its working class followers had rejected socialist ideals long ago. Its allegiances were to Perón and his pragmatic vision of a reformed but not overturned capitalist system. Reading the military journals at the time, one would have thought that Argentina was on the threshold of a revolution. Nothing could have been further from the truth. And for the most part, the fallacies of the "revolutionary threat" of the late 1950s and 1960s would be reproduced again in the 1970s.

By the 1970s, the situation had changed somewhat. With the birth of the Peronist-affiliated Montoneros, and the more radical ERP, (Ejército Revolucionario del Pueblo) Argentina was faced with a guerrilla resistance. Though numbering no more than a handful of student activists in 1970, the Montoneros made their presence dramatically known that year by assassinating General Pedro Aramburu just ten days before the ouster of then President General Juan Onganía.

At their peak in 1974 and 1975 the guerillas—those in uniform—were thought to number approximately five thousand against the Argentine armed forces which numbered 200,000. The guerillas were, at best, able to achieve a momentary stand-off with the state security forces in 1974 and through the first half of 1975, having inflicted 109 casualties and suffered 137 of their own.[33] By October of 1975 and then again in December of 1975, they had been firmly rebuked by the army in assaults against military arsenals. In the words of the army's commanding officer at the time, the failed guerrilla operation "demonstrated the absolute impotence of the terrorist organizations with respect to their presumed military power."[34] During 1976, the guerrillas were reduced to committing random acts of urban terror, and by 1977, had all but ceased to function as an organization. A year after the March 1976 coup, the guerrillas reported two thousand of their own killed—a crippling blow from which they would never recover.[35]

Misperceptions

A Popular Revolution

The military's erroneous impressions about the guerrillas were based less on evidence and more on caricatures of revolutionaries in general. It presumed, first of all, that the rebel units had found significant support within the general population. Borrowing a page from Mao's *Strategies of War*,[36] the armed forces were convinced that the rebel defeats in late 1975 meant only that the guerrillas had staged a tactical retreat. Falling back into base areas with sympathetic populations, they were preparing for a counteroffensive. They would strike again unexpectedly, exploiting the military's moments of weakness, as Mao had suggested.

The presumption that the guerrillas had significant mass support was unfounded. Though the Montoneros' daring exploits attracted some supporters and admirers, they did so at the expense of well-grounded political actions.[37] Ironically, their organizational and behavioral principles were more akin to those of the military than to a reputable, vanguard revolutionary movement. They spoke in terms of combat readiness, firepower, formations, logistical support, and strict obedience. They lost sight of the Maoist principle that revolution is won with the masses; that the revolutionaries should be primarily concerned with the daily, practical problems of the public; and that armed struggle was one component of the process but was no substitute for ongoing grassroots political work.[38] For these reasons, they could never make significant inroads with the working class whom they would have to depend upon were they to assume the leadership role in a left-leaning Peronist movement. In general, their romantically naive visions of achieving an Argentine socialism through Perón and their wreckless armed attacks against military and police installations dissuaded most Argentines from affiliating with them.[39]

Disguised Subversives

The military, by their own pronouncements, had made it clear that, by the end of 1976, the guerrillas could not function as organized combat forces. If so, then in what form would they launch their counteroffensive? Desiring to preserve the image of the cunning revolutionary, the armed forces believed that the rebels, once having won over the population through persuasion and intimidation, had easily infiltrated into legal, social, and political organizations. The general populace was thought to be weak, malleable, and incapable of resisting the rebel's pull. An officer of the navy commented:

> There will be no lasting reorganization or recuperation in our country while there are subversive elements engaged in destroying the country at all levels . . . not while the Argentine adolescents and youth continue to be deceived and subtly taken over by subversive organizations with lyrical siren songs that hide the foreign origin of subversion and the real objectives which they pursue.[40]

The vulnerable public did not and could not become the object of the military's own campaign to win hearts and minds. The armed forces believed that the public had been so thoroughly and successfully "infected" with the "Marxist curse" that there was no choice but to launch a general offensive against the entire population in an effort to weed out the rebels. *The Argentine citizenry had become the enemy.* Here, the Argentine generals were following in the footsteps of Roger Trinquier, a leading French proponent of state terror during the Algerian war, who argued that humanitarian endeavors were wasted on a public that is "infected by clandestine organisms that penetrate like a cancer into its midst . . . ."[41] Colonel Trinquier was one of the first to acknowledge that proper identification of an enemy that is so well assimilated into society would be extremely difficult, thus issuing a license for less discriminate campaigns of state violence like the Argentine "dirty war."

Operating in disguised form, the revolutionaries—with the forced cooperation of various social and political groups—were launching the next phase of the struggle. Each succeeding phase would elevate the level of conflict, moving from numerous but limited engagements to mass insurrection to revolutionary warfare. It was the mission of the armed forces to prevent Argentina from becoming the "single spark that ignites the prairie fire."[42] Again this perception about disguised, then escalating conflict simply conformed to standard Maoist precepts about dispersion, movement, levels of conflict and greater wars.[43] But it had little or nothing to do with Argentine reality.

A Permanent War

The junta was convinced that the chameleon-like transformations of the subversives prolonged their life span. They could survive indefinitely under the protective cover of diverse legal organizations. Ramón Camps, chief of the Buenos Aires Police during the height of the dirty war, and himself personally responsible for the disappearance and death of some two thousand prisoners, stated, "You always have a latent element which awaits an opportune moment to reappear . . . This is the thesis of Vo Nguyen Giap and of Mao Tse-tung."[44] For the generals, the counter-subversive struggle was a permanent, total war against an elusive foe.[45] They were convinced they were participants in a war of global proportions; a third world war between east and west and between two different ways of life. Argentina was one critical theatre of operations. The war was also an irregular one, with the line between belligerents and non-belligerents and between wartime and peacetime blurred. One could never place spatial or temporal limits on the confrontation.

Democratic Vulnerability

Given the enduring nature of this threat, the state would have to remain forever vigilant, and could do so only through an authoritarian political structure. For this reason, the military was not pleased with the resumption of democratic practices in 1984, believing that only authoritarian governments had the will needed to fight the subversives. Characteristically, Camps and soldiers like him came out of retirement to invent new forms of democratic-styled subversion to worry the politicians with. Absurdly they claimed that exiled guerrillas had won the allegiance of European and U.S. officials who were now participants in the campaign to disparage Argentina. In other instances, they would take isolated domestic disruptions and link these to imaginary, global, Soviet-inspired plots.[46] But most significantly, the generals convinced themselves that the revolutionary terrorists occupied legitimate positions within the political, social, economic and legal framework: they were members of Congress, the administration, the courts, the major political parties and the media. Practicing the politics of *"entrismo"* (entering) these rebels inserted themselves into the democratic process so as to undermine and overturn it. Democratic leaders such as Raul Alfonsín had been duped into believing the war against subversion was over. He was wrong; it had only changed form.

Abandoning Politics

Believing themselves to be at war, the Argentine generals were then free to allow the logic of war to mold their views of civil society. This produced a simplistic and dichotomous view of the Argentine polity. All those who refused to demonstrate loyalty to the military and its government were declared in opposition to the regime, the state, and the nation itself. Furthermore, those placed in opposition were treated as implacable enemies of the state who were to be eliminated rather than won over. Typical of states at war, political foes were characterized in dehumanizing terms. They were referred to as "subversives or ter-rorists," terms normally reserved for those thought to be unscrupulous in their tactics and irredeemably immoral in character. Willing to resort to any means to pursue ignominious ends, these foes could not be trusted to abide by negotiated settlements, or indeed be permitted to survive even as a vanquished member of society. Only their complete extermination would satisfy the military's absolutist thirst for total security. Unwilling to admit that relations with political foes could improve, that adversaries on one issue could be allies on another, or that dissidents could redeem themselves, the distinctive character of this view was that it was politically blind and tended "to accelerate compulsively to the point of greatest violence."[47]

Conclusion

The Argentine military's stereotypical conception of the revolutionary movement—one which is ubiquitous, chameleon-like and perpetually lethal—denied it the opportunity to establish support with large segments of the population who themselves were opposed to the guerrillas. The military ended up preying upon the very populations it could have served. As if a participant in a tragic comedy of perceptual errors, the military predicated each of its terrorist acts on a false image of an enemy which did not exist. The wholesale slaughter of fifteen thousand citizens was committed in the name of defending the nation against a threat of global proportions which was anything but global.

The military had incorrectly judged the opposition in terms of its numbers, location, strength, strategies, legitimacy, and purposes. This was a pitiful performance for an institution trained to carefully assess the intentions and capabilities of its foes. But it is understandable, given the fact that judgments were based not on evidence but on preconceptions—ones which themselves were embedded in antiquated and inappropriate doctrines borrowed from others. The military took the easy way out. Rather than designing a new political strategy to overcome the instability of the Peronist years and to build for themselves a new constituency of supporters which could have legitimized their rule, they instead consumed a doctrine of war and resorted to the use of state violence. General Carlos Suárez Mason, former commander of the First Army Corps in Argentina and considered the Adolf Eichmann of his country, said the following when reflecting upon his previous life in the armed forces:

> I like the military way of living. You don't have to think about what you do; you have some regulations you have to follow.[48]

Suárez Mason's comment is revealing in the sense that it displayed an intellectual laziness shared by all the commanders of the armed forces. Unfortunately, his statement does not go far enough. It was not only the controlled, hierarchical environment of the military which was comforting to men like him, but the fact that they all could and did fall back upon a few simple principles to guide them in their behavior. Mason and his fellow officers relied on an ideological "map" which clearly displayed the political world for them. They made little effort to confirm or disconfirm their images of reality. This was manifested in their complete lack of interest in bringing hard evidence to bear against those arrested, tortured, and then executed for political reasons.[49] Specific charges were rarely made. Instead the military relied on a rhetorical litany of accusations about revolutionary activity, subversive connections and terrorist plots for which there was no defense. The ideology which cultivated these propagandistic responses was reassuring to its followers, but terribly costly for the Argentine and Latin American public.

Notes

1. Ernest Duff and John McCamant, *Violence and Repression in Latin America: A Quantitative and Historical Analysis* (New York: The Free Press, 1976), 51.

2. John Simpson and John Bennett, *The Disappeared and the Mothers of the Plaza: The Story of the 11,000 Argentinians Who Vanished* (New York: St. Martin's Press, 1985), 76.

3. The Argentine National Commission documented nine thousand cases but believes the actual figure to be much higher. Some estimates range as high as fifteen thousand and another five thousand who were murdered and identified and thus not classified as disappeared. See The Argentine National Commission on the Disappeared, *Nunca Mas* (New York: Farrar, Straus, Giroux, 1986), 5.

4. R. Cohen, *Threat Perception in International Crisis* (Madison, Wis.: University of Wisconsin Press, 1979), 4.

5. J. D. Singer, "Threat Perception and the Armament Tension Dilemma," *Journal of Conflict Resolution* 2 (1958): 93–94.

6. Duff and McCamant, 25.

7. Raymond Duvall and Michael Stohl, "Governance by Terror," in *The Politics of Terrorism*, 2d. ed., ed. Michael Stohl (New York: Marcel Dekker, 1983), 201–210.

8. Adrian English, *Armed Forces of Latin America* (New York: Jane's Publications, 1984).

9. David Pion-Berlin, "The National Security Doctrine, Military Threat Perception and the 'Dirty War' in Argentina," *Comparative Political Studies* 21 (October 1988): 382–407.

10. K. Knorr, *Historical Dimensions of National Security Problems* (Kansas City: University Press of Kansas, 1976), 84.

11. Clifford Geertz, *Local Knowledge: Further Essays in Interpretive Anthropology* (New York: Basic Books, 1983).

12. For example, Arendt powerfully describes how the Nazis' fictionalized accounts of demonic Jewish plots were turned into cardinal principles of state, turning the extermination of Jews into a matter of historical necessity. She explains: "The assumption of a Jewish world conspiracy was transformed by totalitarian propaganda from an objective, arguable matter into the chief element of the Nazi reality; the point was that the Nazis *acted* as though the world were dominated by Jews and needed a counterconspiracy to defend itself"

[Hannah Arendt, *The Origins of Totalitarianism* (New York: Harcourt, Brace, 1950), 352]. In fact, scholars lament the fact that Mein Kampf was not taken seriously enough at the time it was published. An appreciation for the power of written ideas may have sent warning signals to the rest of the world about Hitler's future intentions.

13. Knorr, 113.

14. Leo Kuper, *Genocide: Its Political Uses in the Twentieth Century* (New Haven: Yale University Press, 1981).

15. Duvall and Stohl.

16. Helen Fein, *Accounting for Genocide* (New York: The Free Press, 1979).

17. Fein, 8.

18. Kuper, 84–100.

19. J. Comblin, *The Church and the National Security State* (New York: Orbis Books, 1979); R. Calvo, "The Church and the Doctrine of National Security," *Journal of Interamerican Studies and World Affairs* 21 (1979): 69–88; Genaro H. Arriagada, "National Security Doctrine in Latin America," *Peace and Change: A Journal of Peace Research* (Winter 1980): 49–60; José Tapia Valdéz, *El Terrorismo de Estado: La Doctrina de la Seguridad Nacional en el Cono Sur* (Mexico: Editorial Nueva Imagen, 1980.

20. David Pion-Berlin, "Latin American National Security Doctrines: Hard and Softline Themes," *Armed Forces and Society* 15 (Spring 1989): 411–429.

21. This author conducted some twenty interviews with military officers, aides to President Alfonsín, congressional staff members, political party officials and human rights advocates. When asked about the impact of the National Security Doctrine, every respondent insisted that it played a fundamental role in shaping the mind set of the Argentine military.

22. Comisión Nacional Sobre la Desaparición de Personas (CONADEP), *Nunca Más* (Buenos Aires: EUDEBA, 1986), 473.

23. George A. Lopez, "National Security Ideology as an Impetus to State Violence and State Terror," in *Governmental Violence and Repression: An Agenda for Research*, ed. Michael Stohl and George Lopez (Westport, Conn.: Greenwood Press, 1986).

24. See General Golbery Do Cuoto E Silva, *Geopolítica del Brasil* (Mexico: El Cid Editor, 1978), 47. Kjellen took exception with the founder of geopolitics, Friedrich Ratzel (1844–1904), who said that the organic metaphor is imperfect and must be so, since states include individuals whose existence could never be reduced to a dependent part of an organism. A contemporary exponent of Kjellen's strict organic view is General Augusto Pinochet. See his book *Geopolítica* (Santiago, Chile: Editorial Gabriela Mistral, 1968).

25. Genaro H. Arriagada, *El Pensamiento Político de Los Militares* (Chile: Centro de Investigaciones Socioeconómicas, 1981), 122.

26. Ibid., 117–118; J. Comblin, "La Doctrina de La Seguridad Nacional," *Mensaje* 25, no. 2 (1976): 98.

27. R. Trinquier, *Modern Warfare: A French View of Counterinsurgency* (New York: Frederick A. Praeger, 1964); Walt W. Rostow, "Guerrilla Warfare in Underdeveloped Areas," in *The Guerrilla and How to Fight Him*, ed. Lt. Col. T.

N. Greene (New York: Praeger Publishers, 1962); Alexis Johnson, "Internal Defense and the Foreign Service," *Foreign Service Journal* 39 (1962): 20–24; Department of the Army, *Field Manual 1-16 Counterguerrilla Operations* (Washington, D.C.: Department of the Army, 1967).

28. U.S. Army, *Field Manual.*

29. Michael Klare and Cynthia Arnson, "Exporting Repression: U.S. Support for Authoritarianism in Latin America," in *Capitalism and the State in U.S.-Latin American Relations,* ed. Richard Fagen (Stanford: Stanford University Press, 1979).

30. Ramón Camps, "Interview," *La Semana* (Buenos Aires) 2 June 1983, 8–11.

31. Michael D. Shafer, *Deadly Paradigms: The Failure of U.S. Counterinsurgency Policy* (Princeton: Princeton University Press, 1988), 136–137.

32. Colonel Mario Horacio Orsolini is quoted in G. Arriagada, *El Pensamiento Político,* p. 186.

33. Richard Gillespie, *Soldiers of Perón: Argentina's Montoneros* (Oxford: Oxford University Press,1982), 215.

34. Daniel Frontalini and Maria Cristina Caiati, *El Mito de la Guerra Sucia* (Buenos Aires: Centro de Estudios Legales y Sociales, 1984), 66.

35. Gillespie, 38.

36. Mao Tse-tung, *Selected Works of Mao Tse-Tung,* vols. 1 and 2. (Peking: Foreign Language Press, 1975), 213.

37. Gillespie.

38. Mao Tse-tung, 147.

39. Gillespie.

40. Joint Publication Research Service, no. 68361, 26 November 1976, p. 5.

41. Trinquier, 49.

42. Mao Tse-tung.

43. Mao Tse-tung, 79–112.

44. Camps, "Interview," 8.

45. Comblin, "La Doctrina," 99; Erich Von Ludendorff, *La Guerra Total* (La Paz, Bolivia: Editorial Renacimiento, 1941); Arriagada, *El Pensamiento Político,* 195–196.

46. Ramón Camps, article in *La Prensa,* 19 May 1986.

47. Arriagada, "National Security Doctrine," 58.

48. Camille Peri, "Getting to Know the Lord of Life and Death," *Mother Jones* 13 (September 1988): 38.

49. CONADEP.

9

Violent Repression
in the Third Reich:
Did It Stabilize Hitler's Rule?

Bernd Wegner

To what extent did violent repression help to stabilize Hitler's rule? The answer to this question is linked to one of the most controversial issues faced by historians of the Third Reich during the last fifteen years, namely, Was Hitler's dictatorship stable? To provide a better understanding of the subject and its wider, historical context, this paper will discuss the general issue of stability before turning to the more specific question of the importance of violence in maintaining stability.

I

During the first two decades after World War II, historians hardly questioned the inner stability of the Nazi regime. For those who had personally experienced the rule of the Third Reich, whatever their role might have been, the daily experience of the omnipotence of National Socialism was vivid enough to make any doubt about the stability and strength of the regime appear absurd. Unlike any other system, except, perhaps, Stalin's Russia, the National Socialist rule was seen as an omnipresent Moloch controlling virtually all key functions of state and society, a precursor of the Orwellian world of "1984." The will and the arbitrary decisions of an overwhelmingly superior "Führer" controlled this world. The National Socialist state possessed and projected a self-image of being all powerful. Thus, for instance, the status of the "Führer" was defined in the late thirties by E.R. Huber, a leading constitutional law expert, as follows:

The Führer unites in his person all the sovereign authority of the Reich;
all public authority, both in the state and in the movement, is derived
from the Führer authority. If we want to describe political authority in
the *Völkisch Reich* correctly, we must not speak of "state authority" but
of "Führer authority." [. . .] Führer authority is not protected by safeguards
and controls, but is free and independent, exclusive and unrestricted.[1]

Given this perception of the Führer's role, which remained the
predominant interpretation even in the early postwar era, historians,
political scientists, and the public naturally concentrated primarily on
questions about the mechanisms by which rule was exercised, and on
how it was possible to convert a modern industrial society as complex
as the Weimar republic into a totalitarian "Führer" state. As signified
by the term "National Socialist Tyranny" (*Gewaltherrschaft*), coercion,
violence and terror were assumed to be instruments of decisive importance
for such a rapid transformation. Similarly, it was assumed that the
regime's maintenance of control until the very last day of the war was
the result of a progressively perfected system of repression. From this
perspective, the failure of the Nazi regime in 1945 was not caused by
its own inadequacy, but by the superiority of its external enemies who
were provoked, it is true, by Hitler's boundless quest for power.

These assumptions remained unchallenged for a long time, partly
because an emphasis on the terrorist character of the regime provided
the survivor generation with an argument to justify their own failures
and their participation in an unjust society. Research since the mid-
sixties has challenged this image of the Third Reich; in particular, the
concept of the regime as a monolithic block designed as a permanent
formation has proven to be deceptive. An increasing number of detailed
studies on various sectors of the state and society have shown that there
was a chaotic labyrinth of authorities and activities, competing with
and fighting against each other behind the facade, maintained by National
Socialist propaganda, of a *"Volksgemeinschaft"* (people's community)
centered on the person of the Führer.[2] A jungle of intertwined and
contradictory responsibilities existed at all levels of the National Socialist
government, making it difficult for historians to determine Hitler's role
in the control of the state. Consequently, two schools of thought have
developed: the "intentionalist" and the "functionalist."

The "intentionalists" hold that Hitler's power "could hardly be exaggerated."[3] The dictator used his power in a planned manner from the
beginning in order to realize his "Final Aims," (*Endziele*) as laid down
in his book *Mein Kampf* long before he assumed power. In particular,
the foreign and war policy of the Nazi state showed Hitler's hand so
clearly, despite all his tactical tricks, that any qualification in characterizing

the way Hitler exercised power is out of the question.[4] It is true that the polycratic structure of the administrative system, which is undisputed even among "intentionalists," impaired, at times, the efficiency of policy implementation; but in the end it proved to be prerequisite for establishing Hitler's absolute rule. Adhering to the principle of *"divide et impera"* (divide and rule) the dictator deliberately had restricted the operational capacity of the state machinery from the beginning in order to emphasize and enhance his personal responsibility and to create a chaos that could only be mastered by him.

The arguments of the "functionalist school" are entirely different. Inspired, particularly, by research done on the subject of domestic state policy of the Third Reich, functionalists portray Hitler's role from the perspective of the regime's exercise of power in practice rather than from the perspective of its ideology. In doing so, they agree with the "intentionalists" on the fact that Hitler gradually was able "to rid himself of all constitutional and bureaucratic restraints," until his position had become absolutely unassailable.[5] The "functionalists," however, hold that the consequence of this unique concentration of power was by no means a consolidation of the government machine as Hitler's conservative allies had hoped.

On the contrary, Mommsen,[6] a leading functionalist, stated that

the system experienced a process of disintegration due to Hitler's haphazard style of leadership which had evolved during his rise to power. While his readiness to improvise and to appoint new men for special tasks had proved to be highly successful during the *"Kampfzeit,"* [i.e. the period before 1933] these methods turned out to have disastrous consequences once they were applied to the governmental machine as a whole. Bureaucratic procedures were ignored and no overall planning or evaluation of priorities in the domestic field ever took place. Instead, an increasing number of ad hoc institutions were created for special purposes, but without clearly defined responsibilities. A general struggle for power ensued, in particular for Hitler's favors at the expense of rivals. This gave rise to emergency situations of all kinds,

which in turn led to a process of what Mommsen calls "cumulative radicalization," based on the assumed *"Führerwillen."*

Mommsen argues that Hitler should be seen as "the initiator of a chain of self-generating impulses which led to the systematic disintegration of the political and social fabric of society."[7] From this perspective, the breakdown of the Third Reich was not just the result of military defeat, but the logical consequence of the regime's excessive dynamism operating without restraints until the collapse of the regime.

The implications of such contrary interpretations of Hitler's power within the Third Reich for the evaluation of the National Socialist policy of repression are obvious. If the Third Reich is seen primarily as "Hitler's state," as it is by the "intentionalists," then the terror exerted by the regime was primarily an instrument, perhaps even the most important one, for stabilizing the Führer dictatorship. However, if the functionalist approach is adopted, the question arises whether the increase of Nazi terror up to industrialized genocide was indeed a process that was controlled deliberately by Hitler (or Himmler) or, rather, an example of the "cumulative radicalization" inherent in the nature of Nazi rule. If the latter is true, the value of terror in stabilizing the system is doubtful. Unfortunately, the following analysis will show that repression in the Third Reich is too complex a phenomenon to answer this question easily.

II

The insight that was gained during the past twenty years into the polycratic structure of the Third Reich has resulted in a re-evaluation of the Nazi terror, and in the addition of certain qualifications to descriptions of its role; but this has not been done in such a way as to make the horrors appear less extensive or less important today than they did in the past. On the contrary, the loss of personal memories due to the gradual disappearance of the generation directly concerned has been replaced, if not compensated for, by an increasingly intensive examination of the various forms and consequences of terror. The subjects of "persecution and resistance" have developed into a prime theme of German historians of the Third Reich as is evident in an abundance of studies on local history. The emphasis today, however, is put much more on repression, persecution and terror *in relationship* to other factors contributing to the ability of the regime to function. Everyday life in the Third Reich is characterized by inseparable combinations of coercion *and* concession, fear *and* hope, threat *and* bribery.[8] Thus, for instance, not all groups within society were equally exposed to the threat of terror, for it was impossible to threaten permanently the entire German people.

Most importantly, a universal terror was not even necessary, as a great deal of the German population, and presumably the majority during the last prewar years, may be assumed to have approved in principle of Hitler's rule, regardless of widespread discontent with the party.[9] The inclination to adapt to the standards of the regime was encouraged by Hitler's success, primarily in foreign policy, but also in his economic and social policies, particularly in reducing unemployment. Even those groups of the population representing potential opponents, such as the over thirteen million voters of the German Social-Democratic Party (SPD) and the German Communist Party (KPD) in 1932, were by no means forced only by brute violence to accept the new order. Instead, the regime attempted to bribe those groups potentially threatened by terror by moral and material means. A typical example is the forced disruption of the German labor unions in the spring of 1933, which was accompanied, not only by the establishment of a National Socialist substitute organization (the German Labor Front), but also by the designation of 1 May as a national holiday, something the unions had striven for in vain for generations.

In addition, open terror against the German population usually was exercised on an exemplary basis only. During the destruction of the organized labor movement, violence was used only against a limited number of activists, most of them socialist and labor union functionaries. Especially in the early stage of the regime, these measures, such as sending people to concentration camps, were often publicly announced in the press to increase the effect of the deterrence: "concentration camps were not intended for *everyone*, but they could be used to incarcerate *anyone*."[10]

There were exceptions to this rule, however, the most important of which concerned the so called "Rassefeind" (racial enemy), which meant primarily Jews, gypsies, and later, Slavs as well. The purely political opponent was regarded as the victim of wrong ideologies and thus as a suitable addressee for propaganda. According to National Socialist understanding, however, every single *"Fremdrassiger"* (ethnic foreigner) was a *"Volksfeind"* (enemy of the people) merely by virtue of his biological existence. As he could not be released from his hereditary role, either by means of deterrence or by re-education, it was necessary to oppress him, deprive him of his rights, and exclude him from the *"Volksgemeinschaft."*[11] The conquest of Poland and large parts of European Russia, beginning in the summer of 1941, brought tens of millions of such "racial enemies" under the yoke of National Socialism—an event which could almost be said to have made likely a further barbarization of the German rule, if not genocide itself.

III

The expansion of Nationalist Socialist terror over vast parts of the continent was possible only because of the control and progressive perfecting of the repression machine of the Third Reich during the years before the unleashing of the war. Within a few weeks after Hitler's appointment as Chancellor of the Reich on 30 January 1933, the most important fundamental rights guaranteed by the Weimar constitution, such as freedom of the press, free speech, freedom of assembly, and privacy of letters had been repealed. Parliament too had been deprived of its central authority in legislation and in monitoring the government. Early in May, labor unions were disrupted, and two months later, all parties except the NSDAP were disbanded or prohibited. Thus it took hardly six months to establish a single-party-state dictatorship in Germany, substantially less time than required in other similar cases (e.g. Italy).

Revolutionary as it might seem at first sight, this process took place within the framework of the existing social and political fabric. The organs of public administration were not abolished and replaced by Nazi establishments. Indeed, the latter developed in parallel with existing government authorities. The cooperation as well as the counter-operation of these machineries working by entirely different rules led to the "dual state" that Ernst Fränkel[12] was soon able to depict so impressively. Nowhere was the dual state's function better exemplified than in the practice of repression. Here, the distinction between the force exercised by the traditional executive organs of government and the seemingly spontaneous street terror of the NSDAP's SA (storm troopers) was practically dissolved from the start. The activities of the latter took place without punishment and were even legitimized by the fact that storm troopers were officially employed as an auxiliary police force.

A similar example of the amalgamation of governmental and non-governmental forces is evident in the case of the SS. Originally a bodyguard and National Socialist Party police force, this organization independently established armed formations in 1933–34 ("Politische Bereitschaften" or "political alarm squads") without any legal foundation. They were employed as an auxiliary police, trained and paid by the regular state police.[13]

Yet this was only the beginning of a much more dramatic development: Himmler's SS managed to establish a monopoly position in the field of internal security of the regime. This monopoly was principally based on three instruments of power at the disposal of the SS: the secret service (Sicherheitsdienst), the police, and the concentration camps (including its armed guards, the so called "Totenkopfverbände"). All of these subgroups expanded rapidly in size and competence. The secret service, for example, founded by Heydrich in 1931, managed to monopolize all intelligence activities within the NS movement by 1934, and in 1938, it began to penetrate the state administration. It had its finest hour in February 1944, when it took over the Wehrmacht's espionage agency, the Abwehr, which, under the command of Admiral Canaris, had been the only counter-intelligence organization not controlled by the SS.[14]

The development of concentration camps was even more remarkable. After the so-called "Roehm Putsch" in the summer of 1934, all camps were put under the command of the SS and a special administration was established, headed by Theodor Eicke, a former commander of the Dachau concentration camp. Using this camp as a model, Eicke, within a few years, developed a centralized and strictly regulated repressive machine.[15] He also organized special armed units, the Death's Head Units (*SS-Totenkopfverbände*), for guarding the camps. By early 1939 its force was almost nine thousand strong. The most important aspect of this development was that, by establishing the concentration camp system, the SS gave itself a freedom of action that was independent of the existing law and administration of justice. This meant that, in practice, anybody could be arrested at any time and sent to a concentration camp indefinitely without any legal proceeding, or even after being discharged by a court. This lack of legal security, more than the calculable, albeit rigid and unjust laws of the Third Reich, helped to intimidate the German people and cripple the forces of opposition.

The SS's most significant power was in its domination and eventual assimilation of the police force. Himmler obtained authority over the police in several steps: first, he gained control over the secret police (*Politische Polizei*) in the German *Länder* during 1933–34; then through his appointment as "*Reichsführer-SS und Chef der Deutschen Polizei*" in 17 June 1936, he integrated the police forces into the administrative structure of the SS. Himmler's aim was to form a complete amalgamation of both organizations, a gigantic "State Protection Corps" (*Staatsschutzkorps*).[16] For at least two reasons, this meant a complete change of constitutional principles. The police traditionally had formed part of the jurisdiction of the German *Länder*. Himmler's appointment as Chief of the German Police constituted a centralization of the police by the Reich's authorities. Here, as in many other fields, National Socialist rule led to an end of federalism. Furthermore, the fusion of police and SS meant the amalgamation of a state authority with an organization of the Nazi Party. Consequently, the SS enjoyed many privileges usually reserved for the public administration, and the police force was threatened with a loss of its character as an organization of public service by becoming an instrument of the Führer's will.

IV

Considering the foregoing, it is of central importance for the understanding of National Socialist repression to ask whether it is justified at all to talk about "*state* organized terror" with regard to the repression practiced by these authorities, which, as with the SS, and to an increasing extent the police, ultimately received their legitimation from the Führer's personal will. There is no doubt that Hitler, according to the National

Socialists, did not derive his authority from his official function as Chancellor of the Third Reich, but from his presumed historical mission as "leader of the German people."[17] Consequently, in the course of his term of office, the title of "Chancellor of the Reich" in contrast to that of "Führer" was less and less frequently used and was eventually dropped altogether. The title of "President of the Reich," pertaining to an additional function assumed by Hitler after Hindenburg's death in 1934, was never used by him at all. Hitler also never felt bound by the formally imposed restrictions on the power of the Chancellor or the President of the Reich. The actions of the Third Reich, and in particular, the activities of the SS, can therefore be considered only to a certain extent as the policy of *government* organs. They can be characterized more aptly as terror activities of a political movement using the governmental apparatus as a means of power.

This conclusion does not alter by any means the moral and legal liability of the German state. It is quite obvious that the effectiveness of the National Socialist terror was greatly increased by "disguising" it as government action. Street terror exercised without restraint and illegal concentration camps existing until 1934 and directed by the SA were replaced by forms of repression that were more and more bureaucratic. Open personal aggression towards ideological opponents gave way to quasi-state organized action which was not less arbitrary, but far more effective.

Psychologically, the utilization of the state's traditional instruments of power facilitated the exercise of terror. Conceiving that they were carrying out their duty in government service enabled personnel to perform their function in concentration camps or extermination camps without entering into a personal relationship with the victims and thus lessened the burden on their conscience.[18] Thus it was important for non-governmental institutions to give themselves a governmental appearance. The SS, for instance, was far-reaching in its adaptations of military customs and behavior, from uniforms to military-like organization of their units and adoption of the military's rules of order and obedience. Theodor Eicke, the Inspector General of concentration camps, had his letterheads imprinted as early as before the war with the saying, "There is only one thing in effect: the order!" He demanded that his men be prepared to exterminate even their closest relatives if they violated the wishes of Hitler.[19] Himmler used to call himself and his men "soldiers" even though the SS, except for the units of the Waffen-SS or Armed-SS, were a mere party organization without any military function. Thus, during a speech delivered in November 1938, Himmler explained the following with regard to the SS Death's Head Units (*SS-Totenkopfverbände*):

The *Totenkopverbände* were established from the guards in the concentration camps. Of course, they have, and I think that is our mission, become a troop; from jailors they developed into soldiers. I am convinced that in all things we do, we'll become soldiers sooner or later. This will be so in administration, it was the case with the guard troops and it is the same with the secret and criminal police. We always become soldiers, not military, but soldiers.[20]

Himmler's words are typical of the tendency within National Socialism to transfer military principles into political life. Soon after World War I, mushrooming paramilitary corps (*Freikorps*) already had demonstrated how political dispute should be conducted like war campaigns.[21] In the ideology of National Socialism, this attitude had then been condensed to "political soldiery" (*politisches Soldatentum*), a key to understanding the policy of repression in the Third Reich.

Central to "political soldiering" was the notion of struggle (*Kampf*) in both individual and collective life. Struggle was not seen as a contest regulated by a set of definite rules and dedicated to achieving an assigned objective as, for example, in sports or in eighteenth century warfare, but as a struggle for existence (*Daseinskampf*). This concept of struggle, influenced by traditions of social Darwinism, is well expressed in Hitler's own book:

As a rule, the [National Socialist] movement will educate its members so that they do not see the struggle as something engaged in with reluctance, but as the personal goal they have striven for. Thus they will not fear the hostility of the enemies but view it as the prerequisite for their own right to exist. They will not be afraid of the hatred of the enemies of our nationality and our ideology but they will yearn for it.[22]

According to this view of "struggle," it was always the stronger one only who could have the (moral) law on his side. Struggle also determined the opponents' historical right to exist. If the German people were not prepared, then, to stand up for their own self-preservation, as Hitler stated ten years later, "it may very well disappear!"[23] Consequently, a National Socialist who took his ideology seriously was a *"Kämpfer"* (fighter, warrior) by nature, and it was in this sense that he called himself a "soldier" or, more precisely, a "political soldier" (*politischer Soldat*).

It is obvious that soldiering of this kind had little in common with soldiering as a military profession. The fundamental difference was the target of their force. The professional military man used force at a clearly defined time, i.e. in war, and against a clearly defined external enemy. The "political soldier," on the other hand, had enemies everywhere, both inside and outside Germany. In his view, Marxism, "plutocracy," freemasonry and Christianity were nothing other than different faces of one universal threat, the focal point of which became the Jew. The Jew was simply the common denominator of all possible adversaries of National Socialism. Because of this view, the SS man's perception of the world became extremely bi-polar and one-dimensional. As a high-ranking SS officer said in 1939, months before the outbreak of the war,

[The SS] is never tired, is never satisfied, it never lays down its arms, it is always on duty, always ready to parry the enemy's blows and to fight back. For the SS there is only one [!] enemy, the enemy of Germany, there is only one [!] friend, the German people.[24]

This totalitarian ingroup-outgroup ideology of the SS abolished the differences between internal and external enemies and, as a consequence, those between war and peace, and between military and civilian life. As the enemy was ever present, it had to be fought at any time and in any place. Thus it is not surprising to find Himmler, for example, in his wartime speeches, comparing the war to the National Socialist struggle for power during the Weimar period. For him, as for many other Nazi leaders, there was no difference in principle between the political and military struggle. They were the same struggle against the same enemy, fought only by different means and on different battlefields.

Thus, repression and, if necessary, extermination of the political enemy was conducted in the uncompromising and brutal manner typical of any war. It is significant that in replying to critical remarks of individual SS members concerning the illegal execution of prisoners in the concentration camps, Inspector General Eicke explained, even before the war, that "the extermination of the state enemy at home is as much a duty as the destruction of an enemy outside at the front and therefore can never be called disgraceful." Any contrary opinion, according to Eicke, was a relic from a bourgeois world that had been overcome by the revolution of Adolf Hitler.[25]

V

The use of coercion and terror not only served the pragmatic purposes of staying in power, it also appealed to the National Socialist's understanding of the nature of social relations. The only possible attitude of the Nazi towards anybody of a different political opinion was to fight him. This meant that the question of how to deal with opponents of the regime was usually decided in favor of the most radical, that is, the most violent solution. During the initial years of the Third Reich, this trend had a stabilizing effect on the regime, if only because it enabled the new rulers to rid themselves of their numerous early opponents, rapidly and permanently. In doing so, they enjoyed support from major segments of the population for whom the impotence of the democratic government, during the Weimar period, in dealing with militant adversaries from the left and the right had been a traumatic experience. They were now prepared to accept the way the new government dealt with those supposed to be "public enemies," even if it was felt to be excessively severe.

The yearning for "strong government," particularly common among the bourgeois middle classes, meant that violent repression was only considered legitimate insofar as it promised to increase law and order. Yet the Nazis' ideologically motivated exercise of power went far beyond that goal to actually contradict it.

It is true that the street terror of the SA was put to an end by the liquidation of the revolutionary wing of the National Socialist movement in the summer of 1934; but it was only an apparent victory for the traditional public authorities. In fact, this was the beginning of the rise of the SS, a power that was designed as the instrument of the "Führer's will," and thereby contributed to the erosion of state authority. This process of erosion was not restricted to the field of internal security. Indeed, by the eve of the war, the SS had already managed to expand its sphere of influence far beyond its central function proper. It had gained considerable influence in such varied fields as military and foreign policy, economic life, and the promotion of culture.[26] What is even more remarkable is how the security organs continuously grew in size even though opposition representing a potential threat to the regime had practically ceased to exist. According to Rudolf Höss, the future commandant of Auschwitz, 75 percent of all political prisoners could well have been released in 1935–36 without harming the Third Reich in the least.[27]

The fact that the repression machine expanded and developed to perfection despite a decreasing threat to the regime appears paradoxical only if one sees the SS and police system of the Nazi regime merely as an instrument for securing its rule. However, it appears quite logical if it is understood (in the sense of the functionalists) as part of that process of "cumulative radicalization" characteristic of the National Socialist system as a whole. The process of "cumulative radicalization" soon developed a dynamism of its own with destabilizing effects on the system. The policy of extermination directed at the Jews and Slavs by the German authorities under the control of the SS in the regions occupied by the *Wehrmacht* is the most striking example. Quite apart from its moral quality and its violation of international law, this policy turned out to be absolutely dysfunctional for Nazi rule and contributed significantly to the military defeat of Germany by making it impossible to have a German victory on the Soviet battlefield. The *Wehrmacht* soldiers had been welcomed as "liberators" by large groups of the population (e.g. in the Ukraine) when they entered the country in 1941. Within a few months, however, a policy of occupation characterized by ruthless economic exploitation, cultural deprivation, deportation, and annihilation, succeeded in destroying any basis for wide ranging collaboration.[28] As a result there was a dramatic increase of the partisan movement. Responding to this self-created crisis, the German occupying power further intensified its policy of repression. The result was unsatisfactory in terms of military success and disastrous in terms of politics since more and more groups of the indigenous population were driven towards the partisans. Many of the military and civilian authorities were quite aware of the consequences of this continuous radicalization. Despite several attempts at a more flexible policy of occupation, they were, ultimately, not able to halt the spiral of violence as they did not dare to call into question its central motive element, the National Socialist dogma of racial superiority.[29]

Within the borders of the Reich, the policy of violent repression did not produce such obviously destabilizing effects as in the occupied regions. Nevertheless, it helped to alienate the German people from the regime, particularly where the established order was attacked too openly and traditional moral standards were openly violated. For example, the Party's actions against the Church met with massive resistance from the people of Bavaria and other regions of the Reich most strongly influenced by Catholicism. The anti-Semitic pogroms of the so-called *"Kristallnacht"* (Crystal Night) on November 9–10, 1938 also provoked predominantly negative reactions, despite carefully prepared propaganda. "Many who sympathized with much of what Nazism stood for obviously felt this was going too far. A feeling of 'cultural disgrace' and damage to the German image abroad . . . combined with anger at the senseless destruction of property and with humanitarian feelings."[30] The "termination of unworthy lives" or "euthanasia" (i.e. the mass extermination of the mentally handicapped) that had been practiced since 1939 had to be stopped officially after it became known to the public, despite efforts at concealment, having provoked heavy protests, especially from the churches. Obviously, at least a part of the population had come to see the National Socialist policy of violence negatively. The repression of actual or presumed "public enemies" had been approved, or at least tolerated, as long as it appeared to be required for stabilizing the regime and seemed to be practiced within the scope of administrative standards and, if possible, governed by law (i.e. the "Nuremberg Laws"). A policy of sheer destruction and physical annihilation, however, was an entirely different matter; it was impossible to make the public accept this policy even by means of propaganda. Consequently, as far as possible, the National Socialist leadership had to conduct its genocide program secretly. The conditions created by the state of war were most suitable. Thus it was no accident that the change from a policy of repression to a policy of annihilation did not occur until the war had begun. Drastic measures of any kind were correctly perceived as being much easier to realize under the cover of wartime exigencies than in peacetime. Apart from that, everybody had to deal with such a host of private sorrows due to the war that any event that was not related to these would attract very little attention. Most importantly, during the war, the National Socialist leadership was offered suitable areas for discreet accomplishment of its bloody "mission" in the occupied regions of Eastern Europe. Thus the war performed the following functions: (1) it released enormous destructive energies and removed any remaining obstacles to violent terror and repression (e.g. considerations concerning diplomatic relations with Western powers), and (2) it became the motor of the radicalization process leading from a purpose-oriented policy of repression to a nihilistic, genocide mania. The general course of war events shielded genocidal acts, enabling the mania to be translated into reality.

Taking advantage of the disintegration of the established order during the war, the SS experienced the most dramatic extension of its power as it expanded the National Socialist terror throughout Europe. Paradoxically, the SS owed this increase in power not only to German victories but also to German defeats. That is, as the bad news from the battlefields increased and became a threat to National Socialist rule, the process of radicalization accelerated. Thus it was no accident that, in the summer of 1944, after the attempted military putsch against Hitler, and after the Allied invasion in Normandy and the breakdown of the central sector of the Eastern front had combined to lead the regime to the brink of ruin both internally and externally, the power of the Reichsführer SS and Chief of the German police reached its zenith. The consequence of this was a further intensification of National Socialist terror, now directed towards supposed "defeatists" inside and outside the *Wehrmacht*.[31] Yet even excessive terror was not able to prevent the regime from going to ruin more rapidly than any other political system in German history.

Notes

1. Quoted by Richard Bessel, *Coercion and Consent in Nazi Germany* (Milton Keynes: The Open University, 1984), 11.

2. Peter Hüttenberger, "Nationalsozialistische Polykratie," *Geschichte und Gesellschaft* 2 (1976): 417–442.

3. Klaus Hildebrand, "Monokratie oder Polykratie?" in *The Führer State: Myth and Reality*, ed. G. Hirschfeld and L. Kettenacker (Stuttgart: Klett-Cotta, 1981), 96.

4. Sebastian Haffner, *Ammerkungen zu Hitler* (München: Kindler, 1978), 58–59; Karl Dietrich Bracher, *Zeitgeschichtliche Kontroversen: Um Faschismus, Totalitarismus und Demokratie* (München; Piper, 1976), 64–65.

5. Hans Mommsen, "Hitler's Stellung im Nationalsozialistischen Herrschaftssystem," in Hirschfeld and Kettenacker, *The Führer State*, 70.

6. Ibid., 71.

7. Ibid.

8. Bessel, *Coercion and Consent*, 5.

9. Ian Kershaw, *Der Hitler-Mythos: Volksmeinung und Propaganda im Dritten Reich* (Stuttgart: Deutsche Verlagsanstalt, 1980), 72–89.

10. Bessel, *Coercion and Consent*, 31.

11. Bernd Wegner, *The Waffen-SS: Organization, Ideology and Function* (Oxford: Blackwell, 1990), 51–55.

12. Ernst Fränkel, *The Dual State: A Contribution to the Theory of Dictatorship* (New York: Oxford University Press, 1941).

13. Wegner, *Waffen-SS*, 64 ff.

14. Gert Buchheit, *Der Deutsche Geheimdienst: Geschichte der Militärischen Abwehr* (München: List, 1967), 428 ff.

15. Martin Broszat, "Nationalsozialistische Konzentrationslager," in H. Buchheim, M. Brozsat, H. A. Jacobsen, and H. Krausnick, *Anatomie des SS-Staates*, vol. 2 (Olten, Freiburg i.Br.: Walter, 1965), 46 ff.; Falk Pingel, *Häftlinge unter SS-Herrschaft: Widerstand Selbstbehauptung und Vernichtung im Konzentrationslager* (Hamburg: Hoffmann and Campe, 1978), 35 ff.

16. Werner Best, "Die Schutzstaffel der NSDAP und die Deutsche Polizei," *Deutsches Recht*, (1939): 44 ff.; Wegner, *Waffen-SS*, 102 ff.; George C. Browder, "SIPO and SD: Formation of an Instrument of Power," (Ph.D. diss.: University of Wisconsin, 1977).

17. Hans Buchheim, "Die SS—das Herrschaftsinstrument," in H. Buchheim, M. Brozsat, H. A. Jacobsen, and H. Krausnick, *Anatomie des SS-Staates*, vol. 1 (Olten, Freiburg i. Br.: Walter, 1965), 13–24.

18. Herbert Jäger, *Verbrechen unter Totalitärer Herrschaft: Studien zur Nationalsozialistischen Gewaltkriminalität* (Frankfurt a.M.: Suhrkamp, 1982), 62–75.

19. Rudolf Höss, *Kommandant in Auschwitz*, ed. M. Broszat (München: DTV, 1978), 74; Hans Buchheim, "Befehl und Gehorsham," in Buchheim et al., *Anatomie*, vol. 1.

20. Bradley F. Smith and Agnes F. Peterson, eds., *Heinrich Himmler: Geheimreden 1933 bis 1945 und andere Ansprachen* (Frankfurt a.M., Berlin, Wien: Propyläen, 1974), 31–32.

21. Richard Bessel, "Militarismus im Innenpolitischen Leben der Weimarer Republik: von den Freikorps zur SA," in *Militär und Militarismus in der Weimarer Republik*, K. J. Müller and E. Opitz, eds. (Düsseldorf: Droste, 1978).

22. Adolf Hitler, *Mein Kampf* (München: Eher, 1933), 386.

23. Werner Jochmann, ed., *Adolf Hitler—Monologe im Führerhauptquartier 1941–1944: Die Aufzeichnungen Heinrich Heims* (Hamburg: Knaus, 1980), 239.

24. Joseph Ackermann, *Heinrich Himmler als Ideologe* (Göttingen: Musterschmidt, 1970), 156.

25. Höss, *Kommandant*, 74–75.

26. Robert L. Koehl, *The Black Corps: The Structure and Power Struggles of the Nazi SS* (Madison: University of Wisconsin Press, 1983); Bernd Wegner, "Der Durchbruch zum 'SS-Staat': Die SS und das Jahr 1938," in *Machtbewusstsein in Deutschland am Vorabend des Zweiten Weltkrieges*, ed. F. Knipping and K.J. Müller (Paderborn: Schöningh, 1984).

27. Höss, *Kommandant*, 66.

28. Jürgen Förster, "Das Unternehmen 'Barbarossa' als Eroberungs-und Vernichtungskrieg," in *Das Deutsche Reich und der Zweite Weltkrieg*, vol. 4, Der Angriff auf die Sojetunion, ed. Militärgeschichtliches Forschungsamt (Stuttgart: Deutsche Verlagsanstalt, 1983), 413–447.

29. Matthew Cooper, *The Phantom War: The German Struggle Against Soviet Partisans 1941–1944* (London: MacDonald and Jane's, 1979), 143–161.

30. Ian Kershaw, *Popular Opinion and Political Dissent in the Third Reich: Bavaria 1933–1945* (Oxford: Clarendon, 1983), 267.

31. Manfred Messerschmidt and Fritz Wüllner, *Die Wehrmachtjustiz im Dienste des Nationalsozialismus: Zerstörung einer Legende* (Baden-Baden: Nomos, 1987), 63–89.

10

The Refractory Aspect of Terror in Movement-Regimes

Stanley K. Shernock

Introduction: Terror as Purposive Action

Taking the Nazi and Stalinist regimes as prototypes, theorists of totalitarianism have variously described terror as "the essence of the totalitarian form of government,"[1] "the most universal characteristic of totalitarianism,"[2] "the vital nerve of the totalitarian system,"[3] and "the linchpin of modern totalitarianism."[4] At the same time, these theorists assert that terror is initiated during periods of relative stability when no crisis would suggest its use,[5] and that it even increases in inverse ratio to opposition.[6]

Robert Tucker[7] prefers to call regimes that follow such a pattern "movement-regimes."[8] In such regimes governmental coercion against behavioral nonconformity, perceived by regime rulers as threatening to the state, is applied *reactively* during both periods of relative stability or consolidation and during periods of mobilization or transformation. However, during periods of mobilization, governmental coercion is applied *proactively* against various categories of regime enemies, as well as applied reactively against behavioral nonconformists. It is the purpose of this paper to analyze the terror during mobilization campaigns against regime-designated enemies. Specifically, the paper examines the anti-Semitic campaign in Nazi Germany after the Roehm Purge and prior to World War II, the vigilance campaign in Stalinist U.S.S.R. against the so-called "Trotskyist-Zinovievist-Bukharinist" conspiracy after the Kirov assassination and during the *Yezhovshchina*,[9] and the rectification campaign

I would like to thank Tim Bushnell, who made a major contribution in revising a much larger manuscript from which the current paper is derived.

in Maoist China against "capitalist roaders" after the purge of Liu Shaoqi and during the Great Proletarian Cultural Revolution. The position taken here is that campaigns against regime-designated enemies, as with all forms of regime-instigated terror, should be viewed as purposive action by regime leaders.[10] However, the intent and consequences of these campaigns should not be viewed as synonymous. To do so implies that regime leaders exercised a totalitarian control that has not been empirically supported, particularly by recent analyses. Purposive action should not be confused with a consistent or detailed plan of action, but rather should be seen as involving a process of action and reaction.[11] Although not necessarily taking on a dynamic or logic of its own, as intimated in the work of Brzezinski[12] and Dallin and Breslauer,[13] terror, once initiated, and even orchestrated, by regime leaders, can proliferate to a point where it threatens not only to undermine particular regime goals, but, moreover, to destroy the very foundations of the regime itself. This paper focuses on the problematical nature of "unmanaged" or "situational" terror, which Dallin and Breslauer[14] define as generally a product of uncontrolled or undisciplined behavior by lower level cadres that is said to be intertwined with purposive terror initiated and intended by the top leadership in their mobilization campaigns against regime-designated enemies.

The refractory aspect of terror in movement-regimes has not only been identified by scholarly analysts, but by repressive regimes themselves which have promulgated statements about the problems of controlling the violence that has been instigated by their own campaigns against designated enemies. In pre-war Nazi Germany, certain regime leaders condemned the "Bolshevistic terroristic methods" used by the SA (Stormtroopers) against various sectors of the population prior to the Roehm Purge, and the "individual actions" by the SA against Jews after the Roehm Purge. In Stalinist U.S.S.R., certain regime leaders made reference throughout the thirties, but particularly during the Yezhovshchina, to the "overzealousness" and "excesses" of the NKVD (People's Commissariat for Internal Affairs) and local party bosses. And, in Maoist China during the Great Proletarian Cultural Revolution (GPCR), Mao and other members of his inner circle condemned the factional fighting and "overenthusiasm about fighting" of radical Red Guards.

While the top leadership in each regime indicated problems in managing their mobilization campaigns against enemies, unregulated terror presented different problems in each regime based on conflicts concerning (1) the definition of the target group, (2) the designation of the agency or agencies involved in the campaign, and (3) the means of dealing with the enemy. In Nazi Germany, after the Roehm Purge more clearly defined which groups were unacceptable targets of terror, "individual actions" against Jews were officially condemned for being the inappropriate means by an inappropriate agency (i.e., the SA instead of a state agency) for dealing with the "Jewish Problem." "Excesses" and "overzealousness" in Stalinist U.S.S.R. were generally attributed to party cadres and police whose failure to investigate properly led to the arrest of scapegoats instead of real enemies. The overenthusiasm about fighting of the radical Red Guards was condemned by Mao and his leadership clique because it was not selective in its targets (i.e., the "handful" of "capitalist-roaders"), too selective in the agency used to fight the enemy (i.e., it did not include workers), and not selective in using the appropriate means of struggle (i.e., employing armed struggle instead of political means).

Shifting Terror Policy: Pragmatic Considerations and Factional Maneuvering

According to recent analyses of the mobilization campaigns against enemies in all three regimes,[15] the most significant factor affecting the course of the respective mobilization campaigns appears to have been factionalism or conflicts among different regime leaders or regime-sanctioned organizations.[16] The fact that different factions invoked the name of the leader has given the impression of a monolithic leadership entirely determining the course of the campaigns. The SA frequently claimed that the actions they took were secretly supported by Hitler and other top Nazi leaders. Politburo members in the Soviet Union not only invoked the name of Stalin in sanctifying their own decisions but also gave rhetorical support to him when actually opposing his policies.[17] Each of the different Red Guard factions also attempted to justify their actions by claiming to be more loyal to Mao.[18] Because those resisting the campaigns had to operate within the framework of the campaigns, accept *faits accomplis*, compromise with terror, or emulate the instruments of terror, an image was created of a cooperative leadership clique orchestrating the terror of the mobilization campaigns. Moderate Nazi officials were forced to accept the inevitability of the Nuremberg Laws while attempting to limit their effects on both those of pure and mixed Jewish background. Pragmatic opponents of the *Yezhovshchina* attempted to undermine the purge by arguing that it should be continued by the police alone without the assistance of denunciations by party members and bureaucrats. Opponents of the Cultural Revolution, both local party and military leaders, organized their own Red Guard forces either to protect themselves or to combat the ravages of the radical Red Guards.

Much, if not most, of what has been defined by both scholarly analysts and regime officials as the "snowballing of terror" or "situational terror" was not the result of some form of internal, independent dynamic of these campaigns, but actually purposive terror instigated by certain radical factions attempting to broaden the scope of mobilization campaigns against enemies. The failure to identify much of the apparently unregulated terror as purposely triggered by radical factions rather than as undisciplined behavior of lower-level cadres not only assumes more consensus than existed among the top leaders, but ignores how the supreme leader can protect his image of infallibility or his responsibility for the negative impact of his mobilization campaign against regime-designated enemies by blaming subordinates.[19] The terror-limiting measures taken in each regime were largely attributable to the lobbying efforts or subtle conflict strategies of pragmatists, who were primarily concerned with economic instability arising from the social disorder that accompanied the mobilization campaigns. Their positions were largely reactions to chaos and were not programmatic; and they were not necessarily opposed to normal repressive measures. The equivocal and often conflicting and shifting messages conveyed in public media statements and official pronouncements seem to indicate fluctuations between pragmatic and radical positions. Whether temporarily in Nazi Germany, ultimately in Stalinist U.S.S.R., or periodically and then ultimately in Maoist China, pragmatists were able to influence the leaders of each of the three regimes to redefine the terror instigated by the radicals as undisciplined excess, and to reduce the negative impacts of their respective campaigns against regime-designated enemies.

A careful evaluation of the mobilization campaigns of the three regimes would seem to indicate that they did not create totalitarian police states, where the secret police is said to replace the party as the prime political mover and only reliable bastion of the state.[20] Given the rhetoric of their leaders about revolutionary spontaneity from below, radicals in each of the regimes attempted to substitute mass involvement, albeit narrowly defined in terms of the rank-and-file of specific militant groups, for institutional means in fighting the enemy. Most significantly, they favored a "mass mobilization" campaign, in which the politicized masses would direct police actions, to a strictly police operation in their struggle against the enemy. In Nazi Germany, radical party members, interested in undermining the SS emigration policy and seizing control of Jewish policy, incited the SA to engage in "individual actions" against the Jews and organized *Kristallnacht* (Crystal Night). In the Soviet Union and China, radical national leaders attempted to undermine cooperation between local political cadres and police by substituting mass mobilization campaigns. The worst unregulated terror occurred when it became a form of "populist" terror.

As was true with the National Socialist movement as a whole,[21] Hitler's Jewish policy did not follow one consistent plan. The pattern of persecution of the Jews was determined by factional rivalry within the Nazi Party leadership over a solution to the Jewish Problem, just as other decisions and policies were the outcome of temporary success of one faction relative to another.[22] Because Jewish policy was so important to Hitler, almost all Nazi plenipotentiaries vied with one another to influence Jewish policy and felt compelled at one time or another to deliver a background report on the "Jewish Problem," as success in Jewish policy was also to take a significant step upward on the Nazi hierarchical ladder.[23] Although at no point did Hitler consider retreating on the Jewish issue, he did not offer any guidance concerning a solution to the "Jewish Problem" during the pre-war years, but instead encouraged the independent and often rival policies pursued by factions within the movement.[24] Notwithstanding his denunciations of "individual actions," Hitler avoided the conflict between the radical Party members and the moderate economic experts.[25]

The two principal instruments of Nazi power during the mobilization campaign, the SA and the SS, despised each other[26] and clashed, even before the Roehm Purge in 1934. The SS had unsuccessfully attempted to suppress SA rebellions in Berlin in September of 1930 and in April of 1931.[27] Later, the SA radicals came into conflict over Jewish policy, not only with moderates in government positions, but also with the SS, particularly the SD subsection of the SS, and the Gestapo, who rarely indulged in the emotional, ad hoc terrorism associated with the SA.[28] Some Jews even looked upon the SS during the pre-war years as a disciplined and relatively reassuring counterweight to the dissolute Stormtroopers.[29]

Jewish emigration, which provided Germany with one of the most profitable sources of desperately needed foreign exchange,[30] was vigorously pushed by the SS from 1935 until the outbreak of the war in September of 1939.[31] The SS's commitment to an emigration policy was pursued, up until 1938, without concern for upsetting other Nazis and without consideration of its ideological implications. In the hope of furthering emigration, the SS encouraged Jewish self-concentration in a few cities, even though the mayors of these cities opposed such concentration,[32] and afforded official favoritism to the revisionist anti-Marxist Zionists, allowing them to build their institutions and disseminate their propaganda,[33] since these Zionists were seen as helping promote emigration. Meetings between the SS and Zionist groups[34] eventually led to the Haavara transfer agreement which permitted Jews to take most of their property from Germany to Palestine, thus circumventing the prohibition against Jews taking capital out of Germany, which had made emigration almost impossible for middle class Jews. After the Anschluss in 1938, Eichmann carried out an assembly line technique for Jewish emigration in Austria which, though ruthless, did succeed in deporting thousands of Jews who would otherwise have been engulfed in the Final Solution.[35]

Party radicals, wanting to wrest control of Jewish policy, protested the SS's emigration policy strongly. Ribbentrop warned that "Germany must regard the forming of a Jewish state as dangerous, which even in miniature would form just such an operational base as the Vatican for political Catholicism." Rosenberg likewise suggested that it would be better to have Jewish reservations in many parts of the world.[36] The arguments were compelling to Hitler, who consequently suspended the transfer agreements between Germany and Palestine. The eventual objective of Party radicals was to thwart any form of emigration and keep Jews as hostages.[37]

In late March of 1933, the SA, apparently without any central direction, began its anti-Semitic campaign, assaulting Jews and boycotting their businesses.[38] In response to the uncoordinated SA actions, particularly the spontaneous SA boycotts of Jewish enterprises, a national boycott was organized in 1933 which was specifically designed to siphon the energies of the Party's radical elements into controlled channels while demonstrating to these radicals the regime's commitment to National Socialist ideology.[39]

The official boycott in 1933 failed to rein in the SA, instead inciting them to additional independent initiatives.[40] At the same time, the boycott had unanticipated negative effects. It threatened foreign trade and provided additional fuel for foreign propaganda, adversely affecting German diplomacy.

The major lesson that the 1933 official boycott taught the Nazi leadership was that concurrent solutions to the "Jewish Problem" and the economic problems was impossible. If Hitler hoped to achieve some measure of economic progress, which would help him consolidate his political position, he would have to postpone his full-scale attack on the Jews. Despite Hitler's inclination to identify with the radical elements in the Party, he would consider a more moderate policy when the practical harm of anti-Semitism to Germany could be demonstrated.[41] Consequently, the moderate forces in government temporarily were able to assert their influence because of economic considerations concerning (1) the need for a low unemployment rate, (2) rearmament, and (3) foreign exchange.[42] In fact, Hjalmar Schacht would not accept his appointment as Economics Minister until he was promised that in economic affairs, Jews could carry on exactly as they had prior to his appointment.[43] For a short time after the boycott, economic considerations not only restrained anti-Semitic practices in cities like Danzig,[44] but many Jewish employers were prevented from liquidating their businesses, since to do so would have harmed the regime's drive for full employment.[45]

Some moderate government officials such as Hjalmar Schacht and Franz Guertner, Minister of Justice, continually tried to curb the excesses of Nazi anti-Semitism.[46] For example, Schacht established a special bureau, the "interference section," in the Economics Ministry to take every possible inconspicuous measure to protect Jewish concerns against Nazi attacks.[47] Jewish emigration declined from 37,000 in the wake of Hitler's takeover in 1933 to 23,000 in 1934. During the first months of 1935, some 10,000 Jews who had fled returned to Germany.[48]

Once the German autarky plan began to take hold, there was less reliance on foreign trade and, therefore, less of a restraint on extremism. At this time, in 1937, Hitler dismissed Schacht, von Neurath, and von Blomberg, the last bastions of moderation. Almost at once boycotts intensified, accompanied by terror and destruction. In a riot in Danzig on October 23, 1937, where the windows of three hundred Jewish businesses were smashed, the Party continued to deny any responsibility, stating that it had a better means of reducing Jewish influence.[49] However, in Danzig, as well as elsewhere, there was no interference from the Party leadership or from economic authorities in Berlin. By June of 1938 there was a wholesale terrorization of the Jewish community which finally prompted an order from the Deputy Fuehrer's office to all middle-ranking Party officials emphasizing that all unauthorized actions against Jews cease because they could only jeopardize the intended total solution to the "Jewish Problem."[50]

Notwithstanding the turn toward radicalism in Jewish policy, there were still some Party officials and Gauleiter who protested the violence of Kristallnacht, the nation-wide pogrom against the Jews in November 1938, and demanded that the major culprits stand trial. On November 20, 1938, Heydrich promised them that severe measures would be taken against these culprits. A few arrests were made and a trial was arranged, but the proceedings turned out to be a travesty of justice. The only sentences handed down were three month sentences for the offense of race-mixing—the Nazi label for the rape of Jewish females by Aryan males. For criminals who had cold-bloodedly murdered Jews, the Parteigerichte (party court) decreed either pardons or warnings.[51] Without the leverage of economic considerations, the radicals had won their victory and situational terror was condoned.

The conflict between pragmatists and radicals during the Yezhovshchina can be traced to the discontent of some initial supporters of Stalin with his collectivization policy. By 1932, according to Bukharin,[52] the predominant view in Party circles was that Stalin had led the country into an impasse by his policy, that he had roused the peasants against the Party, and that the situation could be saved only by his removal from Party domination. Many influential members of the Central Committee were upset over the human loss caused by collectivization and other related Stalinist policies of the early thirties.[53] Besides right-wing Bolsheviks like Slepkov and left-wing Trotskyites,[54] even those originally supporting Stalin's collectivization policy became increasingly rebellious against his agricultural policies, although for practical rather than ideological reasons.[55]

In the summer of 1932, the more liberal elements in the Party, apparently led by Kalinin, introduced a decree, "On Revolutionary Legality," which stated that revolutionary legality was "one of the most important means of strengthening the proletarian dictatorship," and noted "in particular the existence of an increasingly significant number of infringements of revolutionary legality by people in official positions and distortions in its implementation, especially in the countryside."[56]

However, the most significant among the various programs and declarations circulated from hand to hand during 1932 criticizing Stalin's autocratic leadership and lack of Party democracy and calling for his removal from the position of General Secretary, was a 250 page program proposed by Riutin, a former right oppositionist.[57] The program called for a change in Party policy in the direction of greater democratization, an end of the repression within the party, greater consideration of the interests of the workers, abolition of collectives, and granting of economic self-determination to the peasants. Thirty pages of the program were devoted to Stalin's personal characteristics, depicting Stalin as bringing the revolution to the edge of the abyss, and therefore calling for his removal as General Secretary.[58] When Stalin learned of the program, he demanded the death penalty for Riutin and said his program was a direct justification and an apology for the necessity of assassinating him,[59] even though it did not suggest that.[60] While the Politburo decided to expel Riutin and his collaborators from the Party and exile the group to remote cities and *raiony*, Riutin was spared execution.[61] The Riutin affair, which challenged both Stalin's position and policies, is said to have had a traumatic effect upon Stalin.[62] It is particularly significant because it was the beginning of the indirect challenges that Stalin would encounter throughout the next four years, although Stalin was able to undermine the implementation of the modifications to his policies that he was forced to accept.[63,64]

For example, in 1933 at a plenum of the Central Committee which was reconvened due to further pressure to resolve the crisis in the countryside, Postychev, previously not known for his moderation, criticized the blaming of problems of collectivization on wreckers, kulaks, and other regime-designated enemies, and called for, along with others, a shift away from repression towards assistance to the peasant.[65] At first, Stalin appeared to agree with the critique; but later, he transferred control of the machine-tractor stations from Postychev to Kaganovich. Also in 1933, Rudzutak, head of the Central Control Commission, warned Party investigators against asking tricky questions or engaging in petty or captious digging into people's lives and emphasized the right of appeal of Party members found wanting.[66] Again, Stalin, the hardliner, found Rudzutak's position unsatisfactory, dissolved the Commission at the Seventeenth Party Congress, and thus implicitly removed Rudzutak as executor of the Party purge.

The dissatisfaction with Stalin came to a climax at the Seventeenth Party Congress in 1934. Even as Stalin was receiving panegyric after panegyric for his leadership during the crisis years of collectivization, when it came to the balloting for membership in the Central Committee, a significant minority failed to vote for Stalin's election to the Central Committee.[67]

Many Party members hoped that in his new position as Secretary of the Central Committee, which entailed directorship over a whole group of departments, Sergei Kirov would be able to influence a new policy line.[68] Kirov, generally characterized as a loyal Stalinist who was supposedly a moderate,[69] together with Gorki, believed in the necessity of a reconciliation with the people in order to acquire their voluntary cooperation in the political preparation of the country for the coming war rather than in a Stalinist policy of crushing all dissenters.[70] Kirov stood for the abolition of the terror in general and inside the Party and wanted a reconciliation with former oppositionists in the Party, as well as a reconciliation with the people. As the major spokesman for the dissatisfied Stalinists,[71] he, with the support of Ordzhonikidze and Kuibyshev, repeatedly opposed Stalin at Politburo meetings when Stalin demanded severe repression of Trotskyites and other oppositionists.[72] While hundreds of Trotskyites were arrested for real and imaginary connection with Trotsky during 1932–1933, he refused to authorize arrests of former oppositionists, stating that they should be won over ideologically and not repressed.[73] Through his influence, Kamenev, Zinoviev, and a number of other oppositionists were readmitted to the Party in early summer of 1933.[74]

On the basis of reports and information reaching him, Stalin supposedly realized that the mood of the majority of old Party members was really one of bitterness and hostility toward him.[75] He felt that those that cringed before him, protesting devotion, were not as obedient as he wanted them to be,[76] and would betray him at the first change of the political atmosphere.[77] Kirov, who was both popular and independent-minded, came to be perceived as a threat by Stalin. Despite a lack of definitive evidence, most Soviet historians[78] believe that it was Stalin who arranged Kirov's assassination. Even much later, during the 'Great Purge' period itself, Stalin continued to encounter opposition, albeit more subdued and less direct.

According to Rittersporn's analysis of Pravda in early December of 1937,[79] those opposing the mass purges devised a strategy to terminate the purges by disengaging the state apparatus from involvement in them. After stressing the need to strengthen the entire state apparatus in order to bolster the national economy (in 1937 Yezhov had decimated the ranks of economic moderates)[80] and prepare for the imminent danger of war, they argued that the "enemies" of the vigilance campaign had been largely defeated. Consequently, they asserted that vigilance should not be the criterion of the cadre's political trustworthiness. They also argued that eliminating the remaining enemies should be the sole responsibility of the NKVD, implying that state apparatus involvement in unmasking enemies had detracted from their more important functions. In 1938, moderates were able to pass a Central Committee decree forbidding party organs from arbitrarily replacing managers of enterprises, while disingenuously arguing that enemies had been annihilated because of the heroic activities of the NKVD.[81] In essence, the pragmatists attempted to undermine the campaign. For they realized that the Party and state apparatus, by supplying the tangible victims for the abstract categories the NKVD were required to fill, were actually responsible for broadening the scope of the purge. The radicals supporting the "mass mobilization" campaign, however, recognizing the ploy of the pragmatists, retorted in Bolshevik, labeling the moderates as accomplices of the enemy because they did not want to unmask the enemy or call the masses to battle to unmask the enemy, but instead wanted to hide behind the hypocritical position that it was exclusively an NKVD duty.

Still, it was widely recognized that the mass mobilization campaign, by broadening and institutionalizing internal conflict, always ran the risk of creating political confrontation between leaders and led and a global questioning of the system.[82] According to Rittersporn,[83] when the mass mobilization campaign of the radicals led to mass insubordination of workers, the radicals knew how to close ranks with the pragmatists.

Notwithstanding Mao Zedong's charismatic authority in China, his actual power within the Chinese Communist Party (CCP) had diminished by the beginning of the early sixties prior to the Great Proletarian Cultural Revolution (GPCR). Because of the failures of his previous transformation campaigns—the Great Leap Forward and the Hundred

Flowers campaigns—a crisis of confidence in his leadership developed in the Party. This eventually forced him to relinquish his position in 1959 as Chairman of the Chinese People's Republic, which involved policy making and administrative functions, to his named successor Liu Shaoqi. As a result of his diminished role, Mao was not able to assert the type of control he wished over the future direction of China. Mao's opponents in the Party were not as interested in seizing power for its own sake as they were in influencing Mao to endorse more pragmatic economic policies. At the provincial and local levels, conservative civil and Party bureaucracies developed links with both the public security organs and the military which gave them a much greater degree of independence from radical central authorities than in the Nazi and Stalinist regimes. The Beijing Party organization became so impenetrable that Mao was forced to rely on the Shanghai newspaper for his first fulminations against the Beijing leadership, which ushered in the GPCR.

During the GPCR, as well as before the GPCR, Mao was confronted by an opposition which carried on conflict through subtle means. Under the guise of promoting Maoist policies, they attempted to undermine and mitigate the course and effects of the GPCR. They even developed mass organizations of their own to engage in proxy battles with the radical, Mao-sponsored Red Guard groups. These ostensible Maoist groups contributed to much of the factionalism and fighting between the various mass organizations during the GPCR. Mao became increasingly upset as the factional fighting not only threatened the integrity of the People's Liberation Army (PLA), but also contributed to the alienation of workers who sided with conservative factions and engaged in strikes and protested living conditions.

In the other two regimes, moderates had attempted to restrict police powers,[84] but the public security system became not an instrument but a target of Mao's mobilization campaign. The public security system, which among other units included the secret police and armed public security forces, were the primary instruments of law and order in Maoist China prior to the GPCR. After the anti-rightist campaigns of 1957–1958, the public security forces gained an increasingly dominant position over the other two legal organs, the courts and procuratorate. The functions of these forces included the prevention and investigation of both counterrevolutionary and nonpolitical crimes, the arrest of criminals, and other normal police and security roles, but were also used by the Party to keep the populace in line.[85] In fact, they were aligned with local Party cadres and sought to prevent challenge to the Party at the local level.[86]

At the outset of the Cultural Revolution, the courts and the procuratorates, but particularly the unpopular public security forces, were denounced and physically attacked by pro-Mao revolutionaries. The first powerful opposition figure to be purged was Lo Jui-ch'ing, the minister of public security. Following his purge, a number of top leaders in Mao's inner circle, including Hsieh Fu-Chih, the new minister of public security, fulminated against the mission and organization of the former public security system. Particularly attacked were the specialized work and independence of the public security organs which were compared to the OGPU in the Soviet Union and to bureaucratic security organs in bourgeois countries. Through their ties with the local political cadre, they presented an obstacle to Mao's efforts to purge the Party and state apparatus throughout China. Concerned with maintaining law and order, protecting local political officials, and preserving their own positions, they did, in fact, take stern measures against the rampaging radical Red Guards when they confronted them. Consequently, given their superior strength compared to the Red Guards, Mao called in the PLA to seize the local public security offices.[87]

The PLA soon became charged with taking over the courts and procuratorates, as well as the public security organs. Their assigned mission, which was to be primarily political, was confounded by their ill-defined role, shifts in policy from right to left, and by imprecise directives. Furthermore, they were forbidden by central authorities to use physical means in dealing with fractious elements of the mass organizations, and instead instructed to support the proletarian revolutionaries and maintain revolutionary order.[88]

In early 1967, another and ultimately most powerful category of Red Guard group was formed to counter the radical Red Guards in the provinces. However, instead of being organized to defend the local power structure, they were organized by regional military leaders as proxy forces against the radical Red Guards to help restore political and economic order.[89] The PLA itself, having been severely restricted in its actions, had not yet been able to get Beijing to accept its estimation of the severity of the unregulated terror and destruction being wreaked by the radical Red Guards.

During the GPCR, the local Military Control Committees of the PLA favored one or the other faction, although usually the conservative faction, acting prejudicially toward youth of "bad class" background or organizing political instruction meetings as a means of imposing "proletarian discipline" on the radical factions, seeking self-criticism of their members.[90] Once the PLA became involved in police work, it was highly resented and attacked by radical Red Guards. It wasn't until after the Wuhan Incident in September 1967 that an order issued jointly by the Central Committee of the Party, the State Council, the Military Affairs Committee, and the Central Cultural Revolution Group, lifted the restrictions imposed on the PLA so that they could restore the deteriorating law and order throughout the country.[91] The widespread violent struggle had disrupted the economy and threatened the stability of the PLA's organizational integrity.[92] Open physical clashes had led to temporary closing of many production units, construction projects, and transportation facilities. Finally, after the Wuhan Incident, high ranking moderate elements in the PLA persuaded Mao to curtail the chaos of the GPCR and to bring the radical Red Guards under final control. Some radicals were killed, others arrested, and almost all suppressed by early 1968.[93]

Contending Definitions of the "Enemy of the People"

Each of the three movement-regimes began their respective mobilization campaigns as generalized witch hunts which attempted to expose the "hidden enemy." Notwithstanding general similarities, each of the mobilization campaigns unfolded differently, and did not, as Albert Bergesen[94] has suggested, follow specifically identifiable, universal laws of witch-hunting. They involved different ritual activities, served practical as well as symbolic functions, and alternated between abstract and concrete definitions of the hidden enemy. Insofar as each campaign involved an initially ambiguous identification of the enemy, the refractory aspect of the terror was increased.

Even when the social and political identity of the enemy was clarified, unregulated terror could occur because of a lack of specification of which individuals within targeted categories were enemies. In Nazi Germany all within a designated category were defined as enemies, thus indicating that the victims and targets were one and the same. In the other two regimes the situation was different. In the Soviet case, Stalin, on a number of occasions, had to warn against viewing all leaders as enemies; and in the Chinese case, Mao had to distinguish between the leaders and the led of the opposing forces.

In each of the three movement-regimes, the conflict between pragmatic and radical positions often took the form of efforts to redefine the nature of the enemy. Enemies with ascribed characteristics were more readily identifiable than enemies whose identity had to be ascertained by interpreting behavioral cues indicating underlying ideological opposition or revisionist tendencies. It was the definition of the enemy in terms of achieved or behavioral characteristics that broadened the scope of the mobilization campaigns and contributed to the unregulated terror. Consequently, those attempting to limit the scope of the mobilization campaigns and their attendant unregulated terror tended to define the enemy according to ascriptive criteria. In all three regimes, the limiting of unregulated terror was associated with a more concrete and specific definition of the enemy and a reduction of terror and violence.

The Roehm Purge in 1934 not only reestablished a popularly appreciated sense of order in German society,[95] it also allowed Hitler to focus Germans' attention on a single enemy—the Jew, and deflect the SA from their definition of the old elite as an enemy. The SA, which had savagely attacked and imprisoned thousands of Nazi opponents while terrorizing the general population, had broadened their definition of enemies to include German capitalists, the Reichswehr command, and even top Nazi Party leaders. According to Reitlinger,[96] the Jews alone presented a target to which the old party fighters of the SA could direct their animal spirits after the disappearance of the Communists.

The Jews, who were characterized as the incarnation of evil, were labeled as "objective enemies" or "enemies of the people," in contrast to Aryan political criminals, who were labeled "those dangerous to the state," and Aryan nonpolitical criminals termed "*asozial*."[97] However, it was still unclear what the essence of the danger from Jews was. The attempt to unmask Jews in the official boycott of Jewish businesses in 1933 indicated that the Nazis initially viewed the Jewish enemy in terms of his achieved economic status. The boycott was designed, in part, to awaken anti-Semitism among the German masses by unmasking the assimilated and disguised Jews in their community or neighborhood.[98] Yet, it was difficult to determine who and what was Jewish during the boycott. Many of the department stores boycotted were in the hands of German banks and foreign creditors. Most of these department stores employed large numbers of Aryan Germans whose jobs were threatened by the boycott. Each subsequent measure, from the Nuremberg Laws to the *Judenliste*, which untangled Jewish and Aryan names, to name changes themselves, to document stamping, to the marking of the Jew's clothing with a star,[99] was intended to identify Jews and thus make them more visible.

Given the difficulty of identifying the Jewish business firm and the adverse consequences to the German economy of solving the "Jewish Problem" on the basis of that identification, and given, in addition, a need to respond to the renewed outbreak of "individual actions" by the SA who wanted to halt and reverse the assimilation process, the next step involved unmasking the biological Jew. Thus, a new biological, ascribed definition of the Jewish enemy was created in the Nuremberg Laws of 1935. These laws were based on the idea that the Jew was evil because of blood and that his most monstrous crime was the defilement of the purity of the Aryan race.[100] They included new circumscriptions of certain activities which Hitler himself had outlined: (1) no intermarriage, (2) no sexual relations outside marriage with Jews, and (3) regulation of employment of Aryan housemaids in Jewish homes.[101]

The major conflict between moderates and radicals regarding the Nuremberg Laws was the definition to be applied to *Mischlinge*, those of mixed background. Some radicals, who wanted to include those who were only one-eighth Jewish, were essentially attempting to develop a broader definition of the Jew, while moderates were attempting to maintain a more limited definition. The fact that a special provision was made for *Mischlinge* who had one of four grandparents who were "racially" full Jews was interpreted as a victory of the moderates over the rabid anti-Semites like Streicher who wanted to insure as inclusive a definition as possible of the Jew. Some of the moderates, notably Schacht and Frick, supported the de jure discrimination against Jews encompassed in the Nuremberg Laws because they felt it would protect Jews from the continuing frightful, unpredictable and illegal local violence.[102] Frick went so far as to state that the Laws gave the Jews a legal status within the German State,[103] even though they deprived Jews of citizenship, eliminated them from key positions, and restricted their social interaction. However, while the Laws were ideologically pleasing because they presumably struck at the heart of the "Jewish Problem," the radicals, supported by the Nazified middle class,[104] were eager to launch a full-scale attack against Jewish participation in the economy. They claimed that the Jew was an economic parasite as well as a biological one,[105] believing that such an attack, involving the Aryanization of Jewish property, would be the first stage in establishing the economic relationships promised by National Socialist ideology.

As the Jew was removed further and further from German society, as he was forced to assume the pariah role, he became more of an abstract and invisible demon than a tangible enemy. Only when the Jew was virtually removed from German society could he assume the physiognomy of all enemies. For the plausibility of a single conspiracy to be effective it was necessary to obliterate totally the experience with the mythological and ideological enemy. The Nazis were thorough in doing so. The elimination of the Jews from Germany was accompanied by the removal of all reminders of Jewish life in the country. Hilberg,[106] for example, provides a document showing how trade associations sought to erase the Jewish names ("de-Jew" as it was phrased) from all companies that had been Aryanized. The attempt to create a universal opposition between Jew and Aryan by transforming all enemies into Jews was paralleled by the attempt to create a more abstract ideological opposition between Judaism and Aryanism. Largely a product of the nativistic aspect of Nazism, this more abstract opposition evinced itself in all aspects of culture,[107] and even in the physical sciences.[108] All expressions of modernity and of the Weimar Republic,[109] such as impressionistic art, atonal music, psychoanalysis, and relativistic physics, which the Nazis found abhorrent, were all labeled alien and Jewish. The Soviet, American, and British armies were characterized as no more than another manifestation of International Jewry's power.[110] Roosevelt (Rosenfeld!) and Lord Northcliff were transformed into Jews,[111] Stalin into a half-Jew, etc. The English were characterized as a nation of white Jews by the SS,[112] and the Bolshevistic scourge was presented as Jewish orchestrated (and not as pan-Slavism). On July 28, 1942 Himmler urged in a letter to Gottlob Berger "not to issue any decree concerning the definition of the term 'Jew' . . . for with all these foolish commitments we will only be tying our hands."[113] As the Jew became less tangible and visible and more abstractly defined, planned terror was substituted for unregulated and situational terror.

In the Soviet Union, Rittersporn[114] notes that how the term "enemy" was to be interpreted became the major question around which political struggles revolved, and Getty[115] states that throughout 1936 central Party leaders carried out a heated struggle over how to define the enemy.

Stalin's perceptions of potential threats to his power from those who presumably supported him led him to develop a view that hidden enemies were lurking everywhere. Borrowing Molotov's theory of the enemy,[116] Stalin felt that wreckers did not engage simply in sabotage. A good wrecker would wreck only some of the time and do good work the rest in order to gain confidence and to continue wrecking. An ultra-clever wrecker would not wreck at all. He fulfilled and overfulfilled production quotas, waiting for war when he could display his real talents and wreck to his heart's content.[117] Believing that "devils breed in quiet pools,"[118] Stalin told the members of the Politburo, after the concocted Doctor's Plot near the end of his regime was discovered, that, "You are blind like young kittens: what will happen without me? The country will perish because you do not know how to recognize enemies,"[119] At the meeting of the Central Committee in June of 1936, at the beginning of the *Yezhovshchina* itself, Stalin stated that wreckers and enemies "with party cards" could be anywhere, implying that all leaders were suspect.[120]

In stark contrast to Stalin's thesis about the intensity of enemy activity increasing as socialism became stronger, as well as his thesis about the omnipresent enemy, purge opponents at the plenum of the Central Committee in June of 1936 argued that wreckers were few and on their last legs, and that the stronger socialism becomes the less danger faced by hostile class elements.[121] Such a perspective would clear the current cadres of all responsibility for the regime's difficulties. Those seeking to limit the purge tended, as they did at the first Moscow Trial, to

define enemies narrowly as members of a Trotskyite-Zinovievite conspiratorial group in the pay of foreign powers who did not hold responsible
positions at the time[122] and who were already dismissed and imprisoned.[123] Thus, the difficulties of Soviet management were attributed to
aggressive acts by survivors of the old opposition who had been defeated,
and defined as acts external to the apparatus.[124]

Supposedly, according to Getty,[125] Stalin agreed to a limited definition
of the enemy at the first Moscow Trial, and to the exoneration of
Bukharin. But *Pravda*, in writing about trial, stated that enemies had
penetrated Party organizations and had camouflaged themselves by
feigning support for the Party line.[126] Here, as true generally, radicals
purportedly implied that enemies were bureaucrats and local Party leaders
taking advantage of their positions. Although the epithet "Trotskyite"
originally applied to the Left Opposition which had been crushed, and
although Stalin estimated Trotskyites comprised only six to nine percent
of party leadership, the Trotskyite label became increasingly susceptible
to any interpretation and came to be used against anybody,[127] including
rank-and-file Party members.[128] "Trotskyite" was thus transformed from
a concrete, ascribed status into an abstract, achieved status. At the
subsequent trials—the Piatakov trial in Moscow and the Novosibirsk
trial—the radicals were able to put forth their image of the enemy. The
defendants were not only accused of conspiracy and espionage, but of
abuses commonly committed by cadre presiding over the national economy. The accusation of wrecking was introduced into political discourse,
and the enemy was said to be hiding behind the Party card. Thus, the
enemy, as represented by Piatakov, an economic moderate and former
Trotskyite who held high office, was not only former members of the
opposition, but also suspect cadres of today.[129]

The pendulum swung back in favor of those attempting to limit the
purge when, in early December of 1937, the only published part of a
supposedly important Politburo speech by Yezhov during the nominations
to the Supreme Soviet characterized the enemy in terms of the Trotskyite-
Zinovievist-Bukharinist conspiracy in the service of the foreign bourgeoisie.[130] As Stalin became more concerned about impending war, he
began focusing on external enemies, and stated that every internal enemy
is an external enemy,[131] and in March of 1939 he espoused the view
of his critics that "destroyed enemies had just been old oppositionists
who had become secret agents of foreign powers."

In mounting the Cultural Revolution, Mao was concerned about those
who "wave the red flag to oppose the red flag," and "those who were
obeying outwardly and disobeying inwardly."[132] The first category included "capitalist roaders" who intentionally misinterpreted Maoist doc-

trine, such as those who were weakening and nullifying socialist changes effected by the regime by supporting private plots for peasants, material incentives for labor, and concessions to the remaining Chinese ex-capitalists. The latter category included a number of groups with revisionist tendencies that Mao hoped to resocialize. According to Chen,[133] these groups comprised (1) patriotic Chinese who were moved by nationalism instead of Communism; (2) liberals who originally supported Communist proposals because they were dissatisfied with the old social order, but who were not committed Communists and believed in reform instead of revolution; (3) the masses who wanted better living conditions and a better livelihood immediately but were unwilling to undergo the requisite discipline; (4) people who did not subscribe to class struggle but instead wanted Confucian social harmony; (5) intellectuals who were unwilling to subordinate their individualism and independence and who were guilty of veiled expressions of bourgeois and anti-proletarian ideas; (6) those holding traditional social and cultural values, such as attachment to home and family, aversion to collective life and soldiery, and reverence for Confucianism and its way of life; (7) technologists and professional people who resented political interference in their activities and who placed technology and professional competence above political and ideological orthodoxy; (8) the younger generation of Communists who had not experienced the bitter struggle that characterized the early years of the Chinese Communist movement, and who did not share the fiery and single-minded dedication of the veterans; and (9) Communists who would like to see the more moderate and realistic policies, and who were concerned that the more dogmatic approach undermined public support and the Communist regime.

There was confusion and conflict during the Cultural Revolution in China over whether class origin or political consciousness determined class as the Maoists alternated between definitions. The radicals believed that anybody who stood on the Maoist line was proletarian regardless of class origin, while the conservative mass organizations interpreted class according to class origin.[134] According to Stanley Rosen's study of the Red Guard movement in Ghuangzhou,[135] middle school youth in the Red Guard movement aligned themselves with factions according to their class origin, unlike university youth who tended to join the radical Red Guard faction. The conservative Red Guard faction received their strength from the children of Party and military officials, and secondarily from children from worker and peasant families. On the other hand, the radical Red Guard faction received its strength from the children of intellectuals, and secondarily from children of other middle-class origins. The conservative Red Guards, who were obviously favored by the local power structure, developed a "blood line" theory, which not only supported discrimination against "bad class" youth in the selection process for entrance into the Communist Youth League and universities and prevented "bad class" youth from participation in the Red Guard movement, but which defined the enemy of the GPCR as those of "bad class" rather than those who were entrenched bureaucrats. The "bad class" youth, being deprived of participation in the conservative Red Guards, naturally turned to the radical Red Guard faction which stressed Maoist ideology and the purging of entrenched bureaucrats, and condemned the way "good class" youth from the homes of cadre and military officers were attempting to set themselves up as a separate, privileged stratum. Thus, for the most part, among middle school youth involved in the Red Guard movement, class origin became superimposed on factional affiliation and determined the difference in the definition of the enemy. The support for a bloodline position, (as articulated in Jiang Qing's couplet that "when the father's a hero, the son's a good fellow" and "when the father's a reactionary, the son's a bastard") was reversed as the Maoist camp lent support to insurgent activities of the radical Red Guards.[136]

During the early phase of the Cultural Revolution, the enemy was also extremely abstract—anything symbolic of culture alien to the Chinese Communist Revolution, including ideas from Chinese tradition, Western democracy, and modern Soviet communism.[137] Thus, early rebel Red Guard organizations, comprising Beijing university and middle school youth, were recognized by Chairman Mao as revolutionary and proletarian (at their first rally at T'ien An Men Square on August 18, 1966). Similar rebel Red Guard groups that were formed throughout Chinese cities on the basis of those described in Maoist newspapers, roamed through Chinese cities destroying ancient relics, accosting citizens wearing Western or "bourgeois" clothing styles, and renaming buildings and streets. Economic dislocation caused by the Red Guards clogging rail lines forced Mao to call off further rallies in Beijing and discontinue the free food and lodging that had been given to the Red Guards.[138] This campaign against the "Four Olds" was revoked in September 1966 and a new campaign was initiated to focus more directly on political targets.[139]

In the second stage of the Cultural Revolution, the central leadership in Beijing narrowed the definition of the enemy by identifying the enemy as the "handful of capitalist roaders in the Party."[140] A second group of radical Red Guards either were sent out as crack troops to specific provinces to bring down political leaders out of favor with Mao and Lin, or remained in Beijing to demonstrate against opponents at the highest levels. Those sent to the provinces occupied communications stations, surrounded Party offices, demanded the reorganization of Party committees, and helped in the development of provincial radical Red

Guard contingents. Receiving logistic and strategic support from Beijing, they were successful in virtually eliminating the existing provincial Party leadership. They continued their campaign throughout the Red Guard movement as Mao's and Lin's political hatchetmen.[141] Up to the time of the Wuhan Incident, the "handful" of capitalist roaders only included those within the Party and not the military. Despite their continued support for revolutionary change, the Maoist camp did not want to widen the scope of their campaign to include the military. They moved instead to narrow the campaign against enemies by shifting from a "policy of struggle leading to a unity of the revolutionary left to a policy of moderation and unity through a 'great alliance' of all factions."[142]

The Problem of Controlling Terror

During the Cultural Revolution and the Soviet purges, there were tendencies for terror to spread downward to the lower levels of the Party and state apparatus and into the population at large, striking irrelevant targets and creating unwanted social and political instability. The mobilized masses also began to strike at initially untargeted segments of the elite. The case of the Nazi regime was different since, after the initial stages, the targets of the campaign were clearly defined and the problem of control centered more on the level of unregulated violence against that target. Though there were problems of strategy and tactics in limiting the damage and reasserting control over the course of terror, it appears in each case that when a decision was made by the supreme leader to adopt the pragmatic course, terror could rapidly be curtailed.

Contrary to popular belief, the Nazis were interested in stabilizing the terror system after the first years of the regime. Therefore, they did not look favorably upon anonymous or trivial denunciations.[143] During the first three years of the Third Reich there were so many grumblers and rumor-mongers that had been denounced that the authorities had to take drastic steps against the originally officially sponsored habit.[144] Denunciations were so frequent in the early stages of the regime that a sign outside the Gestapo headquarters in Berlin read: "Denouncers will be smacked in the face."[145] Between 1933 and 1934, prosecution for wrongful accusation and libel actually doubled.[146] The regime wanted to end wrongful accusations for a number of reasons. First, the tendency for denouncers to inherit the denounced person's post caused the Party hierarchy some disquiet as it undermined the spirit of *Volksgemeinschaft*. Secondly, it imposed such a strain on manpower and morale that rewards of up to one hundred marks were offered to anyone able to provide information against false informers. Authorities often traced, tried, and executed blackmailers. Because the avalanche of denunciations was so great, informants were finally asked to shed their anonymity.[147] Not until the war did denunciations again increase.[148]

According to Arendt,[149] the type of racial anti-Semitism practiced by the Nazis made the threat of Judaism for all Germans as much a question of their personal identity as of the supposed danger that identified Jews posed for the Germans. Therefore, all Germans presumably feared that the taint of Judaism might be traced to their ancestors. To borrow Erving Goffman's terminology,[150] Germans suffered the fear of the "discreditable" while Jews suffered the fear of the "discredited." However, most Germans did not have a problem proving that they did not have a Jewish grandparent. Proof of ancestry was required only for a position in government or an agency of the Party.[151] Obviously, given the large number of government and Party members, at least a good number of Germans had passed the test of ancestry. Blackmail did flourish in the hunt for Jewish ancestors, especially among high Nazi officials.[152] Heydrich, who was assigned the task of carrying out the "Final Solution," had to fight four libel actions in 1934, 1935, 1937 and 1940 concerning accusations about his Jewish ancestry.[153] Yet, such accusations could be dangerous. Gauleiter Kube wrote an anonymous letter concerning the non-Aryan origins of Buch (chairman of the *Parteigerichte*) and his daughter (who was Martin Bormann's wife); the SS and the Office for Race Policy in the Reich Ministry of the Interior investigated. When they found the allegations untrue, they stripped Kube of his party office and imprisoned him for several years in a concentration camp until Himmler intervened in 1940.[154] As with denunciations, the clandestine search for others' ancestry was not encouraged. Each piece of legislation subsequent to the Nuremberg Laws, which was couched in the language of defensive action in protecting Germans from Jewish pollution, also created increasingly greater social distance between German and Jew. This segregation or enforced apartheid, which was envisioned early on as part of the deassimilation process, facilitated the image of an abstract 'collective' Jew, who was devoid of humanity. This was the ultimate consequence of the Nuremberg Laws,[155] not the terrorizing of the Aryan population.

Throughout the transition period, from the Roehm Purge to the outset of the war, the SA engaged in what the Nazi leadership called "individual actions" (supposedly unofficial actions) against the Jews. While Hitler had thought of and described the Jews for some time as vermin and parasites, it was the shrill voice of Goebbels and subordinated Party and SA radicals that encouraged both the local violence and increasingly severe persecutory measures against the Jews. Because of the vituperative propaganda against Jews by Party people such as Goebbels, the SA felt that their attacks on Jews were what the government secretly wanted.[156]

The Reich government had difficulty in halting these local actions. Hitler was forced to intervene when SA violence interfered with more non-ideological aims, such as strengthening the economy in order to rearm Germany. Thus, "individual actions" were denounced not only by Hess and other pragmatic Nazi leaders,[157] but by Hitler himself.[158] One example of such denounced actions is the sporadic outbursts and destruction of Jewish property in Baden and other districts in the summer of 1935 during one of Goebbels' anti-Semitic campaigns.[159]

Waves of boycotts and terror were incited by Goebbels, particularly in October of 1938, and directed toward gaining control over Jewish policy.[160,161] The vom Rath assassination on November 7, 1938 provided Goebbels with an especially great opportunity to influence Jewish policy. Goebbels, with Lutze and his SA, planned and organized a nationwide pogrom against the Jews,[162,163] which is commonly referred to as *Kristallnacht* because of the many windows of Jewish enterprises, homes, and synagogues that were broken that night. Both Himmler and Heydrich were not informed of the plans for the pogrom until quite late, which greatly angered Himmler.

The event, which was given the appearance of being a spontaneous reaction of the German public to the vom Rath assassination, embroiled many of the members of the public besides the SA. According to Peterson,[164] leaders of the community, even judges and other ordinary citizens, as well as the SA, "behaved like madmen, destroying Jewish property with maniacal zeal and terrorizing families of young and old, who could scarcely believe the hate hysteria of supposedly civilized men." The collaboration between Goebbels and the SA in this event, which was the worst outburst of terror perpetrated against the Jews since the Nazis seized power, indicated that previous "individual actions" by the SA, especially at certain times, cannot be seen merely as violence by lower level cadres. Instead, although not planned as such, they definitely should be interpreted as a means by which Goebbels and other Party radicals, whose vituperative propaganda helped provoke these "individual actions," were able to maintain involvement in Jewish policy.

The SA was not satisfied with what Hitler considered would be their final fling during *Kristallnacht*. Over the next weeks they continued to irritate the SS leadership by initiating continued anti-Jewish actions. Heydrich and Himmler, who became concerned with the threat of a revived SA, finally were able to bring the SA under control in December.[165] In the aftermath of *Kristallnacht*, Jewish policy was radicalized while the SA's participation in dealing with the "Jewish Problem" was ended.

In 1939, Jewish students were expelled from schools, all Jewish enterprises and shops were Aryanized, all wireless sets owned by Jews were confiscated, all Jews were confined by a curfew, etc.[166] In the next two years, Jews were to undergo document stamping, name changes, the marking of their clothing with a star, and finally, deportation to the East. With the outbreak of the war, Goebbels recognized new opportunities in solving the "Jewish Problem" when he exclaimed, "Fortunately, a whole series of possibilities presents itself for us in wartime that would be denied us in peacetime."[167]

Stalin broadened the scope of the mobilization campaign with his thesis that "the stronger socialism becomes the more intense class conflict becomes and the more nefarious the activities of the enemy." This thesis led local leaders to remove those they did not like or found threatening, or to terrorize or blackmail the best of the local Party members according to the needs of the moment.[168] Administrative and economic cadres protected friends through patronage and nepotism and deflected charges onto insignificant scapegoats, including subordinates acting on their orders,[169] while attempting to appear vigilant or zealous. Frightened by repeated warnings of the need for vigilance against enemy treachery or sabotage, local Party secretaries and economic managers deflected suspicion from themselves for the malfunctioning of their administrations by denouncing, often with considerable remorse, some of their subordinates who were deeply implicated, unpopular, or vulnerable because of their dubious associations or their political past,[170] or who were most troublesome because of their critical remarks about the cadres.[171] Later, terrorized cadres, instead of seeking correct allocation of responsibility, simply denounced immediate superiors. When Party leaders became more clearly designated as targets, "[Party] members denounced leaders (and each other) for dubious class origins, long-forgotten sins, and current misdeeds."[172] Again, in turn, secretaries defended themselves and proved their vigilance by expelling and denouncing batches of rank-and-file members. Panic-stricken local party officials even resorted to filling administrative positions with politically "safe" employees of the NKVD.

Unlike in Nazi Germany prior to the war, denunciations in Stalinist U.S.S.R. were not only encouraged, but required.[173] The victim himself was not only required to confess, but also to name accomplices and confederates, even though none existed.[174] People who did not inform[175] and people who showed leniency toward those arrested[176] were themselves arrested insofar as attempts at restraint were prima facie evidence of counterrevolution or subversive intent.[177] (Those merely acquainted with suspects were arrested as well.[178]) Both the Party and the NKVD were inundated with countless denunciations.[179] The NKVD showed little interest in whether the denunciation was motivated by mercenary and personal reasons,[180] and most slanderers went unpunished.[181] Consequently, friends denounced friends,[182] children denounced parents, and spouses denounced each other.[183]

A number of students of the *Yezhovshchina*[184] have insisted that the NKVD arrests were guided by a quota system, in which orders from Moscow specified target figures indicating that so many nameless wreckers or saboteurs lived in a given jurisdiction and should be identified and apprehended. According to Connor,[185] there was pressure on NKVD administrations at the local, district, and provincial levels to fulfill these quotas or go under. Moreover, the more discord the secret police unfolded or discovered, the more indispensable it became.[186] Therefore, it is believed that there was a large degree of NKVD overcompliance[187] that went beyond any clear political purpose. Yet, there has been no conclusive evidence that the NKVD overcomplied with the directives in terms of numbers. The lack of specificity in directives[188] probably led to "considerable day-to-day indecision about whom to arrest."[189] Given the situation, the NKVD was not the least bit interested in real facts and was willing to create a case once they had arrested a suspect.[190] Consequently, there was a lack of coordination and a great deal of inefficiency.[191] Nevertheless, if quotas in fact existed, the arrests made by the NKVD must be seen as purposive terror, despite their arbitrariness.

Many scholars[192] believe the Great Purges of 1936–1938 were motivated by Stalin's desire not merely to replace the supposedly treacherous old technical experts and Old Bolshevik Party cadres with just any elite, but to anchor his power in a new generation of elite who owed its position to him.[193] During the *Yezhovshchina*, Stalin continued to criticize the NKVD for a lack, not an excess, of vigilance. After the Yezhovshchina, at the Eighteenth Party Congress held in early 1939, Stalin scarcely mentioned "excesses," since most of those victimized in the Great Purge were in fact his intended targets—top and middle-level functionaries,[194] particularly Old Bolsheviks; instead he emphasized the success of the purges, especially in creating a new intelligentsia.[195] It was precisely the purging of some of the new elite—the wrong target—that became defined as "excesses" of the purges of the thirties.

While there were certain celebrated cases exposed concerning non-Party citizens, such as in Leninsk-Kuznetsk where a hundred children were arrested as members of a children's conspiracy,[196] the excesses in the purges against lower echelons of the Party and state apparatus by local cadre leaders were more frequently mentioned in the press and in speeches. So little was publicized about the general terror in the society that recent revisionist historians such as Robert Thurston[197] have concluded that only the elite were targeted during the *Yezhovshchina* and that pervasive fear did not exist among the masses. This leads to the conclusion that the official meaning of "excesses" during the Yezhovshchina pertained mainly to Party members; and that Party moderates did very little, if anything, to reduce the terror in the general population.

During the Great Proletarian Cultural Revolution, Mao became extremely disturbed by the situational violence of the radical Red Guards insofar as inappropriate means of struggle undermined the ideological goals of the rectification campaign. Mao wanted the GPCR to be conducted as a political struggle instead of an armed struggle.

Mao supported methods of conflict that included house arrests, transfers, demotions, and temporary dismissals of revisionist elements in the Party and state positions. For the Red Guards during the GPCR, he approved of the use of character assassination and denunciation through the use of *tatzepao* (character posters), sloganeering, seizure of the media, and struggle meetings involving "self-criticism" sessions. These methods were consonant with the significance Mao placed on reeducation, resocialization, and rehabilitation.[198]

While many earlier analysts of the GPCR confirm that these sanctioned methods were used[199] and that the amount of actual bloodshed was exaggerated except in certain areas,[200] Lucien Pye[201] says that human rights violations were rife during the GPCR and that the current Beijing administration admits that there were millions of deaths. Ann Thurston[202] and Stanley Rosen[203] document that beatings, along with other indignities of various types, were commonplace. Humiliation was used as a major form of persecution and was felt by victims as a form of terror. Professors were made to sweep university grounds and clean toilets, while other victims were relegated to a single room in their own homes as the rest of their dwellings were occupied by abusive revolutionary rebels. Both conservative and rebel factions of the Red Guards were guilty of overly enthusiastic and violent retaliation against perceived "bourgeois" enemies.[204] Moreover, according to Thurston[205] there were also incidents not only of "revolutionary" beatings, but also of robberies, extortion and rape. Instead of fostering positive "self-criticism" sessions, torture just short of killing was used to acquire false confessions. Thurston reveals that everyone she interviewed in her study lost through death a relative or friend—from torture, factional violence, suicide, or the refusal to provide medical care to those labeled "counterrevolutionary."[206]

Because of the mass chaos that occurred during the GPCR, the Maoist leadership circle was forced to use different organizational schemes to rein in the uncontrolled actions of his radical Red Guards before resorting to military action. The warring factions of the Red Guards were brought together at Red Guard Congresses in Beijing, Red Guards were supervised by Red Guard military police (called the provost corps), Military Training Groups were established to provide military and political training, Military

Control Commissions led Maoist Thought study groups to develop a common outlook and unity of the factions, and newspaper articles provided guidance in how to carry out the GPCR.[207] To prevent greater instability and give some coherent structure to the GPCR, "three-in-one revolutionary committees" were established in all administrative and production units. These committees included representatives of the revolutionary mass organizations, faithful Party cadres, and the PLA. By September 1968 Revolutionary Committees had assumed power in all provinces, regions, and municipality administrations.[208] However, almost all of these schemes did not work.

The Wuhan Incident in July 1967 occurred during the apex of the revolutionary violence and proved to be the turning point of the GPCR. From mid-July to early August, regional military authorities in Wuhan not only sided with the conservative Red Guard faction in violation of a Central Committee directive to promote unity among revolutionary forces; they also challenged Beijing's authority by assisting in kidnapping Hsieh Fu-chih, the head of the public security system, and Wang Li, member of the Central Revolutionary Small Group, who had been sent by the Beijing leadership to Kuming to improve the chaotic situation there. Troops loyal to Beijing seized control back from the local military forces, and the leaders of the "rebellion" were arrested and brought to Beijing. Given the military involvement in the incident, Mao became concerned with the dangers of "warlordism," and first contemplated a selective purge of the military. However, given the role of the military as the only institution left to maintain order, and given Lin Biao and other pro-Mao military leaders' opposition to such a purge, Mao was forced to decide against such a purge.[209]

Conclusion

In this examination of the mobilization campaigns in three movement-regimes, the problem of unregulated terror has been interpreted as a consequence of factionalism within the regime leadership or as conflict between regime-sponsored organizations, rather than as a product of the inherent logic or failures of totalitarian systems. The problem of unregulated terror only becomes visible when the moderating forces within the regimes succeed in having their definition of reality accepted and purposive terror reduced, if only temporarily.

To analyze the conflict over the definition of the enemy, it is first necessary to distinguish between target groups and victims. Obviously, it might be assumed that where there is unmanaged terror, the number of victims of the mobilization campaign must exceed the number of intended or public targets. In Nazi Germany, this was not an important problem since the intended and public target was all Jews. As a result of the deassimilation of Jews and the relatively narrow definition of *Mischlinge* that was adopted, as well as the threat of libel action for false accusations, the fear of being identified as a Jew did not really affect the Aryan population. The situation in the Soviet Union was different; target groups and victims of the vigilance campaigns of the thirties were not one in the same. While much greater numbers of non-Party victims were not *public* targets of the campaigns, the "excesses" of the purges referred to by certain leaders concerned the thousands of innocent rank-and-file Party members who were not intended targets of the campaigns. During the Great Proletarian Cultural Revolution, victims and targets were also discrepant, although non-targeted victims were recognized as casualties of the rectification campaign, helping bring the GPCR to an end.

In the Nazi and Stalinist cases, moderates attempted to limit the scope of the campaigns by their definitions of the enemy. When the law was used to define the enemy, moderates attempted to manipulate that medium to create narrower definitions of the enemy. In Nazi Germany, moderates sought a narrow definition of *Mischlinge* in the Nuremberg Laws; and in Stalinist U.S.S.R. moderates defined the enemy as former oppositionists who had already been eliminated at the Moscow Trials. In the Chinese case, on the other hand, the Maoist camp itself defined enemies as "the handful" within the Party who had "taken the capitalist road."

In addition, moderates attempted to limit the scope of the campaigns by selecting or accepting an ascribed status for the enemy rather than an achieved status. Moderates in Nazi Germany rationalized the biological definition of the Jew in the Nuremberg Laws as possibly carving out a circumscribed status for Jews in Germany, while the radicals were not satisfied until the Jew was also defined by his presumably parasitic economic status. Such an economic definition, they felt, would lead to the Aryanization of Jewish property. Party moderates in the Soviet Union defined the enemy according to his previous oppositional background because the oppositionists had been essentially defeated, while radicals wanted the enemy to be defined in terms of behavioral indications of potential opposition from all those who were not indebted to Stalin for their position. The PLA and their proxy Red Guard forces tended to view and treat those of "bad class" background as the enemy, while the radical faction of the Red Guards preferred to identify the enemy as all those who did not follow the Thought of Mao Zedong. In the Stalinist and Maoist cases, the ascriptive status criteria would limit the number of victims, whereas in the Nazi case, moderates hoped that the biological criteria would limit the severity of the measures against the Jewish victims.

Although it is true that the police in both Nazi Germany and Stalinist U.S.S.R. developed their own economic empires and were integrally involved in the purposive terror, there is no evidence that, in either case, a zealous police acted independently or in excess of directives received from the top leadership.[210] On the other hand, in Maoist China, the public security organs, who had strong alliances with local political officials, took strong measures against the initial rampages of the Red Guards. Seen as revisionist by Mao, their offices were seized by both the Red Guards and the PLA during the early stages of the GPCR, and they were virtually emasculated during the remainder of the GPCR. With the initiation of the mobilization campaigns against enemies in the three regimes, radicals in each regime were not only suspicious of any form of legal formalism, but did not believe that the police, whose major role had been control and repression, could perform the new proactive function appropriately by themselves. Instead they believed that there was a need for greater participation of the masses in policing.

In Nazi Germany, the radicals in the Party, particularly Goebbels, were concerned about gaining control over Jewish Policy because of its importance in determining influence within the regime, and instigated the Nazified masses, namely the SA, to take action against the Jews. Consequently, they clashed with the SS and attempted to undermine the SS emigration policy.

In Stalinist U.S.S.R. during the *Yezhovshchina*, Party pragmatists attempted to wind down the Party purge by arguing for limiting all responsibility for "unmasking enemies" to the police. This proposal was in turn opposed by the radicals who supported a "mass mobilization" platform, which would involve *all* Party members in the vigilance campaign. The effort on the part of the moderates to transfer full responsibility for the vigilance campaign to the police was not intended as a means of stifling popular control by the Party "rank-and-file," but instead a means of terminating the purges by abdicating the denunciation role for all Party members that was so critically interdependent with the investigatory role conferred on the police. Given quotas to fill and vigilance to prove, the NKVD, unlike their Nazi counterparts, encouraged denunciations among the non-Party masses, and consequently the labor camps were supplied with hundreds of thousands of nameless victims.

Mao and Party radicals in China, upset with the defense of the status quo by and the "specialized work" of the public security system, insisted on a "mass line" during the GPCR. The PLA was first used to assist radical Red Guards in seizing power from the police organs, and then required to stand aside during the initial stages of the GPCR. However, once the GPCR became dangerously chaotic, the PLA, the only remaining institution of social control, had the restrictions lifted that had been placed on it, and it was required to assume a police role. Their involvement in police work and their function in the Military Training Groups and Military Control Commissions brought about sharp negative reactions from the radical Red Guard factions. Once the radical Red Guard factions engaged in armed conflict with the PLA, Mao, concerned with maintaining the integrity of the PLA and opposed to armed struggle, sided with the PLA and put an end to the Red Guard movement.

Thus, in revolutionary, mass-movement regimes engaged in mobilization campaigns against enemies, the problem of unregulated or situational terror would seem to appear when moderates are able to reduce purposive terror by establishing or restoring more institutionalized forms of repressive control in the process of normalizing the political order. They are able to do so by limiting the definition of the enemy to more symbolic ascribed categories which had already been repressed, and by entrusting policing functions to formal and specialized agents of social control who use conventional control mechanisms.

Notes

1. Hannah Arendt, *The Origins of Totalitarianism*, 2d ed. (Cleveland: World Publishing Company, 1958), 474.

2. Zbigniew Brzezinski, *The Permanent Purge* (Cambridge: Harvard University Press, 1956), 27.

3. Carl J. Friedrich and Zbigniew Brzezinski, *Totalitarian Dictatorship and Autocracy* (Cambridge: Harvard University Press, 1956), 132.

4. Merle Fainsod, "Terror as a System of Power," chap. in *How Russia is Ruled*, rev. ed. (Cambridge: Harvard University Press, 1964), 354.

5. Brzezinski, 18, 27; Friedrich and Brzezinski, 150, 155; Arendt, 91, 162.

6. Arendt, 102.

7. Robert Tucker, *The Soviet Political Mind: Stalinism and Post-Stalin Change*, rev. ed. (New York: Norton, 1971), 3–19.

8. Robert Tucker found the concept of totalitarianism wanting because it did not provide a comparative framework within which Communist, Fascist, and Nationalist single-party regimes could be analyzed by their significant similarities and differences, or as three species of a single political genus.(Tucker, *Soviet Political Mind*, 3–19) He therefore proposed a conceptual category he refers to as the "revolutionary mass-movement regime under single party auspices," or, in its shortened version, the "movement-regime." This political type includes: (1) a constructive process of far-reaching change, (2) active participation of the masses, and (3) a centralized revolutionary party that is the foundation of all political authority. What is significant about this definition is the emphasis placed on some form of mobilization.

9. The time of Yezhov, who was head of the Soviet Secret Police, the NKVD, during the "Great Purge" period of 1936–1938.

10. Irving L. Horowitz, *Three Worlds of Development: The Theory and Practice of International Stratification*, 2d ed. (New York: Oxford University Press, 1972), 454–457.

11. Karl A. Schleunes, *The Twisted Road to Auschwitz: Nazi Policy Toward German Jews, 1933–1939* (Urbana, Ill.: University of Illinois Press, 1970); Niels E. Rosenfeldt, "Problems of Evidence," *Slavic Review* 42 (1983): 85–91.

12. Brzezinski, 168–169.

13. Alexander Dallin and George Breslauer, *Political Terror in Communist Systems* (Stanford, Calif.: Stanford University Press, 1970), 7.

14. Ibid., 19.

15. For example, see Schleunes; Gabor T. Rittersporn, "Stalin in 1938: Political Defeat Behind the Rhetorical Apotheosis," trans. David J. Parent, *Telos* 46 (1980–81): 6–42; Gabor T. Rittersporn, "The State Against Itself: Socialist Tensions and Political Conflict in the U.S.S.R. 1936–1938," trans. Brian Singer, *Telos* 41 (1979): 87–105; Stanley Rosen, "The Origins and Development of the Red Guard Movement in China, 1960–1968" (Ph.D. diss.: University of California, Los Angeles, 1979); Stanley Rosen, *Red Guard Factionalism and the Cultural Revolution in Guangzhou* [Canton] (Boulder, Colo.: Westview, 1982).

16. In the Soviet case, according to Rittersporn ("State Against Itself," 96) and J. Arch Getty, (*Origins of the Great Purge: The Soviet Communist Party Reconsidered, 1933–1938* (New York: Cambridge University Press, 1985), 126) there were no distinct camps or Politburo alignments with standardized lines and slogans with which individuals could be consistently identified; and, according to Getty (*Origins*, 126–127), there was no liberal opposition or anti-Stalinist bloc in the Politburo. If positions were stable, about-faces from one camp to the other were frequent.

17. Rittersporn, "Stalin in 1938," 16.

18. Thomas W. Robinson, "The Wuhan Incident: Local Strife and Provincial Rebellion During the Cultural Revolution," *The China Quarterly* 47 (1971): 413.

19. Arendt, who distinguishes between "leaders" of totalitarian movements and "ordinary" dictators or despots, disagrees with the former statement. According to her (Arendt, 374–375), "a tyrant would never identify himself with his subordinates, let alone with every one of their acts; he might use them as scapegoats and gladly have them criticized in order to save himself from the wrath of the people . . . the Leader, *on the contrary*, cannot tolerate criticism of his subordinates . . ." Arendt goes on to say that he assumes blanket responsibility for everything done in the name of the regime to relieve all lesser functionaries of any sense of individual responsibility for their actions. This was certainly not true in the cases of Hitler, Stalin, and Mao, who encouraged criticism and engaged in the purging of movement members.

20. Ghita Ionescu, *The Politics of European Communist States* (New York: Praeger, 1967); Brian Chapman, *Police State* (New York: Praeger, 1970), 114–121.

21. Robert Koehl, "The Character of the Nazi SS," *The Journal of Modern History* 34 (1962): 280; Karl O. Paetel, "The Reign of the Black Order: The Final Phase of German National Socialism: The SS Counter-State," in Edmond Vermeil et al., eds., *The Third Reich* (London: Weidenfeld and Nicolson, 1955), 634.

22. Joseph Nyomarkay, *Charisma and Factionalism in the Nazi Party* (Minneapolis: University of Minnesota Press, 1967).

23. Schleunes, 169–172.

24. Ibid., 258.

25. Helmut Krausnick, "The Persecution of the Jews," in Helmut Krausnick et al., *Anatomy of the SS State* (New York: Walker & Co., 1968), 24–25.

26. Leo Rattner, "The SS: A Study of Nazi Terrorism" (Ph.D. diss.: New School For Social Research, 1962), 19; Edward Peterson, *The Limits of Hitler's Power* (Princeton, N.J.: Princeton University Press, 1969), 126.

27. Rattner, 20.

28. Schleunes, 177.

29. Richard Grunberger, *A Social History of the Third Reich* (London: Weidenfeld and Nicolson, 1970), 26.

30. Bruno Bettelheim, *The Informed Heart: Autonomy in a Mass Age* (New York: The Free Press, 1960), 253; Herbert S. Levine, *Hitler's Free City: A History of the Nazi Party in Danzig, 1925-1939* (Chicago: University of Chicago Press, 1973), 275.

31. Raul Hilberg, ed., *Documents of Destruction: Germany and Jewry, 1933-1945* (Chicago: Quadrangle, 1961), 32; Krausnick, 29.

32. Hilberg, 36–37.

33. Levine, 262.

34. Heinz Hohne, *The Order of the Death's Head: The Story of Hitler's SS* trans. Richard Barry (New York: Coward-McCann, 1970), 331–336, 346–347.

35. Gerald Reitlinger, *The Final Solution* (London: Vallentine, Mitchell & Co., 1953), 9.

36. Schleunes, 206–207, 210.

37. Reitlinger, 8.

38. Schleunes, 71.

39. Ibid., 76, 87.

40. Ibid., 89.

41. Peterson, *Limits*, 33.

42. Schleunes, 167.

43. Ibid., 138.

44. Levine, 138.

45. Grunberger, 457.

46. Schleunes, 150.

47. Peterson, *Limits*, 47.

48. Schleunes, 116.

49. Levine, 131.

50. Schleunes, 234–235.

51. Donald M. McKale, *The Nazi Party Courts: Hitler's Management of Conflict in His Own Movement, 1921-1945* (Lawrence, Kans.: The University Press of Kansas, 1974), 163–168; Peterson, *Limits*, 58.

52. Nicolai Bukharin, [originally anonymous] *Letter of an Old Bolshevik* (New York: The Rand School, 1938); reprinted in R.V. Daniels, ed., *The Stalin Revolution* (Lexington, Mass.: D.C. Heath, 1965), 139.

53. H. Akhminov, "Stalin—Monster or Functionary?" *Bulletin for the Institute for the Study of the U.S.S.R.* 17 (1970): 16.

54. Bukharin, 139.

55. Borys Levytsky, *The Stalinist Terror in the Thirties: Documentation From the Soviet Press* (Stanford, Calif.: Hoover Institute Press, 1974), 16–18.

56. Jonathan Haslam, "Political Opposition to Stalin and the Origins of the Terror in Russia, 1932–1936," *The Historical Review* 29 (1986): 405.

57. Bukharin, 139; Haslam, 396–97; Mary McAuley, *Politics and the Soviet Union* (Harmondsworth, Middlesex, England: Penguin, 1977), 122.

58. Bukharin, 139; Roy A. Medvedev, *Let History Judge: The Origin and Consequences of Stalinism,* trans. Colleen Taylor (New York: Knopf, [1967] 1971), 142–143.

59. Bukharin, 140.

60. Boris I. Nicolaevsky, *Power and the Soviet Elite* (New York: Praeger, 1965), 11; Robert Conquest, *The Great Terror* (New York: Macmillan, 1968), 52; Haslam, 398.

61. Medvedev, *Let History Judge,* 142–143.

62. Haslam, 397.

63. Ibid., 397.

64. Attempts to exculpate Stalin from the role of decision maker (e.g., Alexander Magid, "Did Stalin Rule?" *British Columbia Historical Review* 9 (1963): 168–181; Getty, *Origins,* 126–127) have received little support (e.g., Francis Randall, *Stalin's Russia: An Historical Reconsideration* (New York: The Free Press, 1985), 5; Haslam, 395; Timo Vihavainen, "The Yezhovshchina: Premeditated Social Engineering or the Result of Unforeseen Circumstances? Some Objections to J. Arch Getty's Revision of the Great Purges," *Nordic Journal of Soviet and East European Studies* 2 (1985): 129) Getty (*Origins,* 135), for example, states that Stalin reacted to events as much as he initiated them, but recognizes that Stalin had decided in principle to move against the opposition and leaned further and further in a radical direction.

65. Haslam, 402.

66. Robert H. McNeal, "The Decisions of the CPSU and the Great Purge," *Soviet Studies* 23 (1971): 179–180.

67. Robert Conquest, "The Great Purge," *Encounter* 31 (1968): 82; Medvedev, *Let History Judge,* 156; Levytsky, *Stalinist Terror,* 19.

68. Bukharin, 143.

69. Bukharin; Medvedev, *Let History Judge.*

70. Bukharin, 141.

71. Levytsky, *Stalinist Terror,* 21; McAuley, 130.

72. Medvedev, *Let History Judge,* 157.

73. Ibid., 163.

74. Bukharin, 142.

75. Ibid., 144.

76. Medvedev, *Let History Judge,* 325.

77. Bukharin, 144.

78. e.g., Nicolaevsky, 69–97; Conquest, "Great Purge;" Medvedev, *Let History Judge*, 161; Frederick C. Barghoorn, "New Perspectives on Functions and Developments of Soviet Terror," *Studies in Comparative Communism* 7 (1974): 314; Levytsky, *Stalinist Terror*, 19; Robert C. Tucker, "Stalinism as Revolution From Above," in Tucker, ed., *Stalinism: Essays in Historical Interpretation* (New York: W.W. Norton, 1977), 98.

79. Rittersporn, "Stalin in 1938," 19–21.

80. Getty, *Origins*, 126.

81. Rittersporn, "Stalin in 1938," 28.

82. Ibid., 25.

83. Rittersporn, "State Against Itself," 10.

84. Peterson, *Limits*, 129–132; Haslam, 407, 496.

85. Ralph L. Powell, and Chong-Kun Yoon, "Public Security and the PLA," *Asian Survey* 12 (1972): 1084.

86. Ibid.; Rosen, *Red Guard Factionalism*, 118.

87. Powell and Yoon, 1085–1086.

88. Ibid., 1087–1088.

89. Juliana P. Heaslet, "The Red Guards: Instruments of Destruction in the Cultural Revolution," *Asian Survey* 17 (1972): 1032–1047.

90. Rosen, *Red Guard Factionalism*, 138, 202, 210, 236.

91. Powell and Yoon, 1089.

92. Hong Yung Lee, "Mao's Strategy for Revolutionary Change: A Case Study of the Cultural Revolution," *China Quarterly* 77 (1979): 50–73.

93. Heaslet, 1038–1039; Powell and Yoon, 1090.

94. Albert Bergesen, "Political Witch Hunts: The Sacred and Subversive in Cross-Cultural Perspective," *American Sociological Review* 42 (1977): 220–233.

95. Howard Becker, "The Regimented Man: Interviews with German Officials Under the Nazis," *Social Forces* 28 (1946): 19–24; Joachim Fest, *Hitler*, trans. Richard and Clara Winston (New York: Vintage, 1975 [1973]), 541.

96. Reitlinger, 6.

97. E. K. Bramstedt, *Dictatorship and Political Police: The Technique of Control by Fear* (New York: Oxford University Press, 1945), 103; Theodore Abel, "The Sociology of the Concentration Camp," *Social Forces* 30 (1951): 151.

98. Schleunes, 61, 94, 130.

99. Hilberg, 4.

100. Schleunes, 118.

101. Ibid., 122.

102. Krausnick, 33.

103. Eugene Davidson, *The Trial of the Germans* (New York: Macmillan, 1966), 271; Arthur Schweitzer, "The Nazification of the Lower Middle Class and Peasants," in Edmond Vermeil et al., *The Third Reich* (London: Weidenfeld and Nicolson, 1955).

105. Schleunes, 133, 135.

106. Hilberg, 119–121.

107. George Mosse, ed., *Nazi Culture* (New York: Grosset & Dunlap, 1966), 4.

108. Grunberger, 310; Joachim Remak, ed., *The Nazi Years: A Documentary History* (Englewood Cliffs, N.J.: Prentice-Hall, 1969), 4; Robert K. Merton, "Insiders and Outsiders: A Chapter in the Sociology of Knowledge," *American Journal of Sociology* 78 (1972): 18.

109. Peter Gay, *Weimar Culture: The Outsider as Insider* (New York: Harper & Row, 1968).

110. Schleunes, 4.

111. Leon Poliakov, "The Weapon of Anti-Semitism," in Edmond Vermeil et al., *The Third Reich* (London: Weidenfeld and Nicolson, 1955), 838.

112. Rattner, 54.

113. Arendt, 365.

114. Rittersporn, "State Against Itself," 99.

115. Getty, *Origins*, 131.

116. Medvedev, *Let History Judge*, 34.

117. Adam Ulam, *Stalin: The Man and His Era* (New York: Viking, 1973), 430.

118. O. Utis, (pseud.) "Generalissimo Stalin and the Art of Government." *Foreign Affairs* 30 (1952): 209.

119. Nikita Khrushchev, *The Anatomy of Terror: Khrushchev's Revelations About Stalin's Regime*, with an introduction by Nathaniel Weyl (Washington, D.C.: Public Affairs Press, 1956), 57.

120. Getty, *Origins* 149.

121. Ibid., 138.

122. Ibid., 124.

123. Ibid., 179; Rittersporn, "State Against Itself," 98.

124. Rittersporn, "State Against Itself," 98.

125. Getty, *Origins*, 127.

126. Rittersporn, "State Against Itself," 98.

127. Getty, *Origins*, 125, 140, 145.

128. Rittersporn ("Stalin in 1938," p. 21) gives a different interpretation of abstractness and concreteness in the definition of the enemy and their role in broadening or restricting the purge. In his perspective, the leaders extending the purge used a more concrete, behavioral definition of the enemy and those opposing the purge put forth a more abstract definition referring to a nonexistent opposition.

129. Rittersporn, "State Against Itself," 99; Getty, *Origins*, 128.

130. Rittersporn, "Stalin in 1938," 22; Getty, *Origins*, 183.

131. Rittersporn, "Stalin in 1938," 34.

132. Lee, 63.

133. Theodore H. Chen, "A Nation in Agony," *Problems of Communism* 15 (1966): 18–20.

134. Lee.

135. Rosen, *Red Guard Factionalism*.

136. Ibid., 111, 120.

137. Wen-Shun Chi, "The Great Proletarian Cultural Revolution in Ideological Perspective," *Asian Survey* 9 (1969): 579.

138. Heaslet, 1035.

139. Ibid., 1033–1034.

140. Anne McEwen, "The Great Proletarian Cultural Revolution in Retrospect," *Journal of Contemporary Asia* 17 (1987): 60.

141. Heaslet, 1035–1036.

142. Rosen, *Red Guard Factionalism*, 200; McEwen, 60.

143. William S. Allen, *The Nazi Seizure of Power: The Experience of a Single German Town, 1930-1935* (Chicago: Quadrangle, 1965), 247.

144. Bramstedt, 114.

145. Hans Gerth, "The Nazi Party and Its Leadership Composition," *American Journal of Sociology* 45 (1940): 517–541; reprinted in Robert Merton et al., eds., *Reader in Bureaucracy* (New York: The Free Press), 113; Robert Koehl, "Toward an SS Typology: Social Engineers," *Journal of Economics and Sociology* 18 (1959): 122–123.

146. Grunberger, 108, 121.

147. Ibid., 109, 112.

148. Bramstedt, 142–144; Grunberger, 113.

149. Arendt, 356.

150. Erving Goffman, *Behavior in Public Places: Notes on the Social Organization of Gatherings* (New York: Free Press of Glencoe, 1963).

151. Schleunes, 130.

152. Klaus Epstein, "The Nazi Consolidation of Power," *Journal of Modern History* 34 (1962): 77.

153. Reitlinger, 34; Joachim Fest, *The Face of the Third Reich: Portraits of the Nazi Leadership* trans. Michael Bullock (New York: Random House, 1970 [1963]), 101.

154. McKale, 145.

155. Grunberger, 465.

156. Peterson, *Limits*, 259.

157. Ibid., 135, 258.

158. McKale, 161.

159. Hohne, *Order of the Death's Head*, 330.

160. Ibid., 330, 338.

161. While most students of Nazi Germany have interpreted propaganda as an incitement to violence, Hilberg (*Documents of Destruction*, p. 32) has said that the anti-Jewish propaganda was not an inducement to action, but a justification for it.

162. Peterson, *Limits*, 270.163.

163. Peterson says (*Limits*, p. 20) that Goebbels possibly organized the attack to surprise Hitler, while McKale (p. 161) says that Hitler gave Goebbels an oral command to order the "spontaneous" pogrom. For a more extensive relation of the event, see Lionel Kochan, *Pogrom, 10 November 1938* (London: Andre Deutsch, 1957).

164. Peterson, *Limits*, 270.

165. Schleunes, 244.

166. Grunberger, 518–519.

167. Schleunes, 257.

168. Nadezhda Mandelstam, *Hope Against Hope: A Memoir* trans. Clarence Brown (New York: Atheneum, 1970), 266; Medvedev, *Let History Judge*, 344; Rittersporn, "Stalin in 1938," 10–11.

169. Rittersporn, "State Against Itself," 87–98; Getty, *Origins*, 124, 145, 152–153, 158.

170. Rittersporn, "State Against Itself," 94, 101; Rittersporn, "Stalin in 1938," 11; Getty, *Origins*, 177, 195.

171. Rittersporn, "State Against Itself," 97, 100; "Stalin in 1938," 11.

172. Getty, *Origins*, 178.

173. Levytsky, *Stalinist Terror*, 29; Alexandr I. Solzhenitsyn, *The Gulag Archipelago*, Vols. 1 and 2, trans. Thomas Whitney (New York: Harper & Row, 1973), 129.

174. Medvedev, *Let History Judge*, 340.

175. Joseph Berger, *Nothing But the Truth* (New York: John Day, 1971), 75; Solzhenitsyn, *Gulag*, vols. 1 and 2, 46.

176. Medvedev, *Let History Judge*, 344.

177. Walter D. Connor, "The Manufacture of Deviance: The Case of the Soviet Purge, 1936–1938," *American Sociological Review* 37 (1972): 408.

178. Rittersporn, "Stalin in 1938," 12.

179. Ibid., 12.

180. Berger, 200; Connor, 408.

181. Medvedev, *Let History Judge*, 354.

182. Victor Kravchenko, *I Chose Freedom: The Personal and Political Life of a Soviet Official* (New York: Charles Scribner, 1956), 132–147; Barrington Moore, *Terror and Progress: U.S.S.R.* (Cambridge: Harvard University Press, 1954), 164; Solzhenitsyn, *Gulag*, vols. 1 and 2, 119.

183. Randall, 119; Margarete Buber, *Under Two Dictators*, trans. Edward Fitzgerald (London: Victor Gollancz Ltd., 1949), 14; Mandelstam, 38.

184. Vladimir and Evdokia Petrov, *Empire of Fear* (New York: Praeger, 1956), 73; Arendt, 429; Conquest, *Great Terror*, 316; Robert Conquest, *Inside Stalin's Secret Police: NKVD Politics, 1936–1939* (Stanford, Calif.: Hoover Institution Press, 1985), 60; Mandelstam, 12, 49; Medvedev, *Let History Judge*, 284; Solzhenitsyn, *Gulag*, vols. 1 and 2, pp. 7, 71, 147, 447; Solzhenitsyn, *The Gulag Archipelago*, vols. 3 and 4, trans. Thomas P. Whitney (New York: Harper & Row, 1975), 642; Anton Antonov-Ovseyenko, *In the Time of Stalin* trans. George Saunders (New York: Harper & Row, 1981), 126.

185. Connor, 408.

186. Fainsod, 461.

187. Randall, 137; Alec Nove, "Was Stalin Really Necessary?" *Encounter* 18 (1962): 90; Connor, 409.

188. Barbara G. Katz, "Purges and Production: Soviet Economic Growth, 1928–1940," *The Journal of Economic History* 35 (1975): 571; Connor, 406.

189. Getty, *Origins*, 178.

190. Mandelstam, 316; Solzhenitsyn, *Gulag*, vols. 1 and 2, p. 146.

191. Getty, *Origins*, 177–178.

192. Herbert S. Dinerstein, "The Purge: Permanent Soviet Institution," *Problems of Communism* 3 (1954): 31; Akhminov, 19; Medvedev, *Let History Judge*, 230; Levytsky, *Stalinist Terror*, 25–27; Sheila Fitzpatrick, "Stalin and the Making of a New Elite, 1928–1939," *Slavic Review* 38 (1979): 380, 394–402.

193. Others have refuted this interpretation. Randall (p. 137) states quite explicitly that Stalin did not go on with the Great Purges self-consciously in order to bring the new Soviet middle class, dependent on him alone, into lower and middle power positions.

194. Aryeh L. Unger, "Stalin's Renewal of the Leading Stratum: A Note on the Great Purge," *Soviet Studies* 20 (1968–1969): 326; Levytsky, *Stalinist Terror*, 24–27; Katz, 571.

195. McNeal, 185; Fitzpatrick, 398.

196. Conquest, *Inside Stalin's Secret Police*, 57.

197. Robert W. Thurston, "Fear and Belief in the USSR's 'Great Terror'—Response to Arrest, 1935–1939," *Slavic Review* 45 (1986): 213–234.

198. Arthur A. Cohen, "The Man and His Policies," *Problems of Communism* 15 (1966): 12; Joan Robinson, "The Cultural Revolution in China," *International Affairs* 44 (1968): 226.

199. See, for example, Frederick T.C. Yu, "Persuasive Communications During the Cultural Revolution," *Gazette* 16 (1970): 74, 83–85.

200. See, for example, Heaslet, 1044–1045.

201. Lucien W. Pye, "Reassessing the Cultural Revolution," *The China Quarterly* 108 (1986): 597–612.

202. Anne F. Thurston, "Victim's of China's Cultural Revolution: The Invisible Wounds," *Pacific Affairs* 57 (1985): 599–620.

203. Rosen *Red Guard Factionalism*, 117.

204. McEwen, 60.

205. Anne Thurston, 613.

206. Ibid., 606.

207. Heaslet, 1040–1041; *Chinese Law and Government*, 1977; Rosen, *Red Guard Factionalism*, 107, 136, 224–225.

208. McEwen, 61.

209. Thomas Robinson, "The Wuhan Incident."

210. The reputation, official tenure, and physical existence of the state security leaders and high officials were exceedingly insecure under Stalin. They were under the control of Stalin's Personal Secretariat, headed by Alexander Poskrybyshev. [Leonard Schapiro, *Totalitarianism* (London: Pall Mall, 1972), 61; Randall, 128.]

As was true in Stalinist U.S.S.R., the secret police in Nazi Germany acquired tremendous power. The SS during the last years of the Third Reich has been described as a "state in itself" [Edward Crankshaw, *Gestapo: Instrument of Terror* (New York: Viking, 1956), 92] or as a "subsidiary government" (Fest, *Hitler*, 473). During the last years of the Third Reich, Himmler, who accumulated a number of major positions in the Nazi state, was characterized as becoming the most powerful man in Germany (Rattner, 50). There is little doubt that the SS and its only leader did acquire more independence than their counterparts in the Soviet Union. While Himmler's power and that of the SS grew, there were other centers of power which also grew in influence with Hitler or which maintained countervailing prerogatives. The Nazi Party under the rising star of Martin Bormann became quite a contender for Himmler and the SS during the last years of the regime.

11

Genocidal Targeting: Two Groups of Victims in Pol Pot's Cambodia

Ben Kiernan

In Cambodia today, it is rather common to hear the view expressed that "Pol Pot was worse than Hitler." This is often backed up with the assertions that "the Nazis killed Jews but not Germans," whereas "Pol Pot massacred his own Khmer people" (as well as foreign and minority groups). The first claim is, of course, incorrect, but the second is undoubtedly true, a case of genocide under the definition of the 1948 U.N. Convention. The word "auto-genocide" has even been coined to describe genocide of members of one's own race, but given that Pol Pot's Khmer Rouge leadership did not plan their own deaths, some distinction had to be drawn between their targeted victims and other Khmer people such as their trusted supporters.

This paper will first describe a method used by the Khmer Rouge regime (called "Democratic Kampuchea" or DK) in 1978 to identify its largest and otherwise most indistinguishable group of victims, the mainly peasant population of the Eastern Zone of the country, bordering Vietnam. Previously targeted victims of DK had been partly distinguishable from the masses of the people by their uniforms (defeated Lon Nol regime military personnel), their social behavior (urban dwellers), their relatively light skin color (Vietnamese residents, Chinese and other urban dwellers), or their vocabulary, accent or language (intellectuals, Phnom Penh residents, Cham Muslims). Even so, many did succeed in disguising themselves as peasants or members of the urban poor, groups not initially targeted for severe repression. It was to be much more difficult to identify and mark a vast peasant mass previously distinguishable only for their geographical origin in the country's Eastern Zone. In 1978, the Pol Pot leadership had to devise special measures for this purpose. Interestingly, its measures, like its ideology of "purification," proved not too different from those devised by the Nazis to mark Jews.[1] This paper will conclude with a look at another case of genocide, that committed by the DK regime against a much more distinct group, the Cham Muslims. Here I will look closely at the fate of the Cham populations west and northwest of Phnom Penh. It will become clear that part of the DK project was to destroy the Chams, who cherish their separate identity, from that of the Khmers.[2] This was to be done not only by awesome violence against a third of the Cham population, but also by forced assimilation of the survivors. Those Chams spared were dispersed and dissolved into the Khmer population. They were "disappeared" as a community. This means of their destruction contrasts with the measures DK took to make the Eastern Zone Khmer population appear as a distinct group. The end result was, of course, equally inhuman. Indeed, these two cases are essentially similar—warheads of genocide that were independently targeted but borne on the same deadly missile: national chauvinism and racism, explicit in the case of the Cham, introverted in the case of the eastern Khmer.

The Yellow Star of the East

Pol Pot's Democratic Kampuchea (1975–1979) was organized into six major territorial Zones: the East, Southwest, West, Northwest, North and Northeast. These Zones were ruled with varying degrees of harshness by different committees of the Communist Party of Kampuchea (CPK), while several similar regions were under more direct control by the CPK Center, headed by Pol Pot.[3]

The Eastern Zone comprised the former provinces of Svay Rieng, Prey Veng and eastern Kimpong Cham, plus one district of Kratie province. The Zone bordered on Vietnam in the east and the Mekong River in the west. The major townships were Svay Rieng, Prey Veng, Neak Leung (accidentally bombed by US aircraft in 1973) and the rubber plantation centers of Chup and Krek. Like Phnom Penh, all these centers were forcibly evacuated upon victory in 1975 (or before, in the cases of rural centers seized earlier, like Chup and Krek).

Most of the Zone is rice land watered by the Mekong and Tauch rivers. Prey Veng has always been the second largest rice-growing province in Cambodia. The whole of the East is well populated. According to statistics accompanying the DK government's Four Year (1977–1980) Economic Plan, the population of the Zone in mid 1976 was 1.7 million. This 1976 figure included probably 300,000 or more "new people" (or "deportees," *neak phñoe*) evacuated there from urban areas, mainly Phnom Penh, in 1975. But it did not include another 100,000 or so who had again been evacuated (to the Northern Zone) later the same year. The *neak moultanh,* peasant "base people" in the Zone, probably numbered about 1.4 million.

The Eastern Zone is in some ways the heartland of Khmer communism. In the First Indochina War (1946–1954), the communist-run Unified Issarak Front maintained an extensive military and civilian network there, and benefitted from the aid of communist Viet Minh troops across the Vietnamese border.[4] During the latter years of the Sihanouk regime (1954–1970), local communist rebels kept a low profile, but Vietnamese communist sanctuaries were established along the eastern border of the country. These sanctuaries and nearby Khmer villages were extensively bombed by U.S. B-52s in 1969, and the spread of the Vietnam War to Cambodia in March-April 1970 affected the Eastern Zone first of all. Probably well over 100,000 tons of U.S. bombs fell on the Zone in 1972–73 alone, and took a massive toll in civilian lives. Worse, Pol Pot's CPK "center" faction profitted greatly from the U.S. bombings throughout the country. It used the decimation and massacre as recruitment propaganda and as an excuse for its own brutal, radical policies and its purges of moderate and pro-Vietnamese communists and Sihanoukists.[5] Communist Khmer-Vietnamese cooperation was strongest in the East; the tradition of solidarity between the two communist parties, inherited from both the First and Second Indochina Wars, died hardest there after 1975. There is, however, no basis for describing the Khmer communists of the Eastern Zone as Vietnamese "agents," although this came to be the view of Pol Pot's Democratic Kampuchea government.

The first account of conditions in the Eastern Zone was probably that of a Khmer refugee who fled from the East to Thailand in 1976, reporting that "the Khmer Rouge (in the East) are less brutal than elsewhere" in Democratic Kampuchea.[6] In 1978, a 61 page report based on interviews with later refugees was declassified by the U.S. government. The only references to the East consisted of two brief statements of refugees interviewed by U.S. personnel in Thailand in late 1976. Their report noted:

> One person who came from eastern Cambodia claimed that executions are much fewer because the more sympathetic Khmer Rumdos (Khmer Liberation) are in control there. He noted that they have generally required only that former officers [of the defeated Lon Nol regime] from the rank of second lieutenant upward shave their heads and do forced labor.

The report went on to add that, according to a second account from the East, the Khmer communists there continue to allow Buddhism to flourish, execute people rarely, make people work only a normal working day, and let them eat and dress better [than in other Zones].

It was later reported that the Eastern Zone communist leadership had consciously adopted a policy to this effect. In 1980, Kong, a former member of a DK central government unit stationed in the East, told historian Michael Vickery that the Eastern Zone leader, So Phim, "was known to have said that the purpose of the revolution was to improve the standard of living, not to regress from rich to poor or to force people into misery just to learn how it was to be poor (Pol Pot's policy, according to Kong)."

But the next substantial body of information, from six refugees interviewed in France in 1979, was much more chilling. Five of them said that in 1978 they had witnessed mass executions of Eastern Zone residents who had just been evacuated by Khmer Rouge forces to other zones. The sixth was a former Eastern Zone resident whose DK village cadre, she said, had told her in late 1978 "that we would be all killed . . . but the Vietnamese arrived first, so that Khmer Rouge were unable to kill us." The information provided by these six refugees was corroborated in 1980 by many accounts obtained from Eastern Zone residents inside Cambodia. The conclusion I have reached is that at the very least, 100,000 Eastern Zone peasants and others were murdered in the last six months of the DK regime in 1978. The picture of relative tranquility in the East in 1975 and 1976 at least, followed by mass murder in 1978, is also supported by all other known sustained research on the subject. On the basis of eleven refugee accounts from the East, collected in Thailand in 1980, Michael Vickery concluded that before 1978, the entire East had been a relatively good zone, both for base peasants and new people. It had many good agricultural districts, and the administration there was in the hands of disciplined communists with long revolutionary experience. The zonal authorities did not deprive the population by sending excess rice to Phnom Penh, and urban intellectuals, as such, were not usually mistreated.

Similarly, Stephen Heder wrote in 1980 on the basis of his own interviews with 250 refugees in Thailand, that compared to other Zones such as the Northwest, "conditions for evacuated deportees in the East had sometimes been marginally better or, even considerably better." Timothy Carney, too, has concluded that before 1978, "life in general" in the Eastern Zone was "better than many other areas," although he stresses the relative nature of this judgment.

Some revealing statistics on the 1978 massacres were compiled by Katuiti Honda, who conducted surveys in 1980 on deaths among about 650 people in four small communities of eastern Cambodia. He found that there had been "few victims till early 1978"; 95 of the 111 executions had occurred in that year, compared to 2 in 1975 and 1976.

Stephen Heder describes the 1978 Eastern Zone massacres as "massive and indiscriminate purges of party, army and people alike." Michael Vickery calls them "by far the most violent event of the entire DK period." Timothy Carney agrees that in 1978 the Eastern Zone "probably lost the largest number of people executed in direct response to Central Party orders . . . a heavy toll among villages."

My own interviews with 87 Khmers who lived in the East during the DK period yielded statistics on executions in 1978 in a number of individual villages. The death tolls were, according to the various informants: 100, 240, 50, 100, 600, 80, 70, 100, 23, 200 and 100 people. Also included are accounts of 705 executions in 1978 among the people from one subdistrict, 1,950 from another, 400 from another. These figures, along with the many eyewitness accounts of massacres, Honda's findings of 95 executions in 1978 out of a total of 350 people alive in 1975, and the mass of other evidence, some of which I will present here, all suggest that a total death toll of 100,000 among easterners in 1978 (over one-seventeenth of the population), can safely be regarded as a reasonable conservative estimate. The real figure could be several times higher.

During 1976, a small number of Eastern Zone cadre were arrested by the shadowy Security Service (Santebal) and sent to their deaths in the infamous political prison at Tuol Sleng in Phnom Penh, known as "S-21." The most important was probably the Secretary of the Communist Party of Kampuchea (CPK) Region 24 branch and former member of the Eastern Zone Party Executive Committee, Chhouk. He was arrested in August 1976. Another was the former Eastern Zone military commander, Chan Chakrey, who had risen to Deputy Chief of the General Staff of the Revolutionary Army of Kampuchea when the armed forces structure was centralized in July 1975. These two and others were forced to reveal the names of their closest comrades, who were then arrested in turn, and the spiralling purge eventually led to the CPK Eastern Zone Party Secretary, So Phim, who committed suicide in June 1978.

In the meantime the number of victims throughout the country increased dramatically in 1977; cadres in nearly all villages were arrested and replaced, usually executed, in that year. In the East, two of the Zone's five regions came under the aegis of the CPK's Southwest Zone Party Secretary, the warlord Mok, who was a close ally of the Party "Center" (Pol Pot, Nuon Chea, Ieng Sary, Vorn Vet and probably Son Sen).

The same year, 1977, saw a number of brutal DK incursions into Vietnamese territory and the massacre of thousands of Vietnamese villagers across the border.[7] These unprovoked attacks, which followed a year or more of calm along the border throughout 1976, were carried out by a combination of Eastern Zone regional units, Center units, and Southwest and Northern Zone units sent into the Zone in 1976 and 1977 to stiffen the anti-Vietnamese posture of the Eastern Zone forces and administration.

This pressure from the Center proved largely unsuccessful, however, and it was soon decided in Phnom Penh that the Eastern Zone military and Party organizations could not be trusted and had to be destroyed. Thus began, on 25 May 1978, a massive suppression campaign, and the enormous massacres of the eastern population in the second half of 1978. The Center described the entire population of the Zone as having "Khmer bodies with Vietnamese minds" (khluon khmaer kuo kbal yuon) and set about eliminating it either through mass evacuation or mass murder. The policy appears to have been far more ferocious than that adopted towards the evacuated urban populations in 1975. This was partly because of the long history of social contact across the Khmer-Vietnamese border, and partly because of the less than hostile triangular relationship between eastern Khmer peasants, eastern Khmer communists, and Vietnamese communists. The isolation of the Pol Pot leadership from all three forces led to its decision to attempt the apparent annihilation of the first two. And even, if one is to believe Phnom Penh Radio at the time, of the Vietnamese race as well. The DK Radio claimed on 10 May 1978:

So far, we have attained our target: 30 Vietnamese killed for every fallen Kampuchean. . . . So we could sacrifice two million Kampucheans in order to exterminate the 50 million Vietnamese— and we shall still be 6 million.

It then added, revealing a perceived relationship between this and introverted genocide: "We must purify our armed forces, our Party and the masses of the People."

In 1986, while visiting a Cham Muslim village in Cambodia's Eastern Zone to investigate the DK genocide against the Cham minority, I overheard a conversation in the mosque. Huy Radi, a 32 year-old Cham, was discussing with other men how, in 1978, the DK regime had marked Eastern Zone residents to distinguish them from other Khmers. When questioned by myself and Dr. Gregory Stanton, Radi told of the evacuation of the village to the western provinces in July or August 1978. Boatloads of exactly 100 families were taken up the Mekong from Neak Leung to the southern Phnom Penh suburb of Chbar Ampeou. The 3,000–4,000 eastern evacuees were fed immediately on arrival.

Radi went on:

After we'd eaten, the Organization [Angkar, the CPK leadership] began to distribute clothes to us—in particular, scarves (*kromar*) and blankets . . . The trucks came from Phnom Penh. Those distributing spoke like people from the Southwest Zone do. We didn't know them. They said: "Send someone over from your group to receive the scarves." . . . There were only blue-and-white and green-and-white scarves . . . Everybody got a scarf. There was some shortage of blankets—one per family [only]. But as for scarves, there was one for each person. Whether you were young or old you got a scarf. If there were ten people in a household there were ten scarves [for them] . . . I saw several truckloads. One truck would come and be emptied and then another would arrive. There was not to be any shortage. There were many scarves. No-one was allowed not to have one.

This did not seem unusual at the time. The wide, checked *kromar* are popular with all Khmers, who use them as turbans, sweat bands, hand-towels, and food bags as well as neck scarves. Even the uncommon coloring seemed insignificant. The Eastern Zone evacuees were being taken to the northwestern province of Pursat, and Radi's group "were happy with the gifts Angkar had given us."

The group was taken by train to Prek Tatrau village in Maung district near Pursat. There they joined the local Northwest Zone population. Radi noticed that the locals all wore red or yellow scarves, and he soon discovered that "they weren't allowed to wear blue scarves." "Whatever village we arrived at, there were none of those blue or green scarves." But this fact still aroused no particular interest, beyond a recognition that the Eastern Zone population was being distinguished from the locals.

Radi had already lost an elder brother, killed by the Khmer Rouge for speaking the Cham language. In Pursat, "they killed people even more." Victims were regularly led away for execution, many still wearing their blue scarves. Two elder sisters of Radi's were murdered in Pursat in 1978. Around December of that year, Radi witnessed a massacre of 24 people by a Khmer Rouge squad of 30 armed soldiers at Tuk Chruos in the hills of Pursat.

But it was not until after this, only a few days before DK was overthrown by the Vietnamese invasion, that the easterners in Radi's area realized the significance of the scarves they were all wearing. Some of the locals had warned them. They said: "Don't wear that scarf if you are going far away . . . If you keep wearing that scarf you will be known as an Eastern Zone person, and all the Eastern Zone people are to be killed. They have been brought here to be killed. Because Eastern Zone people are Khmer bodies with Vietnamese minds." Radi only then realized that the Khmer Rouge had made the easterners "put on a killing

sign." Otherwise, the Khmer Rouge would not know "who was who."
"Their killers only had to see the scarves and they would put people
down to be killed." The power of the "killing sign" became clearer to
Radi after the fall of DK. The Khmer Rouge feared being turned in to
the new authorities. To disguise themselves in order to escape popular
vengeance, the killers began to wear the blue scarves of their Eastern
Zone victims. They appeared to believe that this was a victims' uniform,
and so would exonerate them.

Two days later, Stanton and I were interviewing ethnic Chinese victims
of DK, and we came across a man who had been in Pursat when the
Eastern Zone evacuees arrived. Lim Kuy, 48, had lived in Phnom Penh
before DK. In April 1975 when the city was evacuated, he headed south;
then in January 1976 he was again evacuated northwest to Bakan district
of Pursat. In his barber shop on the outskirts of Phnom Penh, we asked
Kuy the following questions:

> Q. Did you see any Eastern Zone people come [to Pursat]?
> A. Yes, I saw them.
> Q. When you saw them . . . how were they dressed?
> A. People from the Eastern Zone wore black clothes except that they
> wore a *Kromar* of that color [he pointed to a blue-and-white-checked scarf].
> That color. They were all wearing that scarf around their necks. All the
> same . . . I asked them, and they said that they had arrived at Chbar
> Ampeou, and the Khmer Rouge had distributed them all one each. That
> scarf, that one over there [he points to a blue scarf again]. Like this scarf,
> only the checks were a bit larger.
> Q. What happened to the people from the Eastern Zone who arrived
> in Pursat?
> A. . . . I didn't see them killed but I saw them tied up. 4 to 10 people
> in a line, and they were taken to be killed . . . While I was riding to
> work I saw them on the truck, a small truck in the forest. They tied up
> sometimes 5 people, sometimes 10 people. It wasn't fixed. I saw it three
> or four times. The Khmer Rouge were riding ponies and they were tied
> up and being dragged behind.

Interestingly, Kuy claims that not only Eastern Zone people were
killed. The killings, he says, were "general," although there is no doubt
from many other sources that easterners were carefully targeted in 1978.
And Kuy was absolutely sure that the Eastern Zone people were easily
distinguishable by their unusual blue scarves. This appeared to be clear
corroboration of Radi's claim.

Kuy and Radi were living in different districts of Pursat in 1978. Our
next source, whom we met two days later in Prey Veng, was a young
easterner who, unlike Radi, had been evacuated to Kuy's district of

Bakan, although almost certainly not to Kuy's village. Unlike the other two, he was an ethnic Khmer. Chun Vun was 18 years old when the DK period began in 1975. The seven people in his family farmed on the bank of the Mekong south of Neak Leung. In late 1978 all of the people in the area had been evacuated to Pursat via Phnom Penh. On arrival at Chbar Ampeou, the evacuees were assembled. Khmer Rouge cadres wearing black pajamas, rubber sandals, and red scarves, distributed clothes, medicine, blankets, mosquito nets and scarves to them.

The interview continued as follows:

Q. What kind of medicine?
A. Traditional medicine.
Q. What kind of clothes? New clothes?
A. They didn't distribute old clothes . . . whether it was a sign for going to the West or not I didn't know. But . . . after we'd lived there for maybe two months, they told us that it was a "password," that this group who are wearing new clothes, it's a sign for "Vietnamese" . . . And that's when we discovered that our new clothes and scarves were a sign of being from the Eastern Zone . . . They accused the Eastern Zone people of being "Khmer bodies with Vietnamese minds."
Q. What color clothes were you wearing?
A. Men wore blue short-sleeved shirts and blue trousers, and new blue-and-white scarves . . . The colors were mixed but the blue was more prominent than the black, and a little bit of white (check) . . . And when we got there they knew the sign of the Eastern Zone people. Whatever clothes they wore they didn't use those scarves in that area . . . When we got there, there was no confusion. And if they saw us from afar they could see by our blue clothes and blue scarves that we were Eastern Zone people.
Q. Did everyone from your group wear blue scarves?
A. No other colors. Everyone was the same. 100 percent the same.
Q. How were the people in Pursat dressed?
A. The Pursat people just wore black . . .
Q. What color scarves did they wear?
A. Their scarves were all red . . . No-one in Pursat wore blue scarves.
Q. Did you have to wear the blue scarf?
A. We had to wear them when we went to work. If we didn't wear them, they would send us to a meeting where they would lecture us. They would ask me "for what reason are you not wearing that scarf? These are scarves given you by Angkar Leu ["High Angkar"]." If we didn't wear it, they would accuse us, because it was a sign for them . . . [The Pursat people] were absolutely not allowed to wear the clothes of the Eastern Zone people . . .

All seven of Vun's family members were murdered in Pursat in this period. He saw them arrested, accused of being "Khmer bodies with

Vietnamese minds," and led away, one by one. Vun, the youngest, would have been executed last, but he escaped into the forest, where he lived with locals for over 3 months until the DK regime fell.

Som Thon was a 17-year-old girl when her family was evacuated with a group of 40 families to the northwest, in August 1978. During a two-day stay at the medicine factory at Chbar Ampeou, she said in an interview in 1987, that each group of three evacuees were given medicine, and a single black shirt, or for a family, some medicine and a blue-and-white-checked scarf. Thon's family received one such scarf. With 14 other families, they were sent by train to the village of Prey Khlaut in Maung district. After three months there, the local Khmer Rouge, who wore only black-and-white-checked scarves, began to selectively murder the Eastern Zone evacuees. They would take the blue scarves from their victims and use them themselves. No other villagers were murdered while Thun was there. Of the 15 eastern families in the village, all had blue scarves, and only 7 people survived into 1979. Twelve families were wiped out in their entirety. Thon's parents were both killed, and she and her sister survived. "The Vietnamese saved us in time," Thon explained.

Sok Mat was evacuated to Pursat with a group of Chams (from Huy Radi's village) in September 1978. He said that when his group of over 1,000 people arrived at Chbar Ampeou, they stayed only a morning. But "everyone—everyone" was given new clothes, medicine, and a blue scarf. He claimed it was a "sign" for the people who were to be "killed off." When he arrived in Pursat, he saw that no-one besides the Eastern Zone evacuees wore blue scarves. After a month or two, such people realized the deadly significance of the blue scarves, and stopped wearing them, Mat said.

Not all 1978 Eastern Zone evacuees went via Chbar Ampeou, or to Pursat or the Northwest. Those from the eastern Kompong Cham area crossed the Mekong at Tonle Bet, and were taken to the Northern Zone. Many thousands of them were murdered there. Initial evidence suggests that, on the way, attempts were made by DK officials at Tonle Bet to "mark" the evacuees in a similar way to those who passed through Chbar Ampeou. For instance, in June 1978, the entire Eastern village of Preal No. 1 was emptied by the Khmer Rouge, and its people were sent across to the Northern Zone. So Samnang, then a 37-year-old peasant, now an agricultural cadre in the State of Cambodia, says that 70 percent of the families who passed through Tonle Bet were distributed second-hand scarves, either purple-and-white or black-and-white-checked. He estimates that four out of five of these people later perished in the Northern Zone.

Uk Prathna, now also a government official, was a rubber plantation worker in the Northern Zone from late 1976. He saw "hundreds, thousands" of Eastern Zone evacuees arrive in his district of Stung Trang in 1978. "Most," he said, "wore blue-and-white-checked scarves, some new, some secondhand." This distinguished them from the locals, whose scarves were red, in the case of the rubber plantation workers, and of various colors (but few were blue) in the case of the members of peasant cooperatives.

Nevertheless, Prathna does not believe that the scarves were a "sign" of Eastern Zone origin, pointing out that the blue scarves were not all new. On this point, though, he corroborated Samnang's story. One may ignore the patchy evidence from these two, possibly biased, State of Cambodia officials about Tonle Bet. On the other hand, Prathna's skepticism about the significance of the scarves, and Samnang's recollection that their color was purple or black, rather than blue, may also be seen as authentic local or personal variations of detail that actually make the general picture look more convincing. Be this as it may, it would not be surprising if the "identification" of victims was more perfunctory in a provincial center like Tonle Bet.

Why were the Easterners given blue scarves, rather than identical scarves of some other color? As noted, blue was an uncommon color for *kromar*, and it would be sure to stand out. But it may have had its own significance for the Pol Pot regime. It is of course the opposite of communist red, the color of the "Khmers Rouges" (*khmaer krohom*). In the 1960s, Prince Sihanouk had often distinguished the latter from the "Khmers Bleus," or rightist Khmer. Worse, in the early 1970s a dissident group of revolutionaries active in the Southwest Zone had called themselves "Blue Khmers" (*khmaer khieu*), and in the Eastern Zone, another anti-Pol Pot force, close to the Vietnamese communists, had been known as the "white Khmers" (*khmaer sor*). The Eastern population in 1978 was also seen as dissident. Is it possible that in making them wear blue-and-white checked scarves, the Pol Pot leadership was associating them with these earlier groups of traitors to the CPK cause?

During World War Two in occupied Croatia, the Nazi puppet regime ordered all Serbs to wear blue armbands as a sign of their alien status.[8] Pol Pot personally visited Croatia in 1950, not long after the war ended, and was surely apprised of this.

Even if one rejects all that, the fact is undeniable that over 100,000 innocent villagers were savagely murdered by the DK regime in this affair. They were targeted for an accident not of genetics but of geography. Their crime was to have been born and to have lived their lives in an area bordering Vietnam and long ruled by a CPK Zone branch which had enjoyed historically close relations with Vietnamese communism.

Favorite Targets: The Chams of Western Cambodia

Kampuchea's Muslim Cham people are descendants of the inhabitants of Champa, a Hindu-Buddhist and later Muslim kingdom situated on the central coast of Vietnam between the third and the eighteenth centuries, before its absorption and conquest by Vietnam. Over 200,000 Chams lived in Cambodia in 1970 (and about 60,000 in Vietnam).

But DK did not see the Chams as sympathetic victims of a common "historical enemy." Rather, they were seen as losers, as a weak link in the DK state. And what happened to them by 1979 was anyway quite unprecedented. Approximately 100,000 Chams perished in DK. Their religion was banned, their schools closed, their leaders massacred, their villages razed and dispersed by Pol Pot's regime. Elsewhere, I have analyzed this genocidal process in detail;[9] here, I will present some of the evidence. This involves a look at what happened to the rather small communities of Chams in Kampuchea's Western and Northwestern Zones, where most of the Eastern Zone deportees were sent in 1978.

The provinces of Kompong Speu, Kompong Chhnang and Koh Kong made up the Western Zone of DK, while Pursat and Battambang were included in the Northwest. The Western Zone is the poorest part of the country. As Pol Pot said in a speech to the Zone's cadres in June 1976, "there are mountains everywhere and the soil does not have much fertility."[10] Inhospitable coastline, mountains and forests in the west dominate low-rainfall, sandy-soil plains in Kompong Speu and Kompong Chhnang; the latter province is watered by the Sap river, which has great fishing potential but floods large areas for several months each year.

There is only one large Cham community in the Western Zone. It consists of three villages of Kompong Tralach district in Kompong Chhnang province, which contained about 5,000 Chams in 1940. Marcel Ner described them as "the most faithful in Cambodia to the Cham traditions," having undergone very little Malay influence or intermarriage.

> In their mosques and Koranic schools the teaching and sermons are in Cham, and knowledge of Arabic is restricted to the alphabet and some formulae. They jealously preserve some Cham manuscripts which tell of their history: several people can read them and even appear to know long passages by heart. The women maintain the authority that Cham customs accord them and at O Russei just as many girls go to school as boys.

Even in 1986, O Russei village was still known to Chams in other parts of the country for its continuing use of the old Sanskrit-based Cham alphabet, and for the fact that its version of Islam involved communal prayer once a week, rather than five times daily as elsewhere in the country. It was even said that many villagers in O Russei were descended from the kings of Champa and still bore their long, Hinduized family names.

Sah Roh was born in Kompong Tralach district in 1949. By 1975 she was married and living in Phnom Penh. Her husband, also a Cham, was a teacher. With her husband, four children and younger sister, Sah Roh was evacuated to the west of the capital in April 1975. The seven of them went to Kompong Speu province with the three other Cham families. They spent four months there. (Meanwhile, two families of Chams from Kompong Tralach had also arrived in Kompong Speu, after being expelled from their native villages by the Khmer Rouge even though they were "base people." Worse, on 5 May 1975, Sen Mathay's father, brother and sister were murdered for speaking Cham and for praying to Allah, and on the same day, Ros Samath's father and brother were murdered for refusing to eat pork.[11] However, Sah Roh had a happier experience.)

Roh's husband was put to work as a blacksmith, making agricultural tools. The rest of the family had to work in the fields, but were given rations which they cooked and ate privately. They had also brought some food with them from Phnom Penh, and so they had adequate nutrition. The Khmer Rouge knew Roh's husband's background but did not harm him. In fact, Roh says: "The Khmer Rouge in Kompong Speu were a bit soft . . . not very tough . . . There were no killings . . . The base people were quite good. We could ask them to help us."

However, in September 1975, the four families of Chams were "selected" to go to the northwest of the country, along with many Khmer families from the area. The move proved to be a disaster. Of the 26 Chams who had left Phnom Penh together, only 13 were to survive the next three years.

On arrival in Bakan district of Pursat province, the newcomers were divided up, one family to each "co-operative." Sah Roh's family was sent to Talo, a co-operative of over 1,000 families. "As soon as we arrived, we had to hand over all our goods and received in return only two sets of clothes each. No property was allowed . . . We ate collectively, gruel and banana leaves, and watermelons." In mid-1976, Roh's husband was taken away "to study," after revealing that he had been a teacher. "No one has heard of him since." Six months later, two of Roh's children and her sister all died within a month of one another. In 1976, more than 10 people were killed in Sah Roh's village, but in 1977 there were many, taken from "everywhere." Seven out of 30 women in Roh's work team died in 1977. And 1978 saw huge massacres of 3,000 new evacuees from the Eastern Zone. Roh was then privileged by being raised to the

status of a "base person." "They put me aside and above temporarily
while they persecuted the Eastern Zone people." There seems no evidence
in Roh's account of Chams being singled out for discriminatory treatment
the way the Easterners were. Yet her fate was tragic and it is worth
recording her poignant comment:

> My husband was picked up first of all. He died, disappeared forever. I
> was seven months pregnant. It was very, very hard, transplanting rice in
> the flooded fields . . . I am left over from that story.

Pin Yatay, in his memoir, *L'Utopie Meurtriere*, records some of the
activities of the Chams in Pursat in the DK period. He describes them
as "the favorite targets of the sadism of the Khmer Rouge" and explains
how they organized themselves into groups to loot the cornfields in
order to survive. "Their fishing community (they lived around the Great
Lakes) had been uprooted by the new regime. For that reason they bore
a fierce hatred for the Khmer Rouge. In spite of their dispersal by the
country's new masters, the Muslim Khmers had succeeded in establishing
a real underground network. They went in small groups to steal the
ears of corn from the fields."

Nevertheless, Yatay makes the point that, if the Chams were singled
out for special discrimination, it only brought them closer to their Khmer
fellow sufferers: "We were famished slaves . . . Among the new people
there was every kind. The persecuted were from all backgrounds. There
were Chams or Islamic Khmers, Chinese, even Vietnamese who had
not gone back to their country. We no longer had any concept of
difference. We were the new people lined up against the old. We shared
the misery and the silent complicity. We did not denounce one another."[12]

To Hosan was also born in Kompong Tralach, but had moved to
Battambang by 1975, when the Khmer Rouge took over. He was then
19 years old, and with his family of 9 people, he was evacuated into
the countryside of Battambang province. They went to Kang Hat village
in Sangker district, where they knew there was a small wooden mosque.
The local Muslim community had left the area, but eleven Muslim
families also came to Kang Hat from Pailin city, including three Chvea
("Javanese") families. The rest were Cham. For the first three months
or so, they were all allowed to practice Islam, but then the mosque was
closed and all religion prohibited by the Khmer Rouge.

Then in early 1976, cooperatives were established, with communal
eating, and it was made clear to the Muslims that they would have to
eat any pork dishes served. These were rare, but Hosan says: "If a sick
pig died, we got pork for three days." The reason Chams had to eat
pork was a decree that "classes" and "living conditions" were to be

"the same" for everybody. Work was collective, Buddhism and Islam alike were abolished, and "whatever the Khmer people did, the Islamic Khmers had to do the same." Hosan said: "There was one man, called Sman, a holy man from Khleang Sbek, who was shot for refusing to eat pork. He said he would absolutely prefer to die rather than eat pork. He was the very first, and we all waited and watched what would happen. Everybody was fearful. Then they used him as a lesson. They killed him because he was the first to protest . . . So we all started to eat pork little by little. We were scared."

When the cooperatives were established in early 1976, the Khmer Rouge called a meeting and the cooperative chief Ham announced that only the Khmer language would be tolerated from then on. Hosan adds: "Not only Cham but any language, for example, Chinese or Lao, was forbidden. You could not speak Cham secretly at home, either. If they heard you, you would disappear. Even at night the militia would come by the houses and listen . . . Some Chams were killed for speaking Cham."

The first harvest under the "cooperative" system was confiscated. "They took it all away in trucks." They would not let us eat it, although production was high. As a result, starvation struck from about March–April 1977. "Nearly half" the subdistrict perished, over 400 people out of a population of 900 families. Out of the 12 Cham families, 4 people died of starvation and disease, including one relative of To Hosan.

In 1978 there was less starvation, but a harsher work regime. A dam project on the Sangker River claimed "at least ten deaths every day" for most of the year. There were also "many secret killings." The result was that in 1979, only about 600 adults had survived out of the 900 families in the subdistrict in 1975. The Chams do not appear to have suffered more than the Khmer, although they were obviously singled out for special treatment, such as the harsh enforcement of the ban on their language and dietary customs.

Hamat was born in Kompong Tralach district in 1943, but later moved to the capital and became a fisherman. When the Khmer Rouge took Phnom Penh on 17 April 1975, "the whole village of Chrang Chamres was evacuated" north to Kompong Tralach. However, Chams from the district like Hamat were not allowed to return to their native villages. The Cham "new people" were divided into groups and dispersed to various villages and cooperatives. Hamat was sent to a co-operative called Stung Snguot. (His mother was separated from him and sent elsewhere.) In Stung Snguot there were 40 Cham families, while the Khmer families included about 10 families of local "base people."

In August 1976, "all the Chams were executed in Stung Sngout," said Hamat. "Not one family remained . . . I saw people taken away, whole files of them . . . If I had not left, I would have died too." Hamat was felicitously transferred to a fishing detail at Longvek, and only returned to Stung Snguot in 1978. He found that even the Cham children there had followed their parents to their deaths. "Dig up the grass, dig up the roots," Hamat remembers the Khmer Rouge saying. He was the only survivor of the 40 Cham families.

Sok Sokhun, a Khmer evacuee from Phnom Penh, lived in the same village, Stung Snguot, throughout the DK period. He claims that between September and November 1976, 10,000 Cham and Chinese new people were executed in the subdistrict of Ampil Tik in Lower Kompong Tralach district. But Khmers also suffered tragically. Hamat says that of 17,000 new people who arrived in the subdistrict in 1975, only 3,000 survived in 1979.

The neighboring subdistrict of Chhouk Sor experienced a similar disaster even though its population was largely "base people." Of a 1970 population of 8,500, only 3,300 survived in 1979. 4,000 of the inhabitants were killed in 1977–78 alone. It is important to record the background to this tragedy.

The Khmer Rouge first took over the area in 1970, according to Ka Chu, a local Cham blacksmith who was then 45 years old. He recalls: "From 1970 to 1972 they used politics, not killing. It was good . . . The people really believed them. They wanted freedom, happiness, and food . . . The Khmer Rouge said that if we don't struggle, our religion and nation will all disappear . . . The U.S. imperialists would take our country and abolish our religion and race, turning us into American nationals. They said that if we don't struggle hard, "be careful or you'll end up like Champa . . . Now that you have come to live in Kampuchea, you must struggle hard." They said: "Do not follow the example of Champa, which did not struggle. That is why you have no country."

U.S. B-52s carried out bombing raids in the subdistrict in this period. In Chhouk Sor, 20 Chams were killed in the B-52 bombardments, and others were killed and wounded in smaller-scale air raids. It was at the height of the U.S. bombing, in June 1973, that the Khmer Rouge cracked down. The local cadres were replaced, and the villages evacuated. Ka Chu's group was sent 30 kilometers into the forest, where all their possessions and labor were collectivized. Starvation began, and continued in 1974 when communal eating was introduced, with "only one pot for the whole village." By 1975–76, the Chams were being forced to eat meals that included pork, on pain of death or withdrawal of the salt ration.

Also in June 1973, religion was abolished, and Cham girls were forced to cut their long hair, "all together like boys." Finally, June 1973 also saw the proclamation of a Khmer Rouge "plan" to the effect that "enemies all have to be smashed . . . not just the Lon Nol enemy but enemies in the subdistrict instead." The latter were called "internal enemies" by the Khmer Rouge. As Ka Chu recalls it, "if they asked you something and you said something bad or in protest, you would disappear that day forever."

In 1974 and 1975, all Chams who had previously held positions such as cooperative chief or work team leader were dismissed from their posts. Ka Chu says: "They lost their rights. Even those Chams who had fought for the Khmer Rouge were withdrawn [from the armed forces] and put on fishing detail. No Chams had freedom or rights then." Around the same time, the Cham communities were dispersed, scattered over 8 or 9 subdistricts in Kompong Tralach, in groups of "2, 5, or up to 20 families per village," according to Sos Men, another local Cham peasant then in his twenties. "No large groups were allowed," Ka Chu concurs; only 20 to 30 people were left in each Cham village. Sos Men adds: "Therefore from year to year we saw their plans get tighter and tighter, but the people of Chhouk Sor subdistrict could find no way to avoid their yoke . . . in January 1974 [we had to work] 14 hours per day. There was no time to rest between 4 a.m. and 10 p.m., except for eating gruel. People's strength withered. Young people all became old."

Local Muslim leaders began to be killed from 1974 onwards. Sos Men names two victims, Mit and Kop. Ka Chu adds the name of his *hakkem* (community leader), Met, and another dignitary, Kon. They were both killed in 1975 after interrogation about their religion. In 1975, about 500 new people, both Chams and Khmers, arrived from Phnom Penh and Battambang town, and over the next 4 years about ten *hajis* were executed. Ka Chu claims to have compiled a list of 150 learned men from Chhouk Sor subdistrict who were killed in the 1970s.

In mid or late 1976, children were separated from their parents. After their first year of life, babies were placed in jungle centers and fed on gruel and milk. At three years of age, they were taken "to study," learning to plant crops, raise dykes, and "not much reading and writing." Sos Men recalls: "After many days, children would miss their parents and family, and run back to play with them. The Khmer Rouge would catch them and beat them. There was no pity at all. Some children were beaten ten or more times for this. Few did not run back (home), because they only got a little gruel to eat and had to work like adults."

However, the "hardest years" were 1977–78. "They would not let us eat our fill . . . and there was no rest from work." In the planting season ten people were assigned to cover each hectare. If the work was not completed, individual targets were set. "If you could not do that, you were accused of being KGB." It was in this period that 4,000 people were killed in Chouk Sor subdistrict.

Conclusion

In his book, *Genocide*, Leo Kuper describes the Nazi regulation that Jews wear a conspicuous Yellow Star on their clothing as "a powerful instrument of police control" which "paralysed the victims with the oppressive feeling of being continuously under public surveillance." Such devices exposed, "by rituals of degradation, the newly established pariah status" of the Jews.[13] There are obvious parallels with the blue scarf imposed on the deported Eastern Zone population of Pol Pot's Democratic Kampuchea. Its major purpose appears to have been bureaucratic identification rather than psychological terror. The apparent aim and end result was still mass murder, but attempts were made by the DK leadership to disguise their intentions from the target population as long as possible.

This was not the case for the Cham population. They were not separated out and forced to carry a distinctive mark. Rather, they were forcibly assimilated. In the West and Northwest of Kampuchea they appear to have suffered less violence and discrimination than the Khmers from the East, so long as they were prepared to prove that they had given up their separate identity. The difference appears to be that the Chams were targeted by DK for essentially social reasons. Their community was to be destroyed because its separate language, large village concentrations, and independent national networks based on Islam interfered with the DK state's ambition for total supervision and control of its subjects. In other words, they were targeted as a group. This involved racist assumptions about them, but did not necessarily require their destruction as individuals, although about one-third of them were killed in four years.

On the other hand, the Khmers of the Eastern Zone were targeted as individuals, which is why the regime determined to keep track of each one of them if possible. They were politically suspect as a result of their former leaders (of the Eastern Zone CPK branch) taking up arms against the DK regime. The Pol Pot regime must have presumed that each one of them had been to some degree influenced by those leaders. That influence would not be removed by dispersing them. They would always be a threat unless they were either watched carefully or simply eliminated. DK chose the first as a temporary measure, then the second.

The United Nations Convention on Genocide states that the crime of genocide consists of acts such as "killing members of the group," or other acts, "committed with intent to destroy in whole or in part, a national, ethnic, racial or religious group, as such." Mass extermination, even total destruction, of separate "political groups" such as the eastern Khmers is not explicitly included. But the phrase "in whole or in part" does appear to define as genocide the systematic mass murder of the eastern part of the Khmer ethnic group. And even without the mass murder to which the Cham people were also subjected, the phrase "as such" appears to cover their destruction *as a separate group* by the Democratic Kampuchea regime.

It was probably inevitable that DK's aggressive raids against Vietnam and its genocidal campaign against minority groups like the Cham would eventually turn inwards with a vengeance on the Khmer people. The national chauvinist crusade which preoccupied Pol Pot's regime not only demanded massive and debilitating sacrifices from its citizenry. It also defined all consequent real or suspected dissent within its chosen framework of race. So the Eastern Zone Khmer population were accused of being insufficiently Khmer (having Vietnamese "minds"), a cruel irony, proof of the bankruptcy and tragedy of chauvinist politics.

Notes

1. Ben Kiernan, "Blue Scarf/Yellow Star: A Lesson in Genocide," *Boston Globe*, 27 February 1989, 13; Ben Kiernan, "Wild Chickens, Farm Chickens and Cormorants: Kampuchea's Eastern Zone Under Pol Pot," in David P. Chandler and Ben Kiernan, eds., *Revolution and Its Aftermath in Kampuchea: Eight Essays*, Monograph No. 25 (Yale Southeast Asia Council, 1983), 136–211; Ben Kiernan, *Cambodia: The Eastern Zone Massacres*, Documentation Series, No. 1 (Columbia University Center for the Study of Human Rights, 1986).

2. Ben Kiernan, "Orphans of Genocide: The Cham Muslims of Kampuchea under Pol Pot," *Bulletin of Concerned Asian Scholars* 20, No. 4 (1988): 2–33.

3. Ben Kiernan, "Conflict in the Kampuchean Communist Movement," *Journal of Contemporary Asia* 10, Nos. 1–2 (1980): 7–74; Michael Vickery, "Democratic Kampuchea: Theme and Variations," in David Chandler and Ben Kiernan, eds., *Revolution and Its Aftermath in Kampuchea: Eight Essays*, Monograph No. 25 (Yale Southeast Asia Council, 1983), 136–211.

4. Ben Kiernan, *How Pol Pot Came To Power: A History of Communism in Kampuchea, 1930–1975* (London: Verso, and New York: Routledge Chapman and Hall, 1985).

5. Ibid., chap. 8.

6. For references to this quotation, as well as others in the following paragraphs, see the introduction in Kiernan, *Eastern Zone Massacres*.

7. Ben Kiernan, "New Light on the Origins of the Vietnam-Kampuchea Conflict," *Bulletin of Concerned Asian Scholars* 12, No. 4 (1980): 61–65.

8. Mark Aarons, *Sanctuary! Nazi Fugitives in Australia* (Melbourne: Heinemann, 1989), 61.

9. Kiernan, "Orphans of Genocide."

10. Chanthou Boua, David P. Chandler, and Ben Kiernan, eds., *Pol Pots Plans The Future: Confidential Leadership Documents from Democratic Kampuchea, 1976–77*, Monograph No. 33 (Yale Southeast Asia Council, 1988), Document 2, 14.

11. *The Destruction of Islam in Democratic Kampuchea* (Phnom Penh: 1983), 111–12.

12. Pin Yathay, *L'Utopie Meurtriere* (Paris: Laffont, 1979), 231–32. See also the English translation, *Stay Alive My son* (Bloomsbury, 1987).

13. Leo Kuper, *Genocide: Its Political Use in the Twentieth Century* (New Haven: Yale University Press, 1982), 125, 127.

12

Genocide of a Religious Group: Pol Pot and Cambodia's Buddhist Monks

Chanthou Boua

Theravada Buddhism was introduced to the Southeast Asian mainland in the third century B.C. and became the state religion in Kampuchea in the twelfth century A.D. Its following in Kampuchea probably reached a peak in the years after independence from France in 1954 when Buddhism became increasingly influential in both state and public arenas. In this period about ninety percent of the Kampuchean population of over four million was Buddhist. Yet, when the regime led by Pol Pot's Khmer Rouge came to power in April 1975, Buddhism was eradicated from the face of the country in just one year. Interviews conducted with twenty nine surviving monks yielded a vivid account of how this was achieved.

Background

As the state religion, Buddhism had important functions in Kampuchean society. The Buddhist monastery in nearly every village was the center for the village's activities. It was a recreational center where villagers would meet to celebrate Buddhist festivals, to play traditional games, or just to exchange remarks about everyday life. It served as a retreat for the aged who needed to meditate in a relaxed and quiet atmosphere. Monasteries also provided shelter for those without homes in the outside world such as orphans and the mentally ill. In the cities, monasteries provided housing for students who came from the countryside to continue their studies. In short, the "have nots" could always turn up at monasteries for shelter and food which had been given to the monks by those who were better off. Thus, the monastery served to a significant extent as a redistributor of wealth.

The practice of Buddhism was not imposed; rather, it was part of a traditional way of life. The Buddhist doctrine was not taught in schools, but everybody had some relationship to the monasteries and respected monks. With modernization and the introduction of Western culture in the 1960s and 1970s, many young people became less interested in Buddhism, but monasteries continued to multiply throughout the country and the number of monks continued to increase. By 1969 when the Kampuchean population was about seven million, there were 3,369 monasteries and 65,062 monks throughout the country. But by early 1976, a year after the Khmer Rouge took control of the country, there were virtually no more monks to be seen.

The Strategy of the Khmer Rouge Before 1975

Soon after the war started in early 1970, the Khmer Rouge, with the support of the National Liberation Front (NLF) and of Prince Sihanouk, took control of substantial areas of Kampuchea, now known as the liberated zones. By 1972 the liberated zone covered about two-thirds of the country's rural territory.[1] Disrupted by war, many villages in the countryside were in disarray or destroyed; laypeople as well as monks were dispersed throughout the country, some to areas controlled by Lon Nol's army and many others to the capital city of Phnom Penh. During this 1970–1975 war, it was not clear what the Khmer Rouge policy was towards Buddhism. While there were signs of attempts to put down or intimidate Buddhists, there were also strong attempts to use Buddhism to gain popular support for the Khmer Rouge. Their intentions toward Buddhism only became obvious to everyone after their victory in April 1975. One Buddhist monk who had lived under the Khmer Rouge since 1972 when his district, Prey Koki, in Svay Rieng Province was liberated, said, "It was different before and after April 1975. Before April 1975 they cajoled us, they were nice to us."[2] Of course, there were regional variations. This account comes from the Eastern Zone of the country where the Khmer Rouge were milder.

As with laypeople, the Khmer Rouge made a clear distinction between monks living in the liberated zones and those living in the city.

They said that monks in the city and monks in the countryside were different. Monks in the city are imperialists; monks in the countryside are proper and revolutionary. Some monks believed them and took part in the revolution with them. They later realized that they had been cheated.[3]

The Khmer Rouge emerged at a time when the people were receptive to their ideas. Many monks as well as laypeople were disillusioned with the past and current governments, those of Sihanouk and Lon Nol, when corruption, oppression and injustice were widespread. Many rural people were naturally attracted to the Khmer Rouge propaganda of national liberation; of freeing the people from the yoke of the imperialists; of setting up a new society where equality would prevail. Hence, monks often supported the Khmer Rouge before their victory in 1975, "because they believed in independence, revolution to free the country from colonization and feudalism, where equality can be restored—no poor, no rich."[4] Another monk who was then in his late forties and had lived under the Khmer Rouge since liberation of his district of Svay Rieng in the Eastern Zone in 1973 said,

> Before 1975 they told the people and monks that our country had not developed because of the feudalist and capitalist system. Now we must carry out a revolution which will liberate us from the imperialist, feudalist and capitalist system. After liberation we'll all be equal, with equal rights and happiness.[5]

Buddhism is usually identified with traditionalism, peaceful coexistence, and non-coercion. However, this was not the first time that Buddhist monks had taken a stand against imperialism and sided with the oppressed. In 1942 a group of four thousand monks took part in a demonstration against French colonialism and for national independence.[6] This incident has been called "the first demonstration to awaken the Khmer conscience."[7]

To win the people over to their side, some Khmer Rouge obviously lied about their intentions towards Buddhism. They tricked the people and the monks and tested their reactions as they went along to see if they could afford to eliminate Buddhism before they achieved total victory. According to a monk who lived in Svay Rieng Province, they said, "Buddhism will not be abolished, it will become more glorious." "But," the monk added,

> in some areas they liberated before 1975, they started to badmouth Buddhism. If this created chaos among the people, they stopped their propaganda and replaced their cadres with new ones saying that the old ones had been disloyal. This happened in 1972–1975 in Svay Yea and Svay Ang Communes not far away from my village. After 1975 they spoke against Buddhism everywhere, and it was dissolved.[8]

In the nearby province of Prey Veng, anti-Buddhist sentiment was already felt in late 1972 by a learned, sixty-year-old head monk (sangkreach), who said,

I realized that they were anti-Buddhism in late 1972 when they burnt my
Buddhist literature. It took three days and three nights to burn it all. It
happened after the battle between Lon Nol and the Khmer Rouge, and
the Khmer Rouge won. Before this they were alright. There were fifteen
monks at our monastery. They explained that we should not join the
monkhood for very long. One by one young monks in their twenties
disrobed willingly and joined the Khmer Rouge army. When they first
came to the village they were good. In 1971, 1972 they were not going
to abolish Buddhism. . . .They stopped having Buddhist festivals in 1973,
but I was allowed to remain; all monks except me were disrobed. People
still brought me food until they were reprimanded by the Khmer Rouge.
They guarded me to prevent me escaping to Phnom Penh. I was taken
for re-education in 1972 when I was asked to promise, by having my
finger printed, not to escape to Phnom Penh. Many monks left for Phnom
Penh, but I was caught.[9]

Indeed many monks escaped to Phnom Penh to avoid the militarization
of the liberated zones by the Khmer Rouge. Monasteries in Phnom Penh
overflowed with monks. In Unnalom monastery, for example, the number
of monks swelled to about one thousand in 1975, up from three hundred
to four hundred in peacetime.

Buddhist monks in some liberated zones became quite political. A
Buddhist organization called "Patriotic Monks" was set up in some areas
to make monks feel that they were participating in national affairs. Some
monks enjoyed the privilege and supported the Khmer Rouge. One fifty-
year-old monk who went back to his village in Baphnom district in
Prey Veng Province (Eastern Zone) when he was evacuated from a
monastery in Phnom Penh in April 1975, said,

Before April 17, 1975, they used religion as a hook. They set up the
Patriotic Monks Committee to work for them until their victory in 1975
when they started to abolish religion. Even those who had helped them
before were in danger. They abolished religion and even abolished lives.
When I first arrived at my village there were Patriotic Monks or head
monks in charge of each district or village. Later on they too were disrobed.
When I first arrived, there were monasteries, and Buddhist ceremonies
were carried on. Each monastery had five, ten, twenty monks. . . . Three
months later they were disrobed.[10]

In order to ensure their popularity with Buddhist monks, the Khmer
Rouge recruited monks as cadres. In Kompong Speu Province after 1975,
"there were two or three monk cadres. They were disrobed too, later
on. Some were killed while some lived and worked like the rest of the
people."[11] In some liberated zones, while they did not openly oppose

Buddhism, they used monks to do work that monks should avoid, such as raising chickens and carrying guns. A monk who lived in Phnom Penh before 1975 told me that they were asked to transport food and ammunition for the Khmer Rouge. They were cajoled to help the Khmer Rouge. "I don't think they supported the Khmer Rouge, but they had to do the work for fear of being killed."[12]

Many monks realized that they had been used by the Khmer Rouge to influence the people, but the power of the Khmer Rouge was so entrenched that there was nothing the monks could do. A monk who was evacuated from the city of Siem Reap to the liberated zone of that province in April 1975 said,

> When I first arrived in the countryside, some liberated monks whispered to me that with these "blackies," these "crows," [terms used to refer to the Khmer Rouge] there was no hope that religion would survive. I did not believe them at first. I went to see the head monk at Chikreng District. He said the same thing. He said they had told lies and cheated the people all along. Wherever they could not influence the people, they brought along monks from other villages and conducted a Buddhist festival [*kathin*], or sometimes put up Sihanouk posters and called a meeting attended by their cadres. They did this to gather support among the people. There were still many monks in each monastery in the liberated zone when I arrived, because they still needed them to politicize and influence the people . . . Yes, they supported the Khmer Rouge but most did so because they had no choice. They had no means to leave the liberated zone. Their movement was restricted.[13]

After April 1975

The Evacuation

Like the rest of the population who lived in the capital and provincial cities, monks were told to evacuate their monasteries and leave the city. In Phnom Penh, Khmer Rouge soldiers in black pajamas ordered the people to leave. They lied, saying that this would only be a temporary move and that the people would be able to return in the near future. The most widespread reason given was that the "Americans were going to bomb the city." It is perhaps not very surprising that people believed this. A sixty-year-old monk who lived at Unnalom monastery in Phnom Penh said,

> The Pol Pot army told me to leave the monastery around three-to-four o'clock in the afternoon. I said it was a bit late; "where am I going to sleep tonight?" They said America was going to drop bombs tomorrow

and I better leave for three days; no need to lock the doors; I would be back.[14]

This account is typical of what happened to the rest of the population. They were tricked into leaving their homes and many people took few of their possessions. People took just enough provisions for three or four days, hoping that they would be able to return. No one could escape the evacuation of Phnom Penh, including the aged and the sick. Said one monk, "My teacher Achar Tang and two old ladies were very sick and refused to leave. They were forced out and died on the way."[15]

Force was used whenever necessary to frighten people out of the city. Guns were fired at those who refused or were reluctant to leave. "In Moha Mundrei monastery, a few monks were wounded" in the firing.[16] I was told later on that a monk, called Souh, refused to leave and hid somewhere. He was found and shot in front of the monastery.[17] So within a few days, Phnom Penh city, with nearly two million people in 1975, became practically empty.

The situation in the provincial cities was less urgent. A monk who used to live in Siem Reap city said,

> Their military cadres came to live with us for over one week after the 17th of April to investigate our biographies including those of aged men and women who lived in the monastery. . . .We did not leave until over a week later, when they told us through a loud-speaker to leave one morning. They did not give any explanation, but there was a rumor that we were leaving for a short time. . . . They told us to leave the keys with them and not to take anything more than we could carry. One hundred soldiers came that morning to guard all around the monastery, and three trucks were waiting for us.[18]

Little change took place within the liberated zones in April 1975. There are very few reports of evacuations at that point in time; however, the monks there were all told to leave monasteries. Monks from the cities, like the rest of the city population, were sent to the countryside—the liberated zones. Known as "new monks," they were usually placed in monasteries with liberated zone monks or "base monks."

Disrobing of Monks

The order to disrobe monks came later that year. Some monks were told to disrobe as early as July 1975. However, the majority seem to have been able to evade disrobing until late 1975 or early 1976, and in some few cases until early 1977. Usually a formal order was given at a meeting which monks were asked to attend. In one such meeting, we were asked whether Buddhism should be abolished or not. I spoke against the abolition of Buddhism. Khmer Rouge cadres and some Buddhist monks started to bang the table letting us know that this was against their policy. Soon after the meeting the order came for us to disrobe, "new monks" first, "base monks" later. I refused for a long time, but finally, after being advised by an old friend that my life would be in danger if I kept on refusing, I disrobed in January 1976.[19]

Consulting monks as to whether Buddhism should be abolished or not was not common. Orders usually came from district leaders or the people in charge of the village, or the chief of the commune. A monk who then lived in Takeo Province in the Southwest Zone said, "Ta Mok's officials gave the order. There was no way out of it. 'monks must disrobe; it's about time other people lived in the monastery'."[20]

Even though the order obviously came from the top to eradicate Buddhist monks, some local cadres expressed both their lack of conviction and their lack of power to do anything. A monk who had been living under the Khmer Rouge in the liberated zone of Svay Rieng Province since early 1972 said,

They called the abbot and Buddhist teachers to a meeting where they told us that there was a plan to disrobe all monks. I asked, "Why? You have been supporting Buddhism all along". . . . They said there was nothing they could do; that it was an order from above. They compromised by disrobing the 45 novices and *bhikkus* and left the abbot and I. . . . A week later they came back and asked us to disrobe as well. There was nothing we could do. We did not want to be seen as opposing their policy.[21]

There was no clear ideological commitment to the abolition of Buddhism in the mind of some cadres. One of them in Kompong Speu Province said to a sixty-four-year-old monk, "Maybe you can be re-ordained when the country is at peace again."[22] Others were more committed ideologically. Cadres from the Southwest Zone are reported to have said: "Kampuchea is a state where there will be no unemployment, and monks are unemployable, so they must be disrobed."[23]

Threats were used whenever needed. The common one was to threaten to send those who refused to disrobe to the Higher Organization (Angkar Leu). Every monk I interviewed agrees that this meant an end to their lives. Killing some monks as a lesson for the rest was quite common. A monk who lived in Kandal Province said,

We refused to disrobe for a while but they took one monk away and two hours later took his possessions away. This was a sign that he was killed. After that, all of us disrobed for fear of being killed.[24]

Another monk in Kompong Speu Province said that around that time,

> three head monks were killed; I don't know for what reason. Their names
> were Bo, Em, and Son. Having heard that, no one dared refuse to disrobe
> when we were told to.[25]

Many monks were taken away for refusing to disrobe. In Takeo
Province, Southwest Zone, a monk who was disrobed at the end of
1975 said,

> they told us to disrobe many times before this, but we refused and some
> monks were sent elsewhere for this. But at the end they came with guns
> and forced us to disrobe. Fifteen monks were disrobed with me. There
> were no more monks after that.[26]

As expected, there seemed to be different treatment of new monks
and the base monks. In some places, the new monks were the first to
be disrobed and were followed by the base monks. A monk who was
evacuated from Phnom Penh to the Southwest Zone said,

> They said all the monks from the city were traitors. They were monks
> during the day and fought for the Lon Nol government at night. So all
> the new monks were disrobed in July 1975. However, three months later
> an order came for the base monks to disrobe also; they said 'for the time
> being.' We all ended up working together.[27]

Another ex-Phnom Penh monk said that in a village of Kompong Cham
Province,

> there was a letter from the district office with an order that all monks
> must disrobe before a certain date. I was the only new monk and of high
> rank. I thought I must obey the order. So I was the first monk to be
> disrobed. There were also forty-six base monks who had been living in
> the liberated zone with them. They thought I was the only one who had
> to disrobe. Four days later another letter arrived with an order that all
> monks, new or base, must disrobe. Those who refuse to disrobe are to
> pack their bags and the Organization will take them to a higher-level
> monastery, the order continued. The head monk was in tears as he read
> the letter to all the monks and the villagers, who were also crying. The
> next morning all monks disrobed. They used their saffron robes to make
> trousers and shirts because they could not find anything else.[28]

In Kandal Province, Region 22, the Khmer Rouge cadres tried to
make disrobing look as if it was a voluntary act.

They called us to a meeting where they showed us a document for us to sign. The document said that we monks have "awakened," that we wanted to leave the monkhood to help rebuild the country. We did not write this document which they had written for us.[29]

None of the monks interviewed volunteered to disrobe. On the contrary, many preferred to die in a massacre. All twenty-nine interviewees were disrobed by early 1976 except for one who remained a monk until January 1977.[30] They were all forced to disrobe under the threat of death. A sixty-eight-year-old monk said that in his village in Svay Rieng Province in late 1975,

there were monks who refused to disrobe and every one of them was taken away. There were 234 monks who were taken away from this area. They collectively decided not to disrobe on the ground that Buddhism has been part of tradition for a long time. The leader of this group was Sar Pueu, who was in his sixties.[31]

The Khmer Rouge central government was definitely behind this policy of eradicating Buddhism. This can be seen in a self-congratulatory note in an eight-page Party Center document dated September 1975 and entitled *About the Control and Application of Political Leadership in Accumulating Forces for the National Front and Democracy of the Party*. This document says,

ninety to ninety-five percent of the monks have disappeared, in the sense that the majority of monks have abandoned religion. Monasteries, which were pillars for monks, are largely abandoned. The foundation pillars of Buddhism are abandoned, the people have stopped going to monasteries, stopped having festivals and concentrate only on making dams and canals, etc. These pillars have disintegrated. In the future they will dissolve further. The political base, the economic base, the cultural base must be uprooted. To this point, the movement will go forward, not turn back. People run away from monasteries to work the land. It is here that we promise that monks and Buddhism are falling by ninety to ninety-five percent. So this special layer has nothing to worry [us] about. So our society has changed tremendously.

Thus, Buddhist ceremonies and Buddhism's role in Kampuchean society were forcefully stamped out by early 1976.

Former Buddhist monks were forbidden to chant, light incense sticks, shave their heads, or meditate. They, as well as laypeople, had "no right to practice Buddhism." They would be reprimanded or taken away if they were seen doing anything resembling Buddhist practice.

After the Disrobing

After being disrobed, the monks were sent out of the monasteries to live and to become part of the production force with the general population. Like the rest of the people, they were sent to perform various tasks such as building irrigation systems, working in artisanal workshops, tending vegetable gardens, making fertilizer, or growing rice. All interviewees reported the hard and long working conditions, the shortage of food, and the oppression and terroristic conditions they lived under. A sixty-year-old monk who had lived with the Khmer Rouge since early 1972 in the Eastern Zone and was later moved with the rest of the population to the northwest of Kampuchea (Battambang Province), said,

> In the Pol Pot time, wherever I lived, Svay Rieng, Prey Veng or Battambang, there were always difficulties with food. I was asked to dig canals and later worked in artisanry, such as blacksmithing, making axes, repairing houses and kitchens and looking after cows and buffaloes. I never had any free time. It was even worse in Battambang. Old people were to grow tobacco, build barns, raise dykes. We had to work so hard, like animals, regardless of how old we were. As for food, we ate rice porridge wherever we lived, with thin soup, with only a few pieces of vegetable to be seen.[32]

Like the rest of the Eastern Zone population, former monks from that region were moved to the Northwest Zone in 1977 or 1978 as part of Pol Pot's plan to suppress the Eastern Zone. "We went to Pursat by train and five thousand of us were dropped in Maung. We lived there for two weeks and over three thousand of us were killed there." Speaking of a time two to three months and a few more displacements later, he said, "By now most of us had died or been killed."[33]

Many ex-monks were being punished or imprisoned for their wrong-doing.

> Around August-September 1976 I was arrested in the middle of the night. They beat me up until I became unconscious. The next morning I regained consciousness. They punished me for two reasons: first, for refusing to get married, and second, for having my head shaved every two weeks and secretly worshipping Buddha. They must have found out. . . . they said that I influenced the people against the Organization's direction and hid my labor force. The allegations were without proof. So the next morning a district committee member arrived and took the six of us, all arrested at the same time, to a village called Krous—a Security office. The door was opened and everyone inside was in shackles. . . . They took us out of the room to be interrogated every three days.[34]

Harsh working conditions, together with a starvation diet, made many ex-monks die of exhaustion. My interviewees thought that the Khmer Rouge were making them work harder than laypeople. Many of them believed that the Khmer Rouge meant to work them to death, and that it was only luck that saved their lives. Often they were told that they had been comfortable and had oppressed the people for a long time. Now it was their turn to work hard. "Their aim was to kill us by exhaustion," said one of them,[35] while another said, "They kept me because I could do what they asked me to do."[36]

Having been in the monkhood for so long, many ex-monks died on the job because they were not accustomed to such heavy labor and lacked the requisite skills. In Kandal Province an ex-monk died while fishing "because he did not know how to use the nets."[37] There were also reports of monks who were taken away for not finishing building a house in the two days they were assigned, for breaking the ox cart while doing a delivery, or for losing a plow. All these were excuses to get rid of them.

The Genocide

It is hard to determine how many monks died during the time of Pol Pot, because they were dispersed throughout the country and many were forced to get married and are now settled down with a family. Many, however, have since made a big effort to visit their old monasteries to say "hello," or to seek out the faith of their fellow monks. But the number of monks who died or have not been accounted for is very high. A sixty-nine-year-old monk who used to live in Saravann monastery in Phnom Penh and was re-ordained in May 1980, said,

There used to be over five hundred monks in this monastery and all were evacuated. Out of these, about twenty are still alive as laymen and four have returned to the monkhood. I don't know what happened to the rest, but most of them must have been killed because I know many of them and they would have come to see me if they were alive.[38]

Another monk who used to live in Neak Vann monastery in Phnom Penh said,

There were 205 monks in 1975. Of these, I have become aware of six still alive. Five returned to the monkhood. One was married in Pol Pot's time and now lives with his wife and children.[39]

According to a seventy-three-year-old monk, the Moha Mundrei monastery in Phnom Penh used to have 660 monks. He said,

I have met only four people so far. Three, including me, have rejoined the monkhood; two are still laymen. The rest I don't know about.[40]

Another venerable sixty-one-year-old monk said that Sompoeu Meas monastery used to have about 150 monks and that,

of these, four are alive including myself. There are two in the monkhood; two are laymen. The rest I don't know about. I know of two who died of starvation. They were Achar Long and Achar Mei Ly.[41]

Unnalom was the biggest and best-known monastery in Phnom Penh. In 1975 there were about one thousand monks there, and all of them were evacuated. A seventy-four-year-old monk who used to live there and has now returned said,

Only two, including myself, came back and joined the monkhood. There are a few more who remain as laymen; perhaps ten or fewer that I have met. There were many learned monks in Unnalom monastery. They all disappeared; I'm sure they died. If they were not killed, they would have died of starvation or sickness. Their names are Hout Tat, So Hay, ...[42]

While base monks were treated better than new monks who were evacuated from the city in 1975, their casualty rates were much higher in some places than in others. An eighty-year-old monk who used to live at Pothesalapruck Monastery in the countryside of Kompong Cham Province said,

There were five monks in my monastery. All of us are alive. I'm the only one who has returned to the monkhood. The other four stay as laymen [43].

At Chompou Priksar monastery in Svay Rieng Province, however, the casualties were high. A survivor of this monastery said,

There were about one hundred monks in this monastery in the old days. Among them, one is alive, besides me. He rejoined the monkhood and now lives in Pursat.[44]

In Reach Do monastery, Siem Reap district, sixty monks were evacuated in 1975. Of these, eighteen are still alive and have not returned to the monkhood because they were forced to get married and now live with their families. Another three, including myself, have been re-ordained. So there are a total of twenty-one people still alive. The rest are unaccounted for, but I know that most of them were killed.[45]

Thus, from these eight of Cambodia's 3,300 monasteries, only seventy Buddhist monks (2.6 percent) were known to have survived in 1979, out of the 1975 total of 2,680. If such a proportion survived in the country as a whole, this would suggest that fewer than 2,000 monks may have survived Democratic Kampuchea out of the previous total of more than 65,000.

Notes

M.I. refers to a monk interview and the number that follows to the monk being interviewed.

1. Ben Kiernan, "Wild Chickens, Farm Chickens and Cormorants: Kampuchea's Eastern Zone Under Pol Pot," in *Revolution and Its Aftermath in Kampuchea: Eight Essays*, monograph no. 25, ed. David P. Chandler and Ben Kiernan (New Haven: Yale Southeast Asia Council, 1983).
2. M.I. 4.
3. M.I. 4.
4. M.I. 4.
5. M.I. 7.
6. Mul Bunchan, "The Umbrella War of 1942," in *Peasants and Politics in Kampuchea, 1942–1981*, ed. Ben Kiernan and Chanthou Boua (London: Zed Press, 1982), 114.
7. Ibid., 120.
8. M.I. 7.
9. M.I. 22.
10. M.I. 3.
11. M.I. 18.
12. M.I. 19.
13. M.I. 28.
14. M.I. 8.
15. M.I. 29.
16. M.I. 6.
17. M.I. 18.
18. M.I. 28.
19. M.I. 19.
20. M.I. 6; Mok, known as the butcher of the Southwest, is still with Pol Pot today along the Thai border.
21. M.I. 4.
22. M.I. 10.

23. M.I. 5.
24. M.I. 20.
25. M.I. 10.
26. M.I. 18.
27. M.I. 21.
28. M.I. 29.
29. M.I. 8.
30. Region 41, Kompong Cham Province, M.I. 14.
31. M.I. 24.
32. M.I. 4.
33. M.I. 22.
34. M.I. 28.
35. M.I. 12.
36. M.I. 9.
37. M.I. 5.
38. M.I. 29.
39. M.I. 18.
40. M.I. 11.
41. M.I. 12.
42. M.I. 8.
43. M.I. 13.
44. M.I. 24.
45. M.I. 28.

PART FOUR

The Social and Political Psychology of State Terror

13

The Rajk Trial and the Captive Mind in Hungary, 1949

William O. McCagg, Jr.

The show trial of the Hungarian Communist László Rajk and of "his accomplices," held at Budapest between 16 and 24 September 1949,[1] signaled the introduction of large-scale, systematic terror in the East European Empire acquired by the Soviet Union after the Second World War.

While this paper is meant in part to counterbalance two books which have implied that the trial was imposed on Hungary by the Soviet Union,[2] its main objective is to suggest how the trial related to a specific consequence of terrorization: to the state of mind that the Polish poet Czeslaw Milosz labeled the "captive mind." The paper, first, seeks to identify the direction of the trial, including the audience meant to be terrorized. In addition, the trial will be examined to see how it was orchestrated to create terror. Finally, evidence will be presented showing the trial's success in the creation of terror.

The Audience

It may be especially useful to determine the intended audiences of the Rajk trial, as there is evidence that the trial was very carefully aimed at one particular audience.

Given the condition of the state in 1949, it was unlikely that the target audience was the nation state of Hungary. Hungary had been stripped of most of its territories and rendered barely economically viable in the Second World War. First, it lost its independence to the Germans and then to the Russians during the war. It regained its sovereignty only in 1947, and then under conditions which allowed Soviet troops to remain in the country. Given the weakened condition of the state in 1949, did the Soviet Union and the Hungarian Communists need to terrorize it?

The same applies if we look at Hungary as a society, rather than as just a state. Between the two world wars, two-thirds of Hungarian society was defined as "peasant" and was locked out of the political picture by inequitable land distribution, ignorance and poverty. Half of those peasants had been beggars and largely illiterate, landless labor. Although the massive land-reform of 1945 drastically changed the economic condition of the peasantry, creating a new nation of small farmers and "peasant" political parties, Hungarian society remained overwhelmingly village-bound, isolated from the outside world, and powerless.

Similarly, prewar Hungary's modern industrial city of Budapest was no island of political strength for the forces of "modernism." Power remained in the hands of landholding aristocrats, supported by the Catholic Church, industrial magnates, and a bureaucratized, ardently nationalist gentry. The substantial Jewish commercial middle class was made to feel ill at ease in the heart of a "Christian nation," and was beleaguered by quasi-official anti-Semitism. The numerically strong industrial labor force had likewise been kept in place by the depressed economy, illiteracy, and poverty, as well as by repression of the Socialist parties. As in the countryside, the war brought massive political change to the city as the Russians eliminated any vestige of aristocratic rule. The war also wreaked extraordinary havoc among the non-aristocratic population in Budapest. The Germans physically decimated the Jewish population, crippling what should have been a strong middle class. Then, during the siege of 1944, the "Christian" middle class, which had compromised itself through its flirtation with Fascism, lost much of its property. The "degentrified" elite of Budapest was thus already a victim of terror before the Communists got there. It did not require so hefty an instrument as the Rajk trial to subjugate it again four years after 1945.

Finally, there had been many other "terroristic acts" directed at the general population in Hungary before the Rajk trial, culminating in the spring 1949 arrest, show-trial, public confession, and judicial condemnation of a cardinal of the Catholic Church.

Thus, when examining the audience meant to be terrorized by the Rajk trial, it is clear that most of the social elements within Hungary had already been well terrorized by the war and the postwar political drama and did not need to be terrorized any further to make them pliant. It is only when one scrutinizes the political actors in postwar Hungary that the target audience for the Rajk Trial emerges.

Since the war, a new center of power had emerged in the country, the Communist Party whose membership was distinctive from the rest of the population. Though it too was, perhaps, not "free of fear" (whatever that might mean), it was invigorated by wild success.[3] At the start, in 1944–1945, the Hungarian Communists had been notably few in number, their party having suffered drastic persecution between the wars. In addition, the Party had a poor reputation in virtually every sector of Hungarian society because of its self-defeating, radical behavior during the 1919 revolution.

But the Communists had enjoyed advantages too in 1944–1945. They had occupied a special position with the "liberation force," the Soviet Army. The Russians had often treated the Communists as the only politically reliable people in Hungary and had bestowed upon them a privileged position in police affairs. Furthermore, in 1945, the Party Center advocated the broadest possible national political unity for a "democratic" (and not even socialist) reconstruction of the country. Consequently, the Communists were able to present themselves as advocating the interests of virtually every element in the population. To workers, they were a most resolute pro-Socialist force; to peasants, they were the institutors of the great land distribution; to the remaining middle-class Jews, they were the most resolute anti-Fascist force in the country; to ex-Fascists, they could offer pardon and redemption.

The results were striking. By the first postwar elections in November 1945, which were won by a small-landholder party, the Communists already had well over a quarter of a million members. Over the next two years, as the party membership rose to 660,000, a perceptibly close collaboration between the Communists and the police broke up the Smallholder Party. Subsequently, in the elections of fall 1947, the Communists emerged as Hungary's largest single party and formed a coalition government of their own. In massive steps, late in 1947 and in 1948, they launched the socialization of the urban economy. Then, in June 1948, the CP absorbed the Social-Democratic Party, bringing the Party membership (at least on paper) well over the million mark to about one-tenth of the entire population.

Thus, long before the Rajk Trial, the Communists became the leading force in Hungary's society. They were a great mass of people, from diverse backgrounds, who had leapt on a bandwagon of power and success and were characterized by their enthusiasm and euphoria. It was these same qualities which would later become the basis of the "captive mind." Of course, no such captivity yet existed in 1948. The Party had been so busy in the takeover years that it had neither time nor institutions for careful training of the new membership; the party had been maintained through sheer momentum.

There was, however, an anomaly in this situation. To many contemporary observers, the Communists seemed to have seized power according to a preconceived design. Their progress seemed remarkably smooth.[4] There are, however, considerable flaws in this "grand design" concept. Not that polished techniques of power seizure were absent, or that the Communists were pure democrats, void of a desire for power and unwilling to lie to get it. In 1945 the Communists apparently had no idea that they could seize power in the immediate future and, in significant ways, rejected such a seizure of power.[5] Further, as they slowly gained power in 1946 and 1947, their intention seems to have been to construct in Hungary a "new type" of national democracy in which they would be the guiding light but not the only force, and in which "revolution" would follow distinctly new, "non-Soviet" lines. Such ideas continued to inspire the Communists at least until the fall of 1948 when the situation changed rapidly. The confusion and change was such that the same top Party leaders who, in September 1948, were resolutely denying the need for Soviet-style proletarian dictatorship in Hungary, were six months later announcing the existence of a proletarian dictatorship "according to the Soviet form."[6] The action, in spring 1949, eliminating all other political parties, collectivizing agriculture, and Sovietizing industry and culture was a radical negation of everything they had promised to do in the previous five years. To cover up this fact, they fallaciously claimed to have carried out a "blueprint plan" for seizing power while tricking everyone.[7]

During the year immediately preceding the Rajk trial, the Communist Party, swollen with euphoric new recruits lured in with promises of national democracy, threw out its old, attractive goals, and instituted their opposite. Given these circumstances, the reason for the terroristic show trial of the Communist, László Rajk, becomes clear; it was not Hungary and her society, but the tenth of Hungary's population which had streamed into the Communist Party that had to be terrorized. Otherwise, the contrast between previous goals and present actions would have ripped the Party apart.

It is often said that the Rajk trial was imposed on Hungary from the outside. This paper suggests that the Rajk trial was perfectly logical and perfectly "native" in terms of what the Hungarian Communist central leadership was then undertaking.

The Trial as an Instrument of Terror

It is logical to look first at matters of personnel and form. As is well known, the "hero" of the piece, Rajk, was, until his arrest on 30 May 1949, the leading "native" among the postwar Hungarian Communist leaders.[8] It is useful to note that his religious background, physical height and attractive outward mien was in sharp contrast to the party's "Muscovite" leader Rákosi, who was of Jewish background, short, bald and notably ugly. More importantly, to understand the trial, it is necessary to know that Rajk knew more people in Hungary and in the Party than did Rákosi who, for twenty-five years, had either been in prison or abroad. Further, Rajk was just as conspicuous as Rákosi in the early postwar years (April 1946 until August 1948); he had been Minister of the Interior in the national government, and as such had played a key public role in the defeat of the Smallholder Party. Consequently, László Rajk was a very useful "villain" for satisfying the supposed need to terrorize the Communist Party.

Known and admired by a vast range of people within the Party, Rajk had risen very high; consequently his arrest as an American Imperialist agent, and Titoist spy, unsettled virtually the entire Party membership. The selection of Rajk's "accomplices" at the show trial was equally astute. His primary "accomplice," General György Pálffy, former chief of the security branch of the Hungarian Armed Forces, was broadly connected among Communists who had been in the wartime underground, and who were socially linked to the old ruling elite.[9] Tibor Szönyi, the third key figure in the trial, was selected because he could be linked to Alan Dulles, chief of the newly organized CIA, through a left-leaning American Quaker, Noel Field.[10] Szönyi was also a close associate of the fairly numerous group of Communists who had spent the war years in the West, and he was the former Chief of the Cadre Department of the CPH. Thus, his arrest threatened all those who had West European Communist connections and to whom the Party had given a job. Finally, Pál Justus was useful in the dock because, as a former "leftist" Social Democrat, his arrest threatened all those who had recently become Communists through the party merger of 1948.

This threat to a large group of Communist Party members recalls the second element of the "captive mind" in Hungary. After the euphoria came a twinge of guilt. The threat also shows how very "Hungarian" the trial was and how neatly it fit the purpose of terrorizing the Communist Party membership.

The Credibility of the Trial

Assessing the credibility of the trial requires a return to the period of the seizure of power and a recognition of how precisely the trial fit with a special "educational" aspect of the Hungarian CP's rise to power—with its "Jacobinism," as it was called at the time, or "Zhdanovism," as we would call it today.

At the root of this "educational" aspect lay the fact that the CPH rejected power seizure at the time of the 1944–1945 "liberation," and in its own eyes did this so blatantly that the deed required explanation.[11] As such, from the very moment of their return from Moscow, Rákosi and his team began issuing remarkably articulate "theoretical" explanations of why their Party was following a "new," "people's democratic" road towards Socialism. By 1945–46 Rákosi and József Révai, the ideological mentor of the Party, were among the most articulate spokesmen in Eastern Europe for the idea that Socialism might and should be pursued in new, national ways.

In 1946, Révai's daily paper, the Szabad Nép, became the oracle of Hungarian politics. Minutely informed through the Party Politburo about what "enemies" the police might "unveil" next, this journal's editorial page began to explain presciently, at every step, the "lessons" of current events.[12]

Revai's "Jacobinism" lent a didactic quality to the Hungarian Communist "take-over" which was really unparalleled elsewhere in Europe. Because events moved more slowly and less brutally in Hungary than in some other places, it was easier for the new members of the Party to ignore disagreeable facts. In addition the Hungarian Party always actively explained the disagreeable facts away.[13] Finally, in early 1949 when the contradictions between promise and actual policy grew too great to conceal, Révai produced his ingenious doctrine that the Party had been acting according to a secret plan, intending to end up exactly where it now was, while all the time saying the opposite so as to trick the opposition!

Revai's "Jacobinism" and his "secret plan" provide some clue as to why the Rajk trial was so credible within the Hungarian Communist Party in 1949. Because of all those careful explanations in the past, the nascent "captive mind" mentality in the Hungarian Party of 1949 was not a terrorized "mind" such as Czeslaw Milosz described in postwar Poland, where former Fascistic poets, or hardened veterans of Auschwitz became docile servants of a cynical CP, but rather a matter of people getting used to riding with the current of a huge river (as one veteran described it), of getting used to the joy of serving, while the Party did the thinking.[14] As a result, when Rajk's trial came up, surrounded as it was with clever explanation and brilliant P.R., it fit in.

The trial was terribly disturbing, of course, but it was perfectly Hungarian. The Party members here were used to being told, oracularly, that the highly unusual was absolutely correct, that the good guys of yesterday were really bad today, that the "people" had to be educated into Socialism, that the Party leadership—and above all Stalin—was wise and good, that all one had to do was quell one's nerves and follow.

Nothing unusual, given the Party's Jacobin record, that László Rajk should turn out to be a Titoist, and an Imperialist spy! What now about the background? Was there material which, with or without Révai's complex explanations, allowed for a credible trial? The record suggests there was.

As Minister of the Interior in 1914–1948, Rajk had come into increasing conflict with the two comrades who governed the secret police, the Muscovite Mihály Farkas, and the former tailor, Gábor Péter, and through them with their immediate chief, Rákosi.[15] Even today the real nature of the problem between Rajk and his colleagues is not discussed in Hungary. It seems probable, however, that the issue was political tempo. Rákosi, Farkas and Péter enjoyed direct and frequent contact with the highest Police and Party circles in Moscow, and were consequently face to face, right up until 1948, with the reality that Stalin favored caution in treading on Western Allied toes. For them, therefore, a slow-paced and behind-the-scenes seizure of power had obvious virtues; whereas Rajk, a man of simpler mind who perceived Capitalist Imperialism as the enemy and Revolution as the immediate goal, and saw no good reason at all not to rock the bourgeois boat.

Whatever the explanation, by the fall of 1947 relations were very bad between these men. This was when Rajk, in an effort to enhance his own control over the likes of Péter, dissolved all political party units within the police. Péter and Farkas reciprocated early in 1948 with a denunciation of Rajk to the Politburo as an "enemy" guilty of "anti-Party and anti-Regime" activity.[16]

It would be a mistake to blow these frictions up into a tale of full-scale factional conflict within the CPH as it rose to power. The leading Communists of that period were so busy then that they literally had no time for in-fighting. The clashes were much more a function of a typical and very important ingredient of the captive mind: what we call "voluntary service by imitation." As noted earlier, the Party did not indoctrinate its new members then, but it did teach them from the top down that, when there were no orders, they should act in a "Communist fashion"—that is, they should carry out their work in exactly the same way as they saw their superiors working. Since Stalin and "the Revolution"—i.e. Marx—could not, of course, provide orders for every situation, a good deal of Communist behavior was therefore governed by libidinous imagination. The whole Party, including leaders such as Rajk, was actually engaged in plunging forward after the manner rather than at the command of Stalin and the Revolution, brushing aside obstacles as if these were "enemies of the Revolution," rather than their own.

If there was little deliberate factionalism in the postwar Hungarian CP, there was a great deal of "brushing aside," because Rajk played politics in a broad range of areas outside the police. He was very interested, for example, in the peasantist "People's Colleges" through which many leftist Hungarian intellectuals hoped to educate village boys and girls into a new national elite. Here Rajk joined hands with the leading Politburo intellectual, the Muscovite József Révai, and by the fall of 1947, with active support from these two men, the students in some one hundred Budapest colleges had become an effective street force, active in the removal of such "obstacles" to "Revolution" as the Social-Democrats. Rajk was fascinated also by the potential of a reorganized "popular front" among the democratic political parties. In 1947 he visited Yugoslavia, where such a front was a principal instrument for furthering the "Revolution." In 1948 and 1949, until his arrest, he was, with Révai's enthusiastic backing, the President of the Front organization in Hungary, seeking to make it much more prominent than it had been so far. Rajk was no particular fan of Marshal Tito, but in the fall of 1947, when Stalin's favoring of Tito was at its height, Rajk sent a delegation of Hungarian policemen for "consultations" in Belgrade.

To repeat, László Rajk was not (so far as we can tell) an active rival of Rákosi for Party leadership; but he was a "Puritan," a disciplinarian among opportunists; and in May 1948, when Rákosi was allowing the CPH to balloon into a million-strong, and by definition flabby, mass Party, Rajk is said to have visited Stalin, with Révai's introduction, and to have expounded his ideas.[17] Stalin was physically as small as Rákosi and, notoriously, did not like tall people. Is it relevant that two months after the reported visit, Rajk was forced out of his ministry and started on the road to his arrest? We do not know, though this seems as good an explanation as any.[18]

As is known, the Rajk trial as actually staged was a fabrication composed largely by Soviet secret police personnel during August 1949, although they wrote it on the basis of "confessions" that the Hungarian secret police had extracted from the large number of Communists it had arrested during the preceding three months.[19] For the Russians it was important to demonstrate that the Hungarian "traitors" had worked through Tito's Yugoslavia. Consequently, all the men in the dock had to confess to a more or less mythical Yugoslav connection; and one former Yugoslav diplomat, Lazar Brankov, was added to the collection. Further, in the spirit of 1936–1937, the Russians felt that the defendants at the trial should confess not just to recent "crimes," construed on the basis of their behavior since the war, but also to the ultimate iniquity of having been Fascist police spies, virtually from the time of their entry into the worker movement long before the war. The consequent distortions were very great.

But now to make our point: from what we know of Rajk's behavior after the war, there was obviously quite enough material here to make a case that he and the "accomplices" had been conspiring to destroy, even to murder, leaders of the Party such as Rákosi and his fellow Stalinists. Many people could tell that the detail of the published trial transcript was not always quite true to history. But who knew for sure what anyone else had done in the political murk of prewar central Europe? Or, for that matter, in the dim-lit quarters of Party Headquarters during the postwar years. Anyone who had been on the scene within the Party during the three or four years prior to the trial would have to acknowledge the possibility that the case was real—that a monstrous thing had actually happened.

All told, despite the Soviet-imposed distortions, the Rajk trial was not just credible within the Hungarian Communist movement of 1949; it was most beautifully tailored to the need we have suggested above, that of terrorizing the Party. It conveyed the unambiguous message that every Communist had to be immediately and eternally on the alert to root out yet further conspiratorial enemy actions from within the Party midst.

From noting the careful aim of the Rajk trial towards its target audience, we can move almost insensibly on to recognition of its limitations and its inadequacies as an instrument of terror. For this trial was not only credible within the Party: it was too credible; the authorities staked too much on it for their own good.

One way to describe this over-investment is to note that the Terror of 1949 did not start just at the edge of the Hungarian Communist Party Politburo, or at the edge of the Secret Police, and then radiate outwards from there: it started inside and up above; and the trial was a product of the experience of terror. The evidence of this has been clear for a long time, though not so often stressed in accounts of the era. It goes back to the nature of the great political turn which affected Hungary and all of Eastern Europe in 1948, and indeed to the character of the revolutionary tactics pursued by Communists all over the world before then.

Was that great turn invented in Hungary? Of course not! It was a function of Stalin's political stance vis-à-vis the West, and of Stalin's relations with Titoist Yugoslavia. And was the so-called revolutionary tactic of the early postwar years invented in Hungary? Same answer! That tactic was a function of Stalin's preference in 1944–1945 for not offending the West, and for not letting violent revolution rock his boat.

And was the international Communist coalitionist tactic of 1945 approved by all the revolutionaries within the Communist Movement? Here, the answer is that they approved, but often did so reluctantly, on

Stalin's credence. After all, what Leninist could approve fully of a tactic which restrained Communists from seizing power wherever they were able to do so during the glorious moment of revolution which, as Lenin had prognosticated, would dawn inevitably at the moment of collapse following an Imperialist war? What about three years later, in 1947–1948, when Stalin had reluctantly to face the fact that his Grand Alliance had failed, that he faced a prolonged conflict with the Imperialists, yet at the same moment had to acknowledge that the forces of unrestrained revolution were stronger by far than they had been in 1945? Did the forces of Revolution approve then of Stalin's caution and reluctance? The well known answer is that they did not. From China and Indonesia, through Yugoslavia and Greece, to France and Hungary and Finland, the Communists of 1947–1948 were, with conspicuous exceptions, more than eager to let the Revolution proceed. And what did this mean for Stalin, and those conspicuous exceptions, the Stalinist Communist leaders who stood close to the Kremlin? It meant that they had been wrong, that they had misled and opposed the Revolution, and that at a not exactly convenient moment (given Stalin's decayed relationship with the West) they had to confront Leninism rampant.

The reader must pardon this string of laden questions. As is obvious, it is a rhetorical device for evoking recognition that the great turn of 1947–1948 in Hungary began with the emergence of terror within the Kremlin itself, and within the Rákosi-ite leadership of the Hungarian Party. Stalin did not impose the turn, or break with Tito just because he wanted to, or just (as so many historians have claimed) because he found it convenient now to do so. He made the break because he had to, because this was the only way in which he could still, in 1948, limit and control the end-of-the-war Revolution. Only by splitting the "real" revolutionaries from one another, on the one hand, and by precipitating in controlled spots some strictly "Stalinist" revolutions on the other, could Stalin, in 1948, defuse the criticism that he had betrayed the cause.

The fear that filled Stalin at that time may have grown slowly. But it was clearly evinced a whole year before the Rajk trial by the death within the Kremlin in August 1948 of A. A. Zhdanov who for three years had seemed Stalin's right-hand man, and by the rapidly spreading purge in the Soviet Party immediately thereafter. And for the foreign Communists it came like a bomb. They had been plunging forward towards power for three years and now, suddenly, it turned out that something was wrong, dreadfully wrong up above.

Whence the final element in the making of the Hungarian "captive mind." At the top of the Hungarian CP, a year after Zhdanov's death, terror had come so suddenly that two of Rajk's most prominent actual associates, József Révai and János Kádár, privately and publicly betrayed him. Behind the scenes, Révai is said to have actually polished the script;[20] and it was Kádár who visited Rajk in prison on behalf of the Central Committee and persuaded him to confess.[21] In public, from the highest pinnacles of Party power, both these well known friends of Rajk endorsed the validity of the court spectacle, which was broadcast day in and day out, live, all over Hungary. No matter that Révai fell deeply ill after he himself had just barely escaped purge in 1949[22] and that Kádár did not escape purge but landed in prison in 1951. Their fear-driven contribution made the trial more than needs be credible.

Nor was it only they in the top Party leadership who, inspired by fear, involved themselves personally in the making of the trial of Rajk. Rákosi, in the summer and fall of 1949, boasted of his personal contribution to the unveiling of the class enemy within the ranks of the Party. He, the Party's foremost leader, committed himself without any reservation to what added up to the murder of an honest comrade.[23]

This sort of unequivocal leadership endorsement of the trial made it all the more effective as an instrument of terror in 1949. From the very top of the Party, down through the ranks, the terror spread, converting the euphoria of the past and the nervousness of the moment into a blind, panicky "voluntary service through imitation." It was in this dramatic fashion that the "captive mind" crystallized in the Hungarian CP. But the good theatre made for a bombshell under the Party leadership a few years later. In 1953, as was inevitable, Stalin died, and with him, the cause of the great Terror disappeared. Thereafter, it was only a matter of time before the question of rehabilitating Rajk arose, and when it did, at the Twentieth Soviet Congress early in 1956, it placed Rákosi, then still in power, in an untenable position. He twisted and squirmed. He even had the gall, in April 1956, to announce the rehabilitation himself, claiming with pathos to have committed murder "by mistake." But in the summer, Rákosi's was one of two heads that Marshal Tito claimed as the price of his reconciliation with Moscow (the other, as is known, was V. M. Molotov's). Rákosi then fell, a suggestive example of how dangerous it can be for political leaders to get overly committed to the use of terror.

Nor was this all. After 1953, once the secret began to leak out that the Jacobin Party had made mistakes—that the good shepherd had been false and murderous—then the overly rationalized Hungarian "captive mind" broke. Disillusionment became profound. In 1955 and 1956 those same new Communists who, in the postwar years, had helped Révai put out the *Szabad Nép*, became the saboteurs of Stalinism, rejecting not just the Rajk trial, but the whole long set of torturous explanations that preceded it.[24] Those same people who, in the early 1950s, had most lightheartedly declaimed the treachery of Rajk, organized, in the early autumn of 1956, a tremendous public funeral for the fallen hero, as spectacular as the trial itself. And this turned out to be the dress rehearsal for the revolutionary demonstration of October 23. The Jacobinism that induced the Hungarian "captive mind" to believe in Rajk's guilt thus led directly to the so-called "counterrevolutionary" explosion of 1956.

Conclusion

In this paper we have studied the Rajk trial of 1949 as an instrument of "designed" state terrorism. We have found first that more than many historians allow, the trial actually was such an instrument, designed not by Soviet mentors, but by the leadership of the Hungarian Communist Party for the purpose of intimidating a particular sector of the rebuilt Hungary's society, the million-strong Party membership. We have found also that as an instrument of terrorism, the trial was in many, many ways magnificently well designed. It crystallized a "captive mind" among the Hungarian Communists which was more passionate, idealistic and "convinced" than perhaps anywhere else in Eastern Europe. But our criticism has been that it was too effective. The Party leadership got far too heavily involved in a matter of judicial murder and had to pay a price when the secret came out. Further, the leadership allowed this trial to meld too smoothly with the Party's overall record, to rank too equally among its revolutionary accomplishments. The result was that when, years later, questions were asked about the trial, the revolutionary accomplishments came equally up for condemnation.

Does this mean that show trials are always a bad idea? Does retribution always follow when a strong-arm regime designs terror as the Hungarian regime did in 1949? Judging from the broader history of Communism, the answer is surely "No!" In the Soviet Union, where the Leninists as well as the Stalinists staged mighty show trials,[25] there have been no explosions such as in Hungary in 1956; and what about China, where the show trial was one of the established methods of power seizure under Mao? In Bulgaria and Czechoslovakia where the Stalinists staged very fancy show trials, nothing happened in 1956; and the Czech trial played but a small role in the upheaval of 1968. In Poland, on the other hand, where the Stalinists staged no major purge trials, something very close to an explosion occurred in 1956. The rules linking terrorist show trials to popular retribution are, at least in this Communist context, highly complex.

Indeed, reluctantly we are inclined to move in the opposite direction, and to suggest that the show trial is probably a very useful device by which rulers of virtually any political complexion may capture the imaginations of the ruled. Suffice it to mention the dynamism in the United States of the Watergate affair. The public trial became of burning interest to the American public, and one may really wonder whether it was the emergence of Truth, or simply his bad show that brought Nixon down. But can we actually recommend trumped-up show trials, culminating in judicial murder, as a method of state control? Perhaps here, the Rajk affair does suggest a negative answer, because it shows how very easily the use of this method can drag politicians down to thuggery. Some people hold that the Hungarian Communists, like the Nazis, were thugs to begin with and didn't have to be dragged down to what happened in 1949. The fact remains that they ended up as thugs, and their cause bears still the stain. The inconvenience of such a stain to any government is more than adequately illustrated by the difficulties the Soviet Government today is having with its own past history.

Notes

1. The English-language transcript of the trial is Hungary, Justice Ministry, *László Rajk and his Accomplices before the People's Court* (Budapest: 1949); István Soltész, comp., *Rajk Dossié: Dolumentum Válogatás* (Budapest: Lang, 1989).

2. See Stewart Steven, *Operation Splinter Factor*, (Philadelphia: Lippincott, 1974), an unreliable account which proposes that the trial resulted from a CIA counter-information plot; and George H. Hodos, *Show Trials: Stalinist Purges in Eastern Europe 1948-1954*, (New York: Praeger, 1987), a valuable semi-memoir which suggests that the trial was "made in Moscow." Another well informed account of the background of the trial appeared too late for consideration in this essay: Tibor Zinner, "The Rajk Affair" in *Études historiques hongroises 1990*, vol. 6, ed. Ferenc Glatz (Budapest: Academy, 1990), 13-32.

3. For the following, see above all, Bennett Kovrig, *Communism in Hungary from Kun to Kádár* (Stanford: Hoover Institution Press, 1979), parts 3 and 4.

4. The most articulate expression of the "great plan" idea is Thomas Hammond, *Communist Seizures of Power*, (New Haven: Yale University Press, 1975).

5. In Hungary the following has long been no secret. See the informed discussion in Bálint Szabó, *Felszabadulás és forradalom*, (Budapest: Budapest Academy, 1975). I presented the relevant material in English in my Ph.D. dissertation, *Communism in Hungary, 1944-1946*, (Columbia University, 1965), and in my *Stalin Embattled, 1943-1948*, (Detroit: Wayne State University Press, 1978). The material remained controversial in the West, however, until other scholars looked at the documents and arrived at substantially the same findings. See, for example, Charles Gati, *Hungary and the Soviet Bloc*, (Durham, N.C.: Duke University Press, 1986), Chaps. 1-3.

6. For the detail of this extraordinary "turn," see Bálint Szabó, *Az ötvenes évek*, (Budapest: Kossuth Kiado, 1986), 28ff.

256   William O. McCagg, Jr.

7. See József Révai, "Népi demokráciánk jellegéröl" in *Társadalmi Szemle*, 4, nos. 3–4, pp. 161–167; translated into English as "The Character of a People's Democracy" *Foreign Affairs*, 27, no. 1 (October 1949).

8. The clearest biography of Rajk is Erzsébet Strassenreiter and Péter Sipos, "Rajk László" which appeared in *Párttörténeti közlemények*, 1 (1969); then later as a booklet; and finally with some revisions under Sipos's name alone in *Társadalmi Szemle* (1983), pp. 76–86.

9. See his biography, György Száraz, *A Tábornak*, (Budapest: Maguetö, 1984).

10. See Hodos, chap. 4; and Flora Lewis, *Red Pawn: The Story of Noel Field*, (Garden City, N.Y.: Doubleday, 1965).

11. There was good reason for the rejection. Stalin explicitly forbade a "forward" policy in Hungary in 1944, recommending instead a fulsome embrace of the reactionary past. One may even question whether a Soviet-backed seizure of power in 1944 could have been sustained against international repercussions after peace returned.

12. It is difficult to know how Révai came to play this "Jacobin" role. Certainly it was important that, although he was free to evoke all the *ideinost'* of Marxism-Leninism, he addressed a political audience largely unacquainted with Marxism and deprived of its old, hyper-nationalist, anti-Semitic, political language. In this sense, the very nature of the postwar political situation in Hungary made him an oracle. Also of importance was the fact that Révai was a very good journalist in a country well known for its journalistic skills. Furthermore, more than any other Muscovite Communist, Révai knew his Hungarian history and was fascinated by the emphasis placed by past leaders on the need to re-educate the public; and he had picked up some Soviet knowledge about mass educational techniques during his many years of exile in Moscow.

13. The appropriate record is Révai's collection of speeches and writings, *Élni tudtunk a szabadsággal* (Budapest: Szikra, 1949).

14. Peter Kende, in CURPH interview no. 563, comp. McCagg, *Communism in Hungary*, pp. 197–211, where other interview testimony is cited.

15. For the following, see William O. McCagg, *The Hungarian Communist Party, November 1944 to March 1946*, (M.A. Thesis, Columbia University, 1960); William O. McCagg, "The Struggle for Leadership in the Hungarian Communist Party, 1944–1948" (34 pp.), and "The Indictment of Laszlo Rajk: A Study of Communist Party Autonomy" (30 pp.), mimeograph essays written in 1961 for the Hungarian Desk at Radio Free Europe in Munich; and McCagg, *Stalin Embattled*, 394, 400.

16. See Sipos, "Rajk," 84; and the news reports from Hungary in *Nyugati Hirnök* (Paris), 20 December 1947; *New York Herald Tribune*, 30 June 1948; by John MacCormac in *New York Times*, 30 June 1948; and *Manchester Guardian*, 17 May 1949. These reports, which seem to have been based on top-level leaks from the Hungarian Communist leadership, are little used but prime evidence of the politics of the day. They entirely jibe with my own detailed readings of the Hungarian Communist press for 1945–1948.

17. See the reports of May 1948 and of 1949, cited in the preceeding note. Though the report about Rajk's trip to Moscow does not appear in the Sipos

biography, it is perfectly consistent with his disappearance from public for a period of weeks during May 1948, just when Rákosi was carrying out the merger with the SDP in a fashion which a Puritan Communist could hardly have approved of. See *Szabad Nép*, 29 May 1948 for the notice of Rajk's "return."

18. Rajk was shifted to the Foreign Ministry in August 1948. János Kádár, who replaced him as Minister of the Interior, claims that, even then, Farkas was denouncing him, on the basis of "information from Switzerland," as having been an American espionage agent. See László Gyurkó, *Arcképvázlat történelmi háttérel*, (Budapest: Akadémiai Kiadó, 1982), 180-181. G. Hodos says that onetime State Security officers told him that in August 1948, the Hungarian Ambassador to Berne forwarded home a report to the effect that Tibor Szönyi, Rajk's future "accomplice," had contact during the war with Alan Dulles of the American OSS via the Quaker war-relief worker, Noel Field. Nine months later the Soviet police organs got their hands on Field and began exerting pressure to have his East European "contacts" (including now Szönyi and Rajk) arrested. The Field connection then became the key "link" on which all the great East European show trials of the 1950s were based. We have no way of knowing how, in August 1948, Farkas got so rapidly from the "Swiss information" about Szönyi to a Politburo denunciation of Rajk, but the fact that he did so suggests strongly some sort of Soviet displeasure with Rajk even then. See Hodos, pp. 34-36.

19. The KGB did, of course, compile the relevant report on the basis of "confessions" that the Hungarian secret police had extracted from the large number of Communists it had arrested during the preceding three months. See Hodos, p. 48, summarizing a large amount of interview material; and Bela Szász, *Minden kényszer nélkul*, (Brussels: Imre Nagy Institute, 1963), passim.

20. Paul E. Zinner, *Revolution in Hungary*, (New York: Columbia University Press, 1962), 148.

21. Hodos, 48ff., especially footnote 5.

22. See K. Urban, "Revai Jozsef" in *Párttörténeti kozlemények* 24, no. 3 (1978): 162-222.

23. Rákosi, *A Békeért és a szocializmus épiteseért*, (Budapest: Szikra, 1951), 166, 172.

24. For the following, see, in particular, Tamás Aczél and Tibor Méray, *The Revolt of the Mind*, (New York: Praeger, 1960).

25. See Marc Jensen, *Show Trials under Lenin*, (Syracuse: Syracuse University Press, 1987).

14

Popular Support for the Soviet Political Trials of the Late 1920s and the Origins of the Great Purges

Dmitry Shlapentokh

Introduction: The Rationale for the Purges

The question of the origin of the great Stalinist purges has generated a lot of controversy among Western historians. The majority have assumed that Stalin's quest for power was the central determinant of state sponsored terror in the USSR of the 1920s and 1930s. Others have seen the Soviet state terror of that time as being primarily a response to the corruption of state and party officials. The following analysis is intended to demonstrate that, while organized from above, the purges of that time were also to some extent a response to popular discontent with corrupt officials, whose standard of living had become much better than that of average Russians.

One of the most important events in the formative history of the Soviet regime was the emergence of the political bureaucracy as a new ruling class that acquired various privileges and used its power to indulge in abuses ranging from corruption to drunkenness and sexual promiscuity. The roots of this bureaucratic indulgence can be traced back to the very beginnings of Soviet rule.

The bureaucracy's privileged position, as well as its growing size,[1] was based upon the absolute control it assumed over the economic life of Soviet society immediately after the revolutionary takeover.[2] During the consolidation of the Soviet rule the "system of food control placed unprecedented power in the hands of the government."[3] The amount and quality of food and other commodities depended upon one's place in the hierarchy, and the bureaucracy was among those groups whose rations were the best.[4] Russia's new masters fully understood the importance of the food distribution network in securing both their power and the standard of living which that power brought. At the same time, their power was far from secure, and they were eager not to repeat mistakes of their predecessors, who absolutely disregarded the basic needs of the populace. The regime did its best to nourish the workers, especially those "whose occupations were dangerous to their health." Among the civilian population, "they were the most privileged." "The second category comprised the workers engaged in hard, but not dangerous physical labor."[5] The population of the big industrial centers, and especially Petrograd and Moscow, was under the government's constant attention. (The Bolshevik government remembered very well what dire consequences food shortages had brought for both the Tsarists' and the Provisional Government's stability.) Due to the government's effort, and despite all hardships, Petrograd was spared the deep famine suffered by the general population.[6] The regime's representatives also made attempts to give priority in supply to public restaurants and children's institutions.[7] The Red Army and Navy, whose dissatisfaction with the old regime was often caused by bad rationing, were also among the best-fed groups of the population.[8] The situation with lodging and clothes was similar; although some of the Soviet dignitaries and the regime's supporters were quite modest in these respects,[9] others were eager to get the best of both clothing and apartments.[10] Even local bureaucrats could occasionally decorate their rooms lavishly by despoiling the rich.[11] The top bureaucrats, their relatives, and foreign "professional revolutionaries" also enjoyed lavish salaries and other material privileges.[12]

Cases of corruption and speculation among the top members of the bureaucracy were not unknown.[13] The opportunity to engage in corrupt practices depended not only upon one's position, but also one's department. Members of the Cheka (secret police) definitely enjoyed greater privileges. For this reason, contrary to the claims of some historians, they never experienced major problems in recruiting personnel.[14] Alcohol played quite an important role in the bureaucracy's corruption. As a symbol of the good life, it was eagerly consumed by the new Russian rulers, both military and civilian.[15] It often became an object of illegal machinations, and practically anything could be gotten in exchange for it.[16] Sexual promiscuity was also not uncommon among the members of the bureaucracy.[17]

Despite their privileges, the bureaucrats' lifestyles were not very different from those of the general populace in the early days of Soviet rule. In the first place, the government was eager to fill the available job slots with workers.[18] Secondly, the standard of living for the majority of bureaucrats was not much better than for the rest of the populace.

Soviet Russia was an extremely poor country which had suffered several years of war. Therefore, even the majority of the privileged elite did not live luxuriously according "to our [Western] standards."[19] Those who did not belong to the very top echelons of the bureaucratic elite often received only a modest ration.[20]

The New Class: Post-Civil War Developments

After the Civil War and the introduction of the New Economic Plan (1921), the situation changed altogether. The lifestyle of the bureaucrats became substantially better than that of industrial workers.[21] State bureaucrats, including both Party members and non-members, became deeply involved in various types of corruption and self-indulgence. The scale of corruption increased dramatically along with the increasing power of the bureaucrats over workers.[22] Although all groups of the Soviet population benefitted from the NEP, the bureaucracy definitely benefitted most.

The monetary privileges for bureaucrats instituted in revolutionary days were substantially expanded, with members receiving constantly increasing salaries. The special shops for the elites, created during the Civil War, also increased in number during the NEP, becoming a Soviet social phenomenon that has persisted until the present day.[23] Members of the bureaucracy and the NEP flooded summer resorts, received "free boxes at the theater" and numerous other privileges, most of which were directly related to their jobs.[24]

Each business trip taken by a bureaucrat was another highly visible indicator of his prestige. Since the time of the NEP, the officials had been accustomed to the most luxurious modes of travel. This tradition continued through the thirties and up to the present.[25] Cars were especially important as symbols of prestige. Every official strove to acquire them, and usually had several. Prolonged struggles sometimes took place between officials over the appropriation of given vehicles. Grigorii Zinoviev, for example, "had appropriated for the use of himself and his staff three magnificent Rolls-Royce limousines which had been the property of the Tsar and later of Kerensky."[26] One of these precious vehicles was taken to be presented to "Commissar Bronstein, the Moscow Controller of Supplies, Trotsky's brother," who accepted the car "with almost indecent alacrity."[27] Lev Kamenev also had four of them and became notorious for his love of expensive cars.[28] One foreign observer wrote that "outside of the government departments long lines of cars are always standing, and in some of those cars may be seen crystal vases containing flowers—how difficult it is to get rid of bourgeois prejudices."[29] He also added that the regime, in their quest to please the bureaucracy, spent currency freely on expensive vehicles.[30] The power and legal privileges enjoyed by bureaucrats enabled them to indulge themselves. The feeling of impending doom that pervaded the Soviet Union of the 1920s ("There were no illusions concerning the transitory character of a pseudosociety which they saw around them.") gave them additional impetus for "embezzlements, thefts and fraud," as well as for "drunken orgies, immorality and prostitution."[31]

The Soviet leaders were not unlike their subjects in their propensity for alcoholic consumption. Some of them were not indulgent and drank and ate what was available to the average Soviet citizen.[32] Others, however, engaged in drinking orgies that could not be afforded by ordinary people. Gambling also became one of the most important preoccupations of the Soviet leaders and often became an integral part of drinking orgies. It seems that Efraim Skliansky, Trotsky's right hand man, was the leading figure engaging in this sort of activity. As Soviet officials acknowledged, "Comrade Skliansky's apartment is a gambling hell."[33]

Sexually promiscuous behavior also continued to be widespread during the NEP. As before, uninhibited sexual relations came to be viewed as a symbol of the revolutionary outlook.[34] However, the revolutionary ideology in general and revolutionary erotic romanticism in particular had mostly begun to dissipate by this time. The spread of prostitution and semi-pornographic literature, as well as the increasing sex-related crime rate, demonstrates this state of affairs.[35] Once again, power and money were becoming fashionable. Bureaucrats and not penniless workers became the most desirable to women. The car became especially important as a symbol of social prestige, and contemporary writers often wrote pointedly about the "car-harem" predilections of the Soviet bureaucracy.[36] Prostitutes, who were ready to sell themselves for "bread and stockings,"[37] were also more accessible to well-to-do bureaucrats than to average workers. The bureaucrat's prestige was increased the most, however, by his deserved reputation as a provider of patronage jobs. In the larger context of economic instability and unemployment, it was within the power of the bureaucrats to offer or withhold jobs. With powerless and submissive trade unions and no law against sexual harassment, "the women employed in Soviet institutions and factories were entirely at the mercy of their chiefs and were frequently compelled to become their mistresses."[38] Members of the Soviet military were known to violate their female secretaries. In one case, one of the bureaucrats raped an employee's wife, who after several days was returned to her husband. Besides engaging in drunkenness and promiscuous sex, the Soviet bureaucrats were also corrupt. The direct embezzlement of state funds was connected with this activity.[39]

While the bureaucrats and NEP men, the new bourgeoisie who appeared in the wake of NEP, definitely improved their standard of living and engaged in various kinds of indulgence, the situation of the workers was more complicated. It was apparent that the gap between workers and bureaucrats had widened drastically. We can see, then, that although self-indulgence by the bureaucracy was not an entirely new phenomenon, having been known since the Civil War, it nonetheless became particularly prominent in the time of the NEP. First of all, it was not motivated by concerns about immediate survival, as was the case during the Civil War; corruption and other forms of illegal activity were engaged in solely for pleasure's sake. Secondly, and more importantly, corruption and self-indulgence on a grand scale became increasingly an exclusive prerogative of the bureaucracy.

The NEP and Beyond: Increasing Popular Resentment

In describing the situation of the workers at the time of NEP, most historians see the workers' lot as having improved. This is only partially true. First of all, the loosening of economic controls brought unemployment that affected workers severely from the very first days of the NEP.[40] Unemployment benefits were not enough to alleviate the problem. Secondly, pressure for greater productivity was increasingly brought to bear on the workplace.[41] At the same time, the chances for upward social advancement were becoming reduced for workers. The stress on efficiency and skills often required a high level of education from those seeking good positions; dedication, an appropriate social background, and even Party membership were not always enough. Since the beginning of the NEP, the government had been doing its best to secure appropriate education for workers' children, giving them preference over the offspring of the well-to-do. The actual results of this strategy, however, were not as good as expected. Financial help, without which most workers' children could not afford to study, was meager and was often eliminated from state budgets.[42] By 1925, the number of students receiving a government stipend had dropped from 67,000 to 47,000, and "the People's Commissariat of Education was threatening to charge tuition fees in institutions under its control."[43]

In the fall of 1927, "the economic situation again began to deteriorate appreciably."[44] By the summer of 1928, workers' salaries in Moscow alone fell by 22 to 50 percent.[45] The workers faced terrible unemployment.[46] "Restrictions were placed on the payment of unemployment benefits in 1927, so that many people who had fled to cities from the poverty and extraordinary measures in the countryside found themselves practically without any means of subsistence."[47] Rents and prices on food staples rose sharply, and pressures on the workers increased.

The workers responded to the deterioration in their living condition with a sharp rise in violent activities, including strikes, which increased continuously in number between 1925 and 1930.[48] By 1930, the country was overwhelmed by workers' strikes, demonstrations, and uprisings on an unprecedented scale. In July 1928, strikes and other disturbances took place in all the major industrial cities of the Union, including Moscow, Leningrad, the coal mining centers of Donbas, Ivano-Voznesensk, and many other cities.[49] The workers demonstrated little fear of the Secret Police (GPU) and often marched to GPU headquarters where clashes between workers and GPU agents and militia regularly took place.[50] In Kolomenskoe, a city near Moscow, a violent strike led to the beating of local union officials.[51] Strikes in Moscow were recorded up until 1930, and during these strikes several people were killed in clashes with the militia.[52] There were also peasant uprisings (at least 150 according to Bukharin) on the eve of collectivization, some apparently with strong nationalistic overtones.[53] In their rebellion against the regime the peasantry definitely enjoyed the support of numerous bandits who inhabited various regions of the country, e.g., the Ukraine.[54] Having started in 1928, the peasant discontent continued unabated until 1930, and workers and peasants often joined together to discuss common strategy.[55] In addition, the Army became unreliable even in the most strategic regions, such as Leningrad and the western districts. It was not only soldiers who came to challenge the current leadership; even "the command staff [according to Voroshilov] was partly unreliable." The same was true of the GPU.[56]

Worker unrest, of course, was not a new phenomenon in Soviet history. However, the unrest of 1928–1929 was in some ways more dangerous for the establishment than the unrest of earlier times. One of the most salient characteristics of the workers' movement of the late twenties was the workers' expression of strong anti-bureaucratic sentiment. There were also influential political groups that could lead workers against the establishment.

People's protests against the privileges and corruption of the bureaucracy were first heard as early as the end of the Civil War.[57] The call for equality was one of the foremost slogans of the rebellious Kronstadt sailors.[58] However, it became a focal point of complaints only at the end of the twenties. The workers, while not homogeneous in their political views, were united in their hatred of the bureaucracy.[59] Workers viewed bureaucrats, including "specialists" ("specialists" were mostly non-Party people with technical or other skills), as useless parasites who harassed women and lived too well.[60]

In the educational policy, the workers saw further proof of the bureaucracy's privileged position. Upset with the inadequate financial help given to poor students, as well as the widespread nepotism, workers began to claim that it was the children of the well-to-do who had greater access to higher education and the best jobs of the future.[61] It is not surprising that many workers, harshly criticizing the bureaucracy, privately held the opinion that bureaucrats, especially "specialists," should "be fired and exiled."[62] Others came to the conclusion that the "egalitarian principles which Lenin had hoped to see practiced did not exist." Many disenchanted workers left the Party.[63]

Gradually workers began to look for political groups that opposed the establishment. Many of them became quite disenchanted with the system as such and became "anti-Soviet," looking for the guidance of a non-Marxist party.[64] Others, however, went to the Left Opposition, mostly centered around Trotsky.

Groundwork for the Purges: Politics of the Left Opposition

In characterizing the political struggle of the late twenties, one should not disregard the Left Opposition as a serious political force. It is true, of course, that by the late twenties Trotsky had already been stripped of his posts, expelled from the Party, and exiled to Alma-Ata. His supporters had also been exiled to various distant regions. By the time of his fall from grace, Trotsky had elaborated his vision of the present Soviet reality as a kind of Thermidor, that is, the counterrevolutionary coup that ended the radical Jacobin phase of the French Revolution. In Trotsky's view, the alienation of the bureaucracy from the masses, as well as the bureaucracy's enrichment and extravagant lifestyle amidst the starvation of the populace, were among the most essential characteristics of Thermidor. Even at the end of the twenties, Trotsky had not lost his hope of being reincorporated into officialdom. For this reason, he refrained from identifying the Soviet regime with that of the thoroughly reactionary regime of the French Thermidor. He merely pointed out that the regime had a tendency to move in this direction.

However, the Left Opposition was not homogeneous. It had its left wing, represented by "Group Fifteen," which believed that a Thermidorian reaction had already taken place in Russia—that is, the Soviet government had already become a repressive government of NEP men and kulaks (rich peasants). They advocated the creation of a new party of the proletariat for a new revolution. In addition to being fragmented, the Left Opposition was also rather small:

According to various sources its active supporters numbered between four and eight thousand. These figures are very small in comparison with the Party's total membership at that time (about a million), but not negligible in relation to the numbers of those who took part actively in political discussions, which meant not more than a few tens of thousands.[65]

Those several thousand people became "the central focus of widespread discontent."[66]

Members of the Left Opposition supported the workers' strikes.[67] The workers responded by protecting Left Oppositionists from GPU agents, marching on GPU headquarters to demand release of Left Oppositionist prisoners, escorting them to railroad stations, and expressing their sympathy in many other ways.[68]

The Left Opposition's position, namely, that of Trotsky, was enhanced by the political split in the top Party leadership, epitomized by Stalin's fierce struggle with the Right. At first, the outcome of the struggle was far from evident, and both sides were in a desperate search for allies. The extent of Left Opposition influence among the masses, and the resulting potential threat to the Party from below, was not ignored. Stalin saw himself as being in a most uneasy position and was especially eager to find supporters, sending emissaries in all directions for that purpose.

Stalin acknowledged the influence of the Left Opposition's political program on his own and he did not exclude the possibility of compromise with some Left Oppositionists, especially with Trotsky.[69]

Stalin had several important reasons for wooing Trotsky. First, he recalled Trotsky's charismatic role in the Revolution and Civil War, and his influence among a substantial proportion of Party members. Stalin also was aware that Trotsky viewed him as a weaker and therefore less dangerous rival than the representatives of the Right. Stalin undoubtedly viewed Trotsky and his grassroots supporters as the potential leaders of a mass movement that could lead to unforeseeable consequences for the regime in the uncertain political situation of the time. Having acknowledged the attractiveness of left political slogans and the potential threat from below that they represented, Stalin started a campaign against the bureaucracy, taking the lead from the Trotskyites.

Stalin was definitely the main figure behind the scene and the campaign's main benefactor. At the same time, Stalin's attack against both non-Party specialists and the Party's bureaucracy took the shape of an anti-bureaucratic drive, wherein Stalin took the egalitarian mantle and became the defender of workers' interests. This strategy was aimed at presenting Stalin as following the road of the Left Opposition. It was intended to split the Left Opposition and draw some of its leading figures and working class supporters to his side.

Stalin's Purges of the Bureaucracy: The Last Agenda in Practice

The purges of members of the bureaucracy in the late twenties were not an absolutely new phenomenon in the NEP period in Russia. In April 1926 Stalin made a strong statement about the disgraceful bacchanalia of "flinging millions of rubles of public money on jubilees and festivals, and spoke of the enormous overhead charges on all business transaction." He also accused the bureaucracy of direct embezzlement of funds. Communists, he said, were more culpable than non-Party men; they regarded the resources of the State as private property. He continued, "an orgy of merry robbery is going on. The happy-go-lucky robbers can be counted by the thousands. And the worst of it is that they are looked upon as 'smart fellows' instead of being made the subject of public opprobrium." In August of the same year Stalin also stated that cutting the cost of the bureaucracy would be a good way to save money for industrial development.[70]

These initial assaults against the bureaucracy were tentative and did not take the form of a political campaign. Moreover, the government often defended members of the bureaucracy, including "bourgeois specialists," against the workers' persistent attacks. The bureaucracy's corruption and their mistreatment of the workers were issues discussed mostly by members of the Left Opposition. However, the years 1928 and 1929 soon brought about a turning point in this respect. These subjects, until then discussed only among the workers and on the pages of underground Trotskyite publications, suddenly were being tackled by official Soviet publications. It was discovered that, in many cities (Smolensk singled out as the most notorious example), the Party and state apparatus had completely degenerated. It was discovered that the bureaucrats, living extravagantly, had squandered state funds and had spent their lives engaged in endless drunkenness and promiscuity.

Investigations took place during the spring of 1928 and on May 18, 1929 the results of the investigation were finally published in *Pravda*. The organizers of the Smolensk affair tried their best to demonstrate Party support of grassroots attacks against bureaucracy. "The result of the investigations were put before a gathering of 1,100 Party members, 40 percent of whom were production workers." Sixty Party functionaries were reported to have been replaced by "mainly worker militants."[71] Commenting on the Smolensk affair, Stalin elaborated upon "shameful cases of corruption and moral degradation." He further called on the rank and file to attack the Party and state bureaucracy, claiming to be appalled by "the fact that Party monopoly was carried to absurd lengths, that the voice of the rank-and-file was stifled, that inner-Party democracy was abolished and bureaucracy became rife." He added, "I think that there is not and cannot be any other way of combatting this evil than by organizing control from below by the Party masses, by implanting inner-Party democracy."[72]

In connection with a massive purge of the Party bureaucracy, the first real political trial was concocted. "On March 10 it was announced that the security police had uncovered a counterrevolutionary plot involving technical specialists and foreign powers at the Shakhty mines in the Donbas industrial complex."[73] The choice of location was not accidental; Donbas was a site of recent industrial unrest. "Fifty-five people were accused of sabotage and treason" and duly punished; several were executed. The Right, too, was eager to appear as the supporters of the workers against the bureaucracy. Thus, they not only rendered no support to Shakhty's victims, but were among those who demanded the harshest punishments. Bukharin voted for the death sentence and later rebuked Stalin for his refusal to support him.[74]

The Rightists' advocacy of NEP, however, made it impossible for them to benefit from the campaign. Rightists opposed intensification of the purge, insisting that the Shakhty affair "was an isolated case."[75] In the eyes of the masses, they were identified as supporters of the bureaucracy.

Official publications were eager to demonstrate the masses' absolute support of both the purges and the resolution of the Shakhty affair. However, historians might reasonably suspect them of not having documented the true public mood. Western historians have reliable sources, including a collection of letters written by exiled Trotskyites, deposited in the Trotsky Archive at Harvard University. Some of them had also been published by Trotsky's magazine, Biuleten' Oppozitsii (Bulletin of the Opposition). They provide scholars with unique documentation of the public opinion on the first big public political trials in Soviet history since the 1921 public trials of the Social Revolutionaries.

Official revelations about spreading corruption in Smolensk, Artemovo, Sochi, and other places, the Shakhty trial, and official calls for democratization stirred the workers, becoming favorite subjects of discussion.[76] With few exceptions workers and grassroots Left Oppositionists who became their allies did not express their doubts about the trials, nor did they question the motivation of the purges.[77] The vast majority asked for the harshest punishment. A certain Pukhas, in a letter to Trotsky, mocked those who viewed the Shakhty trial as an instance of "Bolshevik provocation against innocent people." He would not polemicize against them because they "would not change their minds." The

Shakhty affair demonstrated, he claimed, the deep degeneration of the bureaucracy. Other letters support Pukhas's view, stating that the apparatus was full of the kind of people against whom workers had fought during the Civil War.[78] What concerned the workers and Left Oppositionists was what they viewed as the excessive leniency on the part of the government, both toward Party bureaucrats and toward those involved in the Shakhty affair.[79] This leniency, according to some members of the Left Opposition, demonstrated that the regime was still rightist and pro-bureaucracy.[80] Others, though, assumed that those who were involved in the Shakhty case received what they deserved,[81] and that the Shakhty trial demonstrated that the regime had started to evolve from being Thermidorian (that is, pro-bureaucratic and pro-NEP man) to being egalitarian, democratic, and revolutionary. They insisted that Shakhty and other of Stalin's actions demonstrated that a "turn to the left took place in VKPB," and that they should therefore "completely support" Stalin.[82]

In 1929, the purge of the bureaucracy (at that time directed almost exclusively against supporters of the Right) continued, and culminated in the new public trial of the so-called Prompartiia (Industrial Party). As before, the Party purge was presented as a struggle against the bureaucracy. The Sixteenth Party Conference (1929) identified "the fight against bureaucracy" as the Party's most important goal.[83] The Conference resolution solemnly proclaimed:

> The conference draws the attention of the whole Party and of every Party member individually to the need to wage the most resolute, the most determined, the most persevering struggle against elements of bureaucracy in the Party itself, in the Party apparatus.[84]

Corruption of the bureaucracy and general alienation of the apparatus from the masses were presented as the main reasons for the purge. The Prompartiia trial was a real political trial, in the sense that its victims were accused not simply of wreaking havoc, but of a full-fledged conspiracy to overthrow the regime. Several prominent intellectuals, many either directly or indirectly working for the state, were alleged to have been involved in it. As in the Shakhty case, the Prompartiia trial and the drive against bureaucracy that it was held to exemplify were lauded by official publications. They induced hope in many that the Soviet regime was finally becoming more egalitarian and democratic. (Authoritarianism was still associated with rightist policy, with NEP and "Thermidor".)

These hopes could explain why repression of the right still found sincere supporters. The Prompartiia trial was supported not only by

Maksim Gor'kii[85] (who was at Stalin's mercy and could be suspected of not being free to express a differing view), but also by those whose sincerity could hardly be questioned. An anonymous letter sent to Trotsky's *Bulletin of Opposition* asserted that workers were in complete support of the Prompartiia trial and were only upset that the sentences were not harsh enough.[86] An anonymous Left Oppositionist from Moscow saw in the Prompartiia's victims real counterrevolutionaries who deserved harsh punishment.[87] Trotsky himself gave full support to the trial. The trial demonstrated (he asserted) that the Soviet bureaucracy was full of counterrevolutionaries, and he praised the government for shooting some of them.[88] The Left Oppositionists (many of them in exile, their condition continuing to deteriorate) interpreted the Mensheviks' trial (1931) in the same way.

Conclusion: The Legacy of
Stalin's Triumph over the Bureaucracy

The increase in privilege and the spread of corruption among the bureaucracy were essential elements of the regime since its birth. They contributed much to the regime's instability in the late twenties and early thirties. The political trials and general purges of bureaucracy were to some degree a response to pressures from below, in which the Left Opposition played an important role. Thus Stalin's (and partially Bukharin's, Rykov's, and Tomsky's) rehearsal for the Great Purge, their "revolution from above" in general, had a certain push from below.

By the mid-thirties this push had been consummated; all opposition was routed, and Stalin, having solidified his position, felt no serious threat either from the Party or from below. The anti-bureaucratic drive did not stop the workers' unrest. However, it definitely neutralized many workers and Left Opposition activists, who from then on saw in Stalin a populist egalitarian leader. The legacy of the anti-bureaucratic campaign, however, remained. Despite his unlimited power and reliance on repression, the Stalinist regime could not have survived without a legitimating public image. The puritanism of public officials was one of the image's important dimensions. According to the official image, Stalinist bureaucrats could be tough and cruel, but they were hard-working, close to the masses, and (this was especially stressed) puritanical in their daily lives. Stalin was quite concerned with this image of the Soviet bureaucracy and presented himself so as to conform to it.

The real Stalinist policy, as well as the general development of the Soviet society, was quite different from what was implied by these puritanical anti-bureaucratic images of Stalin's regime. The bureaucracy continued to acquire privileges throughout the thirties, and they have survived up until the present day. Upon crushing the opposition, Stalin's bureaucracy also increased its pressure on the populace, finally launching the devastating Great Purge of 1936–1938.

It was discovered (in retrospect, of course) that the purges of the late twenties and early thirties had led, not to the restoration of the regime in all of its original revolutionary purity (anti-bureaucratic and democratic), but to the entrenchment of "Thermidor" (corrupt bureaucratic authoritarianism). When, however, the Trotskyites (Bukharinists later joined them) and Stalin's supporters among the populace discovered this, it was too late.

Notes

1. Victor Serge, *Year One of the Russian Revolution* (London: Allen Lane, The Penguin Press, 1972), 356.

2. Joseph Ameel, *Red Hell* (London: Robert Hule Ltd., 1941), 68–69.

3. Francis McCullogh, *A Prisoner of the Reds: The Story of a British Officer Captured in Siberia* (London: John Murray, 1922), 207.

4. Ameel, 69.

5. Dorian Blair and C.H. Dand, *Russian Hazard* (London: Robert Hale and Company, 1927), 214.

6. Paul Dukes, *The Story of "St. 25": Adventure and Romance in the Secret Service in Red Russia* (London: Cassell, 1939), 367.

7. F.G. Popov, *1920 god v Samarskoi Guberni: Khronika Sobvtii* (1920 in the Samarskii Province: A Chronicle of Events) (Kuibyshev: Kuibyshevskoe Knizhnoe Izdatel'stvo, 1977), 101; Ameel, 68.

8. Ameel, 28, 30; Dukes, 293.

9. Louis Bryant, *Six Red Months in Russia* (New York: Arno Press and the New York Times, 1970), 145.

10. Dukes, *The Story of "St. 25,"* 193; Princess Paley, *Souvenirs de Russie 1916–1919* (Remembrances of Russia, 1916–1919), (Paris: Librairie Plon, 1923), 242; A. Ransom, *Russia in 1919* (New York: B.W. Huebsch, 1919), 187.

11. Emma Ponafidiana, *Russia—My Home* (New York: Blue Ribbon Books, 1931), 246–247.

12. Claude Anet, *La Revolution Russe* (The Russian Revolution), 4 vols., (Paris: Payot B.C., 1918-19) 3: 248; Dukes, *The Story of "St. 25,"* 314; Pitirim Sorokin, *Leaves from a Russian Diary and Thirty Years After* (Boston: The Beacon Press, 1950), 205; Paley, *Souvenirs de Russie,* 259.

13. A. Gan (Gutman), *Rossiia i Bol'shevizm: Materialy po istorii revoliutsii i bor'by s bol'shevizmom,* (Russia and Bolshevism: Materials on the History of the Revolution and the Struggle with Bolshevism) (Shanghai: V Tip Russkago T-vapechatnago i izdatel'skogo dela, 1921), 232.

14. Roy A. Medvedev, *On Stalin and Stalinism,* trans. Ellen de Kadt, (Oxford: Oxford University Press, 1979), 392.

15. Baroness Sophie Buxhoeveden, *Left Behind: Fourteen Months in Siberia During the Revolution: December 1917–February 1919* (London: Longmans, Green and Co., 1929), 97.

16. Paley, *Souvenir de Russe*, 140–41; Dukes, *The Story of "St. 25,"* 49.

17. Maitre Aubert, *Bolshevism's Terrible Record* (Boston: Small, Maynard & Co., 1925), 14.

18. Albert Thys Williams, *Journey into Revolution: Petrograd, 1917–1918* (Chicago: Quadrangle Books, 1969), 232; Blair and Dand, *Russian Hazard*, 214; Vladimir Koudrey, *Once a Commissar*, (New Haven: Yale University Press, 1937), 43; Sheila Fitzpatrick, *The Russian Revolution*, (Oxford: Oxford University Press, 1982), 81; Ameel, *Red Hell*, 79.

19. Bertrand Russell, *The Practice and Theory of Bolshevism* (London: George Allen and Unwin, Ltd., 1920), 168–169.

20. Serge, *Year One of the Russian Revolution*, 395; Dukes, *The Story of "St. 25,"* 73; Ameel, 68.

21. G.A. "Po Rossii," *Sotsialisticheskii Vestnik*, September 27, 1929, 15–16; Leon Trotsky, *Stalin: An Appraisal of the Man and His Influence* (New York: Harper and Brothers Publishers, 1941), 386.

22. Charles Bettelheim, *Class Struggle in the USSR*, 2 Vols., (New York: Monthly Review Press; Hassocks Harvests Ltd., 1976–78), 2:489; Anna L. Strong, *The First Time in History* (New York: Boni and Liveright, 1924), 59.

23. Michael Voslensky, *Nomenklatura*, (Garden City: Doubleday and Company, 1978), 178; *Novoe Russkoe Slovo*, October 30, 1987; Ameel, 197, 248. Concerning privileges of bureaucracy, see also: Lidiia Shatunovskaia, *Zhizn' v Kremle* (New York: Chalidze Publications, 1982), 28, 39–45.

24. Strong, 171; Lancelot Lawton, *The Russian Revolution 1917–1926* (London: Macmillan and Co., 1927), 165.

25. Ameel, 66, 249.

26. Blair and Dand, 22.

27. Ibid., 222.

28. Aubert, 18; Boris Bazhanov, *Vospominaniia Byvshego Sekretaria Stalina* (Recollections of a Former Secretary of Stalin) (Paris: Tretia Volna, 1980), 2.

29. Lawton, 468.

30. Ibid.

31. Ameel, 99; Lawton, 328.

32. Simon Liberman, *Building Lenin's Russia* (Chicago: University of Chicago Press, 1945), 17, 67, 68.

33. Aubert, 17.

34. Edward H. Carr, *Socialism in One Country*, vol. 1 (New York: Macmillan, 1958), 32, 34.

35. Lawton, 235; *Novoe Russkoe Slovo* September 27, 1987; *Vecherniia Moskva* October 18, 1929.

36. "Pis'mo o prichinakh pererozhdeniia partii i gosudarstvennogo apparata," *Buileten' Oppozitsii* 1929, 16.

37. *Novoe Russkoe Slovo* September 27, 1987.

38. Ameel, 102.

39. Aubert, 18–19; "L. Sosnovskii's Letter to Trotsky," *Biuleten' Oppozitsii* vol. 3–4, (1929): 26–27.

40. *Leningradskaia Pravda* March 28, 1924; Carr, *Socialism in One Country*, 363.

41. Ibid., 389.

42. Lawton, 408.

43. Carr, *Socialism in One Country*, 372.

44. Michael Reiman, *The Birth of Stalinism: The USSR on the Eve of the "Second Revolution,"* (Bloomington: Indiana University Press, 1987), 38.

45. *Trotsky Archive*, T-2502, T-1588.

46. Ibid., T-2704, 1.

47. Reiman, 53.

48. Carr, *Socialism in One Country*, 393; Pavel Dolgorukov, *Velikais Razrukha* (Madrid, 1964), 411–12.

49. Trotsky Archive, T-1928; *Bor'ba za Rossiiu* (Paris), March 10, 1928.

50. Trotsky Archive, T-2949; Concerning the relationship between the workers and the Secret Police in the twenties and thirties, see also, *Novoe Russkoe Slovo*, March 16, 1983; Nadezhda Mandel'shtam, *Vospominaniia* (New York: Isdatel'stvo imeni Chekhova, 1970), 356.

51. Ibid., T-2502.

52. *Bor'ba za Rossiiu* (Paris), July 7, 1928.

53. Trotsky Archive T-2442, T-1897.

54. Ibid., T-2346; Lawton, 213.

55. Trotsky Archive, T-2238, T-2442.

56. Reiman, 33; *Bor'ba za Rossiiu* (Paris) July 21, 1928.

57. Emma Goldman, *My Disillusionment in Russia* (New York: Garden City, 1923), 23–25, 31, 154.

58. Anton Cilega, *The Kronstadt Revolt* (Freedom Press, 1942), 11.

59. Trotsky Archive, T-2238, T-2534, 1.

60. Carr, *Socialism in One Country*, 380; Trotsky Archive, T-1583.

61. Ibid., T-2021, 11.

62. Carr, vol. 5, 380; Trotsky Archive, T-2534.

63. Lawton, 423. Those intellectuals who were not employed by the state received a very meager salary, Ibid., 261; Trotsky Archive, T-1583.

64. Ibid., T-2704, 1.

65. Charles Bettelheim, 2: 376.

66. Reiman, 33.

67. Trotsky Archive, T-2698.

68. Ibid., T-2852, T-2560, T-2021, p. 7, T-2851, T-1572, T-1800.

69. Ibid., T-3980.

70. Lawton, 268–69.

71. Bettelheim, vol. 2, 224.

72. Ibid., 225.

73. Stephen F. Cohen, *Bukharin and the Bolshevik Revolution: A Political Biography: 1888–1938,* (New York: Alfred A. Knopf, 1974), 281.

74. Trotsky Archive, T-1897.

75. Cohen, 281.
76. Trotsky Archive, T-1612, T-2071.
77. Ibid., T-1583.
78. Ibid., T-1332, T-1456, T-1399, T-1612, T-1745, T-1377.
79. Ibid., T-2710; Bettelheim, vol. 2, 224.
80. Trotsky Archive, T-174.
81. Ibid., T-1355.
82. Ibid., T-1335, T-1336, T-1584.
83. Bettelheim, vol. 2, 435.
84. Ibid., 440.
85. Michael Heller and Aleksandr Nekrich, *L'Utopie au Pouvoir* (Utopia in Power) (Calmann-Levy, 1982), 224–25.
86. *Biuleten' Oppozitsii* 19 (1930): 18.
87. "L.T.," "Ob'iasneniia v Krugu Druzei," *Biuleten' Oppozitsii* vols. 25–26 (1931).
88. Lev Trotsky, "Problemy razvitiia SSSR," *Biuleten' Oppozitsii* 20 (1931); Trotsky, "Pis'mo italianskim levym kommunistam storonikam tov. Amadeo Bordiga," *Biuleten' Oppozitsii* vols. 1–2 (1929): 31.

15

The Politics of Paranoia: Jonestown and Twentieth Century Totalitarianism

Helen Fein

Unexpected events which violate our unspoken collective expectations of human nature arouse the need for explanation. One such event is the collective suicide-murder of over 900 Americans[1] in a ministate named Jonestown in the Guyanese jungle in 1978.[2] This mass suicide-murder was precipitated by the investigation of, and visit to Jonestown by Representative Leo Ryan (Dem., Calif.) in November 1978. Ryan was assassinated during this visit by members of Jonestown who were almost certainly acting under the direction of Rev. Jim Jones. This provoked Jones's decision to invoke the suicide ritual.

The development of the People's Temple (hereafter PT) into Jonestown can be linked historically to the development of revolutionary messianic sects during the Middle Ages, which were organized by prophetic leaders who expressed the recurring vision of equality and brotherhood on earth.[3] These leaders proclaimed an apocalypse after the oppressors were destroyed: the prologue to a millennium of justice to begin after the blood ceased flowing. Like these earlier messiahs, Jones offered to the socially marginal and the spiritually alienated the tantalizing promise of a communal loaf which all would share, just as the people had shared the loaves distributed by Jesus.

Revolutionary messianism justifies the demand to rid the world of its corrupters, to purify it by destruction. Modern totalitarianism, whether communist, fascist, or Islamic, is viewed by Norman Cohn as a new expression of such movements. It is a Manichean vision of good versus evil, whether defined in terms of religious or political ideology. National or class enemies are equated with agents of the devil who must be destroyed. From its beginning, Jonestown was a totalitarian state, albeit a ministate, based on Leninist principles. Jones controlled all decision-making. Jonestown successfully claimed a monopoly over the means of violence in its space, maintained entry and exit controls (by taking away the passports of its members), and monopolized the flow of information, keeping most members (excepting a trusted elite cadre with tasks in Georgetown) in total isolation.

Most interpretations of the collective self-destruction at Jonestown focus on explaining Jones's psychological state and Jonestowners' compliance. But one can also relate Jones's paranoia to the paranoid myth he relied on—a myth similar to those used by his political exemplars. Similarly, the methods used to induce Jonestowners' compliance can be compared to the state-produced construction of reality in totalitarian societies which causes people to repress their intuitive perceptions, discredit disbelief and to collaborate in acts of cruelty, betrayal, and violation committed against their fellow citizens.

No better myth has been devised than that of collective persecution to generate both feelings of solidarity and distrust among members of a group so that everyone is prone to suspicion, causing the members to suppress their doubts. The paranoid myth displaces internal dissatisfaction, failure, griping, or rebellion, projecting such aggression onto an enemy—an enemy that is depicted as being within as well as outside of one's society.

The paranoid myth enables authorities to discredit dissent and to deny their own failures which they account for as the consequence of subversion or sabotage. The leadership thus creates the enemy it needs for defining collective identity and cementing solidarity. This paradoxically exemplifies Simmel's thesis that external threats tend to unify groups and lead toward the centralization of power.[4]

In this analysis, I will show how the PT evolved into an authoritarian hierarchy, how PT members collaborated in their own repression, and how the paranoid myth embraced by Jones led to a self-fulfilling prophecy instigating him to invoke his interpretation of "revolutionary suicide." This account will concentrate on the social organization, ideology, and development of the PT from a voluntary community—cult, commune, or movement—into a ministate.

Evolution of the People's Temple and Jonestown

Jones began his career as a preacher in Indianapolis in 1953 without formal training or ordination. He sought and attracted an integrated congregation, a rarity at a time when church segregation was the norm and white intolerance for black participation was widespread. In 1964, he was ordained in a mainstream Protestant denomination, the United

Church of Christ. The following year, he moved to Ukiah, California with a core of about 140 followers from Indianapolis[5] and organized a church in his own residence. In 1967, the congregation moved to Redwood Valley, building a church largely by themselves, which they transferred to San Francisco in 1971. Between 1965 and 1971, church membership increased geometrically, almost doubling every two years, growing from 40 to 772 (according to Church records).[6]

Jones attracted both whites and blacks who came from a diversity of backgrounds. When the PT moved to San Francisco in 1971, it became predominantly black. The blacks tended to be older and less educated than the whites. The latter were more likely to be the disaffected college graduates and dropouts of the 1960s and children of middle-class families who were moved by Jones's idealism. A few observers noted in particular how he reformed deviants and street people—addicts, criminals, prostitutes, the mentally and emotionally impaired or adrift—and converted them and their families to followers.

Jones's preaching and the Temple ritual combined both New Left and unreconstructed Stalinist ideology, atheism, and old-time religion. His performances recalled those of Father Divine (a black minister attracting a similar following) whom Jones had studied. While Jones advocated racial justice and socialism and used profanity freely to curse the authorities, he also led gospel hymns and staged faith healings, purportedly extracting cancers—actually well-aged, malodorous chicken livers—with the collusion of his wife and selected accomplices. The Temple gained a widespread reputation for organizing good works such as taking in foster children, rehabilitating drug addicts and prostitutes, and feeding masses of people. These people, in turn, could be counted on, in response to cues from Jones, to write hundreds of letters and mobilize hundreds of bodies for progressive causes.

Control over the PT was centralized in Jones, and layers of authority were few, resembling patterns of totalitarian control. The hierarchy on which Jones relied was based on a small circle of about ten advisors; ranked below this inner circle was a "planning commission" of 100 members. Although "the church was 70 to 80 percent black, probably two-thirds of the upper-echelon leaders were white."[7] The members of this white elite, selected because of their skills and vocations, were privy to Jones's duplicity (such as his staged faith healings), practiced a double standard (enjoying forbidden privileges, including movies) and were said to share in his belief that the end justifies the means.

Unlike cults and movements which retreat from this world, the PT sought to transform the world. In California, it was actively involved in politics as well as in good works. Jones wooed politicians and the press, exchanging payoffs. He delivered blocs of votes, enlarged by false registrations, to politicians who needed them and in this way often provided them with the margin of victory. In return, he obtained public blessings, public appointments (becoming Chairman of the San Francisco Housing Authority) and letters of endorsement to the government of Guyana from local, state, and national leaders.

Jones began to explore plans for decamping to Guyana in the fall of 1973 in response to defections of some staff members and some critical columns by Lester Kinsolving in the *San Francisco Examiner* of September 1973. Threats of further media criticism, usually suppressed by counter-pressure from PT demonstrators and barrages of phone calls, had also been increasing with the expansion of the PT.[8]

By August 1977, when *New West* published its exposé ("Inside Peoples Temple"), the majority of active followers of the PT had emigrated to Jonestown, Guyana. Although Jonestown was formally a colony in a foreign state, it was effectively a state within a state, maintaining its own border control, armaments, radio, and public relations. Jones formed ties to Guyanese leaders similar to those he had made in California, offering leaders political support and American dollars in exchange for respecting his control and for not enforcing their laws in Jonestown.[9] Some Guyanese leaders were also seduced by Jones's female staff, in affairs scripted by Jones, to guarantee their loyalty. Rather than confronting the state, Jones neutralized Guyanese authority, thus reinforcing his followers' dependence on him. Similarly, he neutralized the United States Embassy in Georgetown, working out a cooperative relationship whereby the embassy staff gave him prior notice of impending visits by relatives of Jonestowners, enabling Jones to brief his congregation members before their relatives' arrival.

Despite its austerity, Jonestown evidently evoked a high level of commitment among most members; only 2 percent of its members either defected with Representative Ryan or escaped after Jones began the suicide ritual. Rep. Ryan himself remarked on the Jonestowners' enthusiasm. The PT exploited the same commitment-inducing mechanisms that best account for the endurance of the longer-lasting utopian communities of the nineteenth century.[10] Members were irreversibly invested in Jonestown, having given up all their worldly possessions, resources, and jobs. Over two out of every ten Jonestowners were aged (199), and three out of every ten were children (276). The great majority of the social security pensioners received under $200 a month, an income guaranteeing them poverty in the United States if they had no other resources.[11] They had renounced familial and other social ties to the outside world, and were physically isolated in Jonestown. Previous friends and acquaintances were tainted by their association with a corrupt, capitalist society. Jonestowners could experience collective transcendence through identification with Jones and with an ideology promising the transformation of this world. Communal sharing, confessions, and rituals of mortification reinforced group values.

As in nineteenth century utopian communities, sexuality was regulated to prevent couples from withholding primary loyalty to the community. These communes usually prescribed chastity, group marriage, arranged marriages, or coupling with the leader. In Jonestown, relationships were forbidden unless approved by a committee. Married couples were discouraged from having intercourse and had to sleep in single-sex dorms. Jones had a free choice of sexual partners, male and female. He systematically broke the bonds between couples and exploited his followers' sexuality to make them more dependent on him and more vulnerable to guilt, self-doubt, and group shaming.

Solidarity was fortified by the myth of persecution reiterated by Jones; defectors were virtually tagged as Judas Iscariot. Since most of the defectors were white and had been prominent among the elite, he may also have fortified racial distrust or justified expression of pre-existing antagonism.

But the perception of gaps between ideology and practice in Jonestown threatened solidarity. Some people turned out to be more equal than others. They enjoyed a better diet, varied tasks, and shared in the exercise of Jones's authority. Three methods were used to control griping and the latent threat of disorder: re-education and group shaming, violence (punishment and drugging), and incentives involving economic gain or increments of authority. In all of these, Jonestowners collaborated. The fear of blackmail (members had signed blank sheets of paper), Jones's legal control of their children, and fear of leaving behind other family members also inhibited potential defectors.

Re-education involves not only self-censure but coercive group persuasion, involving shaming and the threat of exposure to make all responsible for each one. In Jonestown, members were re-educated to blame themselves for their dissatisfactions, to deny the validity of their perceptions and to reconstruct their biographies, just as people of China did when sentenced to "thought reform."[12] In his harangues, Jones accused them of depravity and of harboring secret yearnings for McDonalds' hamburgers and other capitalist delights. The seven deadly sins revealed in their written self-analyses in response to his guiding questions were elitism, intellectualism, anarchism ("doing one's own thing"), lack of willingness to submit to authority, lack of commitment, self-pity, and dissatisfaction.[13]

Public group shaming also reiterated collective values and reinforced fear of deviance. Shaming was supplemented with public punishment. Offenders were beaten with a paddle, brutally at times, in front of the assembly, and still expected to demonstrate their loyalty by repeating, "Thank you, Father," before they left the stage. Violence was sometimes ritualized in mortification ceremonies such as "boxing matches" in which an offender was pitted against a stronger opponent and sometimes multiple opponents. This harsh discipline was defended by Jonestown and its sympathizers as a necessity because of the previously unstructured, anomic, and deviant lives of many congregation members.[14] Shaming by compelling people to perform public sexual acts was another means of punishment. People were humiliated by Jones's orders to perform homosexual and heterosexual acts in public with assigned partners. Some punishments were less public. For incidents of slight mischief, children were publicly paddled and dunked upside-down in a well. Some were also subjected to electric shocks, especially bed-wetters. Adults were imprisoned in "the box," a dark, six-by-three-foot isolation cell. Occasionally, psychopharmacological drugs were administered to keep people quiet.[15]

The ordinary Jonestowners who reportedly applauded these punishments, either enjoying or tolerating such socially sanctioned sadism, were not just victims but were co-perpetrators.[16] Although Jim Jones's son Stephen was disillusioned and disrespectful, and recognized the harm his father was doing, he rejected the demand of his brother Tim to kill their father because he realized how dependent Jonestowners were on him.[17]

There was grumbling within Jonestown, but there were no signs of organized disaffection or rebellion. Jones feared the departure of defectors, for they might discredit Jonestown and incite investigation; this is what happened eventually. Jones coped with threats of defection and of investigation by two alternate strategies. First, he interpreted these threats ideologically and incorporated them into a paranoid myth of persecution to be overcome by heroic resistance, even to the extent of self-destruction. Second, Jones considered removal to a state in which Jonestown would be out of reach of the U.S. authorities.

In the first strategy, Jones linked the course which Jonestowners had chosen to the fight against American imperialism and to revolutionary struggles in the Third World. He directed Jonestowners in rehearsals for the performance of "revolutionary suicide"—a concept of Huey Newton's which originally meant heroic resistance—teaching them that there were no other alternatives.

Jonestowners' susceptibility to the belief that their existence was threatened was reinforced by isolation and weariness. Jones's harangues were broadcast over Jonestown loud-speakers up to six hours a day and sometimes at night. He warned Jonestowners daily to anticipate invasion and torture by the CIA which he said was out to eliminate Jonestown because it was an outpost of socialism.

He especially aroused fears among blacks. Jonestowners were shown films of the Holocaust every week and warned by Jones that the United States was planning the genocide of black Americans. Suicide was idealized as resistance, and escape was denigrated. The self-analyses of Jonestowners previously cited also show that several writers expressed their readiness to die rather than to endure the torture which Jones told them to expect if Jonestown were to be invaded.

During "white nights," Jonestowners were drilled to commit "revolutionary suicide" after being awakened from sleep by sirens. Deborah Layton Blakey, whose warnings of Jones's plans for mass suicide were published in *The San Francisco Chronicle* on June 16, 1978, five months before it occurred, recalled how

> During a "white night" we were informed that our situation was hopeless and that the only course of action open to us was a mass suicide for the glory of socialism . . . We were told everyone would be tortured by the mercenaries if we were taken alive. Everyone, including the children, were told to line up. As we passed through the line we were given a small glass of red liquid to drink. We were told the liquid contained poison and we would die within 45 minutes. We all did as we were told.

Hall observes that this ritual paralleled that of imbibing wine during Holy Communion; Jones exploited this previously rehearsed pattern, attaching a new meaning to it.[18] The edge of the fear of self-destruction must have been worn off by its repeated arousal without consequences. After these drills, Jonestowners would fall asleep, exhausted and relieved. Thus they rehearsed for the final performance.

Jones's second strategy to prevent defection and investigation involved moving the Jonestown community to a location out of reach of U.S. authorities. Jones's choice of the Soviet Union as a haven was fitting in the sense that it was the first model of state socialism in the twentieth century. Jones advocated socialism and practiced centralized leadership. At different times, Jones claimed he was the reincarnation of Christ and Lenin. His self-casting as the new messiah, faith-healer and wonderworker appeared to wane in Jonestown to the extent that he saw himself as the leader of a socialist ministate. Yet his choice of the Soviet Union as a new setting also illustrates his naïveté in supposing that the Soviet Union would tolerate a state within a state as had Guyana.

Jones's perception of a crisis was real to him by all accounts. It was fortified by his lawyers, his investigators, and by the "Concerned Relatives," an organization made up of defectors and relatives of congregation members of the People's Temple which was infiltrated by Jones's agents. But the only federal agency which enforced any regulation against Jonestown was the FCC which imposed a $50 fine for Jonestown's violation of radio operation rules. The U.S. State Department, responding to the testimony of the defectors and their relatives and of Jonestowners, distanced itself, conveyed no warnings, and never opened an investigation. A Customs Service investigation of the transport of guns to Jonestown led to a negative finding in August-September 1977.[19] California welfare officials never checked on the well-being of the foster children there, even though at one time 150 of them were cared for by the PT, and despite reports by defectors and relatives of a regular pattern of child abuse.[20] There is no conclusive evidence that the FBI ever opened an investigation before November 18, 1978,[21] nor is there evidence available to evaluate charges by Jonestown survivors and their friends that the CIA played some role.[22]

Jones was not confronted by any objective threat he could not handle until Rep. Leo Ryan (Dem., Calif.), a member of the House Foreign Affairs Committee, launched his investigation in the fall of 1978. Ryan responded to the request of an old friend, Sam Houston, whose son had died immediately after he left the PT, and to the charges of Deborah Blakely (cited above) and other members of Concerned Relatives. Representative Ryan's visit was accepted by Jones reluctantly on the advice of Charles Garry, a prominent left-wing lawyer appointed as the first attorney of the PT. To Jones's consternation, Ryan arrived with delegations from the media and Concerned Relatives.

During his tension-laden visit to Jonestown, Ryan was feted at a public performance of Jonestowners on November 17. Ryan acclaimed their achievement: ". . . from what I've seen, there are a lot of people here who think this is the best thing that happened in their whole life."[23] This evoked a roar of approval. Yet fears persisted. A few had foiled a public attempt by a male Jonestowner to knife Ryan. Meanwhile, Representative Ryan's staff quietly interviewed Jonestowners and received notes from people wanting to leave. Fifteen members (including Larry Layton, an agent of Jones) began to leave with Representative Ryan and his party on November 18, 1978.

During the loading of the airplanes to take them to Georgetown, Layton began firing inside a plane loaded for take-off. About the same time, a squad of men who had arrived from Jonestown and were standing poised on a flatbed cart attached to a tractor-trailer, fired on the open field, aiming at the Congressional delegation and the media. They killed Representative Ryan and three media representatives on the field, and Layton killed one defector in the plane; ten people were also wounded.

Just before the shooting began,[24] Jones called for the final "white night." Tapes of his last performance indicate that one Jonestowner, Christine Miller, dissented and was shouted down by the crowd; ultimately, she too went along. The children did not cooperate despite previous drills. Their shrieks provoked Jones to order their mothers to shoot the poison down the throats of their children with syringes.

One may ask whether the defection of 2 percent of Jonestown's members was the trigger provoking Jones to order this final act or whether, as many observers view it, it was Jones's apparently worsening physical and mental condition which triggered it. Most accounts attribute Jones's disorders to paranoia and drug abuse.[25]

Did Jones, viewing Jonestown and himself as one, perceive the defectors' escape as a loss of a part of himself and sense that he could only evade disintegration by destroying himself and his creation? Reiterman's report shows how violated and outraged he felt by the incursion of Ryan, as well as by the unannounced visit of the media and the Concerned Relatives delegations.[26]

These and other psychological interpretations are plausible. But one can also put oneself in the place of Jim Jones and view Jonestown as a totalitarian ministate which was actually threatened because the paranoid myth Jones relied on had become a self-fulfilling prophecy. Some Jonestowners who had absorbed Jones's version of reality struck at the outsider, even without Jones's explicit instigation, as had the person who tried to knife Representative Ryan in full public view. A tape of Jones's last speech showed that he anticipated a catastrophe provoked by his followers' aggression; he imagined that they would shoot the pilot and bring the plane down.[27] Preparation for the collective suicide was ordered by Jones before reports of the assassination of Representative Ryan and the others were received from the assassins. The House investigating committee concluded that "some moderate credence [can be given] to the idea of a contingent conspiracy."[28]

The assassination of Representative Ryan was more than murder; it was an act of aggression against the Congress and the U.S. Government that surely would have provoked investigations and an indictment. Jonestown would no longer have been a state unto itself. Jones explained to one follower who (during preparations for the collective suicide) spoke up for an airlift to Russia instead of death, that it was too late to implement that plan. This left collective suicide as the only perceived alternative.

But there is no need, in this instance, to choose between explanations, for the personal and political crisis were one. Jones was faced with a loss of self or a diminished self-image, and Jonestown was faced with a crisis which might have led to invasion, indictment and disintegration.

The crisis was itself provoked by aggression which was, in turn, provoked by the perception of impending doom which Jones had propagated. Thus, the prophecy became self-fulfilling.

The Politics of Totalitarian Paranoia in Macrocosm

The totalitarian empires of this century have sought both to transform reality and expand their power. Totalitarian societies, like Jonestown, maintain loyalty by terror and by creating closed frameworks of reality cognition. They absorb members in associations coordinated from the top, leaving scarcely any time or space for privacy, free thought, or the development of unregimented associations. They also control cognition by controlling information and by coordinating the media of communication so that members are taught to recognize reality only through an ideological lens and cannot confirm their own observations of what is going on.

But inducing loyalty is never enough for social controllers in totalitarian states. Shaming, group coercion, and prompting of confessions, as well as violence and terror, have been used extensively in both the Soviet Union and China since their revolutions. The relative degree of reliance on manipulated group coercion versus terror, arbitrary incarceration, isolation, and killing, differs in different periods. The direct and indirect violence perpetuated during the Cultural Revolution as recounted by Cheng[29]—torture, suicide, and killing—indicate that there is a continuum of means of persuasion from nonviolent to extremely violent.

To cultivate identification, voluntary compliance, and enthusiasm, the "cult of personality"—the ongoing idealization of a paternal and charismatic leader—is regularly drawn upon. But may not that cult itself corrupt the leader? Absolute power itself, justified by ideology and by the desire to maintain control, may lead toward paranoia. One may also suspect that totalitarian states may be vulnerable because there is an element of self-selection involved; perhaps they are more likely to be the offspring of leaders with paranoid tendencies, or perhaps totalitarian states tend to select such leaders.

But the elements of the paranoid script are inherent in the ideology (pitting the damned against the elect) and the development of the totalitarian state itself. The state, which claims to transcend previous social orders, cannot accept error, and blames its failures on enemies within. Failures, internal struggles for power and external conflict provoke leaders' fears that they are unable to control their environment. In order to retain or to expand their influence, leaders commit acts of aggression and project their aggression onto hostile others, arousing threat and counter-threat. This fortifies a collective myth of persecution. Both enemies within and enemies without have to be eliminated. The ideology and the emergent scripts justify and reinforce the fears of a paranoid leader.

While threat may fortify internal cohesion, appeals for solidarity are not seen by leaders as sufficient. For the people are always infiltrated by the enemies of the people or by non-persons in the ideological scripts of state socialism, Nazism, and anti-communist national security states. The practice of Marxism-Leninism, which negates the common humanity of class enemies and enemies of the people before they are annihilated, has regularly legitimated mass murder.[30] Kuper considers whether Marxism is not another warrant for genocide, noting how Marxism "readily yields a conception of guilt by social origin; people are guilty for what they are, rather than for what they do . . . whole groups become expendable for the realization of an ultimate good. . . ."[31]

A unique paranoid myth justified the ideology and strategy of Nazi Germany. Delusions of persecution justified delusions of grandeur and vice versa. German desires for aggrandizement were justified by idealizing the *volk* and their need for *lebensraum*. German preparation for war was presented as a response to persecution by the West which had imposed the Versailles Treaty on Germany. Similarly, the 1939 invasion of Poland by Germany was presented to the German people as a German response to aggression by Poles against ethnic Germans in Poland.

Hitler and Goebbels repeatedly stated that the enemies, among whom were the Jews (who were considered subhuman), were persecuting the Germans (even after the Germans had exterminated the great majority of Jews under German occupation or influence). The extermination of the Jews was a means toward achieving a larger goal based upon another delusion—the creation of a race "of pure blood."

In all, five to six million Jews were murdered throughout Europe to achieve the Nazi ideal. Later, one-quarter to one-half million gypsies, also defined as *artfremde*—alien species—were added to the toll of victims of totalistic genocide. Over one-quarter million "Aryan" Germans were also killed in the drive to create a perfect race.

A Concluding Note on the Future

The paranoid myth is not an inevitable development, but a choice that leaders—especially paranoid leaders—of totalitarian societies are prone to select. The evidence that some leaders of such states can acknowledge failure openly, even if infrequently, as Castro did in 1970 when he publicly accepted responsibility for the shortfall of the Cuban sugar cane harvest, shows that the elaboration of the myth is a political choice.

The swift collapse of the late Khmer Rouge which killed 30–40 percent of Khmers to create social homogeneity may illustrate how fragile is totalitarian rule based in the first instance on terror with no positive incentives or attempts to create new loyalty or use group processes to create cohesion.[32] The Khmer Rouge leaders made no attempt to devise a cult of personality idealizing leaders (none of whom were reported to have any signs of charisma) in order to invoke submission or loyalty. Because of the extent of threat, demoralization, and disintegration of traditional groups, even the external threat precipitated by Vietnam, the traditional enemy, did not unite Cambodians.

The need of totalitarian states to preserve the paranoid myth may diminish with time. This appears to have occurred both in the USSR and the People's Republic of China. However, can one expect that new states will learn from this? My expectation is that such learning is doubtful. We may theorize about the conditions which make the paranoid myth and the use of terror most likely in future cases. Some factors determining whether this path is chosen and the extent to which such states precipitate their own destruction may include: (1) the degree of success in instilling collectivist values; (2) the charisma of the leader; (3) the material and nonmaterial satisfactions afforded members; (4) the presence of safety valves for potential opposition; (5) the strength of external threats; and (6) the inducements or penalties for defection. Some states have fended off serious external threats and fortified solidarity by expelling the disaffected, as did Cuba.

But, it appears that the susceptibility to such beliefs is inherent in human nature and that it is easily evoked by totalistic ideologies and organizations and movements appearing in times of crisis and transition. Both isolation and ideological biases allow followers and fellow travelers to construct consistent and aberrant fictive realities. As long as leaders in command of totalitarian states and total organizations successfully propagate the myth, they will perpetuate a reign of terror and a perversion of human values. These horrors will be forgotten when new movements and leaders arise, promising to bring us a golden age in which they will end inequality and injustice—and also, in California, loneliness and alienation—if we will only yield our wills and our minds to the new messiah.

Notes

1. See United States Congress, House of Representatives Committee on Foreign Affairs (USHR), *The Assassination of Representative Leo J. Ryan and the Jonestown, Guyana Tragedy*, (Washington, D.C.: USGPO, 1979), 6.

2. In addition, Sharon Amos, a staff member in Georgetown, killed herself and her three children after receipt of orders from Jones; however, the majority of the staffers did not. Four members of Jonestown escaped or evaded the last "white night," fourteen had defected earlier with Representative Ryan's party (excepting Larry Layton, Jones' agent), and nine escaped the morning before in a group effort planned for weeks [Ethan Feinsod, *Awake in a Nightmare: Jonestown, The Only Eyewitness Account* (based on interviews with Odell Rhodes) (New York: Norton, 1981), 75–80]. Thus Jones triggered the death of 97 percent of his followers resident at Jonestown. We do not and will never know how many committed suicide "voluntarily" but we do know that 276 or thirty percent of them were children, poisoned by parents and caretakers. Jones's persuasion was reinforced by armed enforcers circling the assembly of Jonestowners, threatening rebels with shooting.

3. See Norman Cohn, *The Pursuit of the Millennium: Revolutionary Messianism in Medieval and Reformation Europe and Its Bearing on Modern Totalitarian Movements* (New York: Harpers, 1961).

4. Lewis Coser, *The Functions of Social Conflict* (New York: Free Press, 1956), chap. 8.

5. Tim Reiterman with John Jacobs, *Raven: The Untold Story of the Rev. Jim Jones and His People* (New York: E.P. Dutton Inc., 1982), 98.

6. Rebecca Moore, *A Sympathetic History of Jonestown: The Moore Family Involvement in Peoples Temple* (Lewiston/Queenston, Canada: The Edwin Mellen Press, 1985), 112.

7. See Marshall Kilduff and Ron Javers, *The Suicide Cult* (New York: Bantam Books, 1978), 61; also Reiterman, 133, 157.

8. Reiterman, 209–240.

9. Ibid., 416–419.

10. Rosabeth Moss Kantor, *Commitment and Community: Communes and Utopias in Sociological Perspective* (Cambridge, Mass.: Harvard University Press, 1972), chap. 4.

11. USHR, 719–774.

12. See Nien Cheng, *Life and Death in Shanghai* (New York: Grove Press, 1986).

13. See *New York Times*, November 29, 1978.

14. Shiva Naipaul, *Journey to Nowhere: A New World Tragedy* (New York: Simon and Schuster, 1981), 149, 226.

15. Reiterman, 482.

16. James Reston, *Our Father Who Art in Hell* (New York: New York Times Books, 1981).

17. Reiterman, 454.

18. John R. Hall, "The Apocalypse at Jonestown," in *Violence and Religious Commitment: Implications of Jim Jones's Peoples Temple Movement*, ed. Ken Levi, (University Park, Penn.: Pennsylvania State University Press, 1982), 33.

19. USHR, 25.

20. Ibid., 34–35.

21. Moore, 394–396.

22. Because of its non-cooperation with Freedom of Information Act suits, there is scant evidence of the role of the CIA; however, several conspiracies have been suggested since the demise of Jonestown: a plot against Guyana, a mind control experiment, and complicity in knowingly allowing the killing of Representative Ryan, co-author of the Hughes-Ryan Act requiring approval of CIA covert operations (Moore, 399–427). As the House committee investigating the assassination only examined this question in its classified report, this cannot be further assessed. "However, the House Committee on Intelligence, after months of study, found no evidence to suggest that the CIA knew about the mistreatment of Jonestown residents, nor that the agency conducted mind control experiments there, as some alleged, nor that it used Jones for its own purpose." (Reiterman, 586). Moore notes that the Committee did not publish a report of its findings (Moore, 363).

23. Reiterman, 494.

24. See the chronology of events in USHR, 6.

25. Reiterman, 445–448; Kenneth Wooden, *The Children of Jonestown* (New York: McGraw-Hill, 1981), 16; Moore, 306–308.

26. Reiterman, 468–539.

27. See *New York Times*, March 14, 1979.

28. USHR, 26.

29. See Cheng.

30. See Robert Conquest, *The Human Cost of Soviet Communism*, Senate Document 92-36, (Washington, D.C.: USGPO, 1971); Maurice Meisner, *Mao's China: A History of the People's Republic* (New York: Free Press, 1977), 107; Hurst Hannum and David Hawk, *The Case Against the Standing Committee of the Communist Party of Kampuchea*, Working Draft (New York: Cambodia Documentation Commission, Sept. 15, 1986).

31. Leo Kuper, *Genocide: Its Political Use in the Twentieth Century* (New Haven: Yale University Press, 1981), 100.

32. Hannum and Hawk, 121–129.

16

Suicides and Suicide Survivors of the Cultural Revolution

Jane Jia-jing Wu

It was October 1972. Mother called me and told me that my brother Jun had died. It was a suicide, said the telegram from the factory where he had worked. To this day I do not remember the exact date or the day of the week. I only know that he died a few weeks before his twenty-sixth birthday. The memory of the shocking news was so painful for me that I unconsciously wiped that important date from my mind.

It is still not clear to us why Jun committed suicide. We had not heard from him for six months before his death. It was during the Cultural Revolution, and none in my family had had the freedom to take off and visit him. Nor had any of us suspected that Jun would fall prey to this political movement. Jun was always a cautious person. He was the only one of the five children in our family who had the "privilege" of being accepted by the Young Communist Youth League. When the Cultural Revolution broke out in the summer of 1966, Jun was a junior in the Physics Department at Fudan University in Shanghai, and I was soon to graduate from the same school and was waiting for my job assignment. At first, we both participated in the student demonstrations and wrote Big Character Posters to help the university Party authority to reform. Our enthusiasm, however, was soon quenched when we learned that we would end up on the blacklists if we continued to participate. The university authority had passed an emergency "rule of collective punishment," which was circulated among the party cadres on campus. It stated that faculty members would be held accountable and considered guilty of a crime against the Party if their children

Special thanks are extended to Tim Bushnell for his valuable assistance in developing some of the ideas for this paper during several long discussions.

participated in the demonstrations. Since our father was one of the faculty who had already fallen a target of criticism, neither Jun nor I could afford to be critics of the university authority. We quickly detached ourselves from the activists and became onlookers. We kept our mouths shut as much as we could and joined the anonymous audience, hoping that no one would spot us.

Jun was a warm person. He loved and cared for people. During those terrible months of the Cultural Revolution, he was always there to cheer us up when he could be physically present. His love for music and literature gave him unlimited resources for amusing us when we felt low. Due to my father's political status at the time, Jun could not get any decent jobs in the research institutes. Nor could he be a school teacher anywhere near Shanghai because we were the outcasts and did not have any powerful connections. After a year's "re-education" in an army camp, he got a job in a small, collectively owned factory in southern Jiangxi. Life was hard there. Yet, Jun made the best of it. He said, "There are flowers wherever you go."

But then, why would such a person who loved life so much end his own life?! Going through the turmoil of the Cultural Revolution, we had already experienced the shock of numerous suicides and suicide attempts among our close friends, neighbors and colleagues. We knew instantly that Jun's death was related to the political movement. But what on earth could Jun, the obscurest of the Obscures, have done which would lead to a political crime?

We learned afterwards that, before his suicide, Jun wrote a letter to Chairman Mao in which he pleaded his innocence of the alleged crime of sabotage. In desperation he appealed to the most powerful and the highest commander of the Cultural Revolution for justice, hoping that Mao would send words down to rescue him from the wrongful charges. The letter had not been mailed out before Jun died. According to the letter, he had been a suspect of sabotaging his factory's production by cutting off the electricity supply. There were two reasons for the allegation. One was that Jun happened to have his desk next to the fuse box. The other was that he was suspected of being a member⁻ of an anti-revolutionary group.

The factory where Jun worked was a small one in rural Jiangxi where the Communist Party set up its first Soviet bases in the 1930s. As a result, people there may well have had a higher level of revolutionary vigilance than people in other places. It was a time when China faced an extreme shortage of electricity. The rural and primitive areas were hardest hit. Due to overload, the factories had been forced to stop production in the middle of the day by a sudden cut-off of electricity. Instead of trying to find out the real cause, the Party leaders in the factory quickly concluded that it was sabotage. It did not matter to them that they themselves had decided to put Jun's desk next to the fuse box. The sudden cut-offs of electricity which they desperately needed for production led them to believe that Jun, the one next to the fuse box, was the Number One Suspect.

Jun did not have a revolutionary family background to clear him. Normally the party bosses did not trust you if you did not belong to a working class or peasant family. Even without such a family, the party could still trust you if you had professional parents who held Party membership cards. Jun was not lucky enough to have either one. Making him still more vulnerable to the accusations of sabotage, Jun had friends who were just like him.

While in the army camp, Jun made friends with several young men who were also college graduates from Shanghai. Somehow they all ended up in the same town where Jun worked. All of them were single men without girlfriends, and they felt lonely. To help pass time, they met once each week for a potluck party. Through these weekly gatherings, the young men kept each other informed of what was going on outside of that little rural town. Unfortunately, when the sabotage issue arose, the potluck parties became a suspicious, anti-revolutionary activity. Jun was then doomed to fall prey to the revolutionary maniacs who refused to listen to reason.

As a suspected anti-revolutionary and saboteur, Jun did not dare to jeopardize our family's vulnerable status by contacting us. Otherwise, the whole family would be implicated in his alleged crimes by this dangerous madness. He stopped writing us. Although we were worried, we could do nothing but pray, hoping that we would see him and find out the reason for his silence when he had his next once-a-year, two-week vacation.

Jun did not live to get his next vacation. The pain he felt under the pressure to admit guilt for a crime which he had never committed must have been so severe that he could not even wait a couple more weeks to celebrate his twenty-sixth birthday. He became one of thousands and thousands of Chinese who committed suicide during the Cultural Revolution.

Understandably, many people find it too painful to recall the most terrifying moments of their lives. Consequently, they choose not to talk about the suicides of their dear ones. For this reason, perhaps, there are no books or articles that deal specifically with the subject of suicide during the Cultural Revolution. Furthermore, we lack access to statistics on political suicides in China that would help in judging the magnitude of this phenomenon. (For the faculty at Fudan University, the community that I know best, I determined that the suicide rate may have been approximately five to six percent. See the appendix for details.) Yet, to understand the political and social behavior of a huge nation such as China, we need to begin with an understanding of the inner experience of key groups of victims and survivors of the most important, formative and traumatic event of the Communist period.

This paper was written, therefore, to shed light on a practically prohibited and virtually untouched subject for historians, sociologists, political scientists, and psychologists. It is based only on my own personal experience and observations, supplemented by several interviews with other suicide survivors. Focusing mostly on the intelligentsia, it will discuss various kinds of political suicide victims, the immediate reactions of their survivors, and the lasting consequences for the survivors.

Categories of Suicide Victims

Dallin and Breslauer wrote, in *Political Terror in Communist Systems*, that under widespread conditions of terror "even conformity does not assure security or survival. Failure to adjust can mean extinction of life."[1] Jun was one of those who died during the Cultural Revolution, not because they committed any real crime, but because they failed to adjust to social norms. Under the rule of extreme Communist terror, friendship was labelled as a bourgeois sentiment against proletarian class love. Therefore, it was disapproved by the Party, and social gatherings were unofficially banned. As a result, any regular social gatherings were looked upon with great suspicion. Perhaps Jun could have taken precautions to remain above any suspicion by isolating himself from his friends. But he was in a small town where there were few people with whom he shared common interests. So he hung around with a few college graduates whom he had met in the army re-education camp. Like most of us, Jun chose companionship over isolation. The consequence was fatal.

Suicides which were related to socializing were not limited to the rural areas. The rate was higher in the cities where government research institutes, schools, and university campuses were filled with college educated people. The victims in this category were mostly university graduates. Some of them chose to be away from their families so that they could have a better career in good universities and research institutes. Others like Jun had little choice because they were assigned to jobs far away from home. Almost all of them were male since there were fewer female students admitted by the universities. The small number of female college graduates in any working unit were likely to establish a relationship with a man soon after their assignment since they were rare in the male-dominated professions. And once a person got into a steady relationship with a person of the opposite gender, that person was less likely to get involved with group activities, thus was less likely to be suspected of anti-revolutionary activities.

The singles (mostly males) and those whose wives were working in different cities developed their own social circles. This was done under the scrutiny of their neighbors, who were also usually their colleagues. The neighbors who were not included in those social groups might feel left out and resentful. Under normal circumstances their resentment would go no further. During a violent political upheaval such as the Cultural Revolution, however, mass hysteria distorted perceptions of what originally were considered normal social activities. Small group gatherings could be interpreted as a political threat to the establishment. And people who participated in those gatherings became potential enemies of the government. Their neighbors and colleagues were mobilized and manipulated by the Party boss to report on the activities of these potential enemies, who were labelled as "members of the Petofi Club," which, according to the Chinese Communists, had toppled the Hungarian government in 1956. Thus, these lonely, single professionals committed the "crime" of organizing "anti-Party clubs." They were immediately isolated from each other by the Party's order and were forced to write individual confessions about their personal and group anti-government and anti-Party crimes which they had never committed. Any discrepancy between the individually confessed accounts among the group members regarding any single specific conversation was manipulated by the interrogators as a means of getting more information and to split the group. Under such tremendous pressure, these lonely men often felt betrayed, abandoned and helpless. Many of them resorted to suicide as a solution.

A second group of suicide victims during the Cultural Revolution was those who were too weak to stand public humiliation, disgrace, and the loss of face. They were primarily women. They had had a relatively easy and comfortable life prior to the turmoil. Many of them were previously respected members or even supervisors of the neighborhood community and could be regarded as the neighborhood elite. They were often educated women and some of them were selected by the local Party authority to lead the lower levels of Chinese society comprising the retired, the unemployed, and people who do not belong to any work unit, such as housewives. The functions they had performed before the Cultural Revolution included helping to settle neighborhood disputes, passing on the Party's policy to the neighborhood by reading newspapers at weekly meetings and organizing the unemployed to find means of self-support. Although they were not government officials, they could possibly be regarded as powerful quasi-officials by the uneducated members of the neighborhood—the wives of the workers or the unemployed.

The women in this group were used to their comfort and security, and the respect which they had so far enjoyed. All of a sudden, the Cultural Revolution broke out. First, their professional husbands fell, having been labelled as enemies of the revolution. Then, to make things worse, the previous grievances against them, which lower status members of the community had previously not dared to voice, now burst into outrage. In such cases, the unruly masses often cut or shaved these women's hair, ripped off their blouses, or smeared their faces with mud. These incidents usually originated from below rather than being incited from above by a Party authority. They often occurred on the spur of the moment and took everybody by surprise. This kind of violent incident was not a continuous occurrence. To the victims, however, the swift fall from great respect to public humiliation was too much to bear. Their fragile sense of identity was destroyed by the violent actions of the mobs. Time to them seemed suspended in one moment of tremendous humiliation. They could not see anything beyond their trauma. After one or two episodes of public humiliation, they committed suicide.

The next category of suicide victims was young students in college. They could be boys or girls in their late teens or early twenties. They became targets not because their fellow students disliked them or resented them, but because they were singled out by their political instructors. These students often had "problematic" family backgrounds. They either came from a former landlord or bourgeois family, or had some relations who had worked for the former Guomindang government. They tended to be serious about their studies, apolitical, and independent-minded. Their differences from others were signalled either by the way they dressed themselves or by the kind of books they read. By traditional Chinese standards, to be different and independent implied social deviation, a behavior people would frown upon. Under Communist rule, their nonconformism was labelled as disloyal to the party. The political instructors did not like nonconformist behaviors and often questioned the loyalty of these students. When the Cultural Revolution broke out, it provided the political instructors excuses to punish these young men and women who refused to be "the docile tools of the party" as the central government encouraged them to be. Through continuous, organized "struggle meetings," the publicizing of "evil thoughts" from their personal diaries in Big Character Posters in the most popular areas on campus, and the revealing of private conversations reported by other students, these young people were made to feel isolated, betrayed, and humiliated. They lost their purpose and direction in life before they could have a chance to realize it. They saw no place for themselves in society. They felt doomed. They committed suicide.

A fourth category of suicide victims of the Cultural Revolution was the "old guards." Almost all of them were men between fifty and sixty years old. For decades, these old Communist cadres dedicated themselves to a cause which finally destroyed their lives. They did not believe in anything except the Party. Now they felt betrayed by it. They could not accept that they were the enemies of the revolutionary cause which they had fought for. They felt trapped and disillusioned. Victims of this group were not ordinary old Communist vanguards. They had been educated, either before or after they joined the Red Army, and held important positions in the professional institutes before the Cultural Revolution. Almost all of them had been through numerous Party power struggles and had learned how to recover. But they failed this time. Although well-weathered, they had never seen anything in Party history as violent as the Cultural Revolution. They felt helpless and in despair.

To make things worse, these "old guards" had much less family support than ordinary people in similar situations. Many of these victims did not get married until the Communists took over in 1949. In 1966, therefore, they generally had children between twelve and seventeen years old in 1966. Since the high schools were the centers of activity for Red Guards, their teenage children became radicals. Besides, years of parental ideological indoctrination had taught them that nothing was more important than loyalty and faithfulness to the Communist Party. The children were encouraged to denounce anybody who was regarded as an anti-revolutionary. Consequently, these teenagers tended to be more "revolutionary" than other children their age. They denounced their own "reactionary" parents as they were taught to do.

Apart from the lack of understanding from their children, the "old guards" also experienced great pressure and lack of support from their own spouses. Because many of them married after they had become government officials, women often married them for their power and status and tended to be opportunists. Through their marriage or through their own affiliation with the Communist Party, these spouses became the beneficiaries of the political system. All of a sudden, the privileges and comfort they had enjoyed as spouses of those cadres were taken away from them. They felt betrayed by these "old guards." And they now resented them.

There were spouses who, like the young children of the cadres, were so indoctrinated by the Communist ideology that they lost their ability to think independently. Even if they did not believe the charges against their husbands, they chose to accept rather than challenge the allegations that their husbands were enemies of the people. They joined forces with their children to denounce the "old guards." The denunciation from their own children and their own spouses cracked the hard core of these "old guards." They committed suicide.

The last group of suicide victims did not become targets of criticism in the Cultural Revolution. They committed suicide because they *feared* that they would become targets. These victims did not have any children and tended to be mostly educated women in their late fifties or early sixties. Most of their lives had been peaceful. When the Cultural Revolution broke out, they could not grasp the violent aspect of the political turmoil. They did not know how to control their lives. They committed suicide not because they were actually attacked, but because they were scared of being attacked someday. In some cases, previously existing physical or emotional problems of the victims also played a role. Consequently, the impact of these suicides on their survivors was less severe than that of the other four groups on their respective survivors.

The Experience and Behavior of Suicide Survivors

It is painful for relatives to confront the sudden loss of their dear ones. It is even harder for the survivors of political suicides. In the Cultural Revolution, injustice was inflicted on the family twice. For political reasons, the victims committed suicide. For political reasons as well, most survivors were deprived of their right to mourn and grieve. That deprivation took from them the opportunity to heal their wounds. It prolonged the process of suffering. Consequently, it created serious problems in their personal development.

In all cultures, suicides are related to shame. They were more so for the Chinese survivors of the suicide victims of the Cultural Revolution. Willingly or unwillingly, most survivors had to denounce their deceased ones, calling the suicides a shameful, anti-revolutionary act. In many cases, the survivors were not in a position to show their real emotions. They were either already targets of criticism or were becoming the accused ones themselves. They had to be extra careful to distance themselves from the suicide mess. Any sign of sorrow would be interpreted as anti-revolutionary and could lead to further troubles. To avoid implication, they repressed their grief, anger, and sometimes guilt.

Generally speaking, the number of open displays of grief by suicide survivors was small. There were, however, a few survivors who had the privilege of showing their grief in public. Most of these people could feel safe because their deceased family members had not been working in the same cities where they lived. Unless they themselves had already become targets, news of their emotional reactions to the suicide would not travel far enough to reach the ears of the Red Guards of their deceased's working unit. Besides, many of these survivors were already low in social status. They had little more to lose.

Even smaller was the number of survivors who had the courage to protest against the political violence by being completely silent. They neither denounced the victim nor showed any emotional reaction. At the "struggle meetings" called to further denounce the dead ones, they kept their mouths shut the whole time. When they were forced to make public statements, they said nothing. By remaining silent, they demonstrated the real strength and dignity of human beings. No matter how feeble they might have looked, their silence sounded louder than the slogans of the survivors who were anxious to denounce their dead ones.

The more "fortunate" survivors were those who could still be regarded afterwards as part of the people. Those in this group, being eager to get ahead and to continue with their successful careers, cut themselves off from the suicides completely. They stayed as far away as possible by vehemently denouncing the dead. Many of them refused to take a last look at their dead family members.

Some of these survivors even reacted to the suicides by more actively conforming to the political trend. Their fear of the loss of membership in the "rank and file of the people" was so strong that it impelled them to a display of political fanaticism. For these people, denunciation became a positive drive. They did not feel fear as they should have. By denouncing their deceased family members, they became oblivious to their own political vulnerability.

In some cases, the survivors felt guilty because they knew that their earlier denunciation had contributed to the suicide. But they did not want to face their guilt. Instead, they looked for glorious political excuses to justify their actions. The act of suicide further reinforced the willingness of those survivors to accept the alleged crimes of their deceased ones as facts.

While unusually extensive denunciation of the victims showed the survival instincts and/or self interest of the survivors, it sometimes reflected true belief in the Communist doctrine. Some survivors believed that their dear ones were the real enemies of the country and therefore, that they deserved to die in the most disgraceful way. This was particularly true for indoctrinated, teenage Red Guards. However, it is hard to believe that adult spouses would completely accept a guilty verdict no matter how shallow their depth of thinking. Could anyone, even as a product of Communist brainwashing, lose all common sense and shut themselves off completely from the tragedy? It is not likely. In most cases, self-interest was the motivation of the survivors who went to the greatest lengths to denounce the dead.

While the surviving adults were consciously hiding their real emotions or unconsciously denying their emotions by enthusiastic participation in the denunciation of the suicide victims, the children of the victims were the hardest hit. Many of them did not know how to handle the situation. They were confused. They needed help. But no one was around. Their surviving parents either denounced the suicide or did not feel it was safe to tell the children their true feelings. Like the parents, the surviving children did not feel safe enough to talk to other people about the suicides. As a result, they tried to avoid pain and confusion by not facing the tragedy. They ran away from it physically as well as intellectually. They ran to places where they could hide from public humiliation or to people with whom they felt secure.

For some teens, the suicide of their parents seemed to offer a solution to the problems they could not resolve. For weeks and months, or even years, before the suicide, the children of the politically accursed felt burdened by the problems of their parents. The tragic experience of a fifteen-year-old girl who felt relieved when she heard about her father's suicide, reflects the dilemma and confusion many teenagers faced. While her father was still alive, this girl did not know what to say about him when other people asked her. During that time, questions about a person's class origin and family background constantly followed them wherever they went. It would be as hard to say that you did not have a parent as to answer them, and such a response would lead to further suspicion. Feeling caught in an unsolvable dilemma, she wished her father death in the tumultuous months before the suicide. The suicide finally relieved her of the burdens of having a "reactionary" parent. Being young and innocent, she believed that death would help solve all her problems.

In order to start with a clean slate, the girl decided to cut the past from her life. She volunteered to go to be re-educated in the remote countryside where no one knew about her father's "crime." Although she was too young to be eligible, she insisted on going, and one month later she left her hometown, the place which bore the painful memory of her father's death and her own trauma. To further demonstrate her determination to start a new life, she completely changed her name. Unfortunately, her efforts to find a new identity did not work for her. Wherever she went, she was forced to bear the cross of having an "anti-revolutionary" father. When her friends joined the army or were admitted as "worker, peasant and soldier" college students, she was left out. No matter how hard she tried, she was denied all possibilities to move on with her life.

When the young children of suicide victims tried to cope with their real-life problems, they were forced to struggle within themselves to sort out the tragic consequences of their parents' deaths. Things did not change for the better for them even after months and years had passed since the suicide. They were still labelled as the "little bastards" of the reactionaries. They felt doomed, cheated and angry. Worst of all, they felt guilty. Remembering that, when they were young radicals, they had denounced their parents, they felt responsible for their parents' deaths. That powerful sense of guilt gripped their hearts. Many nights they would torment themselves by reliving the memory of their parents' suicides. To help ease the pain of guilt, the young survivors began to use denial techniques unconsciously. Although they knew that their parents had committed suicide, they refused to accept the fact. Sometimes they made themselves believe that it was somebody else. Days, weeks, months, and years passed. They hoped that someday their deceased parent would come back.

Another means of denial used by practically all survivors of the political suicides, both adults and children, was never to talk about the suicides. It is sad enough that the survivors did not talk to friends about the suicides because it was not safe. Most did not even talk about them within the immediate family. They chose to avoid the pain by completely wiping that tragedy out of their lives.

The Need for Healing

Denial and escape have not helped ease the pain of suicide survivors. Instead, they prolonged the process of suffering. The Cultural Revolution has been over for more than fifteen years. Yet, the sense of guilt keeps haunting the survivors. The painful memory will not go away. From time to time, the survivors open that sealed off spot in their hearts and peep through. They tremble, shake, and cry. The emotional torment goes on.

It has been nineteen years since my brother Jun died. The pain of the loss is as deep as it was nineteen years ago. Jun was only one of the many thousands of innocent people who died of suicide during the ten-year Cultural Revolution. Using the revolution as an excuse, the maniacs brought the whole country under a reign of terror. That reign of terror killed Jun. It took the lives of my professor and mentor and his wife. It took the lives of my neighbor across the hall, my upstairs neighbor, and next door neighbors. In addition, I lost many other not-so-close friends, while my best friend in college attempted suicide and survived. For awhile, suicides became an everyday phenomenon in my life and in the lives of millions of other Chinese.

Many thousands of Chinese committed suicide during the Cultural Revolution. Yet, to this day, there has not been a single official or unofficial study done about political suicide and the survivors of the political suicides during the Cultural Revolution. The official Party line tells the Chinese people not to look back into those years of "wounds," claiming that dwelling on the negative past would stand in the way of China's modernization and reforms. The truth is that this official denial of one of the most painful periods in modern Chinese history is itself a block to real political reforms. Unless the Chinese people gain their right to mourn and grieve, even belatedly, unless they are allowed to talk openly about the wrongs and injustice of the Cultural Revolution, unless Chinese people in all walks of life can come to grips with their own roles and their guilt during those ten years, the road to a true democratic reform will be long.

The years of terror became a reality only with the compliance of millions of Chinese who followed the official Party line by denouncing their neighbors, colleagues, friends, and family members or by sharing the maniacal political fervor. We were victimizers as well as victims. Therefore, to keep blaming the other people, the Gang of Four and their followers, is not going to help the nation recover from that terrifying time of pitiful and total helplessness. All of those who survived the Cultural Revolution need to start unburdening themselves of their traumatic experience of loss, confusion, pain, and guilt. This, we Chinese have to do ourselves. Every one of us.

The publications of personal accounts of the Cultural Revolution in recent years marked a beginning towards talking about the human pain under extreme terror. Unfortunately, none of the writers have addressed the issue of their own guilt. As a result, the books tend to portray the authors as rising above the Chinese crowd for their cool-headedness and far-sightedness during those ten crazy years. Sometimes the reader wonders why even those who had access to the highest commander of the Gang of Four were just victims of the Cultural Revolution.

The need for unburdening oneself of guilt is probably more urgent with the leadership of the Chinese government. China needs an introspective, self-searching, self-examined leadership who will stop portraying themselves as the victims of the Cultural Revolution. Some of the "old guards" contributed to those years of turmoil. They either complied with the maniacs of the revolution or actively participated in acts of terror by denouncing their old colleagues, which led to political suicides. (Deng Xiao-ping, for example, denounced Gao Gang and Yao Shoushi in the early 1950s, leading to many political suicides.) Until the leaders face their own complicity, they will not be able to understand real democracy.

Denial of traumatic human experience by individuals or by the Party, including the experience of the loss of loved ones to political suicide, is one of the real obstacles to true political reform in China. Hence, this paper is not just an indictment of the excesses of the Cultural Revolution, for sheer indictment is not enough. Nor is it an attempt to expose further the bitter irony in its revelation of the cruelty and weakness of human nature in light of the ideals of socialist character proclaimed by the Revolution. By talking about the devastation and terror that millions of Chinese like me experienced during the decade of political turmoil, I finally have a chance to relieve myself of the pain and the guilt as a survivor of the suicides. Unlike the survivors of suicides committed for other reasons, we, as survivors of political suicides, were deprived of our right to mourn, to cry, or to grieve. Willingly or unwillingly, we repressed our sorrow, pain, anger, and guilt. We either ran away from the suicides or adopted a false personality. Some of us became deadly withdrawn afterwards. What we should have done and did not do was to face our losses and address the tragic consequences. Hopefully this paper can help Chinese who are the survivors of political suicide learn to face the experience of the suicides of their dear ones and come to terms with themselves. Only then will the wound heal. And only then will we be able to move on.

Notes

1. Alexander Dallin and George W. Breslauer, *Political Terror in Communist Systems* (Stanford: Stanford University Press, 1970), 4.

APPENDIX: THE SUICIDE RATE
AT FUDAN UNIVERSITY, SHANGHAI

Since the university archives were not accessible to me when I visited Fudan University in the summer of 1990, I cannot provide precise figures. Nevertheless, I was able to interview historians who participated in a research project on the history of Fudan University, including its history during the Cultural Revolution. Although nobody was willing to commit himself to a definite number for casualties at Fudan, I was told that the total number of successful suicides at Fudan was between forty-three and forty-five. This figure does not include the suicides of spouses of the faculty resulting from their loved ones falling into disgrace. Neither does it include the many unexplained deaths of faculty during this period. It is also important to note that there were many additional suicide attempts which were unsuccessful.

The university authorities claim that, at the time when suicides were committed, the university had a total of over nine thousand members, including students, faculty, workers in the affiliated production lines, and a huge support staff, comprising doormen, janitors, gardeners, maintenance men, kitchen staff, porters, the personnel department, "political instructors," and library staff. Consequently, the total number of suicides represents about .5 percent of the total university population. However, those who committed suicide were mostly faculty members, and the remaining few were students. If the total number of students and faculty is approximately six thousand, then the suicide rate for this group is .75 percent. If the seven or eight hundred faculty are considered separately, the approximately forty suicides in that group yields a suicide rate of 5 to 6 percent.

It should be noted that at Fudan the term faculty includes retired and inactive faculty. These members were largely insulated from the political upheavals on campus. It will be an interesting subject for further research to identify and examine the particular group among the active faculty who were the most susceptible to suicide under conditions of political terror. Indications are that there was a cohort of males of a certain rank who fell prey to the terror and committed suicide in substantially greater proportions.

Coda:
Enter the Demon

Robert A. Solo

Since Cain slew Abel, the killing of man by man has never ceased. No beginning, no end, ceaselessly. And for so many reasons. To satisfy such a variety of purposes. To eat the victim's flesh, to sacrifice him to the gods, for amusement, for the thrill of combat, in the rage of the amok, to take his land, his possessions, his women, to defend his possessions, his land, his women, to terrorize in order to enslave, in order to exploit, in order to break the power to resist, the killing in war, the killing in revolution, the killing in repression, the killing in vengeance; there is nothing new about killing. And yet, in our time there has been a return to a particular kind of killing; or perhaps it is a killing particular to our time. A slaughter of the innocents, wherein a society massively and systematically devours its own, a functionless slaughter of those who are not the enemies of the society, nor in order to enslave or exploit them. Such were the great Stalinist purges of the 1930s. Such was the Nazi Holocaust of the 1940s. Such was the bloodbath visited upon the people of Cambodia by Pol Pot and the Khmer Rouge. Such was China's Cultural Revolution. All of these are to be accounted for, I think, by the re-entry of the demon into our century.

The idea of the demon is very old, antecedent to the idea of the gods or God: very old, and universal and persisting. What then is this idea, deep in the psyche, of the demon? It is the idea of a malignant spirit that takes possession of another being and, hidden within the one possessed, conspires against me, conspires to destroy me, who would pursue me to my destruction. A malignant spirit that can take possession of any other being, that can assume any mask, speak from behind any face, dedicated to my destruction. Such is the idea of the demon.

What is to be done? What options have I in a world where the demons roam free? What shall I believe? Whom can I trust? Not my neighbor. Not my father. Not my brother. Not my friend. Not my teacher. Any and all might be possessed by that crafty demon who waits only to destroy me. From behind the smiles and greetings, from behind that talk and laughter, behind those innocent eyes and gentle gestures, the demon, hidden, could be watching, waiting, poised to destroy me.

Somehow I must fend off the demon. I must find, pursue and destroy him. But which, where, who is he? Not for an instant dare I relax. Always alert, on guard, I must wait for the clue, for the slip, the mistake that will expose him. I must watch for the mark by which to identify him. What mark? What clue? I turn for instruction to my priest, shaman, guru, exorcist, magician, inspired leader, to the one on high. Guide me, I ask. Teach me to know the demon.

Of one thing I am sure. In this fight against the malignant spirit, I must withdraw into myself. Lest the demon know what I suspect, what I intend, I must hide behind my words, behind my smiles, behind my gestures, behind good manners and proper behavior, betraying nothing of myself, but watching, waiting and planning to identify, unmask and destroy the demon. In sum, I myself become a demon. To believe in the existence of the demon brings the demon into existence. In believing in the demon, I am possessed by him and become his creature.

Paranoia, suspicion, superstition are indigenous. Conspiracy exists. There are malignancies of spirit. And yet, for most of us, most of the time, these are only at the rim of our lives. It is when they deepen and spread and move from the periphery to the center, that the demon takes possession. A society demonized is ready for the massacre of the innocents.

History opened the way for the entry of the demon into post-revolutionary Russia. At the helm of the state, controlling society, were the Old Bolsheviks, for generations weaned in the arts of conspiracy and deception. Conspiracy and terror, infiltration and deception had been, for them, imperatives of survival, for they were themselves continuously infiltrated, subverted, betrayed. Those imperatives of survival, that ingrained outlook, those habits of a lifetime did not vanish because, finally, they had conquered. They controlled but they were not transformed. They remained what their lives had made of them, conspirators who everywhere saw conspiracy.

There were good reasons for them to hold their world suspect; perpetually to watch, even among themselves, for malignancy, deception, betrayal. Enmities, festering grudges, unsated vengeance must be hidden in the train of a long and cruel civil war. In the melee of war, civil war and revolution, foreign powers seeking their destruction had introduced into the Russian society, spies and saboteurs and agents of conspiracy. And how to mark out among a people conquered and converted by the garrote and the sword, the loyal and faithful from those who hid hatred and conspiracy behind a facade of belief? And there were those (and the children of those) who had flourished with the old regime, now dispossessed of wealth and status, the engineers, managers, and scientists who could not be dispensed with yet, but whose thoughts and intentions remained forever suspect.

Good reasons for apprehension and suspicion. But with so many good reasons for apprehension and suspicion, who then was not suspect? Who was friend and who was fiend? Beyond some threshold where there ceases to be a boundary to suspicion, or a limit to apprehension, is the domain of the demon. In the 1930s, the Soviet Union crossed that threshold and society was alive with demons. There had ceased to be any basis for personal trust, not father for son, not son for father, not brother for brother. In a world where any and all were suspect, the people turned to their high priest, their grand shaman, their inspired leader, to Josef Stalin that he might tell them the clues to look for, the mark by which to know the demon. Only he who possessed and commanded Russia could not be suspected of plotting to destroy what he, after all, commanded and possessed. Stalin, himself demonized, his world alive with demons, was in hot pursuit of their elusive and malignant spirits. In that pursuit he destroyed his revolutionary comrades, destroyed the communist elites, destroyed the military command and the echelons of its leadership, destroyed all who, it seemed, might have the power to conspire against him.

Within all societies there is a primal tension in the presence of the stranger, the alien, the outsider who dwells in their midst; a readiness to hate difference and turn against those of another culture, language, color or religion. And the Jew, like other minorities dispersed among the nations, has suffered on that account. But aside from and in addition to the hatred and blame visited upon the stranger, the outsider, there is an ancient, deep-sown anti-Semitism of quite another order. For the true anti-Semite, the issue is not the strangeness of the Jew, but that behind his masks, behind his ostensible familiarity, amiability, commonness, patriotism, altruism, dedication, respectability, there lurks the demon. And the anti-Semite inherits, or invents as a complex mythology, the accumulated fantasies of those who would give concreteness to the hidden spaces of the Jew's demonic existence. In those fantasies, the secret power of the Jews pervaded every corner of the world. Their linkage, Jew to Jew, spun the web of the spider around the world. Behind the pretense of being divided among themselves as revolutionaries and reactionaries, on every side of every question, they were united in conspiracy, a perpetual conspiracy of the demons against the gentile, against the Aryan, against the anti-Semite.

Adolph Hitler was a classical anti-Semite. Up from the gutter, inflamed by the basest instincts of *Der Volk*, his triumph ushered into Germany and into Europe an age of the demon. Hitler's assault was easier than Stalin's, for Hitler's demon could be identified by a bloodline, by a circumcision, by the mark of the Jew. Even when all Europe was under his heel, when his powers were supreme, when millions of Jews from every corner of the Continent, helpless and innocent, were being consumed in the flames of his ovens, Hitler never ceased to see and fear the demon Jew, elusive, ineradicable, behind his enemies in England, in the persona of the American president, in all that supported the struggle against him, as the cause of his failures, as the root of his frustration.

And what led the aging hero and master of all China, Mao Tse Tung, across the threshold into the domain of the demon? Whatever it was, he awoke to see the fiend in all those around him, in those closest to him, in those who had served him, in his comrades of the Long March, in the high party cadres, in the organizers and managers of enterprise, in the scientists and scholars, indeed in all those who, in the exercise of their responsibilities or in the scope of their knowledge, possessed some element of thought and power of decision, some element of freedom beyond his reach. And how could he strike at the demons surrounding him, conspiring against him, when they had infiltrated the very instruments of his power? The sly old man reached beyond them to summon the raw and infantile idealism, the energy and ignorance of China's youth to fight against his demons. Thus was launched the terrible rampage over the length and breadth of China called the Cultural Revolution.

The most terrible visitations of state terrorism in this century have thus, without exception, made manifest the demonization of a society. Then, where is he now, this demon? With the termination of the institutional barriers of race, religion and ethnicity in the United states after World War II, with the amazing reconciliation and integration of ancient enemies in Europe into a viable community, with the renunciation of militarism in a Japan that has opened itself to the world, with Vietnam and Afghanistan as lessons for great power imperialism, with the example of Iraq as a check upon aggression, with the decaying walls of totalitarianism in China, with Perestroika in the Soviet Union, with the end of the obsessive blindness of the Cold War, and with all that V.S. Naipaul would call the spreading light of universal civilization, the demon has been in retreat. In retreat, but he has not vanished and will not vanish. He will be sheltered within the closure of the cults and orthodoxies that proliferate in our midst, and will feed upon their jealous fanaticisms. He will find a home in the new nationalisms spawned out of the fragmentation of empires, ethnic enclaves whose raison d'etre is their hatred, fear, suspicion of the Other; he will be nurtured there by the rich harvest of unforgotten wrongs, unshaken grudges, fantasies of grandeur, unsatisfied ambitions, and greed. Be assured, the demon will flourish and, in his time, in some shape or form, he will return.

About the Editors and Contributors

Jonathan R. Adelman earned his M.A. and Ph.D. in political science from Columbia University and is an associate professor of political science at the Graduate School of International Studies of the University of Denver. His edited volume, *Terror and Communist Politics* (1984), was important to the recent development of the comparative study of state terror and repression. Professor Adelman is also the editor of *Communist Armies in Politics: Their Formation and Development* (1982) and the author and editor of many other books on Communist armies and Soviet foreign policy.

Chanthou Boua was born in Kompong Cham Province in Cambodia in 1952. She attended Phnom Penh University, the University of New South Wales, and the University of Wollongong, gaining degrees in commerce and multicultural studies, and has worked on relief programs in Cambodia. She is co-editor of *Peasants and Politics in Kampuchea, 1942–1981* (1982) and author of *Women in Kampuchea* and *Children of the Killing Fields: A Study of Kampuchean Adolescents in New South Wales*. She now lives in New Haven, Connecticut.

Charles D. Brockett is Professor of Political Science at the University of the South in Sewanee, Tennessee, and has his Ph.D. from the University of North Carolina. He is the author of *Land, Power, and Poverty: Agrarian Transformation and Political Conflict in Central America* (1988) and several journal articles on agrarian politics and political conflict, and is a co-editor of *Agrarian Reform in Reverse: The Food Crisis in the Third World* (1987). Professor Brockett's current research focuses on cycles of protest and repression in Central America.

P. Timothy Bushnell received his Ph.D. in economics from Michigan State University in 1988 and is now as assistant professor of economics at Allegheny College. His research has been concerned with transformations in concepts of coordination and hierarchy in the history of management. He worked with Professors Vanderpool and Shlapentokh to organize the November 1988 conference on state organized terror out of which this book grew.

Helen Fein received her Ph.D. in sociology from Columbia University and is the Executive Director of the Institute for Genocide Studies at the John Jay College of Criminal Justice. She is the author of *Accounting for Genocide: National Responses and Jewish Victimization During the Holocaust* (1979) as well as other books and articles on genocide, collective violence and human rights.

Rhoda E. Howard is Professor of Sociology at McMaster University. She is the author of *Human Rights in Commonwealth Africa* (1986) and co-editor with Jack Donnelly of *An International Handbook of Human Rights* (1987). In her published papers, she has dealt with such topics as economic rights and women's rights in Africa, Canadian policies with respect to human rights issues, and general theoretical and methodological issues concerning human rights.

Ben Kiernan gained his Ph.D. from Monash University in 1983 and is now Associate Professor of History at Yale University. He is the author of *How Pol Pot Came to Power* (1985) and co-author or co-editor of several other books on modern Cambodia. He is now working on a book entitled *The Pol Pot Regime in Power*.

William Maley is a Lecturer in Politics at University College, University of New South Wales and a Barrister of the High Court of Australia. He has co-edited *The Soviet Withdrawal from Afghanistan* (1989) and *The Transition from Socialism: State and Civil Society in the USSR* (1991); and is co-author of *The Theory of Politics: An Australian Perspective* (1990) and *Regime Change in Afghanistan: Foreign Interventions and the Politics of Legitimacy* (1991).

William O. McCagg earned his M.A. and Ph.D. degrees in East European history from Columbia University. He is now Professor of History at Michigan State University where he was Director of the Russian and East European Studies Program from 1975 to 1987. He is the author of several books including *Stalin Embattled, 1943–1948* (1978), *Soviet Asian Ethnic Frontiers* (with Brian Silver, 1979), and *A History of Habsburg Jewry, 1670–1918* (1988).

John McCamant received his M.A. from Columbia and his Ph.D. in political science and economics from the University of Washington. He has taught and conducted research in several Central and South American countries and published *Development Assistance in Central America* (1968) and *Violence and Repression in Latin America* (1976). Professor McCamant teaches Latin American area studies and comparative politics at the Graduate School of International Studies of the University of Denver.

David Pion-Berlin received his Ph.D. from the Graduate School of International Studies at the University of Denver and is an associate professor of political science at the University of California at Riverside. He has authored *The Ideology of State Terror: Economic Doctrine and Political Repression in Argentina and Peru* (1989) and numerous articles on repression, civil-military relations, military political thought, and the fall of military rule in Latin America.

Alex P. Schmid is a professor in the political science department and the Center for the Study of Social Conflicts at the University of Leiden, The Netherlands. He is the author of *Political Terrorism: A Research Guide to Concepts, Data Bases and Literature* (1st ed., 1984). In 1988, he drafted the initial research program of a new organization entitled Interdisciplinary Project for the Study of Root Causes of Human Rights Violations. (PIOOM is the Dutch acronym.) PIOOM is designed to be an international promoter and clearinghouse for research results on violent repression.

Stanley K. Shernock received his M.A. in sociology from Indiana University and his Ph.D. in sociology from the University of Virginia. He is now Chair of the Department of Justice Studies and Sociology at Norwich University and became President of the Northeastern Association of Criminal Justice Sciences in 1990. He has published articles in sociology and criminal justice journals on such topics as continuous violent conflict as a system of authority; politics and opportunity in the post-revolutionary generation in China, the U.S.S.R. and Nazi Germany; and conflict between political and criminal prisoners in concentration camps.

Dmitry Shlapentokh received Masters degrees from the University of Moscow and Michigan State University and his Ph.D. in Russian history from the University of Chicago. His dissertation was entitled "French Revolution and Russian Intellectual Life: 19th and 20th Centuries." He is now a fellow at the Russian Research Center at Harvard University.

Vladimir Shlapentokh earned his doctorate in economic sciences from the Institute of World Economy and International Affairs in Moscow and was senior research fellow at the Institute of Sociological Research in Moscow where he was a leader in the development of Soviet public opinion polling and analysis of social values and attitudes. He emigrated to the United States in 1979 and is now Professor of Sociology and Community Health Science at Michigan State University. He has published several books on the Soviet Union including *Soviet Public Opinion and Ideology: The Interaction Between Mythology and Pragmatism* (1986) and *Public and Private Life of the Soviet People: Changing Values in Post-Stalin Russia* (1989).

Robert A. Solo received his Ph.D. in economics from Cornell University and is Professor of Economics Emeritus at Michigan State University. Much of his work has focused on the theory of the state and the evolution of its capacities, both past and potential, for economic regulation and the shaping of technological advance. Among his many books are *Economic Organizations and Social Systems* (1967), *The Positive State* (1982), and *Opportunity Knocks: American Economic Policy After Gorbachev* (1991).

Jeyaratnam Sundram received his B.Ec. from the University of Malaya in 1975. For the next 12 years he worked in the business sector in Malaysia and then in university administration in Negara Brunei Darussalaam. He received his M.A. in 1989 from Michigan State University where he is currently completing his Ph.D. in sociology.

Christopher Vanderpool received his Ph.D. in sociology from Michigan State University where he is now Professor and Chair in the Department of Sociology. The central focus of his many professional articles has been on international law and the relationship of status to political formations in the context of Third World development.

Bernd Wegner was educated at the Universities of Tuebingen, Vienna, and Hamburg. After receiving his doctorate in 1980, he has been associated with the Military History Research Institute in Breisgau, Germany where he is a permanent fellow. He has published *The Waffen-SS: Ideology, Organization and Function* (1990). He is also co-author of *Der Globale Krieg, 1941–1943* (Das Deutsche Reich und der Zweite Weltkrieg, vol. 6, 1990) and editor of *Zwei Wege nach Moskau: Vom Hitler-Stalin-Pakt zum Unternehmen 'Barbarossa'* (1991).

Jane Jia-jing Wu is a native of Shanghai where she graduated from Fudan University in English. During the Cultural Revolution, she worked for seven and a half years in a bicycle factory to be "re-educated." Later, she became a lecturer in history at Fudan University. She is writing a Ph.D. dissertation for the history department at Michigan State University on failure of American policy in China in the 1940s resulting from blindness to Chinese factionalism. She is now a lecturer at Southwestern Missouri State University where she teaches U.S. and East Asian history.